15-28
18-24 Sd 94
277-28

WE VERMONTERS:

PERSPECTIVES ON THE PAST

Edited by

Michael Sherman
and
Jennie Versteeg

Library of Congress Cataloging-in-Publication Data

We Vermonters: Perspectives on the Past/
        Michael Sherman (1944-) and
        Jennie Versteeg (1946-), editors.
            p.cm.
        Includes bibliographic references.
        ISBN 0-934720-38-x
        1. Vermont—History. I. Sherman, Michael, 1944- .
II. Versteeg, Jennie G.
F49.5.W4 1992   92-14662
974.3—dc20   CIP

Published in cooperation with the Center for Research on Vermont, University
of Vermont, with support from the National Endowment for the Humanities.
Managing editor: Susan Bartlett Weber
Cover design by Don Hanson Design
Printed by Capital City Press, Inc.

Table of Contents

vii   **FOREWORD** *by George B. Bryan*

1   **INTRODUCTION**

A STATE OF MIND

7   We Pledge Allegiance to . . . ?
by Frank Smallwood

15   Finding the New World *by Toby Morantz*

29   Incorporating the Frontier: A Perspective on Euro-American Colonization in Vermont *by Richard H. Schein*

47   Defining New England: Revisioning Our Colonial Past *by Marshall True*

53   The Vermont State of Mind: Adventures in Schizophrenia *by William Mares*

59   Good Proverbs Make Good Vermonters: A Study of Regional Proverbs in the United States *by Wolfgang Mieder*

71   Place Names as Footprints of History
by Esther Munroe Swift

WE VERMONTERS

81   Legacies of Contact: Indians, Europeans, and the Shaping of Vermont
by Colin G. Calloway

95   Stocking the State: Observations on Immigrants, Emigrants, and Those Who Stayed Behind *by Samuel B. Hand*

107   We Proprietors: The First Europeans
by Winn L. Taplin

123 The Franco-Americans of Vermont and New England
by Anne P. McConnell

135 Some Intolerant Vermonters *by T. D. Seymour Bassett*

145 Our Patriotic Identity *by Willard S. Randall*

153 Rudyard Kipling, Vermonter *by Robert Stanfield*

165 Dorothy Canfield Fisher's *Vermont Tradition*
by Ida H. Washington

175 Private Lives: Vermonters at Work and at Home
by Connell Gallagher

183 The Roadside History of Vermont
by Peter S. Jennison

MAKING A LIVING

195 The Evolution of Economic Identity
by Jennie G. Versteeg

213 Agriculture and the Good Society: The Image of Rural Vermont
by David Donath

219 Vermont "Mill Girls" *by Deborah P. Clifford*

225 The Granite Workers of Barre, 1880-1940
by Richard Hathaway

239 Vermont's Nineteenth Century Railroad Workers
by Gene Sessions

249 Rails, Trails, and Automobiles: Tourism in Vermont
by Michael Sherman

265 Spreading the News: Newspaper Reporting in Vermont
by Nicholas Monsarrat

GOVERNING VERMONT

277 Inventing Constitutions: The Vermont Constitution and the Print
Revolution of the Eighteenth Century *by Patrick Hutton*

291 Biennial Government? *by Eric L. Davis*

303 Challenges Facing Vermont Women in Government
by Vi Luginbuhl

307 Vermont's Citizen Legislature Can Be Preserved
by William Doyle

313 Regulating Vermonters *by James H. Douglas*

327 The Disinfecting Light: Public Disclosure of Campaign Finances
      by Paul S. Gillies
341 A Hardy Race: Forging the Vermont Identity
      by D. Gregory Sanford

349 **AUTHORS' BIOGRAPHIES**

353 **WE VERMONTERS PROGRAMMING**

ILLUSTRATIONS

  4 *Tree Rhythms* by Luigi Lucioni
 33 The Diffusion of Ideas
 35 Our Shrinking World
 78 Vermont Bicentennial Celebration
 97 "Native Son Rule" Broadside
157 Rudyard Kipling's Residence
192 "Dairy and Creamery Supplies" Broadside
232 Brusa Monument, Hope Cemetery
274 Second Vermont Statehouse
312 Secretary of State James H. Douglas

Foreword

When Winston Churchill admonished that "we cannot say 'the past is past' without surrendering the future," he expressed the guiding philosophy of the "We Vermonters" project. Six years ago, a notable series of presentations called "Lake Champlain: Reflections on the Past," partially funded by the National Endowment for the Humanities (NEH), found a receptive audience in Vermont. Three years later, representatives of the Fletcher Free Library in Burlington (Maxie Ewins and Amber Collins), the Vermont Historical Society (Michael Sherman), and the Center for Research on Vermont at the University of Vermont (George B. Bryan, Samuel B. Hand, Kristin Peterson-Ishaq, and Jennie G. Versteeg) convened to consider the NEH's invitation to propose a new project similar to "Lake Champlain." Still reeling from the exertions demanded by arranging sixty-four programs focused on the Lake Champlain region, this intrepid band decided to leap once again into the churning waters of humanistic programming.

The result was "We Vermonters," a series of general audience history presentations including eight topical segments that, as the NEH grant proposal claimed, examined "the evolving identity of Vermont within the context of international, state, and local events, movements, and values that have influenced its development."

The initial program was presented on 7 January 1990 and the last on 20 November 1991. In the interim, eighty-eight scholars and other experts explored the past and present significance of the Vermont identity. Accompanying exhibits, prepared by Louise Roomet, Virginia Westbrook, and Don Hanson, also educated countless library patrons. This book is not just a tangible reminder of that sunburst of ideas that flashed through the Community Room of the Fletcher Library and illuminated the minds of the approximately 2,500 people who heard the presentations when first delivered. It is also a means of making the series accessible to others who did not attend. A wondrous thing about a book is its longevity. A good book, moreover, clothes its makers and its subject with a sort of immortality, insuring that "We Vermonters" will be something other than what Shakespeare, in his *Tempest,* refers to as a walk "on the sands with printless foot."

Old habits die hard. Two-and-a-half decades have passed since I last appeared in a professional theatrical production; yet nearly every evening at

6:30, I am unsettled by the notion that I have missed a make-up call and should at that moment be in a dressing room. I wonder how many people besides me will think of "We Vermonters" at seven o'clock every Wednesday evening. At those times I will proudly remember my association with the project, its planning committee, and its audience. Warmed by that sentiment, I may, perhaps, be excused for paraphrasing a comment made by Churchill in his eightieth birthday speech in 1954: It was the "We Vermonters" people that had the lion's heart. I had the luck, as project director, to give the roar.

George B. Bryan
Director
Center for Research on Vermont
University of Vermont
Project Director, "We Vermonters"

Introduction

"Just because the cat has her kittens in the oven, that don't make them biscuits."

Countless generations of Vermonters have used, or had used against them, this aphorism to allude to the mysterious quality of local or regional identity. Close to the surface of everyday life in Vermont is the consciousness of an individual and group identity that is linked to where we live. Perhaps we are no different from Americans in other states in this respect. Indeed, our national humor, literature, politics, economics, and history often reflect the local and regional differences that separate us from our fellow citizens. This is true even as we think, act, legislate, and in many other ways insist on a national identity that transcends the boundaries and barriers of state and region.

Americans from their earliest history have been concerned, even obsessed, with questions of national and regional identity. For example, in the 1770s Guillaume-Michel St. Jean de Crèvecoeur, an anglicized Frenchman living in New York, asked in his *Notes of an American Farmer*, "What is this new man, this American?" Like many of his contemporaries on both sides of the Atlantic, Crèvecoeur recognized that geography affected culture and that the physical distance of America from the Old World somehow made a difference in shaping the basic character of Americans. We have been asking about the how and why and what of that difference ever since.

Geography has had its local effects as well, and regional differences emerged early as significant factors in shaping our national history. Only a few years after independence from Great Britain, delegates to the Constitutional Convention of 1787 had to contend with the powerful role of local and regional identities as they labored to create a national charter. Less than a century later, Americans fought each other in a Civil War based largely on the importance, viability, and durability of regional identity and institutions. In our own day, we continue to care about "balanced tickets" in presidential elections, while publications such as *Yankee Magazine* and the enduring popularity of "Lake Wobegone" both reinforce stereotypes and appeal to the popularity of regionalism. We continue to long for clearly identifiable regional images and characteristics in our language, literature, art, and architecture; and we cherish them when we find them in the works of William Faulkner and Robert Frost, the architecture of Frank Lloyd Wright, and the *Dictionary of American Regional English*.

Being the product of transplantations of people from many lands and cultures and the amalgam of many traditions, most Americans are conscious of the tension between our national, regional, and local identities. Because we remain mobile and constantly repeat the migrant activities that created our nation and its smaller political units, we cannot escape the task of repeatedly re-identifying ourselves through our geographical location. Even the peoples who were here before there was an "America" confront this question of local and regional identity as part of their efforts to maintain and renew themselves culturally, linguistically, and politically.

Being a Vermonter at the end of the twentieth century, therefore, is in many ways like being a Texan, New Yorker, New Hampshirite, Minnesotan, or Californian. It means assessing the impact on our lives of a complex mixture of facts, myths, and traditions, of geography and language, and most of all, of history. Are we more or less than where we were born? To what extent did our ancestors or predecessors have their lives shaped by their physical location? To what extent do we continue to shape our own lives by our choice of place, or have them shaped by where we happen to live and how previous generations of Vermonters lived? Asking these questions, are we now any different from our neighbors in other states? Is identity by statehood, region, or even nation in this age of global travel and instantaneous, worldwide—even interplanetary—communication still an effective or useful means of finding a place for ourselves as individuals and groups?

For two years speakers and audiences at the Fletcher Free Library in Burlington, Vermont, discoursed upon, demonstrated, and discussed these and related questions. Planned and sponsored by the Fletcher Free Library, the Center for Research on Vermont of the University of Vermont, and the Vermont Historical Society, the series built upon the successes and unanswered questions of a similar project, "Lake Champlain: Reflections on Our Past," presented at the Fletcher Free Library from 1986 to 1988. Like its predecessor series, "We Vermonters" was funded by a major grant from the National Endowment for the Humanities. And like its predecessor, "We Vermonters" has generated a collection of published essays as a byproduct and permanent resource for future generations of Vermonters, as well as readers "from away."

Limitations of space and format made it impossible for us to include every presentation offered to audiences over the two-year life of the project. Moreover, we have reorganized the sequence in which the papers were presented to give greater coherence to the book. We have, however, included as an appendix a complete list of the programs and speakers. We have chosen not to reproduce all the bibliographic compilations of the project but rely on end notes to offer our readers a guide to resources for further reading and research. Finally, we are unable to reproduce here materials from the exhibits that accompanied, sometimes summarized, and always complemented the research and conclusions presented by speakers and panelists. The exhibit materials have been retained, however, at the Vermont Historical Society and are also documented in notebooks deposited with the Fletcher Free Library and the Department of Special Collections of the Bailey/Howe Library at the University of Vermont.

This volume, therefore, reflects but does not reproduce the series "We Vermonters." We have retained, and we hope emphasized, some of our major themes and goals. Foremost among these was to place the history and experience of Vermonters in a broad national and global context. Most of the essays included here view a topic in Vermont history and culture through a wide lens of national or international events, ideas, trends, and changes, as did most of the public presentations. In rearranging the essays, however, we have placed at the beginning of each of our four sections one or two pieces that particularly establish a national or global context for our theme. Subsequent essays in each section narrow the focus and give the reader details of the Vermont experience. These demonstrate what Vermont has in common with other states and what is—or may be—unique and definitive in its history and character.

Any project of this magnitude and duration owes its successes to many people. As George Bryan mentions in his foreword, the editors were part of the team that planned "We Vermonters" in 1989 and presented it in 1990 and 1991. That team included, in alphabetical order: George Bryan, Amber Collins, Maxie Ewins, Samuel B. Hand, Don Hanson, Kristin Peterson-Ishaq, Louise Roomet, Michael Sherman, Jennie Versteeg, and Virginia Westbrook. Publication of this volume was made possible through the cooperation of the Vermont Historical Society and the Center for Research on Vermont at the University of Vermont. We are especially indebted to Susan Bartlett Weber, Managing Editor for the Vermont Historical Society, and to Kristin Peterson-Ishaq, Coordinator of the Center for Research on Vermont, for their invaluable assistance with the copy editing and production. We offer our gratitude and appreciation to the more than eighty individuals who prepared lectures, presentations, commentaries, and slide shows for the "We Vermonters" series, both those whose work is included in this volume and those not included.

Finally, we thank our audience. For two years, they faithfully attended the "We Vermonters" programs, examined our exhibits, evaluated our efforts, and encouraged us to assemble this publication. By doing so they demonstrated to us that, even in this age of electronic communication, the written and spoken word retain their power and fascination; that in this age of specialization and fragmentation of knowledge, intellectual curiosity and the search for understanding still cross the boundaries of scholarly disciplines; and most of all, that in this age of global communication, homogenized culture, instant news, and short attention spans, a patient and detailed examination of our local and regional past may still provide us some fruitful pathways for understanding our present and planning for our future as citizens of our community, state, region, nation, and planet.

Michael Sherman
Jennie Versteeg

Tree Rhythms. Luigi Lucioni engraving (1953). Courtesy of the Vermont Historical Society, Montpelier, Vt. (VHS A-588).

A STATE OF MIND

We Pledge Allegiance to . . . ?

Frank Smallwood

D riving one day in Malletts Bay, Colchester, I followed a pickup truck with a bumper sticker that read: WELCOME TO VERMONT, NOW GO HOME! This bumper sticker reminded me of Michael Sherman's comment in "Memory, Commemoration, and the Storyteller's Creed": "when some of us complain that the history of Vermont has been and is being buried beneath the 'myth of Vermont,' I think we are saying that the conventions . . . have become too constraining, that they no longer or imperfectly encode the behavior and beliefs of our society."[1] The bumper sticker was a perfect symbol of one of our most prevalent constraining myths—the "us" versus "them" myth, the real Vermonters versus the flatlanders.

REAL VERMONTERS VERSUS FLATLANDERS

In his piece in this book on "Stocking the State," Samuel Hand tells us that flatlander is "a relatively new term that apparently gained currency during the 1960s." It is often used in a derogatory fashion, yet paradoxically our political system has been dependent on flatlanders for well over two hundred years. Originally called New Connecticut, Vermont was settled rapidly by colonists from other parts of New England.

Between 1760 and 1777, the estimated population of Vermont grew from three hundred to twenty thousand. This rapid settlement had a profound influence on our early political life because when the Republic of Vermont was created in 1777 it could not draw upon any indigenous institutional experience nor on native-born political leaders. Instead, Vermont was totally dependent on "flatlanders" from other colonies—the Allens, the Chittendens, Nathaniel Chipman, and the like. Our greatest folk hero, Ethan Allen, was born in Litchfield, Connecticut, and as William Doyle has noted, Litchfield County gave Vermont four governors, seven congressmen, seven Supreme Court justices, and three United States senators.[2]

The influx of outsiders increased rapidly for the next thirty years as Vermont's population grew from 85,425 in 1791 to 154,464 in 1800 and then to 217,895 in 1810. During this period Vermont was the fastest growing state in the nation, and as Charles Morrissey has pointed out, the new inhabitants were very young: two-thirds of all Vermonters in 1800 were less than twenty-six years old.[3]

Hence, Vermont was originally founded and governed by outsiders. Thomas Chittenden, our first governor, was elected nineteen times between 1778 and 1797 primarily because he was one of the few Vermonters who had prior political experience in the Connecticut legislature. After Chittenden died in 1797, he was succeeded by Isaac Tichenor, born in Newark, New Jersey, and known as "Jersey Slick," who served from 1797 to 1809.

As a matter of record, the first fourteen governors of Vermont from 1778 to 1835, a period of fifty-seven years, were all born out of state. It was not until 1835 that Lt. Gov. Silas Jenison was chosen as the first native-born Vermont governor after three days of legislative wrangling and thirty-five ballots.[4]

Vermont's dependence on outsiders for its political leadership has not been confined to just the early years of the state. Since 1950, we have elected ten governors, and only four of them were native Vermonters. Six were born out of state, and three were born out of the country—Joseph Johnson (Sweden), Josiah Grout (Quebec), and Madeleine Kunin (Switzerland). Twenty years ago, in 1972, when I was elected to the state senate, it consisted of fifteen native-born Vermonters and fifteen out-of-staters. In the 1991-92 legislative session, this ratio is exactly the same in the senate, while the House consists of seventy-nine native Vermonters and seventy-one out-of-staters.

Real Vermonters versus flatlanders may be part of our political mythology, but that mythology has never portrayed the reality of Vermont's political life where out-of-staters have played a critical role.

CONSENSUS VERSUS CONFRONTATION

A second major myth about Vermont politics derives from our landscape. Because Vermont is a placid, peaceful, quiet place, we tend to assume that our politics have always been serene. Nothing could be further from the truth. From the very beginning, Vermont was involved in difficult political conflict, and our early history was one of the most tumultuous of any of the American states. The first ninety years of Vermont politics from 1777 to 1860 were marked by continuous turmoil. Some of the major early issues involved:

(1) *Governance:* Would the tight Chittenden/Allen dominance create an oligarchy, or would Vermont develop into a true democracy?

(2) *Ideology:* Once political parties were formed, would the more conservative Federalists or the more progressive Jeffersonians gain control of the state?

(3) *Union:* Would Vermont survive the economic hardships from the Embargo of 1806-7 and the War of 1812? Had we made a mistake when we joined the Union in 1791?

(4) *Social ferment:* Would the political turmoil resulting from the religious revivals and the anti-Masonic movement in the 1830s tear the state apart?[5]

(5) *Moral agitation:* Would the fragmented multi-party movements concerning freedom, slavery, and prohibition that appeared during the 1840s and 1850s paralyze the state?

My basic thesis is that many of our current political debates still center around a number of enduring divisions that grew out of these earlier conflicts. Because we Vermonters are diverse in our backgrounds, heritage, and history, we pledge allegiance to a diverse set of ideas of what Vermont is and what we would like it to be. Four major themes dominated our political development and continue to play a major role in influencing our politics today: (1) Ideology: conservative versus progressive tradition; (2) Unity and scale: local versus centralized control; (3) Freedom: individual rights versus community welfare; (4) Change: traditionism versus modernism.

We Vermonters have been arguing about these issues for the past two hundred years, and we may well continue to argue about them two hundred years from now.

(1) Ideology

From the beginning days of the republic, Vermont has harbored two distinct political ideologies, originally rooted in geography. As Harris Thurber has commented, "The eastern part of the state, the Connecticut Valley, was dominated largely by old line conservative Congregationalists from Connecticut, while in the western half of the state, the Champlain Valley, the more freewheeling sects, with their . . . more radical and social doctrines, held fuller sway."[6]

The basic ideological division between the western (Allen) faction versus the less flamboyant easterners encompassed different attitudes towards political style (aggressive versus conciliatory), religion (free thinkers versus traditionalists), philosophy (radical versus conservative), and even economics (entrepreneurial speculators versus more settled farmers).

When political parties were formed in the 1790s, the preponderance of easterners and professionals (merchants, lawyers and clergy) became Federalists, while the westerners were Jeffersonians. In the election of 1800, Jefferson carried every county west of the Green Mountains, while John Adams carried every eastern county. In 1810, the state legislature created Jefferson County in the center of the state, but in 1814, when the Federalists regained control, they managed to change the name to Washington County.

Later manifestations of the tensions between the radical progressive and the more conventional conservative traditions were evident during the War of 1812 and in the religious and political revivals of the 1830s. From 1831 to 1835, anti-Mason William Palmer was elected to four terms as governor, and in 1832 Vermont was the only state to cast its electoral votes for the anti-Masonic candidate for U.S. president.

The great political clashes of the 1840s and 1850s involving slavery and temperance led to multi-party gridlock as the Whigs, Democrats, Free Soil, and Liberty parties battled for votes. D. Gregory Sanford has commented about this period as follows: "Though the Whigs monopolized Vermont's major elective offices, their control was tenuous. From 1841 through 1853 there had been thirteen state elections, or a total of thirty-nine contests for the three top posts (i.e., governor, lieutenant governor, treasurer). Thirty-three of these were thrown into the legislature when no candidate got a popular-vote majority.... In 1853, it took four days and thirty-one ballots to elect a Speaker of the House, ten days and twenty-six ballots to elect a governor, and . . . after thirty-nine ballots, the legislature declared itself unable to elect a United States senator and the seat remained unfilled for a year."[7]

So much for placid, pastoral stability! Once the Republicans took over, things quieted down, but progressive versus conservative issues remained. In 1915, for example, a "progressive" legislature enacted the direct primary, court reform, and workmen's compensation. However, arguably the biggest progressive issue during the twentieth century has involved the extension of Vermont's proudest claim: participatory democracy. I don't want to minimize Vermont's early achievements in establishing institutions like town meeting government and the like, but we should not exaggerate such accomplishments.

The basic reality is that throughout most of our history the state's political life was dominated by white Protestant males. It was not until the 1970s that the first Catholics, Thomas Salmon and Patrick Leahy, were elected governor and United States senator, and it was not until 1984 that we elected our first woman governor, Madeleine Kunin, whose religious preference is Jewish. Vermont's movement towards full political equality is still in the process of evolution, although it took a great leap with proportional representation in the House and Senate in 1965.[8]

(2) Unity and Scale

A second major political issue that Vermonters have argued about for the past two hundred years has involved the question of scale—to what level of government do we pledge our allegiance? The town? The county? The region? The state? And what if they are in conflict?

Vermont's grassroots tradition has always favored local authorities—the towns, or the "Little Republics," as Gov. John McCullough (1902) called them. As someone who has just chaired the first phase of our legislative reapportionment process following the 1990 census, let me assure you that the town as a political symbol is still astonishingly strong in Vermont today.

Yet, in reality, as Sam Hand's research has revealed, the towns—especially the smaller, poorer towns—have consistently given up power to the state in return for money to pay for basic services, such as roads, schools, and welfare. Centralization has been driven by economics, particularly the economics of equality between the richer and the poorer towns. The most dramatic reversal has taken place in education where the original unit was the local school district. By 1850, our 239 towns contained 2,594 such districts; 103 of them enrolled six or fewer students; 420 between seven and eleven students. By 1860, the overall state average was twenty-nine students per school district, and fierce intratown fights broke out over town consolidation of schools.[9]

Today, as more areas of authority gravitate to Montpelier, there is a new focus in Vermont on devolution and decentralization. The latest push centers on rationalizing and strengthening regions, a concept Gov. Philip Hoff raised when he was first elected in 1963. More recently Frank Bryan and John McClaughry have proposed shire government in *The Vermont Papers*,[10] and in 1991 the first issue of "Regional Democracy" appeared, the newsletter of a new organization that wants to create a more rational system of regions "where government is large enough to govern effectively and small enough to govern humanely."[11] The debate over scale continues to capture our attention.

(3) Freedom

Vermont's third major political conflict has involved the great historic American clash—the rights of the individual versus the welfare of the community. The Vermont constitution places a high priority on individual rights.

Article I asserts that "all men are born equally free and independent, and have certain natural, inherent, inalienable rights, amongst which are . . . acquiring, possessing, and protecting property."

Article II specifies that "private property ought to be subservient to public uses when necessity requires it . . . nevertheless, whenever any person's property is taken for the use of the public, the owner ought to receive an equivalent in money."

Hence, Vermont's historic "natural rights" tradition is based on the assumption that individuals, not groups or communities, are created equal. Yet, our political system is also based on John Locke's social contract theory, which assumes that no rights are absolute. Where, then, do we draw the line between the individual and the state?

Constant bickering over property rights has characterized our politics from the very beginning. Actually, property rights was the critical formative issue that shaped Vermont as the early settlers argued over the validity of the New Hampshire versus New York land grants. Once the republic was organized in 1777, there were continuing battles between the Chittenden-Allen faction, which drew upon the principles of natural justice, and the newcomer lawyers, such as Nathaniel Chipman and Isaac Tichenor, who appealed to common law. When confiscated lands were restored to Loyalist owners, these battles spilled over into legislative disputes about the Redemption Act and the betterments issue.[12]

Our current manifestations of these early conflicts involve Act 250, Act 200, zoning, subdivision controls, and the newly emerging public trust doctrine. What constitutes a legal "taking"? Where do individual property rights give way to the larger interests of the community? The Vermont Natural Resources Council, developers, conservationists, and the Citizens for Property Rights advocate dramatically different positions.

While some of our historic conflicts may be closer to reconciliation, this one appears to be picking up momentum as we enter our third century.

(4) Change

The fourth great issue involves our attitude toward change. To what extent do we want to hold onto our old ways of doing things, and to what extent do we accept new forces of change?

If the letters to the editor in local papers are the measuring rod, there's not much acceptance of change. One of my favorites appeared in the *Burlington Free Press*:

. . . I don't like all the construction going on all over Williston. I do not think it is going to make Williston a better town. There are going to be more people, and more people could mean more drugs and violence, more cars and more traffic . . . and probably more accidents . . . I would rather have Williston stay just the way it is. It's a nice town and I don't want it to change.[13]

While this may be a strong sentiment, there is compelling evidence that throughout most of our history, Vermont and especially its farmers have been willing to embrace, rather than reject, changes in the form of new technology. One of the more insightful analyses of this appears in Frank Bryan's discussion of the "rural technopolity" in the last chapter of his book, *Yankee Politics in Rural Vermont*, published in 1974 and still relevant today.[14]

Despite protestations to the contrary, change has been a constant in our economy and politics from the very beginning—change from a frontier society to self-sufficient hill farms, to potash and lumbering, to sheep farming, to railroads, to commercial dairy farming, to slate, marble and granite quarrying and processing, to state roads, airports, and interstate highways, to a more service oriented economy with a new high-tech base in IBM, Digital Equipment, and all the other recent postwar enterprises.

Hence, the question—where do we go from here?

VERMONT'S POLITICAL FUTURE

Assuming our diverse allegiances on key public issues will continue, what shape will our politics take in the future?

Frank Bryan provides a strong clue in the final chapter of *Yankee Politics* where he discusses two different axioms: the community axiom, a more localized political view, which is supported by the hill people, the old Yankee elite, and the new intellectual and artisan left; and the systems axiom, a more cosmopolitan modern view, which is supported by the farmers, the middle class, and the new technocratic elite.[15]

Bryan's analysis brings us back to the first myth I discussed, because the political distinctions he draws are not based on some hypothetical differentiation between "us" and "them," between natives and flatlanders, outsiders and insiders. Instead, we are all involved in shifting coalitions of old-timers and newcomers, whether our concerns are equal rights, environmental conservation, property rights, constitutional reform, or regional democracy. In dealing with these issues, We Vermonters should try to be:

(1) *Tolerant* of each other's differences. Honest and legitimate divisions should be resolved in an open and civil manner.

(2) *Responsible* in accepting the costs and trade-offs of change. There's no free lunch. If we want to live in a high-tech world, we must make choices about sources of energy and disposal of waste. If we want economic opportunity for our children, we must avoid the "not-in-my-backyard" syndrome.

(3) *Involved and informed*. That was one main aim of the "We Vermonters" speakers series and is a goal of this publication, which includes pieces on the Vermont constitution, the citizen legislature, biennial government, lobbying and campaign finance, women in government, civil liberties, and other issues.

As citizens we have opportunities that can add to our understanding of, and our appreciation for, the different mix of concerns, needs, problems, and allegiances that have contributed to the richness and diversity of Vermont's political tradition during the past two hundred years. If we are careful to use them, such opportunities will continue to contribute to our political growth in the decades ahead.

NOTES

1. In Michael Sherman, ed., *A More Perfect Union: Vermont Becomes a State 1777-1816* (Montpelier, Vt.: Vermont Historical Society, 1991), 178.

2. William Doyle, *The Vermont Political Tradition* (Barre, Vt.: Northlight Studio Press, 1984), 66.

3. Charles T. Morrissey, *Vermont: A History* (New York: W. W. Norton & Co., 1981), 107.

4. Doyle, 106.

5. See David M. Ludlum, *Social Ferment in Vermont 1791-1850* (New York: Columbia University Press, 1939).

6. Harris E. Thurber, "Some Values of the Vermont Community," *Vermont History* 25 (July 1957): 209.

7. D. Gregory Sanford, "The Gilded Age of Vermont Politics," in Jennie G. Versteeg, ed., *Lake Champlain: Reflections on Our Past* (Burlington, Vt.: University of Vermont, 1987), 94-95.

8. Doyle, 202.

9. Samuel B. Hand, Jeffrey D. Marshall, and D. Gregory Sanford, "'Little Republics': The Structure of State Politics in Vermont 1854-1920," *Vermont History* 53 (Summer, 1985).

10. Frank Bryan and John McClaughry, *The Vermont Papers: Recreating Democracy on a Human Scale* (Chelsea, Vt.: Chelsea Green Publishing Co., 1989), 82-160.

11. "RD" (Burlington, Vt.: Regional Democracy Newsletter, Vol. 1, No. 1, Summer/Fall, 1991).

12. Samuel B. Hand and P. Jeffrey Potash, "Nathaniel Chipman: Vermont's Forgotten Founder," in *A More Perfect Union*, 56-58.

13. "Unwelcome Change," *Burlington Free Press*, 15 December, 1988, 15A.

14. Frank M. Bryan, *Yankee Politics in Rural Vermont* (Hanover, N.H.: University Press of New England, 1974), 234-267.

15. Bryan, 255-259.

Finding the New World

Toby Morantz

Europe gave us the term the "New World" towards the end of the fifteenth century. But in reality the voyages of discovery and exploration from Europe opened a number of new worlds for both the native peoples and the Europeans of the fifteenth and sixteenth centuries. In this essay I will tour a few of them and then look more closely at one of the new worlds that developed for the indigenous populations of North America.

The "New World" had, of course, already been known to Europeans at least once by the time Columbus set sail in 1492. The Vikings had a colony on the northern tip of western Newfoundland about one thousand years ago. We know they met the local inhabitants for their sagas talk of the "skraelings"; but their interest, archaeologists suggest, was more in the timber resources than in trade with the local people. The colony was short-lived, it is believed, because of the distance from the main Viking settlements. It was the commercial interests of Columbus and his successors that established a permanent interest in the New World—hence my claim that they "invented" the New World.

The Columbus expedition seeking India was backed by Spain and followed an earlier voyage of the Portuguese explorer Vasco da Gama, who landed in India in 1486. Columbus intended to find a way to India without trespassing on the Portuguese discoveries. He claimed that by sailing westward he could land in India—hence the name the "West Indies" when he thought he had. Columbus not only announced that the new lands harbored an immense and largely unexploited wealth[1] but, unlike da Gama, he sought to colonize and Christianize the lands and people he found. Those who came after Columbus, such as Amerigo Vespucci, writing in 1502 and 1529, and Hernando Cortés who led a thousand-man invasion of Mexico in 1519, both publicized and occupied the lands in the New World more effectively than their predecessors. Thus Europe quickly became familiar with the New World and the increasing European appetite for material wealth in luxury goods did much to shape its ideas and images of this world.

The search for material wealth brought to the Old World new ideas or new formulations of old ideas. The old tripartite division of the world had to give way to a directional geography based on four quarters. Now there was a west to add to the north, south, and east, and an America to add to Europe, Africa, and Asia. In his 1735 classification of life forms, Linnaeus classified all men as one species but had four divisions: Europeans (*albus* or white), Africans (*niger* or black), Asiatics (*fuscus* or dull rust—yellow) and Americans (*rubescens* or reddish).[2] To these he added two supplementary classifications drawn from traditional beliefs—feral and monstrous peoples, i.e., the wild men and the deformed or unusual persons referred to in the classical or travel literature.[3]

The *Law of Nations and the New World* by L. C. Green and Olive P. Dickason shows us the wealth of ideas and questions that flowed from the earliest writings and observations of the new men in the New World. Pope Alexander VI moved quickly, ruling in 1493 that these people "were human and capable of being Christianized."[4] Church doctrine from the time of St. Augustine had insisted that, however strange man was and from wherever he came, there could be no doubt that he was descended from Adam. Acknowledging the Americans as belonging to the family of man was one thing but establishing their position in relation to Europeans was quite another. Were the Americans descended from the children of Noah or did they represent an earlier form of humanity? If, as people believed, the world had been divided among Noah's three sons—Shem having peopled Asia; Japhet, Europe; and Ham, Africa—why had America been left out of this three-fold division of the world? Had man arisen from a state of bestiality or descended from a state of innocence? These were serious theological problems because they challenged Christian dogma and tradition.[5]

Such lofty questions and concerns kept theologians and philosophers busy but did not interfere with the Europeans' notions of how to proceed. No matter their origins, these Americans were to be transformed, civilized, and Christianized. There was much less theological debate than debate as to how that was to be done. As we read in the *Law of Nations*, "Remolding Amerindian cultures was a Procrustean task that was to absorb the energies of generations of officials, missionaries and soldiers,"[6] and that is a story we all know too well.

There was little controversy over the Europeans' rights to Christianize these people of the New World or to try to possess their souls. The possession of their lands, however, did prompt discussion and argument, based on theories formulated two hundred years before Columbus bumped into the West Indies. In the mid-thirteenth century Pope Innocent IV had decreed that all rational creatures, Christians or pagan, had the right under natural law to own property and govern themselves. This view was contested by Hostiensis (Henry de Segusia, c. 1200-1271), a cardinal and noted canonist who claimed that the rights of Christians prevailed over infidels. All power, he argued, had been assumed by Christ on his coming and those who failed to recognize Him forfeited their rights. By the time Europeans encountered the New World, however, the declining influence of a universal Catholic church meant that the law of nations displaced the natural law and each nation developed its own way of exercising its expansionist goals over the territory of the Americans.[7] The questions of possession, territorial rights, and sovereignty became important as each European nation argued for or against the rights of the native inhabitants as the basis of their claims to the territory vis-à-vis other European nations. For example, though the French themselves never specifically recognized Indian rights to their lands in New France, they did argue after the Treaty of Utrecht in 1713 that France could not have ceded title to the lands of the Maritimes to England because the Maritime Indians had been their allies, not their subjects, and therefore had never ceded their lands to the French.[8] It was a principle argued purely from self-interest and did not reflect French policy in action. Many of these issues, of course, continue today in both American and Canadian courts as native peoples press for their territorial claims based on principles formulated four hundred years ago.

Practical, everyday life was equally affected by information passing between the New World and the Old World. This is highlighted by anthropologist Eric Wolf, who shows that Europe's rise to world domination drew the whole world into a complex of global social, economic, and political relations, which make the study of separate societies meaningless. Not only were the princes and merchants of Europe drawn into a web of relations with the New World, so was the ordinary laborer. Whole towns became dependent on trade with the New World. As mercantile activity developed and took on new forms, it affected the lives of the people in the towns and the welfare of their families. For example, between 1670 and 1760 the Iroquois demanded in trade dyed scarlet and blue cloth made in the Stroudwater Valley of Gloucestershire. Wolf comments that this was one of the first areas in which English weavers lost their autonomy and became hired factory hands.[9] Glass and ceramic beads, kettles, guns, and a whole range of items manufactured in European towns were also in demand to fuel the North American fur trade. The raw materials and manufactured goods passing back and forth from Europe to North and South America had enormous consequences for large numbers of people on both sides of the Atlantic.

Perhaps it is time to look at the native peoples' New World or worlds that resulted from the European invasions. The New World for the native peoples was, of course, by this time very much an Old World, because their Ice Age ancestors had crossed over a land bridge formed in the Bering Sea, between Alaska and Siberia, to become the original Americans between 12,000 and 40,000 years ago. Having discussed something of the world views of the Europeans, it would be useful to balance this with a similar look at native peoples' cosmology. This we could do from comments made by priests and others. Archaeologists, though, have also been able to help us understand native perceptions by making a crossover between the supernatural and the material world. For example, the natives have long been mocked for selling off vast tracts of land for a few dollars' worth of beads or simply because of an interest in trinkets. George Hamell, however, has studied what is known about northeastern religions at the time of contact and has shown that the important substances of native copper, quartz crystals, and marine shells—substances that came out of the earth and were imbued with supernatural powers—were used in burial rites in precontact times. These symbolically important substances could be replaced by beads and glass objects of similar coloring and texture.[10] Hence, we now have a reasonable explanation of why native peoples found beads so intriguing. It was not because they were naive shoppers.

Unfortunately, we cannot be privy to many of the perceptions of the sixteenth-century indigenous peoples, for their learning was transmitted orally rather than written. Scholars such as Cornelius Jaenen, however, provide us with whatever the French records will yield from the early writers who recorded native thoughts and reactions to the Europeans in their midst. There were, according to Jaenen, a number of features of French life that the native peoples admired. Marc Lescarbot, lawyer and playwright, writing from among the Micmacs in the very early 1600s, suggested that they were much taken with the daily activities of the French and came from afar to observe them. Similarly, the Algonquins were so amazed at Samuel de Champlain and his men that Champlain commented: "The bulk of the savages who were there had never seen a Christian, and could not get over their wonder as they gazed at our customs, our clothing, our arms, our equipment."[11]

The native people admired European learning and appreciated the products of European technology. Almost all adopted and adapted to their needs products of European technology, such as metal, cloth, and twine, soon after these items were introduced into the trade network.[12] The native people noted with approval that the French respected and took seriously ceremonialism and ritual. Writers of New England history always comment that the loyalty of the Indians to the French stemmed, in large part, from the willingness of French civil, military, and religious leaders to participate in ceremonial acts as preludes to trade and military talks.[13] This was in contrast with the English, especially those of New England, who brought to the New World a distaste for ceremonialism. It has also been suggested by historians such as Kenneth Morrison, who has studied the Abenakis and their relations with the French and the English, that the greater emphasis on ritual in the Catholic church helped sway the native people to Catholicism.[14] But even in secular affairs, the French habit of marking occasions like the birth of the future Louis XIV in 1639 with bonfires and cannon shots "astounded and amazed" the native people so that "they put their right hands to their mouths, which is their method of exhibiting joyous emotion."[15] Jaenen here speaks of a fortunate cultural convergence: the French held views of a sense of occasion and recognition of rank and status, which served them well in their relations with their allies.

Just as the French and English viewed themselves as superior to the native people they encountered, so did the Indians disdain the Europeans who came into their midst. As one example, Father Gabriel Théodat Sagard, writing in 1623-24, reported that the Hurons considered the French "to possess little intelligence in comparison to themselves."[16] Another indication of this feeling of superiority is that the Indians did not learn French; the French learned Huron, Montagnais, and Algonquian.[17] The Indians also thought of the French as physically inferior and at times effeminate, both because of their demeanor and their tendency at times to engage in women's work, such as carrying wood. No doubt it is somewhat jolting for you, as it was for me, to learn that there were occasions when Frenchmen were denied Indian brides. For example, Jaenen reports from a contemporary source that when "'an honest French surgeon' asked to marry an Amerindian maiden in 1618 the native council refused his request." The Micmacs forewarned the French not to "meddle with their women" and threatened they would kill the men.[18] The natives also found the French ugly.[19]

French food did not please the Hurons and, not surprisingly, they also commented on the French habit of drinking blood and eating wood, referring, of course, to the wine and wafers of communion. Native people disapproved of French attitudes and practices of child-rearing with its emphasis on discipline that differed so much from their own.[20] They also criticized French habits of personal hygiene. The custom of carrying handkerchiefs for wiping noses, for example, confused and disgusted native people, and one Jesuit account in 1613 has the natives inquiring "for what purpose do they preserve such a vile thing?"[21]

French morality, especially, came under scrutiny and, as Jaenen notes, the Indians of New France never hesitated to point out the discrepancy between the missionaries' ideals and the colonists' practices.[22] Indians were scornful of European values, especially of French attitudes toward personal property and the accumulation of goods. Thus, Jaenen notes, "They expected the French to have a better developed sense of kin-group belongings, of sharing of goods, of using the goods or utensils of others if there was an urgent need to do so without the formalities of ownership intervening."[23]

Jaenen concludes that overall the native people of New France were not much impressed by the French:

> They were quite unable to understand that in France, where, according to the tales of the Europeans and the few Amerindians who had visited the country and returned to North America, there was apparently an abundance of food, many large towns and many people yet there were also poor people and beggars. . . . The Recollet missionaries found no beggars in the Huron and Montagnais encampments and whatever food was available was always shared, open hospitality being offered to all travellers.[24]

Obviously the world order of the native people changed in many ways for the worse after the arrival of Europeans.

Robert Berkhofer gives us another perspective and shows how "Indian" is a white American construct that kept changing over time and has served over the years to subjugate the native peoples. In his study, *The White Man's Indian: Images of the American Indian from Columbus to the Present*, Berkhofer suggests that we invented the Indian and continue to do so today. He claims that whites still view Indians as "others," as of the forest or a Wild West show rather than as farmers or city dwellers. He asks why, if we no longer think of ourselves as Gauls or Teutons or Anglo-Saxons, we continue to view Indians as unchanged from aboriginal times?[25] That certainly is not the native peoples' image of themselves and their world, but rather a new world constructed for them that persists today.

Incidentally, it is Berkhofer, writing back in 1979, who makes a strong plea for shedding the term "Indian" because it serves only as an ideological image and not the reality. He suggests in its place "native Americans."[26] I personally disagree with "native Americans" precisely for the reasons Berkhofer favors it, because the term identifies the native peoples as being American, as merging with the larger American society, as being no different than Italian-Americans or Asian-Americans. To distinguish them this way seems to me to portray them as any other ethnic group in America, but they are not. They are the original inhabitants of this land, not immigrants, and this fact should be recognized in some meaningful way. In Canada, native peoples are struggling to find some common appellation, and I know that they would never agree to be called "native Canadians," for they are arguing for recognition as separate nations within the state of Canada. Right now, the term gaining favor is "First Nations," but consensus may not be easy as it must be gained among the Indian, Métis, and Inuit peoples.

So ends our brief visit to some of the new worlds that emerged when France and England, following Spain's example, decided to colonize the northern half of America. Let us now examine more closely another New World that developed and how some native societies accommodated themselves to the European imposition. A comparative analysis of this contact between Europeans and native people demonstrates that the effects were not uniform and that cultural, geographic, and historic processes all converged to make the outcome different for different societies.

Until recently the historical literature of the contact period told us that native life underwent immediate and drastic change upon the arrival of the Europeans. These simplistic explanations tended to be based on the presumed superiority of European technology and, in the days before social history was acceptable, did not probe the inner workings of native society to examine exactly what changes took place. Implicit within this presumption of technological superiority is the notion of European superiority in political and economic relations. Historians thus assumed that Europeans dominated every aspect of the contact situation from the start.

We now know this was not true. In fact, we realize that France and England got caught up in the military alliances and political intrigues already in place among native groups and that these were important factors in shaping the Europeans' eventual domination of the North American continent.

This change in our view of history has come with the development of ethnohistory, a merger of history and anthropology. Application of anthropological principles to interpreting historical data has led ethnohistorians to new views of the contact situation and the native peoples' responses to it. Our new methodology leads to the conclusions that there is no unicausal explanation that can be applied to the contact situation for all native peoples and that historians have erred in assuming that new technology was the all-important factor in change. To illustrate the contribution of ethnohistory to our understanding of historical processes, let us take a brief look at social change as experienced by two hunting peoples in two different historic and cultural settings: one maritime people, the Micmacs, and one subarctic-boreal forest people, the James Bay Cree. I will also make occasional references to other peoples.

MICMAC HISTORY

In 1605 the Frenchmen Pierre du Gua the Sieur de Monts and Samuel de Champlain stepped ashore at what they called "Port Royal." Located on the south shore of the Bay of Fundy in the present-day Canadian province of Nova Scotia, it was at that time homeland of the Souriquois, a band of Micmacs. The French leaders established a colony there that practiced subsistence farming to feed itself and engaged in a fur trade with the local Indians to produce revenues for the colony and its French promoters. The Micmacs were the suppliers to this fur trade. Perhaps as much as one hundred years prior to this settlement in their midst the Micmacs were certainly in contact, at least sporadically, with the European fishermen who seasonally arrived along their coastline to harvest cod and obtain fresh water, firewood, and perhaps meat. Thus by the time of the arrival of French settlement and the establishment of fur trade, the Micmacs were quite accustomed to trade, at least to occasional trade.

Maritime anthropologists and historians tell us, however, that the hunting of fur animals, particularly beaver, modified the precontact calendar of subsistence activities and settlement patterns of the Micmacs, who had been more largely oriented to a coastal marine economy. Combining archaeological evidence and inferences based on the climatic conditions and Micmac economic patterns described in the early seventeenth-century data, they suggest that the Micmacs in the years just prior to the contact period were more populous and more sedentary than those of the historic period.[27] Although climatic conditions might have had some effect on population and culture, it was the focus on beaver hunting after sustained contact with the French that drew the Micmacs away from an emphasis on marine resources. Their wholehearted incorporation of the fur trade within their economy is, according to these historic sources, perhaps explained by their desire to obtain the manufactured goods the Europeans offered them.

To obtain European goods, the Micmacs had to alter their round of subsistence activities, based on coastal resources, to accommodate an inland hunt of land-based, fur-bearing animals. Although an interior orientation had always provided the skins and sinews of moose and deer for clothing and tent-ing, the fur trade-based orientation towards the interior was of a different order of magnitude. The precontact hunting of large game animals such as the moose and deer allowed the Micmacs to congregate in larger hunting groups whereas a concentration on smaller fur-bearing animals dictated smaller family units and a longer stay in the interior along lakes and streams rather than in the more forested habitat of the caribou. This change in seasonal activities also drew them away from the coast in spring where the fish resources were more abundant.[28] Thus the altered subsistence settlement was a system in disequilibrium with its environment.[29]

Other changes in the Micmac social order can be attributed to their entry into the fur trade. By the mid-1700s, ethnohistorians tell us, the depletion of resources in the interior forced many Micmac males deeper inland to trap fur-bearing animals, and they left their families at fur trade posts or near other European settlements, where they subsisted on European foods.[30] Thus, "artificial communities" arose at locations convenient for traders, missionaries, and colonial administrators but not necessarily compatible with the principles of a maritime-based community organization nor with the subsistence practices that prevailed in precontact times. In fact, we learn from the archaeological record that the Micmacs abandoned many aboriginal settlement areas. In sum, involvement in the French-sponsored fur trade radically altered precontact Micmac communal social structure, thoroughly undermined political solidarity, and destroyed self-sufficiency. These transformations occurred not immediately but gradually over the first 150 years of contact. By the mid-1700s any aboriginal societal practices that had not been already altered due to the demands of the fur trade had been changed or destroyed. Then in the mid-1700s, English settlers not only stole Micmac lands but hunted the Micmacs down in order to eliminate them. The conflict over land is what ultimately destroyed a large number of Indian societies, particularly in the New England area.

CREE HISTORY

Sixty-four years after the French launched a fur trade in Acadia, the English in 1668 involved the eastern Cree of the James Bay and Hudson Bay in the fur trade. This story unfolds differently, because the Cree did not have to abandon settlement systems or radically alter subsistence practices. They already had an interior adaptation rather than a coastal one and, although they were caribou hunters, they did not have the luxury of concentrating on this one resource. This is clearly seen in the historical records when the daily journals of the Hudson's Bay Company begin in 1736.

The archaeological record in this northern subarctic region clearly indicates that Cree social organization was based on a winter hunting group of several families and that the seasonal shifts in the late precontact times were similar to modern ones indicating, perhaps, a similar resource exploitation.[31] The earliest reference to the size of winter hunting groups dates to 1755 when a trader suggests that winter hunting groups were no greater than three or four families,[32] a size consistent with the prehistoric archaeological findings of Laliberté and those of recent fieldwork investigations.[33] The Cree subsistence economy, as represented in the eighteenth-century documentary records, parallels the precontact one represented in the bone deposits of the archaeological sites, and indicates a mixed economy of caribou, beaver, hare, and fish. Although caribou was the prized food, beaver ranked a close second and, in fact, was a more reliable food source than the small, widely scattered herds of woodland caribou.[34] To engage in the fur trade, the eastern Cree, therefore, did not require a significant shift in resource exploitation and/or habitat as did the Micmacs. Accordingly, the Cree were able to incorporate the needs created by the fur trade within their year-round subsistence strategy. Furthermore, the emphasis on beaver hunting, which prevailed in the eighteenth century meant that the Cree were able to consume the flesh and trade the furs. In the latter half of the nineteenth century, however, declining resources, among other factors, produced a shift in the fur trade to smaller fur bearers such as marten, fox, and muskrat, that is, to non-food animals. This shift to small animals continued in the early part of the twentieth century, combined with a decline of the traditional food animals, beaver and caribou, and a drastic drop in world fur prices, led to a reduction in the size of the winter hunting group from three or four families to a single nuclear family.[35] Once the dire game shortage was over and beaver hunting resumed in the late 1940s, the Cree were able to reinstate two and three-family winter hunting groups.[36]

Changes have occurred in Cree society, many of them caused by the Crees' involvement in the fur trade and many of them parallel to those that occurred for the Micmacs at an earlier period. These changes, however, were the result of a profusion of factors, all having to do with late nineteenth-century developments that brought outside agencies (church and government) and individuals into James Bay.[37] These external factors combined in an assault on the Crees' self-sufficiency and political independence and made them an impoverished, economically dependent people. This situation is slowly being reversed.

Although the Cree eventually reached the same impoverished state the Micmacs suffered some two hundred years earlier, the route they traveled was not the same. It is these differences that make us stop and question the conventional wisdom that involvement in the European fur trade or the introduction of a superior technology necessarily results in instantaneous changes for the weaker society.

CONCLUSION

As the two contrasting experiences with Indian-European contact indicate, the changes that take place in a society must be studied from the point of view of the social and institutional structures. The incorporation of a new technology does not, in itself, lead to dramatic changes within the society. Most often, the so-called new technology was a substitution of foreign materials for indigenous ones, such as metal knives for stone blades or wool cloth for skin clothing. European items made subsistence practices more efficient, perhaps, but did not alter them. The reason Micmac society changed to accommodate the fur trade while Cree society did not is that Micmac social organization had to change in order to produce the beaver skins. For the Cree, beaver was already a staple resource and their social organization was geared to its production. The Micmac chose to engage in the fur trade because they wanted the products of a new technology and were willing to alter their hunting and subsistence patterns to get them. As a result, their social organization had to transform itself, leaving them more vulnerable to later European assault on their political and economic autonomy. Thus, change came from an altered subsistence economy and not as the result of an altered technology. This is a more sociologically sound explanation for change. Not all societies chose this route early in the contact period, as is exemplified by both the Naskapi Indians and the Inuit of eastern Hudson Bay who stayed out of the trade until the 1840s, some two hundred years after the Cree had entered it.[38]

Space does not permit a similar in-depth sociological analysis of other societies. Instead, I direct you to the work of Bruce Trigger who has masterfully crafted the details of Huron history and society. In one of his volumes, *Natives and Newcomers*, he argues that the fur trade strengthened rather than threatened traditional patterns of social organization.[39] Similarly a study of west coast fur trade by Robin Fisher concludes that the fur trade, being a mutually beneficial economic system, brought minimal cultural change to the Northwest Coast peoples and that it was change they could control and to which they could adapt. Later settlement was disruptive, however, because it introduced major cultural and social changes so rapidly that the people lost control of their situation.[40] One can even reach across to southern Africa to find similar conclusions about the consequences of contact. In their article on the Kalahari San, Jacqueline Solway and Richard Lee "challenge the notion that contact automatically undermines foragers. . . . We subscribe to the view of culture as buoyant and capable of modification without transformation."[41]

There are a number of other lessons from anthropology that need to be applied to our analyses of contact situations. For instance, one must begin with the assumption that in a contact situation each group tries to gain the maximum advantages of the trade without destroying the general framework of its own society. One can expect that societies will opt for gradual development by incorporating new elements on their own creative terms rather than choosing abrupt change, unless specific conditions have made it impossible for the society to control the change, such as when disease decimates the population. Similarly, we can expect that each society would attempt to control the changing situation and exercise its dominance over the process of change. There are a number of examples of this. Micmac resistance to English settlement in the early 1700s is one; Huron expansion of their trading network and independence of the French in the 1620s and 1630s is another.[42]

Another problem in the historical literature is how we portray this change. On the surface, in terms of technology, dress, and other outwardly visible manifestations, significant change may seem to have occurred, yet the internal cohesion of the society, achieved through its religious and ideological systems, as well as its political and economic institutions, may remain intact. Anthropologists tell us that one of the functions of a society is to try to provide security for its members and that it does so by producing its "stabilizers."[43] Historians must look for these stabilizers. In the Cree case they can be found, in addition to the social organization described above, in aspects of Cree religion and outlook that are strikingly maintained even today.[44] Thus, historians have to be careful about assuming rapid social change as a result of Amerindian contact with European society.

Another concern must be in the actual practice of developing ethnohistoric accounts. Researchers have tended to accept at face value narrative accounts in the documents without considering if such developments could really have occurred, given what is known about the society at the time. One example is historians' acceptance of the assumption that with the arrival of the Europeans the Indians became dependent on them for food,[45] as if shiploads of European provisions were sent to feed the local Indians. The Hudson's Bay Company, for one, could barely scrape together enough food to feed its European employees, and, in fact, relied on the native hunters for provisions. I suggest that there has been less rigorous examination of such texts and fewer attempts to achieve consistency than one finds in other historical endeavors. The historical data must be balanced with anthropological perspectives on, and knowledge of, the functioning of societies.

In conclusion, I am suggesting that it is necessary for historians to probe the consequences of Indian-European contact, using a longer temporal perspective than one usually finds in the literature, and to seek a complex of sociological factors to describe and explain social change rather than relying on a universal, unicausal explanation. Any sound historical analysis must take into account the processes of incorporation, adaptation, assimilation, and cultural persistence; and historical data must be critically examined with a view to interpreting it in ways consistent with these principles. Otherwise, we will fall prey to ethnocentricism and the erroneous assumption that because some native peoples—such as the native societies that once thrived in Maine, Vermont, New York, and Massachusetts—suffered relatively rapid social disintegration and extinction because of the force of European settlement, all societies so succumbed in the face of the European superiority. I hope I have shown that they did not and that we now have more information and a wider perspective with which to assess the long-term effects of what happened to native peoples when Europeans found an unexpected land mass and created for themselves a New World.

I have hanging on my office wall a bumper sticker that I purchased a few years back at a powwow in Chicago. It reads: "Indians had bad immigration laws." Some might interpret this to suggest that the Indians should have kept out everyone. I say they just were not selective. They did not differentiate among Europeans. They should have encouraged fur traders and kept out settlers.

NOTES

1. Olive P. Dickason, *The Myth of the Savage and the Beginnings of French Colonialism in the Americas* (Edmonton: University of Alberta Press, 1984), 5.

2. Raymond Fogelson, "Interpretations of the American Indian Psyche: Some Historical Notes," in *Social Contexts of American Ethnology, 1840-1984.* 1984 Proceedings of the American Ethnological Society, June Helm, ed. (Washington: AES, 1985), 10.

3. Robert F. Berkhofer, Jr., *The White Man's Indian: Images of the American Indian from Columbus to the Present* (New York: Alfred A. Knopf, 1979), 40.

4. L. C. Green and Olive P. Dickason, *The Law of Nations and the New World* (Edmonton: University of Alberta Press, 1989), 29; see also Dickason, *The Myth of the Savage.*

5. Ibid., 29, 33, 32.

6. Ibid., 40.

7. Dickason, et al., x-xi.

8. Peter A. Cumming and Neil H. Mickenberg, eds., *Native Rights in Canada* (Toronto: General Publishing Co., 1972), 82.

9. Eric R. Wolf, *Europe and the People Without History* (Berkeley: University of California Press, 1982), 4.

10. George R. Hamell, "Strawberries, Floating Islands, and Rabbit Captains: Mythical Realities and European Contact in the Northeast during the Sixteenth and Seventeenth Centuries," *Journal of Canadian Studies* 21 (Winter 1987).

11. Cornelius J. Jaenen, "Amerindian Views of French Culture in the Seventeenth Century," *Canadian Historical Review* 55 (September 1974): 265.

12. Ibid.

13. Ibid., 268.

14. Kenneth M. Morrison, *The Embattled Northeast: The Elusive Ideal of Alliance in Abenaki-Euroamerican Relations* (Berkeley: University of California Press, 1984), 57.

15. Jaenen, 269.

16. Ibid., 271.

17. Ibid, 277.

18. Ibid., 279.

19. Ibid., 271.

20. Ibid., 280, 285.

21. Ibid.; Reuben G. Thwaites, ed., *The Jesuit Relations and Allied Documents: Travels and Explorations of the Jesuit Missionaries in New France, 1610-1791*, 73 vols. (Cleveland, 1896-1901), I, 281.

22. Ibid., 277.

23. Jaenen, 267.

24. Jaenen, 281-82.

25. Berkhofer, 29.

26. Ibid., 196.

27. Patricia Nietfeld, "Determinants of Aboriginal Micmac Political Structure" (Ph.D. diss., University of New Mexico, 1981), 116-24, 363.

28. Nietfeld, 212; L. F. S. Upton, *Micmacs and Colonists: Indian-White Relations in the Maritimes* (Vancouver: University of British Columbia Press, 1979), 20.

29. Nietfeld, 213.

30. Ibid., 445.

31. Marcel Laliberté, "La forêt boréale" in *Images de la Préhistoire du Québec*, C. Chapdelaine, ed., Recherches Amérindiennnes au Québec, 7:1-2 (1978), 96.

32. Toby Morantz, *An Ethonohistoric Study of Eastern James Bay Cree Social Organization, 1700-1850* (Ottawa: National Museum of Man. Canadian Ethnology Service Paper, no. 88, 1983), 106.

33. Edward S. Rogers, *The Hunting Group-Hunting Territory Complex Among the Mistassini Indians* (Ottawa: National Museum of Man. Anthropological Series no. 63, Bulletin no. 195, 1963), 55.

34. Morantz, 25-31.

35. Adrian Tanner, "Game Shortages and the Inland Fur Trade in Northern Quebec, 1915 to 1940" in *Papers of the Ninth Algonquian Conference*, W. Cowan, ed. (Ottawa: Carleton University, 1978), 146-59.

36. Toby Morantz, "A History of Northern James Bay, 1700-1945" (manuscript prepared for the Cree Regional Authority, 1985), 160.

37. See Toby Morantz, "Dwindling Animals and Diminished Lands: Early Twentieth Century Developments in Eastern James Bay" in *Papers of the*

Eighteenth Algonquian Conference, W. Cowan, ed. (Ottawa: Carleton University, 1987).

38. Daniel Francis and Toby Morantz, *Partners in Furs: A History of the Fur Trade in Eastern James Bay, 1600-1870* (Montreal: McGill-Queen's University Press, 1983), 136.

39. Bruce G. Trigger, *Natives and Newcomers: Canada's "Heroic Age" Reconsidered* (Montreal: McGill-Queen's University Press, 1985), 208. A fuller account may be found in Trigger's definitive work on the Huron, *The Children of Aataentsic: A History of the Huron People to 1660*, 2 vols. (Montreal: McGill-Queen's University Press, 1976), 361-62.

40. Robin Fisher, *Contact and Conflict: Indian-European Relations in British Columbia, 1774-1890* (Vancouver: University of British Columbia Press, 1977), xiv-xv.

41. Jacqueline Solway and Richard B. Lee, "Foragers, Genuine or Spurious: Situating the Kalahari San in History," *Current Anthropology* 31:2 (April 1990), 110.

42. Upton, 31-32; Bruce G. Trigger, *The Children of Aataentsic*, 361-362.

43. J. A. Ponsioen, *The Analysis of Social Change Reconsidered: A Sociological Study* (The Hague: Mouton and Co.: Institute of Social Studies, vol. 4, 1962), 57-58.

44. See Adrian Tanner, *Bringing Home Animals: Religious Ideology and Mode of Production of the Mistassini Cree* (London: C. Hurst, 1979).

45. See Rich, 71.

Incorporating the Frontier:

A Perspective on Euro-American Colonization

in Vermont

Richard H. Schein

istory is as much about perspectives and viewpoints as it is about facts. History is always being rewritten; and so it should be as we gain new information and, importantly, new perspectives. This paper proposes to examine the Vermont frontier from the vantage point of an historical geographer. Such a viewpoint involves looking at the Vermont frontier within the larger context of American imperial and colonial expansion; as part of a burgeoning American nation that was increasingly tied by a common desire for commercial prosperity and political independence; as lands that were first claimed and conquered by Europeans and then organized and settled primarily from outside the region; and, finally, as a territory and state that was eventually physically linked with a larger world. These themes together suggest the hierarchical nesting of places and the need for an attention to different scales of historical geographical inquiry.

One example of the ways in which places are nested and the notion of changing scales of inquiry comes from Thornton Wilder's play *Our Town*. At the end of the first act, Rebecca Gibbs has joined her brother George at a bedroom window, gazing into the vastness of a moonlit night. She tells him of a letter received by a friend of hers, addressed to: "Jane Crofut, The Crofut Farm, Grovers Corners, Sutton County, New Hampshire, United States of America, Continent of North America, Western Hemisphere, The Earth."[1] What follows is an attempt to establish the same sort of address for the Vermont frontier at the turn of the eighteenth century in order to connect that specific part of Vermont history to larger issues and distant places.

This paper makes those connections in a two-step process. First, it erects three "straw men" of sorts by briefly examining three general ideas or stereotypes that have come to shape our perceptions and recollections of the past. Introducing and questioning these three ideas or commonly accepted concepts—our image of the New England village, the frontier of Frederick Jackson Turner, and the recent hastening of time-space compression—allows us to see, in part, the foundations of our historical understanding in order to go beyond them. Second, this paper suggests an alternative, historical geography perspective for viewing the Vermont frontier.

PRELIMINARY IDEAS ON THE VERMONT FRONTIER

The first of my straw men is the idealized New England village. The stereotypical image of the New England village is a familiar picture: the town as the basic political unit, focused on a central village. That village has a central common or green, dominated by a Congregational church, and flanked on three sides by large, white clapboard houses. This celebrated cultural landscape is generally acknowledged as the remnant of Puritan utopian settlement ideals. The clustering of houses around a common space, all within the shadow of the church, symbolizes the social and religious nature of the community within. But recent scholarship has shown that the New England village just described is an invention of the eighteenth century. In fact, the Puritan founders of colonial New England very quickly abandoned the idea of living in agricultural villages. "New" England offered them more individual freedoms and greater possibilities to own land. As a result, colonial New Englanders spread themselves over the land, living with their families on individual farms in a pattern that is generally called "dispersed rural settlement."

This does not deny either the existence or the social and political importance of the "town." The town was important and its center was marked by a common and a church or meetinghouse. But individual members of colonial New England society chose to live on their farms at some distance from the central gathering spot, and that central spot did not become the focus of villages as we know them until late in the eighteenth century—precisely when Vermont was becoming incorporated into a greater New England.[2]

But even the meaning of the "town" itself had undergone significant changes by the time lands in Vermont were being eyed by southern New Englanders. The town was no longer just a religious or social or political delineation analogous to the English parish. By the time Vermont was divided into towns, "the town" was also a speculative unit—a block of land to be organized and sold to encourage settlement and make a profit. Benning Wentworth's creation of the New Hampshire Grants is remembered for many things and is ever the subject of scholarly inquiry and reinterpretation. However, one thing is certain. The New Hampshire Grants—those towns created by Wentworth in Vermont—were part of a larger "speculative mania" that gripped New England and, in fact, most of British North America throughout the eighteenth century. Land was one of the few avenues to great wealth at that time. The general sales spree in Massachusetts lands in the 1720s and in Connecticut lands in the 1730s was reinvigorated as a speculative fever in Vermont after the French and Indian War and continued unabated in New York and westward after the Revolution.[3]

In addition to Wentworth's profit on the New Hampshire Grants, most of the original grants in Vermont were soon bought up by speculators, who often sent out canvassers to other parts of the country to promote their Vermont interests.[4] This is an important prelude to examining actual Euro-American settlement in Vermont; for it suggests an organizing and ordering of territory prior to settlement, from places external to Vermont, as part of a larger sphere of American capitalist development where land was a commodity to be owned and traded.

By the middle of the eighteenth century, individuals and families were moving to Vermont and setting up independent farmsteads in a pattern of dispersed rural settlement, all within the political and social context of the town, itself organized and sold by speculative interests primarily outside of Vermont. Soon after the arrival of those first settlers, Vermonters joined the rest of New England and much of New York in creating the New England village as we know it today. The village generally occupied a central location, often at the town center or the earlier designated site of the common and meetinghouse, but the catalyst for the actual development of the village was establishing connections to the larger commercial world of the developing nation after the American Revolution.[5] Within the predetermined settlement framework, those connections were created by erecting a mill or opening a general store. Such enterprises served the needs of a commercially minded population. They provided outlets for grain to be processed and forwarded to an external market and represent the reaching into Vermont of mercantile interests providing the goods of a larger world for the settlers on the frontier. P. Jeffrey Potash has shed some light on this very process in his discussion of the early foundations of Middlebury village in the last decade of the eighteenth century.[6] A store lot sold to a New York merchant in 1789 and subsequent competition between two millers at the falls on Otter Creek acted as catalysts for creating a substantial village, described by Timothy Dwight several years later:

> Several mills had been erected at this spot in 1798. A brewery was established; several stores had been built; a considerable number of mechanics and several gentlemen in the liberal professions had chosen this spot as their residence. An academy also was nearly completed, which was intended to be the germ of a future college. Upon the whole, the seeds of future respectability were already sown here.[7]

The second straw man is the frontier concept of Frederick Jackson Turner, arguably the most important work in American historiography. Despite the claim by many contemporary historians that Turner's frontier thesis is no longer given serious consideration, some scholarship is still couched in Turnerian terms. Perhaps more importantly, however, Turner's ideas live on in the popular imagination and in national mythology. Turner presented his hypothesis to a convention of the American Historical Association in 1893, prompted by the announcement three years earlier by the superintendent of the census that the American frontier was officially "closed." In the opening pages, he wrote: "The existence of an area of free land, its continuous recession, and the advance of American settlement westward, explain American development."[8]

Although Vermont was hardly a "western frontier," it was a frontier at the end of the eighteenth century. Turnerian ideas about what he called "the colonization of the Great West," especially his notions of repeated stages of frontier development, can be and have been generally applied to Vermont.

The idea that every frontier essentially began again—involved the recreation of society and civilization after an initial reversion to social and cultural barbarism—is very much a part of American frontier mythology. But people did not leave home and instantly forget all that they already knew upon reaching a new place, whether that frontier was in Vermont or Oregon. To be sure, exigencies of the frontier experience shaped and perhaps guided many aspects of the new life, but people also brought with them ideas and memories, what is generally called "cultural baggage." To fully understand the historical development of Vermont in the eighteenth century, it must be recognized that the Euro-Americans who first settled here came from somewhere; and in making the journey they did not necessarily leave behind their previous notions of society, polity, and economy. The fact of Vermont migrants' "cultural baggage" is neatly captured in a map adapted from Wilbur Zelinsky's book entitled *The Cultural Geography of the United States* (Figure 1).

Zelinksy has drawn primarily on the work of geographers, linguists, anthropologists, and students of material culture to illustrate the general movement of ideas in the eastern United States. Working from the premise of several colonial American "culture hearths"—most notably in southeastern New England, southeastern Pennsylvania, and the tidewater south—Zelinsky reminds us that ideas diffuse through space as people migrate and connections between places are established. To understand the settlement and development of the Vermont frontier, it is important not to accept simply the mythology of a physical environment so threatening, so overwhelming, as to cause people to "reinvent the wheel." Early settlers in Vermont, just as their counterparts on many American frontiers before and after them, relied on their individual experiences and their collective past to confront a new life in a new place.

The third straw man is related to the Turnerian frontier thesis. It is the notion of a global village, an interconnected and shrinking world, a popular one these days; and it is an idea with firm foundations in the changes that have occurred over the past few centuries. The development of new transportation and communication technologies since the eighteenth century has decreased greatly the friction of distance between places and perceptions of those distances. The effect of changing transport technologies on real distance over the past 150 years—or more concisely, the shrinking of the world—is illustrated in Figure 2.

Figure 2 shows us the world and notes that the best travel speed before about 1840 was ten miles per hour. With the advent of steam locomotives and

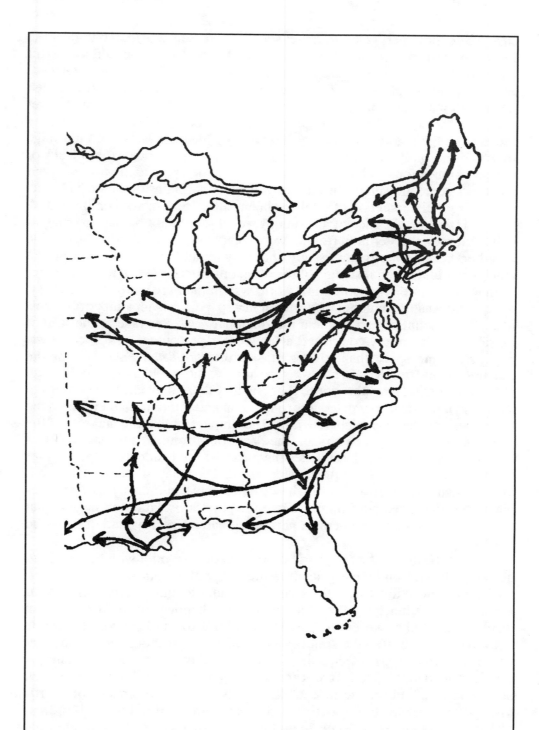

Figure 1. The Diffusion of Ideas. Adapted from Wilbur Zelinsky, *The Cultural Geography of the United States* (Englewood Cliffs, N.J.: Prentice Hall, 1973), 81.

steamships, however, possible travel speeds increased considerably; thus the functional size of the world was made smaller simply by an ability to get around more quickly. Compared to the world before 1840, the world after 1840 seemed a smaller place. Similarly, the invention of propeller aircraft and then jet aircraft made distance even less of a nuisance, and the world seemed to get even smaller as the globe could be circumnavigated in a fraction of the time required in the eighteenth century. Completing Figure 2, we see a final stage in which the globe is reduced almost to a pinpoint through the advent of telecommunications technology, which provides the opportunity to "reach out and touch someone" almost instantaneously. This shrinking of the world is part of the larger phenomenon of what has been called "time-space compression."

However, the idea of a shrinking world should not be used to suggest that settlers on the Vermont frontier were completely isolated from the outside world or, perhaps more importantly, that they wanted to be isolated from the outside world. In fact, residents of the Vermont frontier may have been more acutely aware of their position in a world system than are many people today. A quick perusal of a number of Vermont newspapers provides support for this idea. The amount of national and international news coverage at the turn of the eighteenth century comprised a far greater percentage of a local newspaper's column space than it does in, say, the *Burlington Free Press* or the *Rutland Herald* today.[9] The news reported in those old newspapers, with datelines from all over the world, suggests that there may have been more of a feeling of political connectedness to national and international events of the time than many people might feel now. The simple fact that the majority of the news reported in newspapers of the Vermont frontier was national and international at the very least belies the idea that the residents of the frontier wanted to be isolated from the outside world. They may in fact have found it quite difficult to physically cover the distance between themselves and other places but that need not imply a desire for physical isolation or suggest that they were prevented from being a part of a greater New England or a United States.

Confusing the fact of physical isolation on a frontier with the desire to be isolated on a frontier easily leads to the image of the brave pioneer farmer, far beyond the influence of the civilized world, creating a better life: What Richard Hofstadter has called the myth of the happy yeoman. The yeoman image, promoted by writers such as Thomas Jefferson and Hector St. Jean de Crèvecoeur, celebrated the American farmer's "honest industry, his independence, his frank spirit of equality, [and] his ability to produce and enjoy a simple abundance." The American farmer was seen as "non-commercial, nonpecuniary, and self-sufficient."[10] Thus is created an image of sturdy forebears who liked nothing better than escaping the confines of civilization to feel the dirt running between their fingers as they eked out a wholesome subsistence on the frontier. There may have been some people like that, but for the most part the men and women on any early American frontier were interested in making a living. Robert Mitchell has examined frontier colonization in the Shenandoah Valley in the middle of the eighteenth century. His observations on the commercial foundations of that enterprise are equally

1500-1840
Horse-drawn carriages
and sailing ships—
best average speed:
10 miles per hour

1850-1930
Steam locomotives reach
an average speed of
65 m.p.h.; steam
ships average 36 m.p.h.

1950s
Propeller aircraft reach
speeds of 300-400 m.p.h.

1960s
Jet aircraft move passengers
at 500-700 m.p.h.

1990s
Telecommunications are
instantaneous!

Figure 2. Our Shrinking World. Adapted from Peter Dicken, *Global Shift: Industrial Change in a Turbulent World* (London: Harper & Row, 1986), 108.

applicable to the Vermont experience. Rather than the image of happy yeomen and women, physically isolated from "civilization" and content with their lot, we ought to picture the primarily agricultural colonists of the region as commercially minded farmers trying to produce a surplus for local and external markets.[11] The aim was not just to survive, but to make a profit and achieve a better life. Their counterparts on the Great Plains frontier a century later would be after the same things—hoping to make enough from the harvest to buy a Brussels carpet and some new clothes from the Sears catalog at the end of the year.

AN HISTORICAL GEOGRAPHY PERSPECTIVE

In the first volume, *Atlantic America*, of a proposed three-volume series, *The Shaping of America*, the geographer D. W. Meinig offers a perspective on our collective past that sees the development of the United States as the "human creation of places and of networks of relationships among them."[12] Meinig's model of American settlement and imperial expansion depicts colonial America as a set of discrete points of attachment between Europe and North America, some of which became settlement nuclei; places like Jamestown, Philadelphia, Baltimore, New Haven, and Boston. The most vigorous of the settlement nuclei further developed into regions—like New England or tidewater Maryland or Pennsylvania—which, in turn, acted as eastern bases for eventual westward and, in the case of Vermont, northward American expansion. According to Meinig, the opening of new lands, like Vermont, to European settlement "led to a broad dispersal of the population and the creation of new regional systems, anchored in but grossly distended from the major centers of the seaboard."[13] Thus from the beginning of European-American interest in the lands that became Vermont, the impetus for organization of the territory and settlement of the land came from an already established cultural system, whether it was a European colonial interest centered locally in southern New England and ultimately in London or later an independent American imperial interest developing in the more settled portions of the eastern seaboard to the south and east of Vermont.

The "opening" of the Vermont frontier can then be viewed as an enterprise that was at first wholly orchestrated from outside the state by external political, social, and religious interests.[14] The territory that became Vermont was viewed as an area to be conquered, settled, and incorporated into a larger cultural system whose individual members dictated the initial framework for colonization. One easily overlooked feature of the infamous New Hampshire Grants story so enshrined in the regional mythology is that the grants controversy arose over competing outside interests in Vermont lands. The battle over territory did not at first involve anyone living in the territory but was an attempt to order and control land by men whose political and economic interests were based in earlier settled places. The interests of the New Hampshire and New York governors, the Privy Council, and, eventually, the king represent a "reaching out" of colonial America to draw previously unincorporated lands into the fabric of a maturing colonial system, by designating both specific boundaries within the territory and disputing the nature of the territory itself.

Subsequent to that initial reaching out, there ensued a land speculation period between 1761 and 1776.[15] Ira Allen himself arrived in Vermont from Connecticut in 1773 and laid out lots at Burlington Bay with the assumption that such speculation would pay off handsomely in years to come.[16] Most of the original grants were purchased by speculators who sent out agents to other parts of New England and New Jersey to sell in the interest of a quick profit.[17] The speculative nature of the Vermont frontier made it only one of several such frontiers from Maine to Georgia; one of several developing regions competing for the attention of established seaboard interests.

Alexander Harvey, representing a group of potential settlers from Scotland, arrived in New York City looking for land and traveled to upstate New York and Pennsylvania as well as Vermont before purchasing in the Connecticut River Valley.[18] John Lincklaen, a land proprietor employed by a syndicate of Dutch bankers and active in land promotions in central New York, traveled to Vermont in 1791 to pursue the possibilities of maple sugar production and remarked on the competition between Vermont lands and New York's "Genesee Country."[19] An 1805 ad in a Windsor newspaper suggests that speculators in Vermont were savvy to the general American practice of "hothousing," where initial farmlands in a newly settling territory were offered at little or no cost to promote settlement. Proprietor's agent James Whitelaw was offering any six men fifty acres each, presumably on the assumption that the presence of those six would act as a catalyst for further settlement, prove the suitability of the land for cultivation, and increase the value of the land for subsequent sales.[20] Thus through speculative ventures the Vermont frontier was organized in part from outside the region, and this organization was a component in larger, more general processes that were characteristic of the nation as a whole.

Another example of external organization or interest in early Vermont comes from the journal of Rev. Nathan Perkins, a prominent theologian from West Hartford, Connecticut, who completed a missionary tour of Vermont in 1789.[21] Perkins traveled up the western side of Vermont almost to the Canadian border, preaching to assorted congregations in barns, houses, churches, and even in the open at places like Middlebury, New Haven, Hinesburg, Williston, and Essex. He commented in his journal on many things, including the "raving arminian methodist" preacher he came across at Sunderland, the size of his audiences, and his effect upon their religious enthusiasm, the nature of the women in Vermont, and the general state of religion in what he called "a heathen wilderness," which was, in his opinion, being punished by famine for its transgressions. Perkins's particular dislike for many Vermonters may have been colored by his obvious distaste for the privations of food and drink forced upon his normally cosmopolitan character by the frontier situation. He repeatedly recorded his longing for the luxuries of bed and board in Connecticut and was especially disgusted by the scarcity of good drink on his tour, commenting of Vermonters that "their beer [is] poor bran beer . . . maple cyder is horrible stuff" and that there was "no malt in ye country." Nevertheless, Perkins did manage to reach about fifty new towns in Vermont, preaching on the average six days out of seven.

Aside from the touch of color that Perkins's journal adds to our perceptions of the past, we should be aware that in his evangelical mission he was "appointed by ye association of Hartford county at the instance and request of the General Association of Connecticut." One of his duties while in that appointment was carried out at Essex, where he "gathered and incorporated a church and admitted a member and drew ye form of covenant." Perkins was part of a larger missionary endeavor in which religious interests in more settled parts of the United States felt it their duty to reach out to organize Christianity on the frontier. The General Association of Connecticut was one of many societies sending clergy to newly settled places. Organizations like the Massachusetts Missionary Society, the Berkshire and Columbia Missionary Society, the Connecticut Missionary Society, the Hampshire Missionary Society, the General Assembly of the Presbyterian Church in America, and the circuit riders of the Methodist Church headquartered in Baltimore were all active in the eastern United States. Representatives from these and other organizations ensured that the frontier would be an extension of established practice and that peripheral locations would be immediately incorporated into larger regional and national cultural systems.[22]

In addition to the initial and ongoing influence of external forces and individuals on the Euro-American colonization of Vermont, settlers migrating to the state brought with them cultural baggage from their earlier homes. Through their migration they assisted in the diffusion of ideas from earlier settled cultural hearths. To be sure, they also reacted to their new environments in novel ways, but much of the new society they organized on the frontier was affected by the notions of society they carried with them.

Early migrants to the Vermont frontier often came in families or, through information networks, established migration chains that connected a Vermont community with an older one in southern New England. Thus from the beginning, links of kinship and acquaintance ensured that traditions would not only find their way to Vermont, but would continue to be informed by contacts with the places the settlers had left for Vermont. Bellesiles has written of the early grants settlers that they did not feel isolated from the communities they left behind for they maintained contact with their former neighbors and "by no means" were they cut off from communication. In fact, the general attitude in the early grants towns was that they were an outpost of traditional New England.[23]

That perception of a New England outpost makes sense, for most of those early migrants arrived in Vermont from other parts of New England. Harold Meeks has documented the origins of the earliest white settlers in the state and has pointed out that in fifty Vermont towns the first settlers were from Connecticut, in twenty-seven they arrived from New Hampshire; thirty-four more towns claimed Massachusetts origins for their first Euro-American residents, and three towns were settled from Rhode Island.[24] Those early settlers were crowded out of other parts of New England and, in the late seventeenth century, were blocked from westward migration by the presence of New York, the Iroquois Confederacy, and the Proclamation Line of 1763. Looking to the north for an outlet, they came to Vermont: traveling via the Connecticut River to settle the east side of the state; up the Deerfield River to the Green Mountains and down their western flanks to the Champlain Valley; or up the Housatonic River and through the Berkshires to the western part of Vermont.[25] In some places the migration was a several-year process. Colonists would travel to Vermont in the late winter or early spring to establish their farms but would return home to southern New England for the first few winters until their Vermont farmsteads were well established.[26] Thus, not only were ideas and customs carried to Vermont by migrants, but the yearly return to places of origin reinforced those traditions and the contacts with other places.

Two brief examples point to the diffusion of ideas to the Vermont frontier and to the kinds of cultural baggage people carried with them. The first comes from a small book first published in 1797 by Rutland lawyer and self-proclaimed aristocrat John Graham.[27] On many counts, this is a highly biased and suspect work. Noel Perrin's introduction to a recent reprint of Graham's sketch reminds us that Graham was, among many other things, something of a con man in search of wealth and power through a half-dozen different schemes. Thus Graham's descriptions of the state are intended to show it in the best of lights and to flatter the residents named in the work. Nevertheless, many of Graham's observations are valuable. Among his various descriptions are notes on the types of religious congregations found in Vermont. The list of religious practices includes Baptist, Unitarian, Episcopal, Presbyterian, Quaker, and Congregationalist. None is native to Vermont; all reflect the failure of Vermont migrants to revert to social and cultural barbarism. They preferred to re-create some vestige of the religious life as it was known outside the region.

The second example comes from an 1814 advertisement for a new bookstore in Burlington.[28] The store was offering dozens of books, including Milton, Homer, *Pilgrim's Progress*, Scott's works, Morse's *Gazetteer*, the *Memoirs of Jefferson*, *Silliman's Travels*, *Don Quixote*, and *Lewis and Clark's Travels*, in short, many works indicative of the classic liberal education of the day. The availability of these books alone implies the arrival in Vermont of ideas diffused from educated America and Europe. The fact of their advertisement suggests that there was a market for those books and that a significant number of residents in northern Vermont were connected to cultural systems larger than those of an isolated state.

The idea of connections to a larger system leads to the final component of the historical geographical vantage point proposed here: the claim that, from the time of their arrival, Vermonters on the frontier joined with outside interests to assist in the incorporation of Vermont into the fabric of the developing American nation. That does not mean only that they brought ideas with them and thus created, in effect, a new New England, but that they also actively worked to connect the frontier in tangible and intangible ways with more established centers of settlement.

The agricultural colonists who found their way to Vermont at the end of the eighteenth century were very much a part of a larger capitalist system. They were interested in producing surpluses to sell for profits. They needed markets for their anticipated loads of pearl and potash and for the eventual wagons of wheat, oats, rye, and barley they hoped to produce. The fact that many early settlers may have had a difficult enough time simply feeding themselves should not lead us to believe that they were not interested in selling the products of their labor.[29] There is, however, ample evidence that plenty of early farmers in Vermont did have produce for sale and that they found markets for those goods. Randolph Roth, for example, points out that early Euro-American settlers in the upper Connecticut River Valley carried their own goods annually to markets on the river or to Boston, Springfield, and Hartford. They also carried non-perishable items to their hometowns in southern New England where friends and relatives might hold them for a more "timely sale."[30] The important point to note is that connections were made between the frontier and external markets, connections that served to tie two regions increasingly closer together.

Vermonters looked externally to several different market centers. Those in the eastern half of the state focused on the Connecticut River and overland connections to Portsmouth or Boston and Hartford or New Haven. Eastern Vermonters chose between a southwesterly connection to Troy, Albany, and ultimately the New York City market or the northerly connection via Lake Champlain to the Richelieu and markets at Montreal and Quebec. Those in the upper reaches of the Connecticut River Valley and in north-central Vermont had access to the St. Lawrence River and Canadian markets via the Passumpsic River, Lake Memphremagog, and the St. Francis River Basin. Although the importance of the northern markets, especially to northern Vermonters should not be discounted, eventually, the southeastern and southwestern markets would dominate, as Vermont was, after all, part of the United States and not Canada.

To develop the potential of the southerly connections, attention in Vermont, as in much of the United States, turned to canal building by the 1790s. John Lincklaen, on his visit to Vermont in 1791, noted that "all the talk in Burlington was of a canal to be built from [present day] Whitehall to the North [Hudson] River and that the general opinion was that Canada would also make a canal between St. Johns and Chamblee."[31] The Hudson-Champlain Canal would become a reality in 1823. Meanwhile, on the other side of the state, more than just talk was occurring. That same year a company was chartered to build the Bellows Falls Canal, completed in 1805 and one of half a dozen canals that would eventually make the Connecticut passable far upstream from its natural head of navigation. Not only would such a canal aid in physically connecting Vermont to outside markets, some of the capital for the canal's construction was English and represents the integration of the Vermont economy with an international financial market.[32]

Advertisements in the *Dartmouth Gazette* and the *Brattleboro Reporter* in the first decade of the nineteenth century shed some light on the readiness of those on the periphery of the nation to assist in tying themselves more closely to the seaboard. Lottery tickets for almost $100,000 in prizes were offered to aid in constructing the South Hadley Canal, one of those further improvements on the Connecticut River.[33]

Such means to achieve commercial links were quite common at the time. The rapidity of general frontier advancement in the early years of the American republic combined with the inability of relatively small state and federal government bureaucracies to provide adequate infrastructure for their burgeoning populations and territories led to a crisis in transportation development throughout the country. Governments simply could not keep up with the demand for transport links within and between their jurisdictions. The solution to the problem lay in local government and, especially, private intervention. Throughout the United States, including Vermont, private road, turnpike, and canal companies raised capital by subscription, stock issuances, and even by lotteries. Beginning in 1799, for example, Vermont chartered ninety-one tollroad, turnpike, and plank road companies; about thirty of which were actually put into operation.[34] States also used lotteries to augment impecunious state coffers in an attempt to meet constituents' demands for good roads and canals. Such innovations in road and canal building point to the consuming desire on the part of peripheral settlers with commercial intentions to be a part of larger economic spheres and, conversely, to the readiness on the part of established commercial seaboard concerns to draw the many American frontiers into their economic embrace. The connections between seaboard cities and frontier hinterlands were nicely expressed by Benjamin DeWitt, a member of the Society for the Promotion of the Useful Arts. His 1807 comments shed light on the interconnectedness of city and country at the turn of the nineteenth century in general:

> Let us consider the city of New York as the centre of commerce, or the heart of the State, Hudson's river as the main artery, the turnpike roads leading from it as so many great branches extending to the extremities, from which diverge the innumerable small ramifications or common roads into the whole body and substance; these again send off capillary branches, or private roads, to all the individual farms, which may be considered as the secretory organs, generating the produce and wealth of the state.[35]

Farms generating the produce and wealth of Vermont existed in much the same relationship to external markets, whether those markets ultimately were in Boston or New York. And, as suggested earlier, very often mills and stores acted as the nexus between the Vermonter and the outside world. Mills obviously prepared locally grown grain for market as well as personal consumption. Stores served a somewhat more complex purpose on the Vermont frontier, as on so many others. In a time before banks in Vermont and during a cash-scarce era, general stores often acted as the financial focus of a Vermont community. Payment-in-kind was often accepted in lieu of cash. A sampling of early eighteenth-century storekeepers in Vergennes, Middlebury,

Rutland, and Lebanon, New Hampshire, indicates that wheat, rye, corn, oats, butter, pork, lard, flax, flax-seed, ashes, and cheese, at least, were accepted in exchange for store goods.

In return, Vermont residents could obtain from those stores not only the essentials of frontier existence but produce and manufactures received from Boston and New York and originating in many places around the world: tea, brandy, rum, cloth, coffee, raisins, tobacco, gin, wine, sugar, snuff, dry goods, bottled water, furniture, hats, shoes, crockery, hardware, glass, and all manner of English, European, and east and west Indian goods.[36] Local stores acted as the links between Vermont settlers and national and international trading and production systems. Vermont may have been a frontier at the edge of that world system, but it was still very much a part of those connections spanning the globe. Moreover, many items of merchandise were identified by origins in storekeepers' advertisements, and people knew the extent to which they were connected with outside places.

A final glimpse of Vermont's place in larger economic systems comes from an advertisement for a Burlington druggist in 1814. John Peck was selling medicines produced by Boston chemist W. T. Conway. The Boston connection alone is interesting, but Peck's ad goes on to note that he is one store in an entire network selling Conway's products, a network that included druggists in Plattsburgh, Canandaigua, Worcester, Northhampton, Brattleboro, and Pittsfield.[37] Not only were connections sought and established between Vermont and outside places, Vermont was one point in larger circuits of connectivity that ultimately linked the entire nation. One consequence, of course, was Vermont's increased vulnerability to economic developments elsewhere. Randolph Roth's comments on the Connecticut River Valley's "precarious economy" are apt for all of Vermont at that time:

> It was not insulated from the vicissitudes of New England's economy as a whole. The fortunes of the Valley's settlers, especially those just entering the land markets, depended heavily on interest rates, currency values, land prices, wages and commodity prices in southern New England.[38]

These are a few examples of the connections established between Vermont and the rest of the nation and, in fact, the rest of the world. It might prove useful to examine others. Where, for example, did the capital originate that funded the state's many turnpikes? When did banks arrive in Vermont? Who were the shareholders? Who guaranteed their worth? And what kinds of correspondence links were established? How did the postal system reach into the state and link Vermont with that national information network? The list of questions one might ask is long.

SUMMARY

These examples drawn from Vermont's frontier experience and presented as part of an historical geographical framework are intended to provide a perspective on the past. I have suggested that the early European-American settlement of Vermont not be viewed as an isolated frontier, removed from the confines and constraints of "civilization." Rather, the opening of the Vermont frontier was very much a process of colonization and began as a process of building outposts for a developing nation. Those outposts were initiated and settled from earlier established places. Once in place, frontier outposts did not lose contact with other parts of the country; on the contrary, the people of the frontier viewed themselves as part of a constantly changing and realigning system of connections that tied the frontier into regional, national, and international circuits. It is often suggested that Vermont was "finally" connected to the outside world with the completion of the Champlain Canal and, eventually, the railroads. To be sure, those tangible, physical links between Vermont and places like New York and Boston made such connections indisputable. But they were always there, in perception if not in actual practice. The development of sophisticated transport technologies made the connections easier and effectively shrank distances between places. But the Vermont frontier, from at least the time of its earliest white settlers, was one of several "peripheries," which were settled from and incorporated into a developing American political, social, and economic "core," a cultural system headquartered in seaboard America with connections reaching to places like Vermont.

Such a framework or perspective allows a view of Vermont's history and geography at many different scales and in broader contexts. Certainly Vermont is unique in many of its attributes. The many individuals and specific places and events that ultimately come together to create the special character of Vermont and Vermonters by no means should be ignored. Rather, it should be recognized that Vermont is now and always has been part of a larger world, similar in many ways to other places, part and parcel of general patterns and processes of history. A rich and full appreciation of just who and what Vermonters are must recognize Vermont's place in that larger world, setting the unique attributes of individual circumstance in the larger framework of the global village.

NOTES

1. Thornton Wilder, *Our Town* (New York: Avon Books, 1976).

2. Joseph S. Wood, "'Build, Therefore, Your Own World': The New England Village as Settlement Ideal," *Annals of the Association of American Geographers* 81:1 (March 1991): 32-51; James E. Vance, Jr., "Democratic Utopia and the American Landscape," in *The Making of the American Landscape*, Michael P. Conzen, ed. (Boston: Unwin Hyman, 1990), 204-221.

3. P. Jeffrey Potash, "Toward a 'New Rural History': Patterns of Community Organization in Three Addison County, Vermont Towns 1761-1850" (Ph.D. diss., University of Chicago, 1986), 10-15; Richard H. Schein, "Unofficial Proprietors in Post-Revolutionary Central New York," *Journal of Historical Geography* 17:1 (1991).

4. Michael A. Bellesiles, "Life, Liberty, and Land: Ethan Allen and the Frontier Experience in Revolutionary New England" (Ph.D. diss., University of California-Irvine, 1986), 86-91.

5. For an elaboration of this idea, encompassed in a "mercantile model of settlement," see James E. Vance, Jr., *The Merchant's World: The Geography of Wholesaling* (Englewood Cliffs, N.J.: Prentice-Hall, 1970).

6. Potash, 10-14.

7. Barbara Miller Solomon, ed., *Travels in New England and New York by Timothy Dwight* (Cambridge: Harvard University Press, 1969), 2:289.

8. Frederick Jackson Turner, *The Significance of the Frontier in American History*, reprint edited by Harold P. Simonson (New York: Frederick Ungar, 1980), 27.

9. *Burlington Gazette*, 9 Sept. 1814; *Northern Sentinel*, 11 Aug. 1820; *The Vermont Mirror*, 18 May 1807; *Rutland Herald*, 8 Dec. 1794; *The Vermont Gazette*, 11 April 1805. All in Special Collections, Bailey/Howe Library, University of Vermont.

10. Richard Hofstadter, *The Age of Reform* (New York: Vintage Books, 1955), 23-24.

11. Robert D. Mitchell, *Commercialism and the Frontier: Perspectives on the Early Shenandoah Valley* (Charlottesville: University Press of Virginia, 1977).

12. D. W. Meinig, *The Shaping of America: A Geographical Perspective on 500 Years of History*, vol. 1 of *Atlantic America, 1492-1800* (New Haven: Yale University Press, 1986), xv.

13. D. W. Meinig, "The Continuous Shaping of America: A Prospectus for Geographers and Historians," *American Historical Review* 83 (1978): 1193.

14. The importance of external organization to early Vermont is neatly encapsulated by J. Kevin Graffagnino in a discussion of the Grants controversy before the Revolutionary War. Graffagnino points out that outsiders held the fate of Vermont in their control. See his "'We Have Long Been Wishing for a Good Printer in This Vicinity': The State of Vermont, the First East Union, and the Dresden Press, 1778-1779," in *In a State of Nature*, H. Nicholas Muller,

III and Samuel B. Hand, eds., (Montpelier: Vermont Historical Society, 1982), 66.

15. Potash, 43-45.

16. Ira Allen, "Surveying the Wilderness" in *Outsiders Inside Vermont: Three Centuries of Visitors' Viewpoints on the Green Mountain State*, T. D. Seymour Bassett, ed. (Canaan, N.H.: Phoenix Publishing Co., 1967), 23-27.

17. Bellesiles, 86-91.

18. Bellesiles, 103-113.

19. John Lincklaen, "The Beginning of Ease [1791]," in Bassett, ed., *Outsiders*, 46-49.

20. *The Post-Boy and Vermont and New Hampshire Federal Courier*, 13 Aug. 1805.

21. Reverend Nathan Perkins, *A Narrative of a Tour through the State of Vermont . . . 1789* (Rutland, Vt.: Charles E. Tuttle, 1964).

22. Richard H. Schein, "A Historical Geography of Central New York: Patterns and Processes of Colonization on the New Military Tract, 1782-1820" (Ph.D. diss., Syracuse University, 1989), 225-248.

23. Bellesiles, 113-115.

24. Harold A. Meeks, *Time and Change in Vermont* (Chester, Conn.: Globe Pequot Press, 1986), 7-25.

25. Meeks, 7-47; Bellesiles, 113-114; Genieve Lamson, "Geographical Influences in the Early History of Vermont," *Vermont Historical Society Proceedings* 1921-23, 79-138; William J. Wilgus, *The Role of Transportation in the Development of Vermont* (Montpelier: Vermont Historical Society, 1945).

26. Bellesiles, 113-115.

27. John A. Graham, *A Descriptive Sketch of the Present State of Vermont* (reprint, Bennington: Vermont Heritage Press, 1987).

28. *Burlington Gazette*, 9 Sept. 1814.

29. Joseph S. Wood, "The Road Network and Regional Interaction in Vermont: 1796-1824" (master's thesis, University of Vermont, 1973).

30. Randolph A. Roth, *The Democratic Dilemma: Religion, Reform, and the Social Order in the Connecticut River Valley, 1791-1850* (New York: Cambridge University Press, 1987), 22.

31. Lincklaen in Bassett, ed., *Outsiders*, 46-49.

32. Wilgus, 52.

33. *Dartmouth Gazette*, 8 May 1802; *Brattleboro Reporter*, 6 Feb. 1804.

34. Wilgus, 52.

35. Benjamin DeWitt, "A Sketch of the Turnpike Roads in the State of New York," *Transactions of the Society for the Promotion of Useful Arts* (New York: John Barber, 1807), 199.

36. *Burlington Gazette*, 9 Sept. 1814; *The Precursor* (Montpelier), 18 May 1807; *Burlington Northern Sentinel*, 11 Aug. 1820, 16 March 1821, 1 June 1821, 7 Dec. 1821; *Rutland Herald*, 8 Dec. 1794, 10 Jan. 1810, 5 Dec. 1810; *Dartmouth Gazette*, 3 Jan. 1803.

37. *Burlington Gazette*, 30 Sept. 1814.

38. Roth, 24.

Defining New England:

Revisioning Our Colonial Past

Marshall True

New Yorker driving one of those fancy sports cars zooms through the crossroads of a rural New England hamlet past two elderly gentlemen spending an August afternoon on the front porch. Shortly he returns coming in the other direction, once again past his observers. Finally in a spray of gravel, he whines back in reverse, rolls down his window, and asks the bemused gentlemen, "Say, which way to East Vassalboro?" The old fellows look at one another and one replies laconically, "Don't you move a goldurn inch."

Except for the reference to East Vassalboro, Maine, we would clearly consider this a Vermont joke. In fact, it appears in every New England state, only the place name changes. This leads me to ask "Which way to New England?" While we are at it, what *is* New England, anyway? Maine, New Hampshire, Vermont, Massachusetts, Connecticut, and Rhode Island. Pine cones, granite, and the annual Red Sox fan's lament "Wait till next year." Sugar maples, dairy cows, and the Tunbridge World Fair. There is no apparent end to the talismans of a shared cultural tradition. But where, and what, are the central strands?

New England is rich in cultural, historical, and literary symbols, in myths and stories; yet these are often difficult to reconcile with one another. We think of village greens, white church steeples, and stately elms, but our reality encompasses interstate highways, television evangelism, and parking lots as well. We venerate "Yankee Doodle" and celebrate, in name at least, our English tradition, yet we honor or elect Brennans, Grassos, Kunins, Sununus, Garrahys, and Dukakises as our governors—a testimony to our ethnic and gender diversity.

Similarly, New England's history is rich with odd couples whose stories illustrate the diverse paths our region's forebears have taken. For example, John Cotton, the eminent Puritan divine, defined Congregational orthodoxy in the same town where Roger Williams came to the conclusion that such enforced orthodoxy was a sin and then left to establish a colony at Rhode Island based on religious tolerance. As Amherst's Emily Dickinson embarked on a lifelong experiment in poetic self-examination, in Concord Louisa May Alcott celebrated conventional domesticity in hundreds of works, most notably *Little Women*. While Henry David Thoreau retreated to the banks of Walden Pond to contemplate how man could best live, Frederic Tudor harvested ice from that same pond, shipping it all over the world, and making a fortune.

This diversity reminds us to be wary of too readily accepting simple characterizations of ourselves. We perceive ourselves as belonging to a regional culture, but it appears that there may be as many differences among us as similarities. How can one define New England if New Englanders are so distinct from each other? What, if any, role does regional identity have in a culture that is as transregional as twentieth-century America? Where do we turn to discover the origins and significance of New England as a distinct portion of the United States?

As a historian, concerned with change and persistence in time and space, I would suggest that New England can best be defined as a place (or places), which became a distinct region only over time, as men and women of diverse backgrounds struggled to create lives for themselves in this particular section of North America. I cannot be precise about when New Englanders began to feel different from Southerners or from their neighbors in the Mid-Atlantic region; neither can I tell you how exactly this process was different from identity formation in other regions. Historians do know, however, that the colonial period was critical.

Since about 1960, historians and historical geographers have engaged in a remarkable reworking and broadening of the colonial history of the western hemisphere.[1] No satisfactory synthesis has yet emerged, but I would like to discuss some suggestive findings and areas of study that have a bearing on the problem of how to define and characterize New England. The convergence of new techniques, such as computer-assisted demographic analysis, and new questions about race and gender relations have begun to produce a portrait of an American culture in the process of becoming. Some general themes are clear.

First, each region of the Americas was a new society, facing an unfamiliar landscape, seeking to satisfy material needs and establish a social and political system that would enable people to live together. Each region was tied into a transatlantic commercial network, established as a result of the economic and military aggression of Europeans. Unlike predominantly white European societies, all new world settlers lived in a multiracial and multi-ethnic world, and this was reflected in religious and community values. These societies were exploitative both of the environment and of other people. In fact, status in the "New World" was most commonly derived from an individual's power to exploit others. Finally these societies were colonial; consequently many decisions about how they would be structured were made elsewhere.[2]

If we examine these similarities in the geographic region now called New England and focus on the first century of settlement, we see that New England's New World was invented by the tens of thousands of men and women—European and Native American—carrying out commercial, political, military, social, educational, and sexual transactions in which they had to bridge the cultural barriers of belief, language, habit, and gender that divided them. These exchanges altered ideas, for example, about how to earn a livelihood, conduct one's life, and worship one's god. They also changed the ecological landscape, as new patterns of land use, travel, and agricultural practices imported by Europeans created a new environment in New England.[3]

The name itself, "New England," was given to this region by Captain John Smith who, more than one hundred years after John Cabot's 1497 voyage, regarded himself as the true "discoverer" of this part of the world. A soldier, explorer, and publicist for England's overseas expansion, Smith explored the Atlantic coastline of North America from the mouth of the Penobscot River to Cape Cod. His 1614 expedition of two ships and forty-five men produced the most accurate map of the region made to that time. It also generated a report that assessed the area's colonial potential. In it Smith, a veteran of Jamestown, described how he had found a land "planted with Gardens . . . and inhabited with a goodly, strong and well proportioned people . . ." in short "a most excellent place both for health and fertility." Smith concluded, "I would rather live here than anywhere." His voyage had failed to pay its expenses but, besides giving the region a new name, produced a plan for its colonization.[4]

By 1600, English had began to move into the New World and Smith's efforts, both in Virginia and in New England, should be seen as part of that larger British overseas expansion effort. In the period from 1600 to 1660, 240,000 to 295,000 Englishmen, including numbers of Scots and Welsh, poured out of England. This migration began slowly, perhaps 30,000 in the first three decades, but it became a flood thereafter, reaching 6,500 to 8,000 per year. The emigrants went to five destinations. Beginning in 1603, 70,000-100,000 went to Ireland, joining a contingent of earlier Elizabethan emigrants; some 50,000 went to the Virginia and Maryland colonies on the Chesapeake after 1607; after 1612 some 3,000-4,000 settled Bermuda; beginning in 1620 some 20,000-25,000 went first to Plymouth and then to Massachusetts Bay; and also beginning in the 1620s a huge number, 110,000 to 135,000, went to the small islands of the Caribbean: Barbados, St. Kitts, Nevis, and Antigua.[5]

Unlike much of the migration to other destinations, the movement to New England, Massachusetts Bay and surrounds in particular, was "short, sudden, and carefully organized."[6] In a dozen years between 1630 and 1642, 20,000 moved to Massachusetts Bay. We know from traditional accounts that this great migration had a strong religious flavor, although it is far from clear that all those who emigrated did so for religious reasons. This emigration was also unusual in that seventy percent of migrants came as members of established families, including both independent farmers and artisans. David Cressy, in his study, *Coming Over*, examines many aspects of the early English migration to New England and argues with a fresh eye and compelling analysis that English "roots" as well as American circumstances shaped the society and culture of early New England.[7]

The land to which the migrants traveled was not, of course, a trackless wilderness. Native peoples—misnamed "Indians" by Columbus—had shaped the environment of New England for millennia prior to the arrival of Europeans. They had carried on extensive trade with the Europeans who had earlier reached their shores and remained part of New England's colonial heritage. Puritans and New Englanders defined their fear of the wilderness in terms of their Indian enemies and, obviously, the land upon which generations of New Englanders lived was taken, in one way or another, from natives. Although statistics are uncertain, populations prior to the arrival of the Europeans were substantially larger than early settlers estimated. Most historians now accept an estimated range of 126,000 to 144,000 native people in coastal New England at the time of Captain Smith's expedition. The most dramatic consequence for the native peoples was that European diseases found "virgin soil" in a population that lacked immunities. The result was cataclysmic depopulation that reached ninety percent in some regions.[8]

Restoring native peoples to their rightful place in defining New England has produced exciting works in the field of ethnohistory. Two excellent books are William Cronon's *Changes in the Land: Indians, Colonists, and the Ecology of New England* and Neal Salisbury's *Manitou and Providence: Indians, Europeans, and the Making of New England 1500-1643*. Cronon attempts to move history beyond the customary boundaries of human institutions into the larger environmental context in which it takes place. To do this he examines not only changes in the way men and women organized their lives but also fundamental changes in the region's plant and animal communities as the shift from Indian to European dominance occurred in New England. Cronon presents a powerful argument that Indians and Europeans worked together in transforming the landscape, although each culture placed different demands on the resource base and had differing expectations about the quality of their lives.[9]

Salisbury looks at the complex of early native-white exchanges prior to and during the first generation of European settlement in the region. His work is one of the first and one of the most successful attempts to see the Indians as active participants in the shaping of early New England. Salisbury carefully assesses their role in the commerce, agriculture, and thought of the region. He demonstrates conclusively that the history of New England is simply unimaginable without the Indian.

Thanks in part to weakened Indian resistance, particularly after the bloody Pequot War of 1637, the men and women who came to Massachusetts Bay thrived. The population of the region grew rapidly, in part due to the sex and age distribution of the initial group of immigrants. Population doubled in the first generation, and by 1660 between 55,000-60,000 inhabitants of English descent lived in the region, most of whom were born in North America. By the early 1640s New England consisted of five separate colonies: Plymouth, Massachusetts Bay, Connecticut, New Haven, and Rhode Island. The early

New Hampshire settlements at Portsmouth and Dover were still considered part of Massachusetts Bay.

The natural population increase testifies to the unique way in which the great migration allowed or compelled women to be active participants in the enterprise of building a society. One of the ways New England was unlike other New World settlements was that the Puritans and Pilgrims brought their wives and daughters with them. Yet all too often the early women settlers remain faceless and nameless in the records. Laurel T. Ulrich's *Good Wives* redresses that balance and restores to the women of New England their rightful role as participants and actors in the building of a New World society. Women, Ulrich concludes, worked in trade, conducted diplomatic negotiations during Indian wars, advised and scolded their husbands and children, and fulfilled dozens of roles to which historians have paid too little attention.[10]

In part out of religious conviction and in part out of civil concern, the migrants to New England brought with them a commitment to create a society as close to the traditional English commonwealth as they could. This society—to the lament of the ministers—rapidly declined from its ideals and models. The commercial world, the interconnectedness of farming and market activity, the need for military defense, and population growth with its demand for more land challenged even the most successful communities.

For those interested in the early social history of New England, Kenneth A. Lockridge's study of Dedham has become something of a classic in the literature. First published in 1970, *A New England Town* has been both model and foil to numbers of other town studies that have enhanced our understanding of the early history of New England. Lockridge's study remains one of the best. It is an exciting inquiry into the lives of ordinary people and a powerful argument that much can be learned from a careful look into local history.[11]

Other towns had more severe problems. The most spectacular example was Salem Village in 1692. In *Salem Possessed*, Paul Boyer and Stephen Nissenbaum offer a powerful and eloquent analysis of a New England town in crisis. Church, town, and family in Salem failed as institutions in the witchcraft crisis of 1692. Boyer and Nissenbaum examined the masses of local records pertaining to late seventeenth-century Salem and discovered tensions and conflicts that simmered just under the surface of life in early New England.[12]

In conclusion, New England can only be defined as part of a story of human creativity. Native Americans and Europeans were forced to adjust to one another as strangers, enemies, and as collaborators and converts. Men and women attempted to accommodate themselves to environmental change by adapting and forever altering—in small and large ways—what they thought they knew. Institutions, from church and school to militia and merchant house, moved in new directions under the pressures of settlement. This colonial crucible of change and adjustment shaped the entity that we today know as New England.

NOTES

1. See D. W. Meinig, *The Shaping of America: A Geographical Perspective on 500 Years of History*, vol. 1, *Atlantic America, 1492-1800* (New Haven: Yale University Press, 1986), and Jack P. Greene, *Pursuits of Happiness: The Social Development of Early Modern British Colonies and the Formation of American Culture* (Chapel Hill: University of North Carolina Press, 1988). I have also been deeply influenced by the ideas of T. H. Breen; see his essay "Creative Adaptations: Peoples and Cultures," in Jack P. Greene and J. R. Pole, eds., *Colonial British America: Essays in the New History of the Early Modern Era* (Baltimore: Johns Hopkins University Press, 1984), 195-232.

2. Jack P. Greene and J. R. Pole, "Reconstructing British American Colonial History," in Greene and Pole, eds., *Colonial British America*, 1-17.

3. Breen, "Creative Adaptations," 198-215; also see works cited in the notes that follow.

4. Philip L. Barbour, *The Three Worlds of Captain John Smith* (Boston: Houghton Mifflin, 1964), 303-19.

5. Here I follow Greene, *Pursuits of Happiness*, 7-8.

6. Greene, 19.

7. David Cressy, *Coming Over: Migration and Communication between England and New England in the Seventeenth Century* (Cambridge: Cambridge University Press, 1987), especially 292 ff.

8. Neal Salisbury, *Manitou and Providence: Indians, Europeans and the Making of New England 1500-1643* (New York: Oxford University Press, 1982), 22-30.

9. William Cronon, *Changes in the Land: Indians, Colonists, and the Ecology of New England* (New York: Hill and Wang, 1983).

10. Laurel Thatcher Ulrich, *Good Wives: Image and Reality in the Lives of Women in Northern New England 1650-1750* (New York: Oxford University Press, 1980).

11. Kenneth A. Lockridge, *A New England Town: The First Hundred Years, Dedham, Massachusetts, 1636-1736*, enlarged edition (New York: W. W. Norton, 1985).

12. Paul Boyer and Stephen Nissenbaum, *Salem Possessed: The Social Origins of Witchcraft* (Cambridge: Harvard University Press, 1974).

The Vermont State of Mind:

Adventures in Schizophrenia

William Mares

This is not a lecture, not a speech, not tablets from on high. It is more a rumination, which is fitting because a class of ruminants, to wit, cows, dominate our landscape and mythology. I called this piece "Adventures in Schizophrenia," because in laymen's terms it means a split personality, and that is what characterizes Vermont and Vermonters in this last decade of the twentieth century.

When Frank Bryan and I wrote *Real Vermonters Don't Milk Goats* in the early 1980s, we set out to have a good time.[1] In a humorous vein we tried to define "real Vermonters" by their opposite, the straw men and women flatlanders, people from away, with alien values, dress, and deportment. Their superficial traits made easy and delicious targets. I was particularly good at picking out these idiosyncrasies, since I was a flatlander—being still some years shy of the twenty-year residence admission rule for joining the Newcomers Club.

Now some of what we wrote seems dated—sadly so. As Robert Oppenheimer, one of the developers of the atomic bomb, once said: "The earth is moving even as we walk on it." Videos hadn't even appeared then; now they dominate the shelves of the mom and pop stores. The lottery was in its infancy. "Crack" was something that happened to ceiling plaster, and the homeless lived on sewer grates in New York and Washington, D.C., but never in Burlington. At that time, my friend Jim Fraser had T-shirts made saying, "I love living in Chittenden County because it's so close to Vermont." Now we ask if all of Vermont is becoming Chittenden County.

In *Real Vermonters* there's a passage called "It's a Fine Line" that bears re-reading in the current context:

Vermont is a land of fine lines—the lines between winter and spring, hard and soft maple, well-grazed and over-grazed. Not much separates a good sugar day from a bad one, ripe apples from over-ripe, snow from freezing rain. . . . The "fine line" applies to people even more than to seasons, scenery or sugaring. It's a fine line between humor and ridicule, between politeness and rudeness, between public and private, between neighborliness and intrusion, between the real and the superficial. And . . . for all the apparently clear-cut differences between Real Vermonters and Flatlanders, every year that fence between them grows more rickety.[2]

I would like to propose four salient values that in my opinion have infused and suffused Vermont over the years. Then I would like to examine how they have changed in the recent past.

First, I would say that Vermont has been egalitarian. That is, the poor and the rich could live side by side with relatively little friction. The spread in wealth was not so great as in other regions. Those who had it didn't flaunt it. Vermont was an economic backwater, protected by an inhospitable climate.

Vermonters shed more blood per capita in the Civil War than any other state—and this sacrifice was arguably directed more at expunging slavery than at preserving the Union.

Second, Vermonters have a strong sense of community. Vermont was founded not by royal charter, nor by congressional action, but "in a state of nature." It grew out of its people and its towns. In Vermont there came to fruition, in greatest measure, the sense of community that Alexis de Tocqueville called the "habits of the heart."

Third is the will to control one's life, to go one's own way, a certain contrariness. It can mean the right to be left alone, the right to do anything one damn well pleases.

Let me pause for a moment to consider these last two conflicting, yet possibly complementary impulses—one to engage, the other to withdraw; one to help those in need, the other to tend to one's own knitting. When I was interviewing former Gov. Philip Hoff for an article recently, I pointed out this paradoxical pull of the Vermont temperament. "Paradoxical—yes!" said Hoff, "But contradictory, no! Independence is absolutely dependent upon toleration and caring for others. It's the cement that holds communities together."

Fourth, Vermonters prize a working landscape—one with farms and productive forests. Vermonters have long been dependent on the land for their sustenance. In the last one hundred years, dairy farming has become Vermont's binding metaphor, an image that calls to mind nourishment—nurturance of the land and of people for each other. The rest of us owe a big debt to the farmers, however distant, who are the underpaid landscape gardeners of Vermont. In 1937 George D. Aiken said: "Two classes of people are dependent upon agriculture for their living—those who live off farming, and those who live off the farmer."

Vermont is beautiful, it has been said, because the environment is healthy and Vermonters have historically built with a knowledge of natural limits. Hence have come the native roots for Vermont's strong environmental ethic.

Now I would like to look at those values in relation to today's reality and to some of the antithetical forces arrayed against them.

VERMONT EGALITARIANISM

In 1989 I served as a member of the Governor's Commission on the Economic Future of Vermont. The opening words of our report's "vision" are relevant here.

> As Vermont nears its bicentennial year, economic prosperity is greater and more widespread than at any time in 100 years. Average per capita income, at 93 percent of the national average, has not been so high since 1880. But, in fact, there are two Vermonts. The people in one Vermont are affluent and healthy, with access to good education, decent housing, and the high satisfaction of living in a natural environment that is the envy of most Americans. The other Vermont is peopled by those who have missed the prosperity train; their economic circumstances are stagnant, their prospects narrow. This Commission believes that without positive action, the gap will widen, the minority will grow and, inescapably, prosperity will diminish for all, with a corresponding decline in Vermont's ability to preserve natural resources and historic values.[3]

We see what Jeremy Ingpen calls the emerging "lifestyle economy," or what John Kenneth Galbraith calls "the living industry." The resort industry has increasingly become merged with the real estate industry; second homes and their construction and maintenance play an increasing role in our overall economy. Irony abounds when condominium developers peddle "total recreation" while year-round residents are struggling for life itself—spending ever more on food, housing, and health care. This trend pushes the traditional resource-based industries like farming, mining, and forestry to the margins. In more and more towns the average folk simply cannot afford the essentials of life. Yet statistical averaging, like physical isolation, hides the depths of the problem.

SENSE OF COMMUNITY

We are like the character in Doctor Dolittle, the Pushmi-pullyu, which was a donkey at both ends. More and more towns are becoming bedroom communities as adult household members commute as much as fifty miles to work in Essex Junction, Montpelier, Rutland, and Norwich. They leave in the dark and come home in the dark.

The long-standing practice of luring down-country folks north to buy up abandoned farms has grown to grotesque proportions and sometimes has had ludicrous side effects: A New York celebrity builds a ten million dollar "Christmas house" in Arlington, and a Chittenden County subdivision built on farmland makes home buyers agree not to pile firewood in the yards. The traffic continues to grow. What kind of community are we building when the traffic lines in and out of Burlington seem endless? What kind of community are we building when the first thoughts or words out of a citizen's mouth are: "Let John do it!" or "I gave at the office." Average citizens, always the backbone of local government in Vermont and the glue for communities, even those with the willingness and time to help, are being worn down by the complexity of the issues, by litigiousness, and relentless demands.

Then comes development and its growing impacts beyond isolated, discrete town boundaries. Landfills, pipelines, water sources, and transportation have increasingly regional effects. Yet Vermont's governmental structure makes it difficult to assign responsibility for regional impacts. How do you balance the desire for local control with the need for larger solutions?

The "not-in-my-backyard" syndrome, alas, is not alien to Vermont. At the same time, however, there is a readiness in Vermont to reach out to solve the world's problems, as the slogan says, to "think globally, act locally." We ban CFC's in auto air-conditioning; Mayor Bernie Sanders never felt the need to apologize for giving Burlington its own foreign policy; and in one of her state of the state speeches, Gov. Madeleine Kunin spoke of her "global warming strategy."

ABILITY TO CONTROL OUR LIVES

Despite the brave efforts of Ben and Jerry's Homemade to stop the cutting in the Amazon rain forest by selling Rainforest Crunch, or Sanders's foreign policy, it is at least arguable that Vermonters have less control over their lives than in the past. In January 1990, hundreds of people gathered in Barre to denounce Act 200, the omnibus planning law passed by the legislature in 1989, as a creature of the devil, the ultimate thief of "local control." They proclaimed that anyone who supports it should be voted out of office. "Local control" has become an emotionally charged phrase, the way "neighborhood schools" were a defense against bussing to achieve racial integration in the 1960s.

Also disquieting is the pace and spread of development—the future shock that many natives never felt. Many immigrants fled what Alvin Toffler described as the "shattering stress and disorientation that we induce in individuals by subjecting them to too much change in too short a time."[4] Thus the rallies against Act 200 are partly a rebellion against "loss of local control" and partly a cry against anyone who would crimp the freedom Vermonters have enjoyed for over two hundred years.

A Working Landscape

To preserve their land and its productivity, Vermonters have worked hard to save agriculture from the assaults of developers, from trends in national milk and grain prices, and from environmental pollution. The Vermont legislature, like the Congress, passes new farm legislation almost every year. As the actual farm constituency drops, however, the emotional one grows. We try to balance property rights of farmers with the rest of our desire for pretty scenery. As a legislator, I argued in the late 1980s against the first-in-the-nation state farm subsidy, because I thought it set a bad precedent. But I applauded when our Economic Commission recommended a two percent increase in the rooms and meals tax to help pay for farm preservation.

As agricultural practices and costs change, we must still ask: Can we afford to keep that land open? Through a variety of devices like current use taxation, working farm tax abatement, land trusts, and so forth we have tried to keep farms operating, even as the number of farms continues to decline from 30,000 forty years ago, to 2,400 in 1989. What happens to the land that gets converted? It grows condos and more development. In Essex, the former Lang farm has become "Lang Farm Center," with two exits slated for it on the proposed circumferential highway.

More and more, we ask—as we must: how much can the land itself tolerate? The travel industry people tell us they must go to four-season resorts or they court disaster. But when that happens, how does the land recover? And what happens to the people who used to live off it?

Pyramid Mall is the metaphor for everywhere else. For over thirteen years, this proposed monster mall has hovered over Chittenden County threatening all that is good about Vermont. Out there, at Tafts Corners in Williston, the Pyramid land sits undeveloped, while the other three quadrants grow like Topsy. Look at University Mall in South Burlington—already larger than Pyramid's proposed first stage. A cynic might say that while everyone focused on Pyramid, the same net amount of development and more occurred elsewhere or nearby.

It may be too melodramatic to say Vermont is at a crossroads. It is surely correct to say Vermont and Vermonters are riven with contradictions. I see impulses to join in America and to run away; to build four-megabit microchips and heat with woodchips; to have an integrated fiber-optic network and still talk baseball and weather at the post office; to provide for all but preserve the neighborhood from the homeless, trailers, and condominiums.

I see a state that used to be one of the more conservative, now arguably the most liberal of states. I see conflicting impulses to hide in paradise and proclaim that paradise. We want to believe that we are a special world. We say our state is prettier than the rest; our garbage smells better; we are more humane. But, being within a day's drive of sixty million people, we know that you can run, but you can't hide. We are torn between "I am my brother's keeper" and "We paid at the office."

Maybe it's just Vermont growing up, and this is all a graceful retreat from being different, or a graceful surrender to the homogenized values and tastes of the rest of America. "Yet every man kills the thing he loves," said Oscar Wilde, a hundred years ago. Can we have both the convenience of interstate highways and the isolation of dirt roads? Can we promise to heal every wound, right every wrong, and still leave people alone?

For over two hundred years, Vermonters have struggled with the contradictory tendencies of urban and rural life, being on the frontier and wanting to be in the mainstream, clinging lovingly to their separate identity and wrestling with their national identity. In 1990, on the eve of the bicentennial celebration of our becoming one of the United States of America, we once again appear to be at a turning point in our history, and I am reminded of one of the fabled mixed metaphors and garbled clichés now called "gillyisms," which used to pepper the speeches and conversation of the late state senator, Gilbert Godnick: "We'll burn *that* bridge when we get to it."

NOTES

1. Frank Bryan and William Mares, *Real Vermonters Don't Milk Goats* (Shelburne, Vt.: New England Press, 1983).

2. Bryan and Mares, 86.

3. State of Vermont. "Report of the Governor's Commission on Vermont's Future: Guidelines for Growth" (Montpelier, 1988).

4. Alvin Toffler, *Future Shock* (New York: Random House, 1970).

Good Proverbs Make Good Vermonters:

A Study of Regional Proverbs

in the United States

Wolfgang Mieder

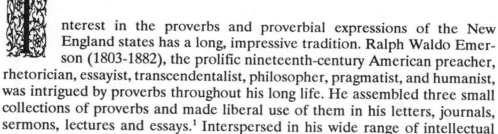nterest in the proverbs and proverbial expressions of the New England states has a long, impressive tradition. Ralph Waldo Emerson (1803-1882), the prolific nineteenth-century American preacher, rhetorician, essayist, transcendentalist, philosopher, pragmatist, and humanist, was intrigued by proverbs throughout his long life. He assembled three small collections of proverbs and made liberal use of them in his letters, journals, sermons, lectures and essays.[1] Interspersed in his wide range of intellectual and literary products are theoretical observations on the proverb as a genre, which are as valid to proverb scholars today as they were in Emerson's time. He defines and characterizes proverbs as the "language of experience," which "gives comfort and encouragement, aid and abetting to daily action."

To Emerson proverbs are "rules of good householding" whose "practical wisdom" teaches us "worldly prudence." They are "metaphor[s] of the human mind" expressing "moral truth" and transmitting "their commentary upon all parts of life." In his early lecture on "Ethics" (1837) he reduces all moral codes of conduct to proverbs, and in his significant essay on "Compensation" (1841) he makes the following acute and all-encompassing observation:

> Proverbs, like the sacred books of each nation, are the sanctuary of the intuitions. That which the droning world, chained in appearances, will not allow the realist to say in his own words, it will suffer him to say in proverbs without contradiction. And this law of laws, which the pulpit, the senate and the college deny, is hourly preached in all markets and workshops by flights of proverbs, whose teaching is as true and as omnipresent as that of birds and flies.[2]

Approximately one hundred years later another American author, the poet Carl Sandburg (1878-1967), echoed this high esteem for proverbs in his epic poem "Good Morning, America" (1928). In section eleven he characterizes the American melting pot via its speech: "A code arrives; language; lingo, slang; behold the proverbs of a people, a nation."[3]

Mindful of a people's collective wisdom expressed in proverbs and wishing to record those texts current in New England, I assembled about five hundred of them under the title *Yankee Wisdom: New England Proverbs.*[4] It was difficult to find proverbs that are truly indigenous to this six-state region, but such texts as "Hitch your wagon to a star" (coined by Emerson in 1870) and "If you don't like the weather in New England, just wait a minute and it will change" obviously have their origin in this area of the country. Scholarly attempts to collect Vermont's proverbial stock by three professors of the University of Vermont show that this little state of ours has contributed significantly to language and folk wisdom. Leon Dean (1889-1982), Vermont's renowned folklorist and former editor of the *Green Mountain Whittlin's* folklore journal, published small lists of proverbs from time to time. Muriel Hughes (b. 1903) presented her collection, "Vermont Proverbs and Proverbial Sayings," in *Vermont History* in 1960, and I benefitted from this previous work in my two collections of about one thousand sayings with the titles *Talk Less and Say More* and *As Sweet as Apple Cider: Vermont Expressions.*[5]

My own collections are based on original field work during the past fifteen years, on the gleanings of Dean and Hughes, and on painstaking investigations of the regional literature of such Vermont authors as Rowland E. Robinson (1833-1900),[6] John Godfrey Saxe (1816-1867), Dorothy Canfield Fisher (1879-1958), Walter Hard (1882-1966), Allen R. Foley (1898-1978), and others. I have concentrated on collecting primarily those proverbs that are not necessarily known throughout the United States.[7] Most of the texts are current only in Vermont or more broadly in New England. The difficulty of deciding whether a certain proverb is, in fact, from Vermont can be seen in such texts as "Sap runs best after a sharp frost," "The world is your cow, but you have to do the milking," and "Every cider apple has a worm." They sound as if they originated in Vermont, but why not in New Hampshire or upstate New York?[8] Only through careful research on each proverb might the actual origin come to light. For many such texts, however, the proof of a source in Vermont, or any other state for that matter, would be impossible. What is important is that I collected the proverbs I listed in my books in Vermont. Most collectors of the proverb lore of a single state preface their collections by the caveat that the title of "X (any state) Proverbs" would actually be better expressed as "The Proverbs Current in X," and that also holds true for the proverbs from Vermont under discussion here.

I must add one more caveat before looking at a number of Vermont proverbs in more detail. There is some danger connected with deducing national or regional characteristics from folklore in general and proverbs in particular. Obviously many of the proverbs in the various state collections do not describe the typical person or mores of a given state. However, proverbs in general do reflect the world view of their users, and with caution one could perhaps say that a collection of proverbs from a particular state mirrors some stereotypical values of its people.

In the case of the five hundred proverbs that I collected from oral and written sources from Vermont, many deal with cows, maple sugaring, independence, thriftiness, and taciturnity, all of which seem to be part of the Vermont scene and psyche. Others I collected express a good dose of the dry humor for which Vermonters supposedly are famous. Above all, the proverbs reflect in concise and picturesque language a way of life that appeals to "real" Vermonters and so-called "flatlanders" alike. That does not necessarily make them Vermont proverbs, but it makes them proverbs used in Vermont as expressions of traditional folk wisdom.

A good case in point is, of course, the appearance of the proverb "Good fences make good neighbors" in the 1914 poem "Mending Wall" by Robert Frost (1875-1963).[9] More than one scholar has falsely concluded that this proverb originated with Frost and that it could thus be considered a Vermont or at least a New England proverb.[10] But as early as 1640 we find the quite similar text, "A good fence helpeth to keepe peace between neighbours; but let us take heed that we make not a high stone wall, to keepe us from meeting."[11] From the same year comes the similar proverb "Love your neighbor, yet pull not down your hedge," which Benjamin Franklin cited in his *Poor Richard's Almanack* for 1754.[12] There is also the medieval Spanish proverb "Una pared entre dos vecinos guarda más (hace durar) la amistad," which Ralph Waldo Emerson recorded in English translation in his journal of 1832 as "A wall between both best preserves friendship." One might well conclude that Frost encountered this text in Emerson and that it as well as the other English proverbs already cited inspired him to formulate the more poetic "Good fences make good neighbors." But no such luck, for the proverb in this exact wording appeared for the first time in *Blum's Farmer's and Planter's Almanac* for 1850, published annually since 1828 in Winston-Salem, North Carolina. It was cited again in Blum's almanac for 1861,[13] and the discoverer of these two early references believes that the proverb might have found its way into Blum's almanac as a quote from a New England almanac or farm journal. Be that as it may, we now can verify that the proverb was known on the east coast of the United States at least six decades before Robert Frost used it in one of his most famous poems. We can assume, therefore, that he must have heard it in oral communication in New England and perhaps even in Vermont.

Even if Frost did not coin this proverb, however, his poem certainly was instrumental in making it one of the most commonly used American proverbs. Furthermore, because Frost is famous as a New England and especially Vermont poet, and because the poem's central metaphor is the typical stone wall of this region, Americans have long considered the proverb to have a New England origin, or as we Vermonters would have it, it is a proverb grown on Vermont soil. As someone who feels unabashedly chauvinistic about his beloved Vermont, I would give a lot to locate the proverb "Good fences make good neighbors" in a Vermont publication prior to 1850. Unfortunately I have not yet had any success, but "Hope springs eternal" as the proverb says.

In the poem "Mending Wall," Frost as the narrator joins his taciturn neighbor during the yearly ritual of repairing their commonly held stone wall and questions the need for this labor since, in the absence of cows, the wall serves no apparent purpose. The neighbor simply continues to work and responds twice by merely quoting his father's authoritative saying that "Good fences make good neighbors." In this "dialogue," if one can call it that, Frost has captured the tight-lipped taciturnity for which the stereotypical Vermonter has gained some fame throughout the United States.

There must be some truth to this characterization of Vermonters if they themselves have come up with the short proverb "Talk less and say more." I recorded this proverb in oral use in Vermont about ten years ago, and I have not located it in any other of the dozens of published Anglo-American proverb collections. Sticking out my proverbial neck here, I am willing to declare this to be an indigenous Vermont proverb, one that encapsulates the world view of independent Vermonters. There are other proverbs that praise taciturnity in Vermont, as for example "Few words are best," "Say nothing and saw wood," "He can't speak well who always talks," "Nobody ever repented holding his tongue," "Be silent or speak something worth hearing," "What you don't say won't ever hurt you," "Turn your tongue seven times before speaking," and "Never cackle unless you lay." But none of them has the paradoxical wit, biting satire, and linguistic pun of "Talk less and say more," and I am thankful to my New England Press publishers for suggesting this proverb as the title for my collection of Vermont proverbs.

Obviously Vermont farmers do not mince many words with or about their cows, but it should not be surprising to find a large repertory of proverbs quoted by them that express everyday wisdom by couching it in cow metaphors. Thus the proverb "It is a lean cow that gives the milk" gives advice concerning frugality; "It isn't always the bell cow that gives the most milk" warns that appearances might be deceptive; "Don't swallow the cow and worry about the tail" reminds people not to get bogged down with minor matters; "If cows lie down before noon, it will rain soon" contains a weather prognosis based on everyday observation; "Every cow needs a tail in fly time" remarks on the usefulness of seemingly unimportant things at certain times; "A good cow may have a bad calf" shows that a good farmer may have a bad son; "The world is your cow, but you have to do the milking" expresses the need for self-reliance and serious work; and "Cursed cows have short horns" states that quarrelsome people will be controlled in a rigorous manner.

Many times these "cow" proverbs are clearly regional variants of more general proverbs. Thus the farm proverb "Milk the cow which is near" probably replaces the overused and clichéd "Take time by the forelock." "Cows prefer the grass on the other side of the fence" is a more realistic image than the general "The grass is always greener on the other side of the fence." "You can't sell the cow and have the milk too" corresponds to "You can't have your cake and eat it too." "A man may kiss his cow" is a more drastic version of "Each to his own." And while Vermonters also use the proverb "It makes a difference whose ox is gored," they prefer the regional variant "It makes a difference whose cow is in the well."

Speaking of wells, it should not surprise us that Vermonters refer to this all-important water resource in several proverbs. For example, "It takes more than one well to make a river," "You can never tell the depth of the well from the length of the handle on the pump," and, of course, the often heard "You never miss the water till the well is dry."

It is particularly interesting to see how Vermonters have dealt with the popular proverb "You can't judge a book by its cover." Over the years I have recorded such variants as "You can't judge a book by its binding," "You can't judge others by yourself," "You can't judge a man by his overcoat," and "You can't judge a horse by its harness." These texts can all be reduced to the structural formula "You can't judge X by Y," and one quickly realizes how such a proverbial pattern can yield a multitude of proverbs depending in each case on the social environment and world view of the speaker. A uniquely Vermont text, of course, is yet another "cow" proverb, namely "You can't judge a cow by her looks."

An even more general version of this proverbial structure is based on replacing the verb "judge" by any variable. This pattern could be summarized in the formulaic pattern of "You can't 'verb' X 'preposition' Y." Such texts express certain impossibilities and unrealistic dreams or wishes, arguing in a typically didactic fashion for the adherence to common sense in our aspirations. I have collected the following variants in Vermont: "You can't hang a man for an idea," "You can't make a whistle out of a pig's tail," "You can't get wool off a frog," "You can't swing a cat by a bull's tail," "You can't put a quart in a pint basin," "You can't build a house from the top down," and "You can't put an old head on young shoulders." The pattern can also be expanded into longer and more descriptive texts as, for example, "You can't always tell by the looks of a toad how far he can jump," "You can't expect anything from a pig but a grunt," and "You can't mow hay where the grass doesn't grow." It is important to notice with these variants the explicit predominance of farm animals and rural metaphors, reflecting the traditional agricultural life of Vermont and the value system of stability, slow change, and status quo.

Farming and sugaring were major livelihoods for old-time Vermonters and to a certain degree they continue to play an important role in the economic structure of the state. Little wonder that many proverbs deal with planting and harvesting, often transmitting old farming rules based on generations of experience and observation. Even though the landscape and demographic make-up of Vermont are changing to reflect a more urban environment, one can still hear many proverbial rules concerning farming and gardening: "If the corn has thick husks, there will be a hard winter," "Plant your corn when the leaves of the oak tree are the size of a mouse's ear," "Sow dry and set wet," "Snowy winter, plentiful harvest," "Plant cucumbers the first Sunday in June before sunrise," and "Town Meeting is time to put in the potatoes." There is even the local planting proverb "It's time to plant corn when the icicles fall off the ledge on Snake Mountain," while others reflect more generally on the hardship and the importance of farming. For example, "It's a rare farm that has no bad ground" and "If the farmer fails all will starve." But proverbs on planting and growing are not always just straightforward rules. Some contain wonderful bits of folk humor as, for example, "Your corn will never grow until you lie naked at night" and "Time to plant beans is when it is hot enough nights so that Hannah sleeps without a sheet on her."

Maple sugaring has also given us folk maxims based on decades of experience with this "sweet" work. Some texts refer explicitly to the hard labor involved in sugaring, namely "A gallon of syrup is worth one day's labor" and "You boil at least thirty-two gallons of sap to make each gallon of syrup." Other proverbs contain information on when the sap runs best as, for example, "When the sun is bright on the snow and warm on your back, the sap will be running," "Warm days, cold nights, make sap run right," "Sap runs best after a sharp frost," "Sap runs better by day than by night," and "When the wind is in the west the sap runs best." There are even proverbs that comment on the particular sweetness of the sap: "The older the tree the sweeter the sap," "Sap run during the daytime is sweeter than that run at night," "The first run of sap is the sweetest," and "The higher you tap the sweeter the sap."

Regarding the scientific value of these proverbial observations, one of the leading maple syrup researchers from the University of Vermont has assured me that they contain truth borne out by years of scholarly analysis. Even the colorful and typically Vermont proverb "Trees differ as much for sugar as cows differ for butter" has scientific validity to it. The actual excitement of starting the sugaring in early spring after a long Vermont winter is expressed in the poetic gem of folk wisdom "A sap-run is the sweet good-bye of winter." Finally there is the proverb "The true Vermonter never loses his taste for the sweet of the maple," which shows our personal delight in this golden product, or is it by chance a tongue-in-cheek advertisement to get people outside of Vermont to buy this natural, sweet syrup that is unrivaled in quality by syrup produced in neighboring states?

We would expect many references to the weather and the seasons in a state that historically depended to a large degree on agriculture. Vermonters are fond of such general weather observations as "Winter's fog will freeze a dog," "A late snowstorm is a poor man's fertilizer," "A cold wet May fills the barn with hay." "March rains serve only to fill the ditches," and "A late fall means a hard winter," which doubtlessly are applicable to other New England regions as well. However, the more general proverb "In New England we have nine months of winter and three months of damned poor sledding" also has a specifically Vermont variant in "Vermont has nine months of winter and three months of damned poor sledding." The same is true for the New England proverb "We have two seasons: winter and Fourth of July," which in Vermont is usually cited as "Vermont has only two seasons: winter and the Fourth of July." It is not certain whether Vermont can claim to have originated these texts, but the local weather guide "Snow on Mount Mansfield and in six weeks the valley will be white" is without doubt indigenous to Vermont.

We can also observe the contrast of regional flavor versus general proverbial wisdom in the following proverb pairs. While most Americans know the weather proverb "One swallow does not make a summer," which has its origin in Greek antiquity and was translated into many languages including English, the Vermonter might at times prefer to quote the regional proverb variant "It takes more than one robin to make a summer." Rather than quoting that old standby proverb "The early bird catches the worm," a rural Vermonter might well decide to specify the generic bird and expand the standard proverb to include a farm metaphor: "The early robin looks for worms behind the early plow." Instead of the classical Latin proverb, "Gutta cavat lapidem," which appeared in English translation as early as the thirteenth century as "Constant dropping wears the stone," Vermonters often cite the expanded version "Constant dripping wears away the hardest stone" or the more regional variant "The constant creeping of ants will wear away the stone" to express that important virtue of perseverance so characteristic of this area. Or rather than quoting that old Biblical proverb "For everything there is a season,"[14] which lacks in metaphorical rhetoric, one will most likely hear a true Vermonter observe that "The time to pick berries is when they're ripe" or "Time to catch bears is when they are out." And why cite the overused sixteenth-century proverb "Beauty is only skin deep" when the proverb "Beauty does not make the pot boil" so convincingly reminds us that glamorous outside appearance does not necessarily feed the farmer and his family?

Yet it is not only by rephrasing existing proverbial structures that Vermonters have created some of their distinctively regional wisdom. Numerous proverbs in common use in this state start with a traditional proverb text and add a modifying phrase beginning with the conjunction "but." Such texts mirror the independent and free spirit of Vermont folks who do not just accept what everybody else says or believes. Speakers of the English language have used the proverb "A new broom sweeps clean" since the middle of the sixteenth century to indicate that a new person in control usually makes changes in personnel or procedures, often referring to this new boss simply with the shortened metaphor "new broom." Yet in Vermont people like to caution that the old or traditional way of conducting business is not necessarily always bad by expanding this standard proverb to "A new broom sweeps clean, but the old one finds the corners."

A similar refashioning of the common proverb "Money makes the mare go" reflects Vermonters' legendary thriftiness. Too much money quickly and perhaps too easily earned brings worries and problems, a fact that is dramatically expressed in the innovative proverbial statement that "Money makes the mare go—but not the nightmare." The thrifty and hard-working Vermonter much prefers such proverbs as "Dirty hands make clean money" or "Take care of the dimes and the dollars will take care of themselves."

All of this is not to say that Vermonters do not realize that we need some money to overcome poverty and to attain a modicum of happiness. With typical Vermont wit, a resident of this state once took the proverb "Poverty is no disgrace" and changed it to "There's no disgrace in poverty, but it's damned inconvenient," while another local person expanded the proverb "Money won't buy happiness" to "Money won't buy happiness, but it's nice to choose your way to be unhappy." These acute observations by a local wit have caught on, that is, they have gained currency among the people and reached a level of acceptance as traditional wisdom so that we can consider them proverbs in their own right. This is also the case with the witty elaboration of the Biblical proverb "Love your neighbor as yourself"[15] to "Love your neighbor as yourself, but no more"—a startling piece of wisdom that is echoed in an even more egocentric but honest expansion of another popular proverb: "Charity begins at home and usually stays there."

Proverbs are rarely saccharine in their content. Instead they "call a spade a spade" and "let the chips fall where they may," to quote two proverbial metaphors for the honesty of proverbs in describing human behavior and relations. They do so with much humor or even satire by employing traditional vocabulary. Perhaps it is exactly the apparent simplicity of proverbial language that makes it so appealing linguistically in contrast to the sophisticated expressions that we usually read and hear in the mass media or workplace. Of course, many proverbs have become clichés through frequent use, and a well-known proverb like "A dog is man's best friend" is no exception. But even the most tired cliché can come to life, as in this expanded variant: "A dog is a man's best friend, but a good cow is more help at the table." This tells it straight, and the honesty of the juxtaposition of the dog as a friend and the cow as a food source expresses in plain language basic emotional, physiological, and economic needs.

Folk speech in general delights in paradoxical statements that often employ a witty wordplay or pun. These proverbs usually require a bit more mental agility than straightforward short proverbs, such as "A squeaking pig gets fed," "Wishes can't fill a sack," and "Mud thrown is ground lost." In contrast, the longer and more involved texts indicate the enjoyment that people find in playing with language.

Proverbs are never a mere joke, but always a concise statement of an apparent truth, albeit couched in a humorous or playful tone.[16] Two examples of such proverbial paradoxes that concern money and thriftiness are "If you don't do any more than you are paid for, you won't get paid for any more than you do" and "He who buys what he does not need will sometimes need what he cannot buy." A particularly successful pun based on the two almost homonyms of "neat/need" and "tight/tidy" gives us the proverb "It is better to be neat and tidy than to be tight and needy." This also refers to the Vermonters' preoccupation with thriftiness. An anonymous folk poet of sorts certainly was at work here, basing his or her text on the standard proverbial structure of "It is better to . . . than . . .," using parallel structure with end-rhyme in the two halves of the text and also creating a simple word play. Proverbs are esthetic modes of expression passed down primarily through oral tradition. Such devices as structure, rhyme, rhythm, and alliteration all make them easy to memorize and reproduce.[17]

Notice as a final paradoxical example the proverb "It won't be warm till the snow gets off the mountain, and the snow won't get off the mountain till it gets warm." Can't you just see a frustrated Vermonter stricken by cabin fever after a long winter standing in front of the house and gazing at the snow-covered mountain, wondering whether spring and warm weather will come. We could, of course, simply state that this is a "catch 22" situation, but this Vermont proverb expresses with resigned irony the bare fact that the weather will do whatever it sees fit.

My final examples of Vermont-grown proverbs clearly express a dry humor, based on deep insights into the human psyche. What a delight it is to hear a Vermonter insist on the wisdom of such proverbs as "Keep a thing seven years and it will sort of do," "If it ain't broke don't try to fix it," and "Use it up, wear it out, make it do or do without" as the wastefulness and throwaway mentality creeps relentlessly into the valleys and mountains of this state. And can't you just imagine an old-time Vermonter arguing with someone who is in favor of such mercantile change by pointing out that "You can't keep trouble from coming, but you don't have to give it a chair to sit in." Seeing one of those giant new homes that city folk are building in Chittenden County might lead to the observation that "A small home is better than a large mortgage" or even more ironically to "Half the dwellers in glass houses don't seem to know it."

In the right context we can also imagine the humor or irony of such proverbs as "Sometimes the cheese is blamed when the fault is in the ventilation," "How beautiful it is to do nothing and then rest afterwards," "It's nice to sit and think, but sometimes it's nicer just to sit," "No matter how tough the roast beef is, you can always cut the gravy with your knife," "A warm-back husband and a warm-foot wife should easily lead a compatible life," and "There's no help for misfortune but to marry again." These texts express in vivid images basic human concerns, and they are ever mindful of the human comedy that plays out on the stage of our everyday existence.

Knowledge of and adherence to some of the proverbs discussed here might well help everyone to cope with the complex world that is changing the villages and towns of Vermont. Many of the proverbs current in Vermont reflect those old Yankee virtues of ingenuity, perseverance, independence, thriftiness, and common sense. It is the Puritan ethic, the value system of hard work and fair play, which the early settlers took with them as they moved across the country. These values helped establish the foundations of the American world view or psyche. In Vermont we still use such proverbs as "If you want to get to the top of the hill, you must go up it" and "Keep straight and you'll never get into trouble or grow round-shouldered" to reaffirm the conviction that self-reliance, determination, and human decency make life worth living. Expressed directly and without any embellishment, a Vermonter might laconically say "Live while you live and then die and be done with it." What counts is what kind of person we are while we act as responsible citizens of one of the last rural strongholds in the United States.

The wisdom and conscience contained in our regional Vermont proverbs should encourage us to maintain and treasure the uniqueness of Vermont life. Yet while the one proverb "Good fences make good neighbors" helps us preserve our cherished personal independence and freedom, we must be careful not to twist this proverb into the shortsighted and chauvinistic anti-proverb of "Bad neighbors make good fences"—a thought-provoking variation of that famous "Vermont" proverb that concludes the poem "Spite Fence" (circa 1980) by Richard Eberhart (born 1904).[18]

Many of the proverbs current or even coined in Vermont could be guiding lights of folk wisdom for preserving traditional values in this state, while we try to cope with the demands and challenges of change. They reflect life experiences and human insights that have been valid for many generations and centuries. They still contain plenty of truths, wisdom, and knowledge about what makes life so special in Vermont. It is, therefore, with legitimate justification that I conclude this essay with a proverbial variation of Vermont's most precious proverb: "Good proverbs make good Vermonters."

NOTES

1. Ralph Charles La Rosa, "Emerson's Proverbial Rhetoric: 1818-1838" (Ph.D. diss., University of Wisconsin, 1969).

2. Wolfgang Mieder, *American Proverbs: A Study of Texts and Contexts* (Bern: Peter Lang, 1989), 143-168.

3. Wolfgang Mieder, "'Behold the Proverbs of a People': A Florilegium of Proverbs in Carl Sandburg's Poem 'Good Morning, America,'" *Southern Folklore Quarterly* 35:160-168; Carl Sandburg, *The Complete Poems of Carl Sandburg* (New York: Harcourt Brace Jovanovich, 1970), 329.

4. Wolfgang Mieder, *Yankee Wisdom: New England Proverbs* (Shelburne, Vt.: New England Press, 1989).

5. Muriel J. Hughes, "Vermont Proverbs and Proverbial Sayings," *Vermont History* 28 (1960): 113-142, 200-230; Wolfgang Mieder, *Talk Less and Say More: Vermont Proverbs* (Shelburne, Vt.: New England Press, 1986); *As Sweet as Apple Cider: Vermont Expressions* (Shelburne, Vt.: New England Press, 1988).

6. See Ronald Baker's *Folklore in the Writings of Rowland E. Robinson* (Ph.D. diss., Indiana University, 1969).

7. See Wolfgang Mieder, Stewart Kingsbury, and Kelsie Harder, eds., *A Dictionary of American Proverbs* (New York: Oxford University Press, 1992); Archer Taylor and Bartlett Jere Whiting, *A Dictionary of American Proverbs and Proverbial Phrases, 1820-1880* (Cambridge: Harvard University Press, 1958); Bartlett Jere Whiting, *Early American Proverbs and Proverbial Phrases* (Cambridge: Harvard University Press, 1977); and Bartlett Jere Whiting, *Modern Proverbs and Proverbial Sayings* (Cambridge: Harvard University Press, 1989).

8. Harold W. Thompson, "Proverbs and Sayings [from New York]," *New York Folklore Quarterly* 5 (1949): 230-235, 296-300.

9. Robert Frost, *The Complete Poems of Robert Frost* (New York: Holt, Rinehart and Winston, 1964), 47-48.

10. George Monteiro, "'Good Fences Make Good Neighbors': A Proverb and a Poem," *Revista de Etnografia* 16 (1972): 83-88.

11. John A. Simpson, *The Concise Oxford Dictionary of Proverbs* (Oxford: Oxford University Press, 1982), 98.

12. F. P. Wilson, *The Oxford Dictionary of English Proverbs* (Oxford: Clarenden Press, 1970), 494; Frances Barbour, *A Concordance to the Sayings in Franklin's "Poor Richard"* (Detroit: Gale Research Co., 1974).

13. Addison Barker, "'Good Fences Make Good Neighbors,'" *Journal of American Folklore* 64:421.

14. Ecclesiastes 3:1.

15. Matthew 22:39.

16. Wolfgang Mieder and Alan Dundes, eds., *The Wisdom of Many: Essays on the Proverb* (New York: Garland Publishing, 1981); Archer Taylor, *The Proverb* (Cambridge: Harvard University Press, 1931); reprinted with an introduction by Wolfgang Mieder (Bern: Peter Zang, 1985).

17. Shirley L. Arora, "The Perception of Proverbiality," *Proverbium* 1 (1984): 1-38; Neal R. Norrick, *How Proverbs Mean: Semantic Studies in English Proverbs* (Amsterdam: Mouton, 1985).

18. Richard Eberhart, *Collected Poems 1930-1986* (New York: Oxford University Press, 1988), 400.

Place Names as Footprints of History

Esther Munroe Swift

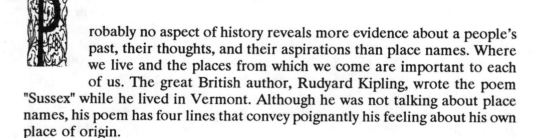

robably no aspect of history reveals more evidence about a people's past, their thoughts, and their aspirations than place names. Where we live and the places from which we come are important to each of us. The great British author, Rudyard Kipling, wrote the poem "Sussex" while he lived in Vermont. Although he was not talking about place names, his poem has four lines that convey poignantly his feeling about his own place of origin.

> God gave all men all earth to love.
> But, since our hearts are small,
> Ordained for each one spot should prove
> Beloved over all.[1]

It has always seemed to me that those lines explain, in part, why all people cherish and then vehemently defend their particular stories of how their place names came about. Many times I found stories of name origins that had long been accepted but which were perhaps not correct. Often the real story behind the name proves to be more interesting than the wrong one. But trying to disabuse anyone of a favorite place-name story is just about as easy as selling snow in Alaska. One is usually well advised not to try.

One of the best examples of a cherished story of doubtful authenticity concerns the origin of the name Burlington. Queen City residents have always claimed with pride that the name came from the British Earldom of Burlington, which was held by the Boyle family. The family included many illustrious members both in England and Ireland, but its best known residence was the famed Burlington House in London. Richard Boyle, third earl, was a talented architect and a great patron of the arts. In addition, he was something of a political figure, having been at different times a member of the privy council and treasurer of Ireland. He is the one most often referred to in the Vermont Burlington story. However, it seems probable that Benning Wentworth, who granted the charter for the town, would have been more interested in flattering a live earl than a dead one. In 1763, when the town of Burlington was created, Richard Boyle was ten years dead and the earldom was held by John Boyle, a minor literary figure who fancied his talents were somewhat greater than, in fact, they were. Nevertheless, because he was a friend of many literary lions—Samuel Johnson, Alexander Pope, Jonathan Swift—John Boyle was quite well known. In addition, the Boyle family was related by marriage to just about everyone of any consequence in the British establishment. Benning Wentworth was himself related to many of the same families and ultimately used most of their surnames or titular names for towns he created in New Hampshire and Vermont.

The romance of the Earl of Burlington story notwithstanding, there is another explanation I have always felt to be a very real possibility. Burlington was granted on 7 June 1763 along with nine other towns, including neighboring Colchester. With no computer, photocopier, nor typewriter to accomplish the paper work, the land office must have been a nightmare that day. There were ten charters, ten lists of grantees (each numbering sixty-odd names) and all the attendant charts, plans, and surveys to be kept straight and matched to their desired names. The Burling family of New York City was wealthy and politically prominent, a combination that always appealed to Wentworth. Over a period of years, the Burlings shared in eleven Wentworth town grants. Nine members of the family are listed among the grantees of Colchester. But no Burling name appears in the Burlington list. The question is: did the town names or the grantee lists get swapped and should Colchester really have been named Burlington and Burlington Colchester?

I often think of place names as a tapestry composed of many threads and colors from a rich storehouse of materials, blended into an intricate mix of wonderful figures or images. Thus it is with our Vermont place names. Looking at the individual threads and colors, one can trace many of the events of history and the people who shaped our state. This shaping process still goes on as politicians, public relations people, and pressure groups come and go. For example, in the southern part of the state there is a small body of water that had been Ray's Pond as long as anyone could remember until the area became popular with people "from away." Then the name seemed hardly dignified or appealing enough. So Lake Rayponda it became.

In 1893 the village of Sodom in the town of Calais got its post office and for some years local folk got their mail addressed to Sodom, Vermont. Eventually some of the more educated or religious among them decided they really didn't care to receive their mail at an address associated with wickedness. Adamant was finally chosen as being symbolic of the granite quarried near the village. Today the sole reminder of the state's most flamboyant postal name is nearby Sodom Pond.

Vermont acquired and lost a good many place names through the efforts of the railroad and the postal authorities. Because trains could not climb hills very well in the 1850s, depots were built in the valley, convenient for the railroad, and villages grew up around the depots. In some cases this way of making new towns badly confused travelers. Best known are the stories about all the passengers who bought tickets for Burlington and, when they got off, found themselves in a place called Essex Junction. Montpelier was similarly situated. Montpelier Junction was created for the convenience of trains. In fact, it, too, is actually located in a different town.

Postal history has had an enormous impact on our place names. For nearly one hundred years almost any settled community could get a post office just by asking for it. Some of the offices never did even five dollars' worth of business during a year's time. Little by little those smaller offices were closed, thereby depriving the state of some of its more interesting names such as Florence, Grange, Maples, and Pearl. The closings have continued up to the present. Unfortunately, some of the recent post offices that have been abolished bore Vermont town names. As a result, sometimes one has to guess or read the entire ZIP code directory to find what a postal name might be for a town. Weathersfield has a choice of Ascutney or Perkinsville. A good many towns have ended up with a compass direction as the first name of the only post office. For example, Royalton is post office South Royalton. Dover has a choice between West and East Dover, but no Dover.

Almost everyone has been affected by twentieth-century trends among postal authorities, government agencies, and even typesetters and typists. It has become standard practice to drop the apostrophe and often the following "s" if they were part of a place name. The result is both obfuscating and bothersome to the historian looking for meanings. Recently Vermont Public Radio began announcing that it transmits from Rutland's "Grandpa Knob." This leads one to ask whether Knob is a surname or a geological name. In fact, the name is Grandpa's Knob, which is self-explanatory even if we don't know who Grandpa was or what he did that caused the hill to be named for him.

Vermont is not just the sole New England state without a seacoast; it is also the only one of the six states never to have been a separate British colony. Both these circumstances contributed to its population patterns and to its names for towns, villages, hamlets, localities, roads, rivers, mountains, and ponds. By the mid-eighteenth century, Great Britain had already had colonies on this side of the Atlantic for more than a century and a half but had established no permanent settlements in the 9,000-odd square miles that is Vermont. For years the Indians and French had moved back and forth in the area. At different times the British and colonial militia had fought with both. A few of those sojourners left their footprints in names for topographic features. One of the oldest and best known is that of our biggest lake. The great explorer, Samuel de Champlain, modestly wrote in his travel journal: "It is called Lake Champlain." Unfortunately, names for other topographical features have been more problematic. For example, if a fellow named Jones lived on one side of a hill he called it Jones Hill, while Smith, living on the other side, was just as liable to call it Smith's Hill. Meanwhile, someone else discovers that the old town records show the same hill as Mount Tug and for him that is its name forever. All this makes one realize that place names, like beauty, are often only in the eye of the beholder.

Both Gov. Benning Wentworth of New Hampshire and the several royal governors of the New York colony felt their respective articles of authority entitled them to grant towns in the Green Mountains. A kind of one-upmanship resulted as both New Hampshire and New York rushed to divide up the territory. Wentworth acted first and on a grand scale. Beginning in 1749 with Bennington, which he named for himself, he created 128 Vermont towns before the King's Council ordered him to desist in 1775.

Many of those towns still proudly bear their original names, given to honor a primary grantee or to curry favor with the king's cabinet or the privy council. Although few of those members of the British nobility and aristocracy would ever see the mountains or walk the valleys of Vermont, their names still mark our map. Some grantees chose their own town names, and many Vermont towns were named either for the hometown in another colony or for the English home of a forefather. In 1777 there were so many towns with Connecticut origins, the newly declared independent state started to call itself New Connecticut until the founding fathers realized that the name was already used for part of the area that has become Ohio.

Quite early, the shore of Lake Champlain and the Winooski River Valley were recognized as prime lands for settlement. In those areas Wentworth granted towns to some of the men who subsequently became founders of our state. Among them were the Allens and Thomas Chittenden, but Wentworth named no towns for them. Vermont later honored Chittenden with both a county and a town name, but the Allen brothers never achieved that kind of official recognition. Ira Allen is the only one of the brothers whose name is associated with any Vermont town. The first of them is the town of Ira. The records are confused and it is not certain that Ira ever was really chartered by Vermont. For years it was known only as the District of Ira, probably because Ira Allen, as the state's surveyor general, knew where the unchartered lands were. The status of the district was thrashed out in several legislative sessions. Eventually it seems to have been accepted as a town only by virtue of the fact that it existed, people lived there, and it was not claimed by any of the adjoining towns.

Ira Allen's other town, which he really did buy, was Irasburg. He later gave it as a wedding present to his wife, as he wrote to his brother: "I have married my favorite Miss Enos and brought her home." When he transferred the title for Irasburg to her he said: "In token of the affection I have for Jerusha Enos Junior." She was the daughter of General Roger Enos, Sr., for whom the neighboring town of Enosburg was named. Many years later Jerusha was to say that at the time Ira gave her the town, she "didn't think it was worth a rush."

Vermont's assertion of independence from both the colonies and Britain in 1777 and its refusal to acknowledge the authority of either New Hampshire or New York meant that it had to find its own way to finance its defense and participation in the War of Independence. The first source of ready money was the confiscation and sale of lands held by Tory sympathizers. When that money ran out the Vermont General Assembly set out to market the remaining ungranted land. With typical Yankee shrewdness, peddlers were sent downcountry with blank charters and land descriptions. A down payment could be made on a grant and the rest would be due when the grantees were ready to take up the land. Many of the parcels were sold to companies of Continental troops.

Some indication of the salesmanship that went into the land marketing endeavor can be seen in the case of the town on the Canadian border now known as Brighton. The grantees asked that their parcel be named Gilead, indicating that they expected it to be their promised land. When they actually got to Vermont and saw what they had bought, they petitioned to have it called Random, for that was exactly what it was: a random purchase out of the lot offered for sale. Random it stayed for fifty years. By then the town had grown to a population of one hundred and didn't appear to have much chance of attracting more people with Random as a name. The town, therefore, petitioned the legislature again to change the name to Brighton, honoring the Rhode Island birthplace of one of the town's grantees, Col. Joseph Nightingale.

Vermont acquired a few of her place names from what could be called Ethan Allen's French connection. He had become good friends with the distinguished Frenchman J. Hector St. John, who is best known today as the author of *Letters from an American Farmer*. St. John de Crèvecoeur, as he called himself in some of his correspondence, suggested that, in view of Vermont's French-sounding name and to acknowledge France's aid to America during the war, it should have some French cities and towns. The state eventually adopted three of his eighteen suggestions: Danville for the noted French geographer and cartographer, Jean d'Anville; Vergennes for Comte de Vergennes, France's minister of foreign affairs during the American Revolution; and St. Johnsbury for St. John himself.

Early Vermonters do not appear to have been the least bit bothered by the recurrence of place names in totally different locations, apparently because they derive from different sources. For example, we have a town of Wells in Rutland County, which was named for Wells in Somerset, England. Far to the east in Newbury, Orange County, is the village of Wells River on the river of the same name. Zadock Thompson wrote in 1824: "Wells River had its name long before any settlement was made in Vermont, but we have not ascertained why it was so called."[2] Subsequent research reveals exactly where the Wells River got its name. Between 1761 and 1763 four Wentworth grants in that area were made in part to Samuel Wells, who had been born in Deerfield, Massachusetts, but had moved to Brattleboro. Written sixteen years after Thompson's title, Benjamin Hall's *History of Eastern Vermont* had a seven-page biography of Samuel Wells. Among other things Hall noted that Wells had stayed loyal to the Crown throughout the Revolution but that he had also remained loyal to Vermont and its interests, hence his lands had not been confiscated as had those of most Tories. By a special act of the legislature, Wells's estate was entered for probate in 1783, just as though he had never held any Tory beliefs.

If one is so-minded, it is possible to do a tour of the United States and the rest of the world without ever leaving Vermont. To visit only a few places, begin in Albany, go on to Algiers, the Alps, and Athens, and continue through the alphabet to Woodstock, Worcester, and Zion.

If one is more inclined to follow whimsical pathways in Vermont, begin with Bagnal and then go on to choose among such wonderfully evocative places as Flypot or Tin Pot, Goose Green or Goose City, to name a few. For mountain people the choices are equally diverse. In addition to the high peaks, whose names are familiar to everyone, you may choose smaller and less familiar names like Breakneck and Hurricane, Thousand Acre and Terrible, Raspberry and Butternut, Bald and Horrid, Aldis and Ames, Bare and Mile, Flower and Blueberry, Lone Tree and Long, Dutch or Dusty Ridge, Galusha and Laisdell.

As an example of how names change, let me tell a personal story: A brook on my property has always been there; it runs all year long (even under its winter cover of ice), and as early as 1770 it powered an up-and-down saw-mill. In later years it ran a small grist mill and foundry. When we bought the property, it still had the ram that pumped water to run the acetylene lighting plant in the house. There is no evidence it ever had a name, so I call it Swift's Brook. If the apostrophe and the final "s" are ever lost, future researchers will assume it was so-named because it is, in fact, swift-flowing.

In conclusion, here is a second example of how place names come about. This incident happened when the book *Vermont Place-Names*[3] was published. Much of the time during the research for the book I had the same secretary. She had typed some of the manuscript, so I took her one of the first copies. She went straight to the index and searched diligently, then looked up and said, "But, Mrs. Swift, they've left out Happy Acres." I explained it was just a personal nickname for our place in Vermont. Her response stopped me dead. "But isn't that the way you always said place names happened?"

NOTES

1. Rudyard Kipling, *Five Nations: The Years Between and Poems from History* (New York: Doubleday, 1940).

2. Zadock Thompson, *History of Vermont: Natural, Civil and Statistical, in three parts* (Burlington: Chauncey Goodrich, 1842), part 3 *Gazetteer of Vermont*, 186.

3. Esther Munroe Swift, *Vermont Place-Names: Footprints of History* (Brattleboro: Stephen Greene Press, 1977).

Vermont Bicentennial Celebration, Montpelier, Vt., August 17, 1991. Courtesy of Vermont Historical Society, Montpelier, Vt. (F-EX VT Bicentennial 1991).

WE VERMONTERS

Legacies of Contact:

Indians, Europeans, and the Shaping of Vermont

Colin G. Calloway

In recent years, historians and ethnohistorians have increased their efforts to understand Native American cultures and how European contact affected Native American societies. But we still pay little attention to how the Indian past and presence affected non-Indian society. Perhaps no state has been portrayed as more "un-Indian" than Vermont, and when Indians do figure in Vermont's past, they usually play a minimal role. Along with the French in Canada, the heavily forested mountains, and the mud in springtime, they act as "obstacles" to the settlement of the Green Mountain State. I intend to take another look at Vermont's past and offer some thoughts on how continual border contact between Indian inhabitants and European colonists may have helped shape the region's history and character. I shall concentrate on Vermont but draw examples from a wider area that includes Maine and New Hampshire where the conditions of contact were similar.

A recent book on the history of the American West, called *The Legacy of Conquest*, advances an interpretation of western history and society that emphasizes as determining themes the conquest of Native Americans and the rape of the environment.[1] I choose "contact" instead of "conquest" as a determining theme in Vermont's history to emphasize the multi-dimensional nature of the interactions that occurred between natives and newcomers in northern New England. Conquest was a major part of the story here, and its legacy was one of undeniable tragedy for the native inhabitants; but it was by no means the whole story and it took a variety of forms other than armed aggression.

As the Norman invaders of Anglo-Saxon England found after 1066, conquest often changes both the conquered and the conquerors. Many of the European colonists who came to Vermont were already products of an Old World heritage and a New World experience of living in Massachusetts or Connecticut. Movement to the North Country added other ingredients to the mix of influences that molded the people and the society they made, and some of these influences came from the Indian people who already lived here.

A first legacy of contact that we need to consider is the size of Vermont's Indian population when European settlers first arrived. The relative sparseness of the Indian population here meant that European settlers did not encounter the massive resistance they met elsewhere; it also gave rise to the myth that Vermont had no native inhabitants. But both the *fact* of low population density and the *fiction* of no native population were themselves products of contact. Old World diseases, transported by European migrants and transmitted to Indian peoples who had little or no immunity to the new germs, spread rapidly through Indian country and penetrated the Green Mountain valleys long before European settlers themselves arrived.

We will never know the exact Indian population of Vermont before the epidemics nor the full extent of the havoc that the diseases caused, but certainly diseases decimated the native population and opened the way for European penetration of Vermont. The depopulation that occurred armed subsequent later arrivals with a convenient justification for dispossession: how could the land one acquired belong to Indians if there were never any Indians here in the first place? By the nineteenth century, the myth of Vermont as an empty no-man's-land prior to white settlement became enshrined as truth. New England congressmen and reformers voiced their criticisms of U.S. Indian policies in the south and west, righteous in the knowledge that such things "had never happened here."[2]

Having recognized once and for all that Indians did—and do—inhabit Vermont, we should consider what effects that Indian presence exerted on the course of Vermont's history. As James Axtell has done for colonial America in general, we might ask: Would Vermont have been the same if there had been no Indians here?[3]

One way to answer that question is to take a look at some of the old histories of Vermont, which were written as if there were no Indians here.[4] Without Indians, Vermont's human history is very short—three or four hundred years instead of the ten thousand plus years described by William Haviland and Marjory Power in their book *The Original Vermonters*.[5] Vermont history traditionally celebrates the European pioneers who settled the Green Mountains but often neglects the Indian pioneers who settled and shaped the land for thousands of years before.

We can all think of things that Vermonters adopted from Indians, which have become part of the culture of northern New England. Many Algonquian Indian words have entered the American English language and, as John C. Huden's lists demonstrate, there are thousands of place names of Indian origin in New England, hundreds of them Abenaki names in Vermont and New Hampshire.[6]

We know, too, that Indians enriched our diets with corn, squash, pumpkins, and maple sugar. European colonists adopted Indian techniques of fishing, farming, hunting, and gathering.[7] Indians also passed along useful medical skills and health remedies, and native healers like Molly Ockett were widely respected by Indians and colonists alike.[8]

Indians influenced the way we dress and travel, passing along to us moccasins, snowshoes, toboggans, canoes, and an extensive network of trails and watercourses in and around the region. We think of Indians as the eager recipients of European technology and, in some cases, so indeed they were. But as John McPhee makes clear in his eulogy on the birch bark canoe, Europeans were equally quick to borrow the technology of the Indians. Europeans rowed their way to shore, backwards, but once they began to travel northern New England's lakes they faced forward, plying light birch bark craft with paddles of ash and maple.[9] An Italian traveler who visited the Penobscots at Old Town, Maine, in 1785, commented at length upon the inroads made by European culture on the Indians' dress, appearance, and way of life, but missed the irony of the fact that he himself departed Old Town in a Penobscot canoe.[10] Indians borrowed selectively from European technology; European colonists returned the compliment. But the fact that Europeans wore moccasins and paddled canoes did not automatically turn them into Indians, nor did Indians who dressed in white man's clothing cease being Indians.

The legacy of contact is more than place names and sporting goods, and my purpose is not just to compile a list of Indian "contributions."[11] Rather, it is to consider Indians and Europeans as co-participants in the shaping of Vermont. From first encounters Indians and Europeans interacted and reacted and exchanged knowledge and skills. Contact, cooperation, and confrontation left lasting impressions that were often more subtle and less apparent but more far-reaching than pulling on a pair of moccasins. Through intermarriage, interaction and imitation, Indian influences shaped Yankee character and society. The English made frequent efforts to educate Indians in what they called civilized ways, but in northern forests it was often the Indians who handed out a practical education.[12]

Normally, we think of distinct lines dividing Indian and Yankee society (the shadow of Francis Parkman looms long). Yet time and again the lines broke down in the forests of northern New England and cultural barriers proved to be porous at best. Initially and in theory, New Englanders regarded Indians as the savage antithesis of the civilization they were trying to create, and defined themselves in opposition to Indian country and to what they thought Indians were. Indians were agents of the devil (or worse still of the French) and Indian country was a howling wilderness. Struggling to find their unique identity and apprehensive of the lure of Indian life, transplanted Europeans announced they were "civilized" not "savages," farmers not hunters, Christians not pagans, settlers not nomads, and so on. But part of the process by which Europeans became American involved rubbing shoulders with the Indian inhabitants of the country they occupied and altered.[13]

Puritan ministers railed against the forest and its savage inhabitants, but in northern New England Indians and Europeans often found themselves sharing the forest. Indians and settlers sometimes mixed freely, even promiscuously in the eyes of Puritan Bostonians. Frontier settlements breathed the air of Indian country and absorbed elements of Indian culture. Vermont was a war zone for much of the eighteenth century as England and France and their respective Indian allies battled for North American supremacy, but imperial strategies masterminded in Paris and London and colonial policies spelled out in Montreal and Boston often lost much of their impact in the valleys and villages of the Green Mountains. Between wars, at the local and the individual level, Indians and colonists got on with the immediate and daily concerns of survival and making a living. That usually entailed coexistence, not conflict, with one's neighbors. Not for the last time, dictates and desires from distant capitals meant little in Vermont.

Indians and Europeans lived side by side at numerous locations throughout Abenaki country and throughout the centuries of contact. We know little about the dynamics of this coexistence, but we get glimpses into communities in the making that included Indians in their population or their peripheries. Nineteenth-century town histories that begin with recollections of the last few Indians still in the area when the first settlers arrived merely reveal the edges of webs of interactions that existed in communities where guarded cooperation was a way of life. When Susanna Johnson first arrived in Charlestown, New Hampshire, the most northerly settlement on the Connecticut River in 1744, she found nine or ten English families living there, and she remembered vividly that "the Indians were numerous and associated in a friendly manner with the whites. . . . There was such a mixture on the frontiers of savages and settlers, without established laws to govern them, that the state of society cannot easily be imagined." Not far away, in Gorham, Maine, about the same time, the settlers likewise were heavily outnumbered by the surrounding Indians and found it was in their best interest to keep on good terms with their neighbors.[14] The end of the French and Indian wars did not produce the total expulsion of the Abenakis. Rather, incoming English settlers met Indians coming home now the danger of war was over and, in Gordon Day's words, "English and Indians mingled in frontier communities from Lake Champlain to the upper Androscoggin River."[15]

Political and ethnic differences that divided empires sometimes seem to have evaporated in North Country communities that grew up around the very bastions of empire. Tiny frontier outposts like Fort Number Four, Fort Dummer, Fort St. Frédéric, or Richmond Fort in Maine served as the front lines of empires, but they also had wider social and economic functions. Soldiers and settlers, priests and traders, adventurers, captives, and Indians from a dozen tribes congregated at these places. People traded, married, attended baptisms and burials, exchanged news from Europe and from Indian country, gossiped and danced.[16] During the American Revolution, exposed frontier communities like Peacham and Newbury saw scouts, deserters, Indians, militia, and settlers come and go, and the upper Connecticut remained a source of confusion and consternation to the British throughout the Revolution as they tried to figure out and assure the loyalties of Indians who moved between the upper valley and Quebec, and of Vermonters whose allegiance seemed to hang in the balance.[17]

Direct documentary evidence detailing instances of cooperative interaction is slight as the records inevitably concentrate on more dramatic and urgent issues of conflict. But in just about every area of contact between

Indians and Europeans we can find evidence of joint participation in the shaping of the region's history.

Our mythology attributes discovery and exploration of northern New England to courageous individuals like Samuel de Champlain. A statue on Isle La Motte shows Champlain striking a heroic posture standing in a canoe. Yet below him an anonymous Indian, who presumably did the paddling, points the way. The exploration of North America was always a joint endeavor, carried out by Europeans who often did not know where they were going or what they were seeing, and by Indians who had nothing to discover since they had been there all along. Indians showed the way, provided food and shelter, acted as liaisons with neighboring tribes, and provided information for European cartographers.

Some Indian guides even spoke to the explorers in their own languages. One of Champlain's guides in 1604 was a Micmac Indian named Messamouet, who not only had been to France but had stayed at the home of the governor of Bayonne.[18] The English Pilgrims at Plymouth in 1620 owed their survival in large part to Squanto, a Patuxent Indian who had been taken across the Atlantic and lived for a time in Cornhill in London. Squanto was introduced to the Pilgrims by Samoset, a displaced Pemaquid Abenaki from the coast of Maine, who had picked up the English language from sailors. Samoset "came bouldly amongst them, and spoke to them in broken English, which they could well understand, but marvelled at it."[19] In fact, both the English and the French made a practice of kidnapping Indians in the hope of producing bilingual guides for future expeditions. In 1605, Captain George Waymouth abducted five Abenakis from the coast of Maine and took them to England. Two of the Indians returned home as guides and interpreters with later expeditions.[20]

Not only did Indian guides show Champlain the lake he named after himself, but they may also have led him into an unnecessary conflict with the Mohawks, an encounter that had far-reaching effects on later Franco-Iroquois relations and on the course of colonial history.[21] Indians guided English and French troops throughout the colonial wars and Abenakis led Benedict Arnold through the Maine wilderness on his march against Quebec in the Revolution.[22] By the time Henry David Thoreau recruited Penobscot guides for his jaunts through the Maine woods, Indians had been keeping intrepid explorers from getting lost for over two hundred years.[23]

The first introduction of Christianity into northern New England was also a product of interaction. Without Indians in substantial numbers as potential converts and congregations, there would have been no missionaries. The Indian souls that evidently needed saving attracted missionaries from France and England. Once established, Catholic missions in turn attracted Indians, influencing if not determining population movements and relocations among the New England natives. Missionaries brought their Old World religious rivalries and added a spiritual dimension to the European struggle for dominance in the region. The French lost the struggle but the French influence in northern New England endured.

As James Axtell shows, conversion was not a one-way street. The meeting of cultures in colonial North America produced a three-sided contest in which French, English, and Indians all tried in various ways to convert one another.[24] Jesuit missionaries wrote home enthusiastically about their success in converting the Indians but in some cases they themselves were the converts. Sebastian Rasles, for example, spent thirty years of his life in Indian country. He lived in Abenaki villages, traveled the Indian seasonal round by snowshoe and canoe, ate Indian food, mastered the Indian language, participated in Indian councils and wars. Rasles confided to his brother: "As for what concerns me personally, I assure you that I see, that I hear, that I speak, only as a savage."[25] When missionaries slept in Indian beds and dreamed in Indian languages, one wonders who was converting whom. English missionaries did not immerse themselves in Indian society to anything like the same extent—and English missionary efforts were not nearly so successful.

The Indian inhabitants of Vermont and the earliest European colonists to arrive in the area were both members of small folk communities, which followed a seasonal round of farming, hunting, and fishing, with trade as a supplement. In the North Country, population pressure remained relatively light for a relatively long time, and it was not difficult for natives and newcomers to coexist and for the Indian and European economies to overlap. Indians and Europeans traded things they had for things they needed. The fur trade in its early years was essentially a relationship of mutual benefit and the participants took pains to ensure that the exchange continued without interruption. European traders knew there was no fur trade without Indians, and they edged north up the Connecticut and Merrimack valleys because they knew that was where the Indian customers were. Fur trading and barter exchange between Indians and Europeans remained an important part of the cash-poor economies on the northern New England colonies for generations, and at places like Fort Number Four trade between Indians and English was a more frequent activity than war.[26]

The fur trade also illustrated how cooperation could become an instrument of conquest. The fur trade promoted debts, alcoholism, and dependence among its Indian participants, further weakening Indian capacity for resistance to the influx of settlers.

The Indian fur trade and existing Indian trade networks attracted the French and maintained the French empire in North America. Indian customers/allies were the essential ingredient that allowed the numerically weak French in Canada to challenge British America for so long and over such a wide area. Without Indian furs and Indian souls to harvest, the French influence in Vermont's history and culture would not be what it is. Indians thronged to French trading posts like Chambly and as early as the first decade of the seventeenth century both Henry Hudson and Bartholomew Gosnold met Indian traders on the Maine coast who spoke French.[27]

Today, in the face of a global environmental crisis, we invoke the memory of the original inhabitants of this land as symbols and reminders that it was once possible to live well without destroying nature. But it would be wrong to suggest that Indians left no mark on the land, either before or after contact with Europeans. As William Cronon has shown in his book, *Changes in the Land*, the ecology of New England was shaped by Indians and Europeans alike.[28] The northern fur trade illustrates how they were co-participants in a complex eco-system. Under the demands of the fur trade, Europeans and Indians jointly depleted beaver and other game, which formerly abounded in the northern forests, and joined hands in linking Vermont to the markets of Europe. By the end of the eighteenth century, Samuel Williams reported, "the beaver has deserted all the southern parts of Vermont, and is now found only in the most northern, and uncultivated parts of the state."[29] Once the beaver was gone, the fur trade was over, and the way was open for the influx of settlers and lumbermen whose destruction of the habitat further depleted Vermont's wildlife population.

As population pressures increased, so did competition for the best land. European settlers portrayed Indian subsistence strategies as wasteful and determined to make better use of nature's bounty by turning the forest into what Cronon describes as "a world of fields and fences." However, the lands they selected for cultivation were not usually untouched wilderness; often they were meadows that Indians had previously cleared, planted, and hoed. While colonists edged out Indians, so their domesticated horses, pigs, and cattle edged out wolves, raccoon, and deer. Increasing competition for prime lands usually eroded more peaceful patterns of contact, but hardship also fostered coexistence and dependence. In the winter of 1800, a group of Abenaki Indians living near Troy and Potton built their camps alongside the newly arrived settlers. The Indians were on the brink of starvation, since the moose and deer, "which formerly abounded here" had been destroyed, and they resorted to making baskets and birch bark containers for sale in the settlements.[30]

The "Indian Wars," with the Abenakis as key players, restricted the options and affected the lives of Indians and Europeans alike in Vermont. Resolute Abenaki resistance to English expansion kept most of Vermont as Indian country through much of the eighteenth century. Vermont's relatively small population in modern times has less to do with Abenaki resistance in the eighteenth century than with the westward migration of New Englanders in the nineteenth century, but the Abenakis initiated that now time-honored Vermont tradition of discouraging flatlanders from settling here.

The "French and Indian Wars" are usually depicted in clear-cut terms. Anglo-Saxon pioneers and British redcoats battle for supremacy against the French and their Indian allies. But in the North Country these wars assumed their own character. Elsewhere armies clashed in epic struggles, but here the fighting was small-scale, localized, and fought by men who, whether Indians or colonists, were part-time soldiers with their thoughts on their homes and one eye on the hunt or the harvest. Conflict here lacked clear-cut lines of racial allegiance. Vermonters and northern militia may have been Indian fighters, but they also fought alongside Indians, as the colonial authorities recruited Indian allies to counter the Abenaki threat.[31] Fort Dummer, built as a defense against Grey Lock in 1724, is remembered as the first permanent white settlement in Vermont, but significantly many of its garrison in the first twenty years or so were Indians.[32] North Country skirmishes often involved men who

recognized each other as former neighbors or even former playmates.[33]
European colonists learned to adapt to Indian-style forest warfare.[34] Guerilla
warfare and close association between Indians and colonists produced a new
kind of frontier soldier in Rogers' Rangers and the Green Mountain Boys.
History and legend remember Rogers Rangers and the St. Francis Abenakis
as implacable enemies and yet, only twenty years after the Rangers torched St.
Francis, New Hampshire, Rangers and Abenakis were serving together on the
upper Connecticut River during the American Revolution.[35]

A by-product of the wars was the surprising number of people from
New England who crossed cultural boundaries as captives and lived, temporarily or permanently, as Indians. The literature on captives and captivity
narratives is quite extensive,[36] and it is clear that the Indian way of life
exerted considerable attraction for many colonists. Indians experienced little
difficulty in adopting and absorbing young non-Indian captives into their society. Titus King, taken captive from Massachusetts in 1755, was dressed and
painted like an Indian by the time he made it across Vermont. He resisted
becoming Indian but noted the ease with which younger captives underwent
the transformation: "in Six months time they Forsake Father and mother,
Forgit their own Land, Refuess to Speak there own toungue and Seeminly be
Holley Swollowed up with the Indians."[37]

Some Europeans became almost completely "Indianized." In Maine, the
Baron de Saint Castine married an Indian woman, gave up wealth and position
in Europe for life among the Indians, and "preferred the forests of Acadia to
the Pyrenean Mountains that encompass the place of his nativity."[38] Other
individuals returned from captivity to the colonial settlements deeply affected
by their experience living as Indians. Like Phineas Stevens at Fort Number
Four, they dealt on equal terms with Indians and Europeans and were known
and respected in both societies. Most colonists never lived *with* Indians but,
near Indians in Indian country, they often appeared to outsiders to live *like*
Indians. A French visitor in the 1790s thought the settlers in the Maine
backcountry "resemble too much the natives of the country whom they have
replaced."[39]

By the time the colonists asserted their independence and their identity
as Americans, Indians and Europeans had been in contact in northern New
England for generations. The contact seldom occurred across tightly drawn
racial battle lines. More often, it occurred and recurred through porous
cultural borderlands. If we look beyond the "Indian wars" that have so long
dominated the history of interethnic contact in northern New England and
begin to scratch the surface of what was going on when Indians and Europeans
were not killing and scalping each other, the "Indian/white frontier" begins to
resemble a sponge rather than a palisade. English captives lived in Indian
villages and did not always want to come home. French missionaries spent their
lives among Indian congregations. European traders operated in Indian
country, cultivating Indian customers and taking Indian wives for the valuable
kinship ties they provided. European explorers and travelers followed
predetermined Indian routes, in Indian canoes, paddled by Indian guides.
Settlers and Indians lived in proximity and cautious coexistence. European and

colonial soldiers served alongside Indian warriors. Indian converts lived in mission villages. Indian students sometimes attended English colleges. Indian women married European men. Indian trappers, laborers, and basket-makers frequented European settlements. Individuals who had been exposed to both cultures sometimes favored their original culture, sometimes shifted their cultural allegiance, and sometimes operated as intermediaries between Indian and European worlds.

Such interactions between Indians and Europeans had important ramifications for questions of identity. The phenomenon of the Abenaki with less than one-quarter "Indian blood" is nothing new: Joseph Louis Gill, "the White Chief of the St. Francis Abenakis," was the son of two English parents and assured captive Susanna Johnson that he had "an English heart." Yet in his identity, family ties, and cultural and political allegiance, he was Abenaki.[40] As settlement pushed north, the lines dividing Indian and European became blurred. To judge by the characteristics attributed to a new breed of Yankee heroes, northern New Englanders no longer defined themselves in opposition to Indians and Indian ways. Certain "Indian" traits ceased to be signs of "savagery" and became instead appropriate virtues for European colonists in a northern New World environment. Like James Fenimore Cooper's Leatherstocking, Yankee frontiersmen combined the best of Indian and European and exemplified the mix of cultures that occurred. Robert Rogers, who attained fame for his exploits as an Indian fighter, attributed the early education that fitted him for his military service on the frontier to his upbringing in a New Hampshire settlement "where I could hardly avoid obtaining some knowledge of the manners, customs, and language of the Indians, as many of them resided in the neighborhood and daily conversed and dealt with the English." Even Ethan Allen took time off from acquiring Abenaki lands to proclaim his love for his Indian neighbors and his skill in hunting and fighting, Indian style.[41]

The mix of Indian and European over generations of border contact contributed to what anthropologist Margaret Mead termed the "mongrelization" of the American people. In northern New England as across the continent interethnic marriage was common and extensive. The French reputation for intimate associations with Indian peoples is well known. Back in 1690, Cotton Mather denounced a war party of French officers and Abenaki warriors as "half Indianized French and half-Frenchified Indians." Almost twenty years ago, historian Wilbur Jacobs asked, "Could it be that many of us are really part Indian and we don't know it?"[42] To judge by the massive increase in Indian population over the past two decades, even as recorded by the U.S. Census, that question has been answered with a resounding affirmative. Some of tonight's audience are, I am sure, of Abenaki heritage and know it. Some no doubt have Indian ancestors of whom they are unaware. As a native of Old England, I may be the only person here who can claim without a shadow of a doubt that I have *no* Abenakis in my family tree—but then again what became of those Abenakis who were kidnapped on the coast of Maine in 1605? I don't know what they did after they "discovered" England.

Contact in Vermont broke down ethnic barriers as well as reinforced them. North Country inhabitants might see themselves as Europeans fighting

Indians, as British fighting French, and as Americans fighting the British, but to some degree they and the society they produced were products of the mix of all these. The mythology of New England maintains that its citizens are as white as its churches, and that every family had an ancestor on a ship called the *Mayflower*. Yet what makes America, and Vermont, distinct is not exclusiveness but interaction, and in particular, I think, the encounters of European colonists and Indian inhabitants. As this series of programs recognizes and illustrates, Vermont's history is not the unique experience of settlers of English descent; it is the shared history of various European and Indian peoples who lived and died here and left their mark on the state and on each other. Rather than neglect its non-English history and its Indian past and presence, Vermont can, in fact, lay claim to centuries of interethnic interaction. Like Tennyson's Ulysses at the end of a lifetime of travels and encounters, Vermont can say: "I am a part of all that I have met."

NOTES

1. Patricia Limerick, *The Legacy of Conquest: The Unbroken Past of the American West* (New York: W. W. Norton, 1978).

2. For discussion of the impact of disease see Colin G. Calloway, *The Western Abenakis of Vermont, 1600-1800: War, Migration, and the Survival of an Indian People* (Norman: University of Oklahoma Press, 1990), chapter 2.

3. James Axtell, "Colonial America Without the Indians: A Counterfactual Scenario," in his *After Columbus: Essays in the Ethnohistory of Colonial North America* (New York: Oxford University Press, 1989), 222-43.

4. An important exception is Walter Hill Crockett, *Vermont: The Green Mountain State*, 5 vols. (New York: Century History Co., 1921).

5. William A. Haviland and Marjory W. Power, *The Original Vermonters: Native Inhabitants Past and Present* (Hanover, N.H.: University Press of New England, 1981).

6. John C. Huden, "Indian Place Names in Vermont," *Vermont History* 22 (July 1955): 191-203, and "Iroquois Place Names in Vermont," *Vermont History* 25 (Jan. 1957), 66-80; idem., *Indian Place Names of New England* (New York: Heye Foundation, Museum of the American Indian, 1962), xiii. Huden's list would have been less complete without the assistance of eight Abenakis, whom Huden gratefully acknowledged.

7. Faith Harrington, "Sea Tenure in Seventeenth Century New England: Native Americans and Englishmen in the Sphere of Marine Resources, 1600-1630" (Ph.D. diss., University of California at Berkeley, 1985). For Indian agricultural

practices see Howard S. Russell, *Indian New England Before the Mayflower* (Hanover, N.H.: University Press of New England, 1980).

8. *A Narrative of the Life, Adventures and Sufferings of Henry Tufts* (Dover, N.H.: Samuel Bragg, June, 1807), 69-71.

9. John McPhee, *The Survival of the Bark Canoe* (New York: Farrar, Straus and Giroux, 1975), 55.

10. Antonio Pace, trans. and ed., *Luigi Castigliani's Viaggio: Travels in the United States of North America 1785-1787* (Syracuse: Syracuse University Press, 1983), 37-41.

11. For such studies see Wilbur R. Jacobs, "What We Owe the Woodland Indians," in his *Dispossessing the American Indian: Indians and Whites on the Colonial Frontier* (New York: Charles Scribner's Sons, 1972), 151-72; and James Axtell, "The Indian Impact on English Colonial Culture," in his *The European and the Indian: Essays on the Ethnohistory of Colonial North America* (New York: Oxford University Press, 1981), 272-315.

12. James Axtell, "The Scholastic Philosophy of the Wilderness," in *The European and the Indian*, chapter 6.

13. Axtell, *The European and the Indian*, 303-04, 308; John Canup, *Out of the Wilderness: The Emergence of an American Identity in Colonial New England* (Middletown, Conn.: Wesleyan University Press, 1990).

14. "A Narrative of the Captivity of Mrs. Johnson," in *Indian Narratives* (Claremont, N.H.: Tracy and Bros., 1854), 131; Hugh D. McLellan, *History of Gorham, Maine* (Somersworth, N.H.: New England History Press, 1980, facs. reprint of 1903 ed.), 36-38. Robertson's Lease, dated 1765, indicates the coexistence of Abenakis and settlers at Missisquoi, National Archives of Canada, RG68, reel 3945, liber A, folio 179.

15. Gordon M. Day, *The Identity of the St. Francis Indians* (Ottawa: National Museums of Canada, 1981), 52.

16. For example, Pierre-Georges Roy, *Hommes et Choses du Fort St. Frédéric* (Montreal: Les Éditions des Dix, 1946), 268-312; *Collections of the Maine Historical Society*, 2d series, 23 (1916): 233-35.

17. *Collections of the Vermont Historical Society* 3 (1943): 268; Calloway, *Western Abenakis of Vermont*, chapter 11.

18. *Dictionary of Canadian Biography* 1 (Toronto: University of Toronto Press, 1966), 506.

19. William Bradford, *History of Plymouth Plantation* (2 vols. Boston, 1912) 1: 198-99; Alden T. Vaughan, *New England Frontier: Puritans and Indians 1620-1675* (rev. ed., New York: W. W. Norton, 1979), 69-70.

20. Henry S. Burrage, ed., *Early English and French Voyages* (New York: Charles Scribner's Sons, 1932), 377-79; Bruce G. Trigger, *Natives and Newcomers: Canada's 'Heroic Age' Reconsidered* (Kingston and Montreal: McGill-Queens University Press, 1985), 130.

21. Ray Gonyea, "The 1609 Champlain Expedition," in *The Original People: Native Americans in the Champlain Valley* (Clinton County Historical Association, 1988), 26.

22. John Joseph Henry, *Account of Arnold's Campaign Against Quebec* (Albany: Joel Munsell, 1887), 31-32, 74-75.

23. Henry David Thoreau, *The Maine Woods* (New York: W. W. Norton, 1950), 18-19 and passim.

24. James Axtell, *The Invasion Within: The Contest of Cultures in Colonial North America* (New York: Oxford University Press, 1985).

25. Kenneth M. Morrison, *The Embattled Northeast: The Elusive Ideal of Alliance in Abenaki-Euroamerican Relations* (Berkeley: University of California Press, 1984), 178.

26. Peter A. Thomas, "Bridging the Cultural Gap: Indian/White Relations," in John W. Ifkovic and Martin Kaufman, eds., *Early Settlement in the Connecticut Valley* (Historic Deerfield, Inc., 1984), 5-21; Calloway, *Western Abenakis*, 25, 142, 160-61, 170.

27. David B. Quinn and Alison M. Quinn, eds., *The English New England Voyages, 1602-1608* (London: Hakluyt Society, 1983), 117; Samuel Purchas, ed., *Hakluytus Posthumus or Purchas His Pilgrims*, 20 vols. (Glasgow: Maclehose and Sons, 1905-1907) 13: 346-47.

28. William Cronon, *Changes in the Land: Indians, Colonists, and the Ecology of New England* (New York: Hill and Wang, 1983).

29. Samuel Williams, *The Natural and Civil History of Vermont*, 2 vols. (2d ed. Burlington, 1809) 1: 121, quoted in Cronon, *Changes in the Land*, 106.

30. Hemenway, *Vermont Historical Gazetteer* 3: 315.

31. *Collections of the Maine Historical Society*, 2d series, 9 (1907), 4-5.

32. Myron O. Stachiw, ed., *Massachusetts Officers and Soldiers, 1723-1743: Dummer's War to the War of Jenkins' Ear* (New England Historical and Genealogical Society, 1979), 164, 177, 185, 248, 260.

33. Francis Chase, ed. *Gathered Sketches from the Early History of New Hampshire and Vermont* (Claremont, N.H.: Tracy, Kenney & Co., 1856), 65-68; McClellan, *The History of Gorham, Maine*, 36; Charles E. Clark, *The Eastern Frontier: The Settlement of Northern New England, 1610-1763* (New York: Knopf, 1970), 263.

34. John K. Mahon, "Anglo-American Methods of Indian Warfare, 1676-1794," *Mississippi Valley Historical Review* 45 (1958-59): 254-75.

35. Calloway, *The Western Abenakis of Vermont*, 209-10, 213-16; Colin G. Calloway, "Sentinels of the Revolution: Bedell's New Hampshire Rangers and the Abenaki Indians on the Upper Connecticut," *Historical New Hampshire* 45 (1990): 271-95.

36. For example, James Axtell, "The White Indians of Colonial America," *William and Mary Quarterly*, 3rd series (1975), 55-88, reprinted in *The European and the Indian*; Alden T. Vaughan and Daniel K. Richter, "Crossing the Cultural Divide: Indians and New Englanders, 1605-1763," *Proceedings of the American Antiquarian Society* 90, part 1 (Oct. 1980), 23-99; Alden T. Vaughan and Edward W. Clark, eds., *Puritans among the Indians: Accounts of Captivity and Redemption, 1676-1724* (Cambridge: Harvard University Press, 1981); Laurel Thatcher Ulrich, *Good Wives: Image and Reality in the Lives of Women in Northern New England, 1650-1750* (New York: Oxford University Press, 1982), chapter 11; Colin G. Calloway, "An Uncertain Destiny: Indian Captivities on the Upper Connecticut River," *Journal of American Studies* 17 (1983): 189-210; and Colin G. Calloway, comp., *North Country Captives: Selected Narratives of Indian Captivity from Vermont and New Hampshire* (Hanover: University Press of New England, 1992).

37. *Narrative of Titus King of Northampton, Massachusetts* (Hartford: Connecticut Historical Society, 1938), 13-14, 17.

38. Reuben G. Thwaites, ed., *New Voyages to North-America by the Baron de Lahontan*, 2 vols. (Chicago: A. C. McClurg, 1935) 1: 327-29; *Dictionary of Canadian Biography* 2 (Toronto: University of Toronto Press, 1969), 4-7.

39. Quoted in Gregory H. Nobles, "Breaking into the Backcountry: New Approaches to the Early American Frontier, 1750-1800," *William and Mary Quarterly*, 3rd series, 46 (Oct. 1989): 644.

40. John C. Huden, "The White Chief of the St. Francis Abenakis—Some Aspects of Border Warfare 1690-1790," *Vermont History* 24 (July 1956): 199-210; (Oct. 1956): 337-55; "Captivity of Mrs. Johnson," 158-59.

41. Canup, *Out of the Wilderness*; Jacobs, "What We Owe the Woodland Indians," 165; Robert Rogers, *Journals of Robert Rogers* (London, 1765), vi-vii; Charles A. Jellison, *Ethan Allen, Frontier Rebel* (Taftsville, Vt.: The Countryman Press, 1969), 137.

42. Alden T. Vaughan and Edward W. Clark, eds., *Puritans among the Indians: Accounts of Captivity and Redemption* (Cambridge: Harvard University Press, 1981), 137; Jacobs, "What We Owe the Woodland Indians."

Stocking the State:

Observations on Immigrants, Emigrants,

and Those Who Stayed Behind

Samuel B. Hand

n the course of the "We Vermonters" project, many different participants defined "Vermonter." Consider the position of my colleague Wolfgang Mieder, whose paper is included in this collection. Wolfgang was born in Leipzig, Germany. He has been at the University of Vermont since 1971, which means that he has lived in Vermont longer than most of his native-born students. Nonetheless he lamented he could never be a true Vermonter. He couldn't even take satisfaction in being a flatlander. He was doomed by birth to be forever a foreigner. Wolfgang has worked out a hierarchy, a caste system. And he has relegated himself to some humble station. Perhaps not an untouchable but certainly tainted for life by accident of birth. This view is not unique to Wolfgang. I immediately think of Frank Bryan, who compensates for not having been born in Vermont by claiming to have been conceived in Vermont.

Let's play with definitions for a while. When I first arrived in Burlington, there was an IGA grocery store at 52 Colchester Avenue, across from the Fleming Museum. J. Kinsley Thomas ran the place and posted a notice stating that he didn't take foreign checks. I assumed that the notice was to alert any Canadian patrons that they were to pay in cash. Retired University of Vermont archivist T. D. Seymour Bassett once mentioned that he had discussed the sign with Mr. Thomas, and Bassett swore to me that Mr. Thomas defined a foreign check as any check not drawn on a Chittenden County bank.

Flatlander is a relatively new term that apparently gained currency during the 1960s. Before then the generic term was outsider, meaning anyone not born in Vermont. Even if your parents were born in Vermont and you

what does "Vermonter" mean — even if grew up there still not one if not born there came back to live in Vermont, you were an outsider. Take Allen Fletcher as an example. Fletcher's father was born in Ludlow, Vermont, but Allen was born in Indianapolis, Indiana. A successful banker, he sold his banking interests in 1905, moved to Vermont, and became a farmer in the Billings-Webb tradition. He was elected four times to represent Cavendish in the Vermont House of Representatives and once to represent Windsor County in the state senate. In 1912 he was elected governor and served the then customary single two-year term. He was one of Vermont's better governors, and in 1916 he entered the Republican primary for U.S. senator. Former Gov. Edward Smith, who was born and died in St. Albans, was outraged that Fletcher would even be thinking about making the senate race. Look at the broadside illustration included here. In it Smith pronounces that "I believe our high offices in Vermont should be kept for Vermonters."[1] An appropriate, if ironic, footnote to Smith's comments is the fact that nineteen of the last forty-five Vermont governors were born out of state, and three of them were born out of the country.

The reason for discussing place of origin is, of course, to explore to what extent where people come from has forged something we can call the Vermont character. To what should we attribute the "fact," as Calvin Coolidge noted, that Vermonters "are an indomitable people . . . a race of pioneers, who have almost beggared themselves to serve others?"[2]

The Spring 1990 issue of "Vermont Bicentennial" commented on a series of 1990 debates as to whether Vermont should leave the federal union. The editor suggested that by voting 999 to 608 to secede "Vermonters once again proved that Revolutionary War General John Burgoyne was right. Over two hundred years ago, the British general declared that Vermonters were 'the most active and rebellious race on the continent.'"[3]

The "Vermont Bicentennial" editor used the term "race" to denote a more diverse, less homogeneous, more heterogeneous ethnic and religious population than either Burgoyne or even Coolidge imagined. Matthew Buckham, president of the University of Vermont, writing in 1901, observed that "the same law which sent much of the best Anglo-Saxon blood from Great Britain to America, India, and Australia, sent some of the bravest and most resourceful men and women of the older New England colonies up to Vermont."[4] Vermont in his view was populated by the best of the best.

Until after the 1930s it was quite fashionable to use race to denote nationality. Vermont exceptionalism was indebted to the relative absence of immigrants from eastern and southern Europe, Asians, and blacks. While the rest of the United States was receiving "wretched refuse from Europe's teeming shores," Vermont remained a Yankee "kingdom." The best Anglo-Saxon bloodlines that had originally stocked Vermont survived undiluted. This theme of Anglo-Saxon supremacy was an international phenomenon that can be detected from the earliest Vermont commentators up to the present. It is less fashionable now than it once was. During the early decades of the twentieth century, it wore a mantle of scientific respectability.

Mingled with panegyrics to Vermont superiority were lamentations over the state's high rate of emigration and deep concern over the sources of its

"Native Son Rule." Courtesy of Vermont Historical Society, Montpelier, Vt. (Broadside C328.33 N213).

NATIVE SON RULE

Would Have Barred Nearly One Half of All The Senators in the 1912 Congress

In his now celebrated attack on Allen M. Fletcher. candidate for United States senator, Ex-Governor E. C. Smith made the following statement:

"I believe our high offices in Vermont should be kept for Vermonters ....There is not a state in the Union that would tolerate the introduction of outsiders to its high offices."

A casual survey of the congressional directory for 1912 suggests the fact that the statement as regards U. S. Senators is perhaps unfounded in fact. The following appears from the official record:

Joseph F. Johnston of Alabama, born in North Carolina;
James P. Clarke of Arkansas, born in Mississippi;
George C. Perkins of California, born in Maine;
Simon Guggenheim of Colorado, born in Pennsylvania;
Duncan U. Fletcher of Florida, born in Georgia;
Hoke Smith of Georgia, born in North Carolina;
W. B. Heyburn of Idaho, born in Pennsylvania;
W. E. Borah of Idaho, born in Illinois;
Shelby M. Cullom of Illinois, born in Kentucky;
Albert B. Cummins of Iowa. born in Pennsylvania;
William S. Kenyon of Iowa, born in Ohio;
Joseph L. Bristow of Kansas, born in Kentucky;
Obadiah Gardner of Maine, born in Michigan;
Knute Nelson of Minnesota, born in Norway;
Moses E. Clapp of Minnesota, born in Indiana;
William J. Stone of Missouri, born in Kentucky;
James A. Reed of Missouri, born in Ohio;
Joseph M. Dixon of Montana, born in North Carolina;
Henry L. Myers of Montana, born in Missouri;
Norris Brown of Nebraska, born in Iowa;
Francis G. Newlands of Nevada, born in Mississippi;
Jacob H. Gallinger of New Hampshire, born in Ontario;
Frank O. Briggs of New Jersey, born in New Hampshire;
James E. Martine of New Jersey, born in Plainfield;
Porter J. MacCumber of North Dakota, born in Illinois;
A. J. Gronna of North Dakota, born in Iowa;
Thomas P. Gore of Oklahoma, born in Mississippi;
Robert L. Owen of Oklahoma, born in Virginia;
Jonathan Burne of Oregon, born in Massachusetts;
George E. Chamberlain of Portland, born in Mississippi;
George T. Oliver of Pennsylvania, born in Ireland;
George P. Wetmore of Rhode Island, born in England;
Robert J. Gamble of South Dakota, born in New York;
Coe I Crawford of South Dakota, born in Iowa;
Charles A. Culberson of Texas, born in Alabama;
Joseph W. Bailey of Texas, born in Mississippi;
George Sutherland of Utah, born in England;
Miles Poindexter of Washington, born in Tennessee;
Francis E. Warren of Wyoming, born in Massachusetts;
Clarence D. Clark of Wyoming, born in New York.

This shows that nearly one half of the senators were born outside the states which they represent.

The list includes men of national force and mental stature. It includes the leaders of every senate with which they have been connected. **No one but Ex-Governor Smith has ever raised the point of their unfitness** because they happened to be born in states other than those they represented.

WHY DOES GOVERNOR SMITH DESIRE THE RE-ELECTION OF SENATOR PAGE?

WHY DO THE RAILROADS INSIST ON HIS RETURN TO WASHINGTON?

WILL SENATOR PAGE ANSWER?

Thousands of people in Vermont desire to know what Senator Page has stood for and what he has created in the way of constructive legislation during his eight years' service in Washington.

Senator Page, what constructive measure have you proposed, stood behind and pushed to a successful issue?

THE ALLEN M. FLETCHER SENATORIAL CLUB

NORTHFIELD, VT.

newer immigration. Descendants of the original pioneers were leaving the state in large numbers. Soon after the Civil War more than forty percent of native-born Vermonters were living in some other state. Rowland Robinson, one of Vermont's fabled and favored native-son authors, wrote in his 1891 history of Vermont "to fill the place left by this constant drain on its population, the State for the most part has received a foreign element." Robinson conceded that the foreign element "keeps the [State's] numbers good" but feared it "poorly compensates for her loss." His particular concern was how the heavy French-Canadian immigration "may finally work in the Protestant mass with which it has become incorporated." The Ferrisburgh sage was not optimistic: "The character of these people is not such as to inspire the highest hope for the future of Vermont, if they should become the most numerous of its population."[5]

Let us step back and view immigration to the United States and Vermont in its more cosmic dimensions as one component of a great migration. It was not until 1820 that the United States began to count immigrants entering the country. From 1820 through 1950, they numbered forty million. In 1820 the entire population of the United States was 9,638,000. In 1950 it was 150,000,000. Immigration, along with a steady birthrate and greater life expectancy, conspired to increase U.S. population almost 1,500 percent. By contrast, Vermont in 1820 boasted 236,000 souls and in 1950, 377,747, a growth of only sixty percent.

Another way of noting the impact of the great migration on Vermont is through the electoral college, an indicator of Vermont's relative size and political weight. In 1820 Vermont cast eight of the nation's 235 electoral votes; in 1952 it cast three of 531. Keep in mind that three is the minimum number of electoral votes and the electoral college is weighted to favor the less populated states. It is not my intention to beguile you with more numbers, but I want to mention that Vermont's relative decline is shared with the rest of northern New England. Obviously the impact of the great migration upon Vermont was different than it was on New York or Pennsylvania or, for that matter, Montreal or Rio de Janeiro. The impact was not necessarily less profound, but New England was not the recipient of massive immigration at the height of the great migration and the impact here was different.

This great migration, the movement of vast human populations throughout the globe, was the product of an almost infinite variety of forces. Some of the sweep was derived from local and temporary influences, which changed in character with variations in time and place. Some involved more push and some more pull. One example many of us are familiar with is Redfield Proctor's effort to recruit stonecutters from Carrara, Italy, to work for his Vermont Marble Company in Proctor. Carrara stonecutters also worked in the Barre granite sheds. Some migrated north from Proctor; others were enticed by their former countrymen who wrote home telling of new opportunities.

Other forces promoting migration were more enduring and more broadly manifested. European population growth was the strongest. From 1530 to 1680, the population of England doubled. This growth, depending upon your perspective, was either the impetus or the result of dramatic social and economic change. The first proprietors and European settlers of Vermont were mostly descendants of British migrants to New England during the second half of that period.

Population growth did not occur simultaneously throughout Europe. It is convenient to think of growth as moving in an easterly and southerly direction. In southern and eastern Europe, however, the causes and the timing of growth remain less clear than in northwestern Europe. Italian population studies claim that, in the early nineteenth century, growth was in the range of 0.3 percent per annum. By the 1880s it had soared to 1.1 percent. The key to growth was the decline of the deathrate. Through most of this era, the deathrate and the birthrate both declined. But the deathrate declined more rapidly than the birthrate.

In the general area of eastern Europe, which nurtured the ancestors of today's Vermonters of Polish, Russian, and Jewish descent, the rate of natural increase shot up from 0.4 percent in the 1850s to about 1.5 percent in the early twentieth century.[6] So that we have a general sense of what these figures mean, the lowest rate, 0.3 percent, exceeds Vermont's growth rate after 1830.

Population growth cannot be isolated from other phenomena, particularly industrialization and urbanization. Although we suspect differently today, until recently we assumed you could not have one without the other. Indeed, once the movements reached a critical mass, total population growth was paralleled by a decline in the agricultural population. This agricultural drop was more than compensated for by urban growth, even in Vermont. It was true everywhere except for some isolated regions of eastern Europe.

A classic Vermont illustration of how this operated can be glimpsed from some consequences of the opening of the Champlain-Hudson and Erie canals in 1825. These canals linked Vermont to New York City and the American west. The Erie Canal shortened the journey between Buffalo and New York City from twenty to six days and reduced freight charges from one hundred dollars to five dollars per ton. There were comparable reductions for Vermont. Translated into specific market terms, it meant that Vermont farmers could buy western grain more cheaply than they could grow it. One consequence with which we are familiar is the conversion by Vermont farmers to sheep raising. Rather than grow grains to feed themselves, their livestock, and their neighbors, they would grow wool to feed the textile mills of southern New England. Sheep raising was less labor intensive. It required fewer hands to attend to more acres. It made the large Vermont farm family an economic liability. It stimulated further migration.

Where did the emigrants go? Mostly to the cities. Vermont farm girls were among the first Lowell textile mill workers. Thus Vermont supplied both raw material and workers for the mills. The Erie Canal (and after 1849 the railroads) that made it so cheap to import western produce also made it cheap to export native Vermonters. Some Vermonters who went west settled farms. And, in a neat twist of fate, they produced crops so efficiently that American grain exports forced eastern Europeans off their farms. Many of these eastern Europeans in turn migrated to the New World. Most Vermont emigrants, however, even those who moved west, seem to have ended up in cities. Just a few examples are Allen Fletcher's father of Indianapolis, Stephen A. Douglas of Chicago, Myra Colby Bradwell of Chicago, Frederick Billings of San Francisco.

One of the historic distinctions between Vermont and most other states is that Vermont never spawned any truly large cities. It is true that Vermont's largest population centers grew more rapidly than the rest of the state. In 1830 the ten largest towns held about eleven percent of the state population and in 1950 over thirty percent, but by national or international standards, this was small. By 1920 there were twenty U.S. cities with populations larger than Vermont, and most states would soon boast two or three cities that housed a majority of their state's citizens.

We boast contrarywise. Vergennes prides itself on being the second smallest and sometimes the smallest city in the nation. Burlington is the smallest biggest city in the country. No other state claims a largest city as small as Burlington. We have pursued and manipulated numbers to support claims that we are the most rural state in the nation. This has been conscious and deliberate.

Thomas Jefferson alleged that "those who labor in the earth are the chosen people of God, . . . whose breasts He has made His peculiar deposit for substantial and genuine virtue."[7] As a corollary, Jefferson also suggested that the proportion of rural folk to urban folk was the rough measure of virtue to corruption in any society. For many Vermonters, Jefferson's dicta have been articles of faith. Insofar as immigration contributed to urbanization, it posed a threat to rural piety and genuine virtue. Cities were corrupt by their very nature. They symbolized the unwashed, the dishonorable, the alien. Cities housed the Jezebels and the Shylocks of society.

In 1857, after a fire destroyed the Montpelier statehouse, there grew a movement to relocate the capital to Burlington. It failed, of course, and leading the opposition was George W. Grandey (Vergennes). Grandey was a highly reputable politician. He was then Speaker of the House and in 1870 would serve as Republican state chairman. Grandey wrote bitterly of "that great JEWrusalem of V[ermon]t the 'Queen City of Lake Champlain' called Burlington by the rustics and barbarians." He went on to question, presumably facetiously, whether it wasn't "time her greatness and superiority . . . were acknowledged by the dwellers in the *rural districts* of the state?"[8] We ought to note parenthetically that in 1857 Burlington was not yet officially a city.

If by designating Burlington as "that great JEWrusalem of V[ermon]t," Grandey intended to suggest it housed significant numbers of Jews, he was wide of the mark. If he intended to convey the impression that Burlington's population was more heterogeneous (included a larger percentage of non-native-born Vermonters) than other Vermont towns, he was on target. By 1857 it had become apparent that Vermont's foreign element was growing, and it was definitely not growing uniformly throughout Vermont. By 1860 the five counties bordering Lake Champlain housed thirty-eight percent of the state's population and sixty-two percent of the foreign-born. Subsequent immigration modified that pattern only slightly while further emphasizing immigration's contribution to urban growth.[9]

At least equally significant, the Catholic church was establishing its organizational presence and succeeding in retaining larger numbers of communicants. By the time Rowland Robinson was writing his history there were already thirty-nine townships, including Robinson's beloved Ferrisburgh, with Catholic churches.[10] Although not all foreign-born Vermonters were Catholic, most were. And by 1870, eighty-three thousand Vermonters, just over twenty-five percent of the state's population, were either foreign-born or children of foreign-born. Burlington was the most Catholic community of all, with over half its population reported as Roman Catholic.

Eighteen-seventy was the year of a state constitutional convention, and one of the amendments up for adoption was women's suffrage. The *Burlington Free Press* didn't think women's suffrage was a very good idea. According to its editor, "the foreign masses in one solid phalanx will vote according to the instruction of their religious teachers." Furthermore, "American women" would not be "an offset to this foreign element," and women's suffrage would lead to an "alarming increase in our foreign vote."[11] If this was indeed the real source of *Free Press* opposition, opposition must have hardened with each passing year. By 1910 there were 117,344 Vermonters who were either foreign-born or children of foreign-born (32.9 percent), and their numbers were still rising.

This was a particular concern of most members of Vermont's congressional delegation. Speaking in support of immigration restriction (1887), U.S. Sen. Justin Smith Morrill noted that, while "many of our citizens of foreign birth are notable men . . . being mostly of the stock of the original Anglo-Saxon race," he was deeply disturbed over the admission of others whose "inherent deficiencies and inequities [render them] as incapable of evolution, whether in this generation or the next, as is the leopard to change his spots." Singling out the Irish as exemplars of this depraved genre of immigrant, Morrill thought "the time has arrived . . . when it is more necessary to look after what the future character of the American people shall be than to the growth and vastness of its numbers."[12]

William Dillingham, Morrill's successor in the U.S. Senate, was also a strong proponent of immigration restriction. Chairman of a 1907 congressional commission that produced a forty-one-volume study of immigration, it was his responsibility to report the findings to the Senate. It is from that report, not directly from the forty-one volumes, that I have attempted to reconstruct Dillingham's attitudes. The commission study, called the Dillingham Commission Report, was very important, however. It is still consulted and debated, contains data on settlement patterns available nowhere else, and provided the principle for immigration restriction by quotas based on national origins. That principle governed U.S. immigration policy from 1920 until 1965.

The national origin quotas restricted immigration to a percentage of any particular nationality living in the United States prior to 1890. Translated into practical terms, it meant large quotas for old immigrant stock from western Europe and much smaller quotas for new immigrant stock from eastern and southern Europe. Numerically the new immigrants entering Vermont were insignificant. The significantly high numbers were from Ireland and Canada. This raises the question of why Vermont senators, particularly

Dillingham, played such a prominent role in immigration restriction, especially when their efforts left Irish and Canadian immigration (the principal threat to Vermont Anglo-Saxon hegemony) virtually untouched.

My first impulse is to admit I don't know. But I'm going to suggest some explanations anyway. The most obvious concern was for retaining what had become the American identity, language, culture, tradition, religion, even costume. Since 1890 immigrants had been arriving from Europe in unparalleled numbers and from regions most alien to American tradition. Sheer numbers and the inclination to perpetuate their Old World interests made these new immigrants increasingly difficult to assimilate. America was the great melting pot, and immigrants were expected to recast themselves into Americans. The groups most inclined to perpetuate Old World interests were those whom American society was most adamant in rejecting.

This was most apparent in the nation's largest cities, but it was visible even in Vermont. Barre Italians constituted Vermont's largest labor union and published a prominent anarchist newspaper. Burlington possessed a sizable non-English-speaking population. Indeed writing in 1952, a former Burlington resident described the Queen City as having been the last surviving eastern European Jewish *shtetl* in North America. (If only George Grandey could have been alive.) According to Philip Rubin's "Boyhood in Vermont," the Burlington Jewish community, juxtaposed alongside a much larger and unassimilated French-Canadian community, was buffered from having to assimilate American ways.[13]

Although Senator Dillingham did not speak directly to conditions in Vermont, his suspicions of an increasingly urban, increasingly non-Protestant America permeated his rhetoric. Dedicated to what sociologists have labeled the agrarian myth and historians like to call the Yankee kingdom, Dillingham produced national figures to refute the claim (in his eyes it was a canard) that cities grew more from migration from rural districts "than by the movement of the [new] immigrant class."[14] That foreign-born contributed the major share of the increase in the U.S. urban population was a potent argument for immigration restriction. For contextual purposes, it is useful to keep in mind that urbanization was occurring as rapidly in parts of Europe as in the United States and would have occurred even more rapidly in Europe except for massive rural migrations to the United States and elsewhere in North and South America.

By 1920, with half the population of the United States urban, the descendants of the Green Mountain Boys perceived themselves as one of the few remaining bastions of the rural culture that traditionally defined Vermont. And this carries us to the Vermont Commission on Country Life organized in 1928 and remembered for its 1931 publication *Rural Vermont: A Program for the Future, by Two Hundred Vermonters.*[15] The plan to organize the Vermont Commission on Country Life was brought forward by University of Vermont professor H. F. Perkins who had fathered Vermont's eugenics survey. For our immediate purposes it is sufficient to note that both the eugenics survey and Commission on Country Life were concerned with conserving the quality of Vermont's "human stock." The commission's study, which enjoyed the status of a semi-official report, "revealed" Vermont had been *first settled* by "sturdy British stock."[16] I emphasize "first settled" because it suggests the absence of a previous Indian population. Vermont writers such as Frederic Van de Water and Dorothy Canfield Fisher, a prominent member of the Country Life Commission, specifically denied Indian settlement.

The commission report went on to note that Vermont was originally peopled by "a sturdy British stock augmented in recent years by a slow influx of French-Canadians and small numbers of other nationalities." The good news was that "this influx has been slow enough to be better assimilated in Vermont than in the rest of New England and there is prospect of its decreasing."

Let me share two commission recommendations with you:

1. Vermonters be encouraged to keep and study their own family records with a view to arousing their pride in the achievements and high qualities of their ancestral stock so . . . [as to] guide them in their choice of mates.

2. That the doctrine be spread that it is the patriotic duty of every normal couple to have children in sufficient number to keep up to par the "good old Vermont stock."[17]

This "good old Vermont stock" was celebrated as "one of the most reliable seedbeds of our national life." In 1937 the Vermont Historical Society published a compilation by Dorman B. E. Kent of the one thousand most prominent Vermont men and women.[18] This was a compilation of not merely prominent Vermonters but *the most prominent* Vermonters. Kent's eligibility criteria mandated the subject be born in Vermont. He did not require the subject live in Vermont. Eighty percent of his entries achieved distinction after they left Vermont. This theme of Vermont as seedbed of our national life remains fashionable. Charlie Morrissey's bicentennial history of Vermont plays heavily upon it.[19]

If you are wondering whether there was an urban counterpart to the *Rural Vermont* study, there was not. Perpetuating rural America was central to the commission's vision of the great society. It was rural Vermont that provided the "most reliable seed beds of our national life." Furthermore it was:

not beyond reason to hope that the tide of population may be turned back again to the fields, that the old towns of the State . . . may regain their prestige, and that the State as a whole, instead of being saved from actual loss only by the commercial centers and quarrying towns, may take her place again as one of the most healthfully vigorous and progressive of the American nation.[20]

Since the 1930s the political, economic, and demographic patterns that constitute Vermont have significantly changed. The state planning office estimates that approximately 50,000 people left Vermont between 1985 and 1990 and about 100,000 people have moved in. Vermont, however, still has not experienced the immigration patterns of many other states. Migrants to Vermont seldom come directly from Europe or Latin America, most are flat-landers, and we have the fewest African-Americans of any state in the nation. Nonetheless, we now possess a more varied population than has ever been here.

Stereotypical elements of the popular Yankee images and symbols mask change in Vermont and continue to retain their potency. It is difficult for me to believe that the writers for the Bob Newhart show didn't read Dorothy Canfield Fisher's *Vermont Tradition*. If you pick up a copy of the January, 1988, *Report of the Governor's Commission on Vermont's Future: Guidelines for Growth*, you might think from the cover that our choice is between pastureland and plowed fields.

The concept of Anglo-Saxon, has, however, undergone transition. And this brings us full circle to the recent issue of the "Vermont Bicentennial" mentioned above: the issue that commended the vote to secede from the United States as evidence that Vermonters were still "the most active and rebellious race on the continent." This sent me scurrying to my copy of *Mr. Dooley in Peace and War*, and I would like to finish with a quote from that source. Both Mr. Dooley and the editor of the "Vermont Bicentennial" appreciated the fact that labels could be inconclusive as well as exclusive. They seem to have had much in common.

Mr. Dooley was a character created by Finley Peter Dunne. Mr. Dooley defined an Anglo-Saxon as a "German who forgot who was his parents." Dooley was a philosophic Irish-born bartender who had an opinion on everything. He spoke in a brogue that can be difficult to understand so I'm going to resort to standard Anglo-Saxon English at the sacrifice of some humor. This was written in 1898. I leave you to ponder its significance.

> I tell you when the Clan and the Sons of Sweden and the Banana Club and the Circle Française and the Polish Benevo-lent Society and the Russian Sons of Dynamite, and the B'nai Brith . . . and the Sons of Holland Society and the Afro Americans and [all] the other Anglo-Saxons raise their Anglo-Saxon [read Vermont] battle cry, it will be all day with the eight or nine people in the world that has the misfortune of not being brought up Anglo-Saxons.[21]

NOTES

1. "Native Son Rule." Broadside Collections of Vermont Historical Society, Montpelier, Vt., B'side C 328.33 N213.

2. Bennington Speech, September 21, 1928.

3. "Vermont Bicentennial" II, no. 4 (Spring 1990).

4. *The Vermonter* VI, no.6 (1901): 6.

5. *Vermont: A Study of Independence* (Boston: Houghton Mifflin, 1892), 330-332.

6. Philip Taylor, *The Distant Magnet: European Immigration to the United States* (New York: Harper and Row, 1971), 51-54.

7. *Notes on the State of Virginia, 1781-1785*, Query XIX.

8. Grandey to C. K. Field, February 6, 1857, Sheldon Museum, Letter File 857156.1.

9. T. D. Seymour Bassett, "Urban Penetration of Rural Vermont" (Ph.D. diss., Harvard University, 1952).

10. Vermont Congregational Conference, *Supplement to the Minutes of the Ninety-First Annual Meeting of the Congregational Ministers and Churches of Vermont, held at West Randolph, June 1887, with Chart and Map* (Montpelier: 1888).

11. *Burlington Free Press*, 9 February and 10 March, 1870.

12. *Congressional Record*, 50th Cong. 1st Sess., 1888, Vol. 19, pt. 1: 58-62.

13. Philip Rubin, "Boyhood in Vermont," *Jewish Frontier*, January 1954, 23.

14. *Congressional Record*, 63rd Cong., 3rd sess., 1915, Vol. 52, pt. 4: 3635.

15. *Rural Vermont: A Program for the Future, by Two Hundred Vermonters* (Burlington: Vermont Commission on Country Life, 1931).

16. Ibid., 11 and 31.

17. Ibid., 31.

18. Dorman B. E. Kent, *Vermonters* (Montpelier, Vt.: Vermont Historical Society, 1937).

19. Charles T. Morrissey, *Vermont, a Bicentennial History* (New York, W. W. Norton, 1981).

20. *Rural Vermont*, 384.

21. Finley Peter Dunne, *Mr. Dooley on Ivrything and Evrybody*. Selected by Robert Hutchinson (New York: Dover Publications, 1963), "On the Anglo-Saxon," 18-22.

We Proprietors:

The First Europeans

Winn L. Taplin

espite the elegance of my title, it contains two misleading terms: proprietors—the nominal and legal owners of large tracts of land in the colonial and pre-Revolutionary eras—and Europeans. First, few Vermont proprietors ever visited Vermont. Those few who did travel to Vermont came only to take a look at their holdings with no intention of settling on them. Second, the early colonial settlers of Vermont were not Europeans—they were Americans.[1] Great students of colonial America such as Charles M. Andrews, Louis B. Wright, and Max Savelle have demonstrated convincingly that as Europeans came to English colonial North America, a new people—Americans—quickly emerged.[2] There were many reasons for this. Scholars like Colin Calloway have demonstrated one of the most important reasons for this early emergence of a new American people—the multidimensional influence of the Indians on the newcomers.[3] Others included distance from the homeland, differences in climate and soil, a distinctly changed economic life, and new social and political organization. Thus, Anglo-Saxon settlers to America had become an identifiably separate group long before serious colonial migration to Vermont began. By about 1760, Americans understood that the British victory over the French in North America was definitive. With the French threat removed, colonial "Americans" began flocking to Vermont, principally from older New England colonies.

Let us first take a look at how this influx worked. By the middle of the eighteenth century family farms in coastal Massachusetts, Connecticut, and parts of New Hampshire were turning out more people than a farm could support. As the fertile lands in these older settlements became scarce, residents looked for new lands. As Americans before and since have done, they sought their fortunes on the frontier—in this case the New Hampshire Grants, what we now call Vermont. The grants had been a dangerous border region between French and British colonies, populated almost exclusively by Native Americans living in low density groups and the scene of continual skirmishes between the rival empires. In the 1760s, with peace, the grants immediately became a rapidly growing frontier. Compared to the gradual development of coastal New England, one historian calls the move into Vermont a "quick, massive on-slaught."[4] There were indeed some Europeans among the early settlers of Vermont as the towns of Groton and Ryegate were settled by immigrants who came directly from Scotland. Fundamentally, however, the colonial and revolutionary era settlement of Vermont was done by second, third, and fourth generation Americans. So we must discard our title. Perhaps we can find another before we have finished.

PROPRIETORS

Even though our title is gone, let us still look at proprietors and the proprietary system. One might even call this section, "Proprietors, A Forgotten Link in Vermont History," for eighteenth century settlers moved to Vermont through the mechanism of a proprietary system that was already well-established in New England. It was the basis for land distribution—the means by which Vermont settlers obtained title to homesteads and farms.

At its most fundamental level, the proprietary system was a device used to build England's colonial empire. In North America, it began when lands there were claimed in the name of the English king. The king held title and it was from him that all later titles stemmed. Proprietorships originated in royal grants that bestowed broad territorial and political powers on a single person or a small group. The well-known proprietary grants of Pennsylvania to William Penn and of the areas that are now New York, New Jersey, and Vermont to the Duke of York are examples. These grants brought with them a responsibility for the grantee to organize and promote the settlement of the granted area.

The proprietary system evolved in America as a means to promote the occupation and development of the king's lands. By 1732, the whole Atlantic seaboard had been granted or chartered by the Crown. The classic statement, "Lo the poor Indian," could justifiably have been used at that early time, for Native Americans, of course, were not consulted regarding this grand colonial enterprise. Many Native American groups did, of course, enter into agreements with white settlers that, on our side at least, looked like contracts for the sale of land. As William Cronon and other scholars have noted, however, Native Americans conceived of these agreements as applying "only to very specific uses of the land," whereas the English settlers interpreted the sales "as a fuller transfer of [property] rights than the Indian communities probably ever intended."[5] The result was a clash between the proprietary system and Native American life.

The grants to individuals and groups were gradually incorporated into the evolving royal colonial governments. In New England, it became practice for the colonial government—or governors—to grant townships to a body of individuals called proprietors. Much of Vermont, both east and west of the Green Mountains was granted by Gov. Benning Wentworth of New Hampshire. Many of these same lands were also granted by the royal government of New York. Thus arose the great early Vermont political problem—validity of land titles.

Once the United States declared independence and royal governments lost control of colonial areas, the system had to change. The Vermont Republic, therefore, took it upon itself to grant townships in areas not already granted by Governor Wentworth. Whether the grants were made by a representative of the Crown or by the independent state of Vermont, the proprietors to whom they were made had a responsibility to develop their towns. This proprietary system, as it was applied to northern New England, is best described in Charles E. Clark's *The Eastern Frontier.*[6]

Generally, proprietors paid for the land they received and accepted certain responsibilities to survey the area, establish town government, and move people onto the land. Often a time limit was imposed for compliance. As Clark describes it, "the proprietors usually chose a committee to tend to the survey and, in most cases, to go to the township to determine generally the likeliest locations for the home lots, pastures, meadow lands, and water power sites. . . . The next step was to assign each home lot—except the three reserved for religious and educational purposes—to a proprietor, usually by drawing."[7] The proprietor, of course, regained his investment by selling the plots assigned to him to potential settlers or land speculators.

Proprietors varied in occupation and status. In some cases they were well-to-do merchants and professional men, often with important political connections, who saw a profit opportunity.[8] Some of their names can be found on several Vermont town charters and as Vermont became populated, more prosperous residents of older towns became proprietors of newer ones. Many local Vermont historians have made efforts to track proprietors of their towns to figure out who was who on the town charter. Such study can reveal a lot about the origins of a town, but it can also be a tricky business. Not only were some investors proprietors of several Vermont towns, but one Vermont historian claims that false names were sometimes used to mask extensive ownership by one person within a township.[9]

Individuals of more modest means also invested with high hopes, perhaps, of earning for themselves "the good life of a country squire" by settling on their proprietary holding. Clark points out that "the realities of financing a frontier settlement"—the need to continue investing to support surveys, ministers, public works—often proved to be beyond the means of some individual proprietors. Thus, the number of proprietors often diminished as one proprietor after another sold his share to the more affluent.[10]

In the independent state of Vermont, the land granting process was used for both political and economic ends. Issuing charters, of course, brought income to the state from the proprietors who invested in the towns. Grants of land were also used outright to curry favor with members of the Continental Congress and Continental Army. As a result, on several occasions Continental Congress delegates who were proprietors of Vermont towns or investors in Vermont land took pro-Vermont positions. Roger Sherman of Connecticut was probably the best known of these delegates. Jonathan Arnold of Rhode Island, a large holder of Vermont land patents, also pressed pro-Vermont positions at Congress. One three-man committee that Congress set up in 1782 specifically to consider New York complaints against Vermont had as a member Eliphalet Dyer of Connecticut, a proprietor under Vermont grants.

In early 1783, the Continental Congress was seriously considering sending Continental troops to quell disturbances in Vermont. General Washington opposed the project, however, and New York delegate Alexander Hamilton wrote home that another reason not to expect any effective military action was that "a considerable part of the army is interested in grants of land . . . under the government of Vermont." Hamilton may have exaggerated, but from a political standpoint, Vermont made skillful use of its self-proclaimed land-granting power to gain influence with selected Congressmen and military officials.[11]

In addition to investors and individuals of influence, there was a third important category of proprietors who were granted Vermont lands—veterans of colonial wars. Proprietary grants to veterans went back to the early 1700s. But the contribution of colonial troops to the British victory in the 1750s was considerably greater than in earlier struggles with the French, and the demands of veterans were greater. It is not surprising, therefore, that Wentworth used such grants to settle veteran claims against his government.[12]

Proprietors who were veterans more frequently settled on their grants than did other proprietors. Newbury, Vermont, is a case in point. It was granted in May 1763 to a group of mostly French and Indian War veterans, organized by Jacob Bayley and John Hazen, well-known in Vermont history because of their development of the Bayley-Hazen Military Road in the American Revolution. At least twenty of the seventy-four proprietors, an unusually large number, actually settled in Newbury. The organizational meetings of the proprietors of Newbury were held in coastal New Hampshire and selectmen were elected before any of the grantees had moved to Newbury.

Usually, proprietary control of a town stayed with the investors, outside Vermont, until their duties had been met and they disbanded. An unusual aspect of Newbury was that enough proprietors settled in the town that they were able to bring proprietary control with them to the new community. The final formal proprietary meetings were actually held in Newbury. The proprietary organization seems to have withered away as town government was established and a functioning community evolved. In other towns, a common complaint among new settlers was that town proprietors were too far away to act promptly on civic or land distribution issues. In some cases, to meet this difficulty, the proprietors appointed individuals who had settled in the town to act in their stead.[13]

Newbury's neighbor, Corinth, Vermont, was more typical. Only one of the town's sixty proprietors actually settled there. This particular proprietor has always been of special interest to me for he happens to have been an ancestor of mine, Col. John Taplin, another veteran of the French and Indian War. Colonel John, born in Charlestown, Massachusetts, in 1727 was typical of many other early Vermont settlers for he brought numerous close relatives to Vermont to settle near him. The story handed down in the Taplin family is that he told his seven sons that he wanted them all to live within the sound of his dinner horn. In fact, the area where the colonel and his sons settled is still known in Corinth as Taplin Hill, although no Taplins live there now.[14]

This question of proprietors and their relationship to Vermont settlement has been neatly put by David Ludlum in his classic work, *Social Ferment in Vermont*. "As few of the original proprietors ever visited their holdings," Ludlum writes, "lands were disposed of in cheerful ignorance of locality or worth. To the actual settler, however, was involved prosperity or poverty; happy residence or a further migration north or west."[15] In this statement, Ludlum has clearly shown how the proprietors' interest differed from that of the settlers. Historian Randolph Roth has more recently echoed Ludlum's view. He says that generally the ambition of those who came to settle Vermont was "contentment with a middling farm and a secure future." Historian Roth believes that "the poor and the frustrated were outnumbered . . . by those whose ambitions were fully realized on the Vermont frontier."[16]

But I prefer Ludlum's expression—"happy residence or further migration." It reminds us of the migrations from Vermont that began early in the nineteenth century and continued in waves throughout the ensuing 150 years. These few words echo into our own day, with the almost unprecedented influx of new immigrants to Vermont beginning in the 1960s. Have any five words better described the whole Vermont experience than "Happy residence or further migration"?

Thus far, I have described white settlement in early Vermont in rather clinical terms—proprietary systems, land titles, grantees, and speculators. To flesh out this picture, I will discuss two themes that seem to me to define important aspects of life in colonial and revolutionary Vermont. Through the years, the Vermont story has become, in modern public relations terms, "packaged." Unfortunately, some historians have taken leading roles in creating the package. Although all Vermont histories tell us that our predecessors faced harrowing difficulties contending with natural and human threats to their security and well-being, there has been nonetheless a tendency in the packaged myth to look back at early Vermont as a benignly bucolic setting for testing rugged individualism. Let's look for reality and real people.

A HARSH LIFE

Life in Vermont in the Anglo-American settlement era was hard, rude, and coarse—even in terms of that period. Perhaps we can get behind the myth if we talk about several early Vermont settlers whose stories have come down to us through images such as those in "The Story of Old Vermont in Pictures."[17] Probably the most widely distributed first-hand account of what an early settler faced in Vermont is Seth Hubbell's *A Narrative of the Sufferings of Seth Hubbell and Family*. Hubbell's was the second family to settle in the town of Wolcott. Of his 1789 journey from Norwalk, Connecticut, to his new home, he wrote:

> My team was a yoke of oxen and a horse. After I had proceed-
> ed on my journey to within about one hundred miles of
> Wolcott, one of my oxen failed, but I however kept him yoked
> with the other till about noon each day, then turned him
> before, and took his end of the yoke myself, and proceeded on
> in that manner.[18]

In Seth Hubbell's story, he notes that his family reached Wolcott one day behind "Esquire Taylor" and his family.[19] Once a town was opened up by the proprietors, there was frequently a race to be the first family to settle there, and the "bragging rights" associated with being a first settler have been passed down through generations. The museum of the Stowe Historical Society, for example, has on display the hand sled used on the Luce family's journey to Stowe. They were the town's first permanent settlers. Oliver Luce had come from Hartland, Vermont, with his wife, two small daughters, and a little furniture. According to Bigelow's *History of Stowe*, "there being no road passable for even an ox team," Luce drew his family on a sled himself for the last six miles of the way. The Luce family arrived on 16 April 1794. The Moodys, from Maine, arrived one day later.[20] There are still several Luce and Moody descendants in and around Stowe. Two hundred years later, one day's difference allows the Luces to remind the Moodys gently which was the first family to settle Stowe.

One of my own ancestors was a first permanent settler of a Vermont town, and his family's experience also demonstrates the difficulties of the times. He was Capt. Samuel McDuffee of Bradford, Vermont. Like so many other early Vermont settlers, he had soldiered in the colonial wars against the French. He settled in Bradford in 1766. His wife Elizabeth joined him shortly thereafter. A Bradford town history reports that she trekked alone on horseback from Connecticut to Bradford "with only marked trees to guide her through the wilderness" for the final sixty miles. On her arrival "Elizabeth McDuffee planted a small apple tree which she had brought with her all the way from Connecticut, perhaps," as the Bradford historian conjectures, "that her tomorrow might have some tangible continuity with her yesterday." Alas, Elizabeth's husband did not survive and flourish as well as her apple tree. In 1781 Samuel McDuffee attended a wedding across the Connecticut River in New Hampshire. On the return trip he fell from the boat and drowned.[21]

The Connecticut River features in another first person narrative of settlement in Vermont. Asa Burton was an early Vermont preacher and educator, who served at various times as a trustee of the University of Vermont, Middlebury College, and Thetford Academy. His description of a boyhood winter trip from Norwich to Quechee Falls further dramatizes the nature of life for early Vermont settlers. Burton wrote,

> There was no gristmill nigher than at the falls on Quechee
> River in Hartland; no roads, and only a foot path. Our road
> was the Connecticut River, in canoes in the summer and on the
> ice in the winter. That winter in January we went from home

in the morning with a handsled and several bushels of grain to go to Quechee to get it ground. It was cloudy, and soon began to storm, and small, round hail fell all day. This rendered drawing our sled as difficult nearly as on bare ground. But at night we arrived at the mill, and after a day of pulling with all our strength our grist, we had to encamp on the floor in the mill. At dark the hail turned into rain, and through the night it rained very powerfully.

Next morning streams and rivers had risen, ice broken up; water on the ice in Connecticut River was knee deep most of the way, which rendered that road impossible. We had to leave our grist and return home by land, no path and no track, and to wade through streams often up to our middle; and the snow was all full of water, and not any better than wading; at last we arrived home.[22]

When he wrote that account in 1817, Burton added,

I mention this incident, which is only one among many [of] that day, to show what labors, hardships, and fatigues [we] had to endure at the first settlement of this country. At this day, people would think, both old and young, if they had to go through such fatigues, it would kill them.[23]

I have said that the times and conditions of life were coarse. There are few descriptions of life as it was lived on early Vermont farms and in early Vermont villages. One of the earliest is a commentary that John Clark made in 1785 about Clarendon, Vermont. He wrote of his disappointment to find in Clarendon vice "predominant, irreligion almost epidemical. . . . Sabbath disregarded, profanity, debauchery, drunkenness, quarrelling by words and blows and parting with broken heads and bloody noses."[24] Clark clearly had little hope for the redemption of Vermont, and twenty years later he might still have been discouraged, for a writer at that time complained of "disorders at a Methodist camp meeting in the vicinity of Windsor in a 'country' [apparently referring to Vermont] where the grossest indecorums between the sexes, is habitually practised and countenanced." Nor was our state capital spared criticism. Another cleric, administering a revival there, called the morals of Montpelier's inhabitants deplorable and said that "profanity was the common dialect."[25]

The rudeness of early rural Vermont is apparent, too, in a story that has come down through my family. One of the early Taplins on Taplin Hill in Corinth had some sheep who tended to stray down the road and occasionally damage a neighbor's garden. (Fences were not yet as universal as they later became on Vermont farms.) The neighbor complained but to no avail. On one of the visits, the neighbor slit the tendon in one hind leg of each sheep, and slipped the other hind leg through the slit. Three-legged, presumably bleating their agony, the sheep hobbled home. The next morning, when the neighbor arose, he found that each of his pigs had a wider mouth than usual. Irate, the neighbor rushed up the hill and started to berate Taplin for cutting his pigs. Taplin is reported to have listened patiently until the neighbor began to wind down and then to have said, "Well, I reckon that when your pigs saw those funny looking sheep run up the hill for home, they just split their mouths laughing."[26] The story may be apocryphal, but it is consistent with the way early Anglo-Americans in Vermont dealt with life.

POLITICAL AND MILITARY DIVISIONS

My second theme is actually a variation on the most widely known aspects of colonial and revolutionary Vermont history. Almost any reading about Vermont history will include accounts of both the fight between New York and the Green Mountain Boys and the later Revolutionary struggle. These events meant that for its first twenty-five years of Anglo-American settlement, Vermonters had not only to face a harsh existence, but had momentous political and jurisdictional issues swirling around them as well. Many have studied and written about these events, and rather than take another look at them, I would like to see what this divisiveness meant to some individual Vermonters who played significant roles in early Vermont but who are not much noted in history books.

First, however, consider two background factors. Immigration to Vermont continued throughout the American Revolution. After Vermont became an independent state, and as its frustration grew over exclusion from the United States, its stance between the combatants became neutral. Vermont thus became a safe haven for Tories and military deserters from the coastal states. In the early 1780s, for example, Arlington, Vermont, had so many Loyalists among its inhabitants that it became known as "Tory Hollow."[27] While there remained many staunch supporters of American independence in Vermont, the continued arrival of Tories reinforced Vermont's neutrality. In fact, the overall tenor of Vermont's population was such that in 1780 leaders in the state undertook serious negotiations with British authorities in Canada for a reunion of Vermont with the British.[28]

A second significant factor is that in September 1781, the independent state of Vermont actually cut a deal with the British to establish Vermont as an independent royal colony under the Crown. The change of government was to take place in late October 1781. Overall during much of 1781 the British appeared to be doing quite well militarily. It seems that Vermont made an agreement with the British partly, at least, to assure that it would be on the winning side. But, most important, the British assured Vermont of virtually every political goal it had sought without success from the Congress—confirmed individual land titles, acceptance of Vermont's large territorial claims against New York and New Hampshire, local self-government, an elected lieutenant governor, and open commerce through the St. Lawrence River. News of the British military debacle at Yorktown, however, caused the Vermonters to call for a delay at the last minute. The Vermont message to Canada said, in effect, "You know, if this is to work, you British have got to win." The plan was finally dropped only when, more than a year later, it became clear that the British were unwilling to make the investment that would have been necessary to achieve military victory against the United States.[29]

What did all this mean to individual Vermonters? Political and military divisions became the key element in the way life played out for many of them. Justus Sherwood was one. Sherwood was born in 1747 in Newtown, Connecticut—one of fourteen children. He apparently had some education as a surveyor. In 1771, like so many other young people, he headed for the frontier—the New Hampshire Grants. Soon after he arrived, Sherwood married Sarah Bottum and started farming in New Haven, Vermont. By 1774, he was a local official in New Haven and was well started as a land speculator. Whenever he had spare cash, he purchased lots or farm sites in the Champlain Valley from the Onion River Land Company. Sherwood's participation in the Green Mountain Boys' campaign to assure that Vermont residents held their lands was consistent with his investments.

Until the American Revolution, the only fight that seems to have interested Sherwood was the one between New York and his fellow residents of the New Hampshire Grants. But as Vermont's struggle over land titles melded into the American clamor for independence, Sherwood—like so many of his friends and neighbors—could not avoid a political choice. He chose the king. By 1776, he was publicly voicing his doubts about the wisdom of military campaigns by the colonists against British forces in Canada. His outspokenness brought him first a public flogging and later arrest and sentencing to the notorious Simsbury Mines in Connecticut. Sherwood never saw the inside of this dreaded place, for he escaped before his three guards could deliver him. As a fugitive, he worked his way surreptitiously back to his farm in New Haven. Once home, he sent his wife to live with her parents in southern Vermont. Her family, the Bottums, were supporters of American independence and Sherwood was confident that Sarah would be safe with them. To protect his farm from confiscation, Sherwood deeded it to one of Sarah's brothers. Then Sherwood fled behind British lines. Incidentally, Sherwood's farm still flourishes about a mile and a half due north of the village of New Haven, and the Bottum family, descendants of Sherwood's brother-in-law, still farm it.

When British forces under Sir Guy Carleton retired from Lake Champlain to Canada in late 1776, Sherwood went with them. Because he had knowledge of the Champlain Valley he was selected in the spring of 1777 to lead a small party on a scouting foray into American-held territory in Vermont and New York. His trip proved productive. He sketched and reported on fortifications at Ticonderoga and Mount Independence; he scouted conditions at Fort Ann and Fort Edward in New York; and he visited and debriefed informants loyal to the Crown in both Vermont and New York. Sherwood's return to Canada in May 1777 coincided with General Burgoyne's preparations for a major invasion southward through the Lake Champlain and Hudson River Valleys. One biographer of Sherwood believes that it was his information that led to the British success in positioning cannon overlooking Fort Ticonderoga in such a way that American general Arthur St. Clair was forced to abandon both Ticonderoga and Mount Independence without a fight.

Sherwood's scouting trip was productive in a second way. He was close enough to his old home in New Haven to chance a visit to his brother-in-law to obtain news of his wife Sarah and his children. To his joyful surprise, Sherwood found his wife was there with a new daughter whom Sherwood had never seen. But Sherwood's overnight visit created a predicament for Sarah and the Bottum family. For when Justus left New Haven the next morning, Sarah was unknowingly pregnant once again. As Sarah's condition became more evident, however, she and her family could not explain that the father was Justus without bringing censure on themselves for having harbored an active supporter of the Crown. It was to be many months before Sherwood learned of Sarah's new pregnancy and of the embarassment he had created.

Sherwood's knowledge of the North Country, his success in scouting activities, his energy and intellect, and a knack for the business led him inexorably into intelligence work. He was made Commissioner of Prisoners and Refugees and then Chief of the British Secret Service in Canada. Sherwood established his headquarters on North Hero Island where he built what became known as the Loyal Blockhouse. It is not widely realized that a leading Revolutionary War intelligence center was located in Vermont. In fact, the Loyal Blockhouse was probably second only to Washington's and Sir Henry Clinton's headquarters in the volume of intelligence activity that passed through it. The Loyal Blockhouse became the first haven for refugees fleeing the American states and the first holding area for captured prisoners. This afforded Sherwood an early opportunity for debriefing both refugees and prisoners.

Sherwood's most important intelligence operation was what historians now call the Haldimand Negotiations—named for General Frederick Haldimand, the British commander in Canada. These were the talks aimed at returning Vermont to British sovereignty. It was Sherwood who carried out the actual negotiations for the British. His counterparts for Vermont were Ira Allen and Joseph Fay. Thus, there were actually Vermont land speculators on both sides of the negotiating table who had a great deal to gain personally by assuring that the validity of the old New Hampshire Grants be recognized.[30] Of course, Sherwood wanted this done under British sovereignty.

Sherwood's story reflects disruptions typical of those in the lives of settlers who at various times took positions supporting New York governments or the British Crown. Early in the Revolution, it became impossible for Loyalists and Tories such as Justus Sherwood to stay in Vermont. During and after the American Revolution, Loyalists streamed into Canada. By 1784, Sherwood had been assigned to organize resettlement in Upper Canada where he eventually moved himself. He found many old associates from Vermont living around him. In the nineteenth and twentieth century emigrations from Vermont led to the cities and to the west, but a third emigration pre-dated these—the exodus of refugees from Vermont to Canada in the 1780s. These days we usually think of political or religious refugees as East Europeans, or Jews, or Vietnamese escaping virulent political, religious, or economic discrimination. But two hundred years ago it was Anglo-Americans in Vermont who were persecuted for dissident political views, and they became refugees. "Further migration" was a necessity for them.

Post-war reconciliation proved relatively easy for some Loyalists who managed to return home following the interruption of war. It never came fully, however, to Col. Thomas Johnson of Newbury. Johnson, like so many others, was a French and Indian War veteran. He had also been a proprietor of the town of Haverhill, New Hampshire, where he lived for a short time. But by 1770, he had moved across the river to Newbury where he opened the town's first tavern. Newbury historian Frederic Wells estimates that by the time of the Revolution, and because town "founding father" Jacob Bayley had suffered some reverses, Johnson was the wealthiest resident of Newbury.

Johnson had served with the Newbury militia against the British during the Burgoyne campaign in 1777 and, in fact, had led an unsuccessful attack against Mount Independence after it had been abandoned by St. Clair and occupied by the British. But in March 1781 Colonel Johnson was captured by agents of Justus Sherwood. Over a period of months, Johnson convinced his captors that he was actually loyal to the Crown. On his agreement to serve as a resident agent in Newbury and, secretly, to provide information to Sherwood through a courier, Johnson was allowed to return home. This was not an unusual operation for Sherwood, who regularly sent out scouting parties to take prisoners for interrogation and who surveyed both prisoners and refugees for likely candidates to become resident agents reporting to him from Vermont towns.

How well did Johnson serve the British? There are some indications that he disclosed his role as a British collaborator to Gen. Jacob Bayley, who was probably the most significant supporter of American independence in the upper Connecticut Valley. But fellow citizens, possibly jealous of Johnson's material success, spread tales of the lenient treatment he had received from Sherwood while other Vermont prisoners languished in British jails. Certainly the British thought that Johnson was loyal to them, for when Sherwood sent a raiding party to capture General Bayley in 1782, its members consulted Johnson before taking action. At the same time, there is some evidence that Johnson warned Bayley that the British were nearby. However he received word of his danger, Bayley avoided capture.

In 1976, Robert Maguire of Shoreham, Vermont, wrote in *Vermont History* about the British Secret Service's attempt to kidnap Bayley. But, even with extensive British and American archives now available, Johnson's intelligence role has not become completely clear. And it certainly dogged him for the rest of his life. Maguire recognized the impact that wartime episodes could have on the life of a Vermonter and wrote that despite Johnson's later prosperity and repeated election as Newbury town representative, "the consequences of his double role during the Revolution afflicted him for the remainder of his days."[31]

CONCLUSION

Earlier I discussed the myth of Vermont history, particularly regarding the three decades before statehood. I find it interesting that out of the harsh life and political and military divisiveness that were the reality of Vermont in the late eighteenth century, both fiction writers and historians led the way throughout the nineteenth century in turning the Vermont experience into an uncomplicated and unified struggle by brave pioneers for supremacy over first and foremost New York, but also over the British, the Indians, the wilderness, and the climate. These tale spinners quoted generously from Ethan Allen, our most famous historical character, who steals the scene in any version of Vermont's history during the settlement and revolutionary eras.

In 1781 Allen wrote with typical defiance and bluster that Vermonters were ready "to retire. . . . into the desolate caverns of the mountains, and wage war with humanity at large."[32] Allen may have believed this himself and the Vermont myth as Allen proclaimed it became accepted by most Vermonters and by non-Vermonters as well. This myth has undoubtedly played a role in the current view that much of the U.S. seems to hold of Vermont—the sturdy pastoral country built by brave patriots on a worthy rural heritage. It appears to have been important to Vermonters of the nineteenth century to avoid the fact that many of the state's early leaders—for reasons that were quite understandable and defensible—had been planning to unite Vermont with Great Britain, or that many people in Vermont—perhaps a majority—had been more loyal to the Crown than to the idea of American independence. I am reminded of how the South, after the Civil War, gradually convinced itself (or at least the Southern *white* population) that the war had been a glorious lost cause. Over time this myth became quite readily accepted by people outside the South as spread, for example, in popular works such as *Gone With the Wind*.

As for the Vermont myth, during this century, historians have finally led the way in sorting out and accurately describing many of the varied political forces that were at play in newly settled Vermont. We now see more clearly that in the period of white settlement a lot was going on that did not involve Ethan Allen and that his view of the world was not necessarily typical of the experience and opinions of those around him. It is always refreshing, for example, to go back to Wells's *History of Newbury*, published in 1902, and see how well this local historian came to understand and explain the contending, and often murky, political forces when few other historians were even mentioning them.

Many who came to the Vermont frontier, even during those difficult years, managed to enjoy what David Ludlum called "happy residence." On the other hand, the Revolutionary War meant "further migration" for many Vermonters. Loyalists such as Sherwood never returned to Vermont. Other Loyalists such as Col. John Taplin, somehow managed to remain on their lands with their families. Since the divisiveness of the American Revolution, for the Anglo-American families who have stayed in Vermont through seven and eight generations, the bonds to the land and to Vermont have become strong. Myth or no myth, a Vermont way of life and a Vermont attitude developed. During the nineteenth and twentieth centuries, other peoples came to Vermont and joined the Anglo-Americans. They adopted the Vermont myth and became latter day Green Mountain Boys. They not only became neighbors of the Anglo-Americans, they became Anglo-Americans.[33] And together, whatever their heritage, Vermonters continue to learn the old stories and to sing loud praises to the Green Mountain Boys and to their scene-stealing founder who really did lead the way for the rest of us to "happy residence."

NOTES

1. See Samuel B. Hand's paper, "Stocking the State: Observations on Immigrants, Emigrants, and Those Who Stayed Behind," in this volume.

2. Max Savelle, *The Foundations of American Civilization* (New York: Henry Holt and Co., 1942), 302-326; Louis B. Wright, *The Colonial Civilization of North America, 1607-1763* (London: Eyre and Spottiswoode, 1949), 244-272; Charles M. Andrews, *The Colonial Period in American History*, 4 vols. (New Haven: Yale University Press and London: Oxford University Press, 1934-38).

3. See Colin G. Calloway, "Legacies of Contact: Indians, Europeans, and the Shaping of Vermont," in this volume.

4. Charles E. Clark, *The Eastern Frontier: The Settlement of Northern New England, 1610-1763* (New York: Knopf, 1970), 355.

5. William Cronon, *Changes in the Land: Indians, Colonists, and the Ecology of New England* (New York: Hill and Wang, 1983), 65-68.

6. In addition to Clark's work, two classic studies of New England settlement provide insight into the proprietary system: R. H. Agaki, *Town Proprietors of New England Colonies* (Philadelphia: University of Pennsylvania Press, 1924); and Lois K. Mathews (Rosenberry), *The Expansion of New England* (Boston: Houghton Mifflin, 1909). William Cronon, *Changes in the Land*, 54-75, discusses understandings of land ownership and proprietary rights held by native Americans and early European settlers.

7. Clark, 183.

8. Clark, 181.

9. Frederic P. Wells, *History of Newbury, Vermont, From the Discovery of the Coos Country to Present Time* (St. Johnsbury, Vt.: Caledonian Company, 1902), 37-38.

10. Clark, 184.

11. Winn L. Taplin, "The Vermont Problem in the Continental Congress and in Interstate Relations, 1776-1787" (Ph.D. diss., University of Michigan, 1955), 211-12, 277. Charles A. Jellison, *Ethan Allen, Frontier Rebel* (Syracuse, N.Y.: Syracuse University Press, 1969), 235.

12. Clark, 334-5. Matt B. Jones, *Vermont in the Making* (Cambridge: Harvard University Press, 1939), 40-41. Jones implies that most of the veterans who were grantees were land speculators.

13. Wells, 16, 21-29. Mathews (Rosenberry), 134-35.

14. Town of Corinth History Committee, *History of Corinth Vermont, 1764-1964* (Corinth, Vt.: Town of Corinth, 1964), 37-46.

15. David M. Ludlum, *Social Ferment in Vermont, 1791-1850* (New York: Columbia University Press, 1939), 9.

16. Randolph A. Roth, *The Democratic Dilemma: Religion, Reform, and the Social Order in the Connecticut River Valley of Vermont, 1791-1850* (New York: Cambridge University Press, 1987), 24.

17. *The Story of Old Vermont in Pictures* (Montpelier, Vt.: National Life Insurance Co., 1991). This pamphlet reproduces forty-four charcoal and crayon drawings of historical episodes in Vermont history by artists Roy F. Heinrich and Herbert Morton Stoop, commissioned by National Life in the 1930s.

18. Seth Hubbell, *A Narrative of the Sufferings of Seth Hubbell and Family* (Bennington and Hyde Park, Vt.: Vermont Heritage Press, 1986), 2.

19. Hubbell, 3.

20. W. J. Bigelow, *History of Stowe, Vermont (From 1763 to 1934)*, 2d ed. (Stowe, Vt.: Stowe Historical Society, 1988), 9-10.

21. Harold W. Haskins, *A History of Bradford, Vermont* (Bradford, Vt.: Town of Bradford, 1968), 40-41.

22. Asa Burton, *The Life of Asa Burton Written by Himself* (Thetford, Vt.: The First Congregational Church, 1973), 8-9.

23. Burton, 9.

24. Ludlum, 20.

25. Ibid., 20-21.

26. The author heard this story about 1950 from his father, Winn L. Taplin, Sr. The latter was a descendant of a Taplin family line that stayed in "happy residence" on Taplin Hill.

27. Mary Lou Thomas, "David Crofut of Arlington, Vermont, His Descendants and Possible Ancestry," Unpublished Manuscript (Arlington, Vt.: 1977), 1.

28. Taplin, "Vermont Problem," 195. Jellison, 269.

29. Taplin, "Vermont Problem," 219-223. Jellison, 278-282. Charles T. Morrissey, *Vermont, A Bicentennial History* (New York: W. W. Norton, 1981), 97-98.

30. Winn L. Taplin, "The King's Green Mountain Spymaster," in Edmund R. Thompson, ed., *Secret New England, Spies of the American Revolution* (Kennebunk, Me.: New England Chapter, Assoc. of Former Intelligence Officers, 1991), 113-33, 216-18. Ian C. Pemberton, "The British Secret Service in the Champlain Valley During the Haldimand Negotiations, 1780-1783," *Vermont History* 44 (Summer 1976): 129-140. Three Canadian biographies of Sherwood have been written from a Loyalist viewpoint: Mary Beacock Fryer, *Buckskin Pimpernel, The Exploits of Justus Sherwood, Loyalist Spy* (Toronto and Charlottetown, P.E.I.: Dundurn Press, 1981); Ian C. B. Pemberton, "Justus Sherwood, Vermont Loyalist" (Ph.D. diss., University of Western Ontario, London, Ont., 1972); Lt. Col. H. M. Jackson, *Justus Sherwood: Soldier, Loyalist, and Negotiator* (Ottawa, 1958).

31. Wells, 93-102, 119. J. Robert Maguire, "The British Secret Service and the Attempt to Kidnap General Jacob Bayley of Newbury, Vermont, 1782," *Vermont History* 44 (Summer 1976): 141-167.

32. Ethan Allen to Samuel Huntington, President of Congress, March 9, 1781, in Sir Henry Clinton Papers, Ann Arbor. Quote in Charles A. Jellison, *Ethan Allen, Frontier Rebel* (Syracuse, N.Y.: Syracuse University Press, 1983), 268. See also John Pell, *Ethan Allen* (Lake George, N.Y.: Adirondack Resorts Press, 1929), 211-12.

33. See Hand, "Stocking the State."

The Franco-Americans of New England and Vermont

Anne Pease McConnell

The images we have of Vermont—in popular publications like *Yankee Magazine* and *Vermont Life*, in regional art, and in much of our literature—prepare us to see our state as the essence of "Yankee" culture. Accents that evoke a British origin and white clapboard Protestant churches reinforce this image of Vermont as New *England*, and it is hard for us to see beneath this quaint and durable shell the presence or impact of the descendants of New France, the Franco-Americans of New England. John Gunther, one of the more perceptive observers of culture and society in the mid-twentieth century, had the same problem. In his 1947 book, *Inside U.S.A*, Gunther wrote:

> The Vermont Yankee is, one may say safely, the most impregnably Yankee of all Yankees. . . . In New Hampshire the Puritan strain has been severely diluted, but in Vermont overwhelming evidence of nonconformist origin is still to be seen on every hand. And Vermont has fewer French Canadians, fewer foreign-born, fewer big towns. . . .[1]

This and other travelers' accounts and guidebooks attest to the "invisibility" of our Franco-American population.

The journalist and novelist Jacques Ducharme, in his personalized account of the Franco-American experience, struggles, even as a Franco-American, to reconcile his existence with the Yankee image of New England:

> The notes on my desk . . . seem alien. The titles and authors are at odds with my surroundings. *Histoire des Canadiens-Français* can have nothing to do with New England, and names such as Hamon, Magnan and their like have nothing of the Yankee in them. If I leaf through my notes, however, I see names of cities that I know—Lowell, Manchester, Woonsocket, Lewiston.

There is a contradiction somewhere. Apparently New France
has come to New England.[2]

For Ducharme, "anything 'French' seems alien in New England." Even
in Canada, he adds, Frenchness is considered picturesque and quaint rather
than natural.[3] The traditional French versus English, Catholic versus Protestant conflicts of Old Europe seem to be epitomized by the simultaneous
French and English presence in our region.

The invisibility of Franco-Americans was, until recently, perpetuated in
our public schools. The first textbook I examined after my arrival in Vermont
in the mid-1970s, was a social studies text and workbook published to com-
memorate the 1776 bicentennial and developed for use by Vermont and New
Hampshire students. The text included *one* sentence about Franco-Americans
in its nearly three hundred pages.

Yet it is easy to discover the great Franco-American presence in our
state, for so long a sort of way station between Quebec and New England.
After all, in the 1980 census, thirty-seven percent of Vermonters said they were
of French-Canadian descent, making them in all probability the largest single
ethnic group in the state. This represents as well the highest percentage of
Franco-Americans in all the New England States.

The impact of Franco-Vermonters may be seen everywhere. How many
of you have waited at a light behind a truck with mudguards that read "Charle-
bois Truck Parts?" What about the Bushey (Boucher) and Benway (Benoit)
taxis? A crane on a construction site may belong to a Côté, and we pass businesses such as Contois Pianos, Beaudoin Radiator, and Frémeau jewelers, or
the offices of the Winooski family of lawyers, the Niquettes. Open the newspaper and there they are, more French names: most members of the Burlington and Winooski fire departments and many police officers; the mayors
of both cities; public defenders, prosecutors, defendants and witnesses;
someone on nearly every page. I often ask my students to open the telephone
directory to a page in the "L's." Nearly every entry is French.

You can't always tell a French name, however. Many Quebec immigrant names have evolved, for various reasons. Anglos often wrote French
names using English phonetics on hiring forms and official documents, for
instance. Thus my friend Carl Zeno's name is really Lusignan, and my
mechanic, whom I thought was of Spanish origin with a name like "Cota,"
turned out to be a Côté. Your friend Pelkey might well be Pelletier, and those
"Italians," Tatro and Parizo, are really Tétrault and Pariseau. My favorite is a
family named "Centerbar" for Saint-Hubert. All your friends named Shortsleeve
and most of those named Greenwood and Drinkwine are Franco-American.
They represent another common transformation: literal translation of the
name. Thus many Hopes may have been L'Espérance and Whites have been
Leblancs.

Because these essays explore the character of Vermonters, I would like
to concentrate now on the elements that have helped determine the Franco-
American character, while trying to avoid too much generalizing. We will,
therefore, skim all too rapidly over much of the early history of the French in
Vermont to concentrate on the last 150 years, ending with some speculation
about the future.

Most Franco-Americans can claim descent from settlers who came to this continent long before other European forebears. Though never numerous compared to the population of the thirteen English colonies thriving in warmer climes and under different economic and political conditions, nevertheless those Franco-Americans explored, charted, named, and laid claim to most of the rest of North America. They also succeeded in defeating the British in battle for decades before finally succumbing on the Plains of Abraham, outside of Quebec City, in 1759. Then, although the anti-Catholic and francophobic British wanted nothing more than to convert and assimilate their new subjects as soon as possible, they dared not try it as long as there was a threat of rebellion against British rule in North America. England offered liberal terms to the defeated French, including religious and language rights, to convince them not to join the rebellion of the colonies to the south.

The region surrounding Lake Champlain—"discovered" and named in 1609 by the great "Father of New France" himself, Samuel de Champlain—was claimed by the French, who sent settlers to both sides of the lake in the seventeenth century. Most of these returned north after the 1759 conquest, so there is no documented continuous line of habitation by the French in this region.

French-Canadians began coming to Vermont and New England in small numbers in the early nineteenth century to farm land that was usually richer and less subject to extreme weather than many farms in Quebec. A greater number arrived in 1837 and 1838, *Patriotes* fleeing the British army after an armed rebellion. Vermonters supported their cause, and the celebrated Ludger Duvernay, journalist and rebel, was received with great honor in Burlington. It is he who gave the Queen City the distinction of having the first French-Canadian newspaper published in New England, *Le Patriote de Burlington*.

It was not until the development of waterpower, however, and the building of great cotton and woolen mills in the Northeast that French-Canadians came to the rest of New England in great numbers. Impoverished by crop failures, economic depressions, and the scarcity of good farmland, many of them listened avidly to the descriptions of money to be earned and jobs to be had to the south. Whole villages sometimes pulled up stakes and emigrated together. More often, one or two members of a family came first, established themselves, obtained housing, then sent for the rest. As the labor movement grew stronger, and as more established immigrant groups such as the Irish demanded better pay and shorter working hours, mill owners found the hard-working Quebec farmer and his family an attractive new source for employees, and intensive recruiting began in Quebec. Emigrants crossed the border on foot, in carts, or later by train, bringing only those belongings they could carry. Camille Lessard-Bissonnette, in her novel *Canuck*, describes in graphic detail the fatigue of the travelers, the noise and confusion of their arrival, and their first view of a generally grimy mill town.[4]

In addition to the material goods they carried across the border, the immigrants from French Canada brought with them a culture that had withstood the assimilationist efforts of the British for a century and techniques for *la survivance*, survival. This cultural "baggage" enabled the French-

Canadians to retain their distinct identity in New England but also became a source of conflict, misunderstanding, and denial of opportunity. Most new arrivals were from rural areas, the peasant culture of which was encouraged and idealized by the intellectual elites (the clergy, educators, and professionals). This insured that most émigrés would be preserved from the "taint" of English Protestant influence in their new surroundings. Traditional values discouraged extensive schooling and considered education not particularly useful except for those who were to enter a profession. Boys, especially, left school as soon as they were strong enough to do significant work on their fathers' farms.

But we must never fall into the trap of assuming that a people not learned in the classical sense is not an intelligent and creative society. The traditions, arts, crafts, and oral literature of this group offer endless riches to those who take the trouble to discover them. Of course, in describing these traditions, we must also be careful not to fall into the other trap of regarding them as "quaint" and "picturesque." Franco-Americans have a functioning, living culture, which helps its members survive and which changes and adapts to new conditions. With these caveats in mind, let us examine some of the traditions that even my young Franco-American students still identify as family activities.

People, especially family, are of paramount importance in the culture. Horace Miner, in his sociological study of the Quebec parish of St. Denis de Kamouraska, points out that the farmers of that region usually did not even consider traveling where they had no kinfolk to visit.[5] The family still is often close-knit, and even the most far-flung branches may take precedence over non-family members in association and even in hiring. When any of my Franco-American friends is introduced to another Franco, the first order of business is an examination of their respective family trees and villages of origin in Quebec. They almost always find some connection, however tenuous, between their families. This is not surprising, considering that most of the millions of Francos on our continent are descended from a group of about ten thousand original settlers.

Most social activities are family-oriented. A *veillée* at home with one's friends is a common occurrence, and no one waits to be entertained "electronically." Guests bring musical instruments, the kitchen table becomes a platform for the fiddler, and almost everyone contributes a song, a story, or a vigorous broom-dance before the evening ends. Aspects of holiday celebrations are good examples of the survival of old French-Canadian traditions. Some examples are *La fête des Rois* (Epiphany), with its king and queen chosen at random by placing a bean and a pea in a special cake; and the blessing bestowed by a father on his family each New Year's Day.

Traditional foods are delicious, but they were meant to keep farmworkers going in the coldest weather. Hence the calorie and cholesterol counts are mind-boggling and foods such as *tourtière* or *fèves au lard* are now eaten only on special occasions. Traditional handcrafts remain alive in beautiful household articles—woven, embroidered, or quilted—and church decorations. The language of French North America is rich and expressive, and its oral tradition became the foundation for a distinctively American style of modern literature.

Folk medicine is still practiced among Franco-Americans, and they still use home remedies, secret cures, and powerful religious objects, though more to "hedge one's bets" than to express a real belief in them. Many people, however, still place much faith in *l'eau de Pâques* (water gathered from a stream just at dawn on Easter Sunday) as a cure for disease, a protection against disaster, and a guarantee that a woman will find a husband.

In traditional French-Canadian society, the church encouraged respect for the father as the authority in the family and exhorted women to be docile homemakers and mothers (of innumerable children). In literature, the women are often portrayed as exhausted, silent drudges; but some are imposing matriarchs, and in reality even the most traditional wife, since she was better educated than her husband, participated fully in the financial affairs and transactions of the family.

Work was important not so much as a source of wealth or status but as a way to provide for the family's needs. The family worked together on the farm, and those who left for the lumber camp or mill town usually turned their wages over to the head of the family, who returned to them a small allowance.

What was the life of Franco-Americans like, once they arrived in New England? First of all, they continued to work hard, and in Vermont more than in most other states, many continued to farm. Although Vermont has the highest percentage of Franco-Americans in the United States, Gérard Brault, in his analysis of urban areas with high numbers or percentages of Francos, lists no Vermont cities.[6] It must follow, then, that a good number of Franco-Vermonters lived in rural areas. Other immigrants were tradesmen, and Saint Joseph Parish in Burlington, the first French-Canadian national parish in New England (1850), was founded to fulfil the needs of a growing population even before local mills were in full swing.

As the huge influx of Franco-Americans came to New England at the end of the nineteenth century, however, most ended up in the mill towns—the *Petits Canadas*. Often the entire family worked together, at least when they were getting started. The new immigrants, frequently considering themselves temporary residents who were here only to earn enough to revitalize their farm in Quebec, worked diligently and even happily in the literally deafening, lint-filled mills.

The former workers of the Amoskeag mill in Manchester, New Hampshire, telling their stories in *Amoskeag* by Tamara K. Hareven and Randolph Langenbach, describe dirt, cockroaches, noise, lint, low wages, and long work hours.[7] They did not love the place, but they did their work well, and many stayed, until the company cut them adrift and closed the mill rather than meet labor union demands. Most worked six-day, eight-hour-per-day weeks, and one Manchester informant says his father worked seven days a week for twenty-five years. Shamefully, no one has done a project like *Amoskeag* to record the lives and experiences of the former workers in Vermont mills, although Ralph Nading Hill described the work and life of Lucette Varin, who worked in the Chace Mill in 1949. Varin's life sounds very much like that of her nineteenth-century predecessors elsewhere in New England, with its routine of early rising and long work hours.[8]

As each *Petit Canada* grew, the mill workers were followed by tradesmen, artisans, merchants, and professionals, so that most transactions the members of the community needed to make could be done in French with "their own people." After an initial accusation of desertion and treason leveled at the emigrants, the Catholic church in Canada adopted a "messianic" ideology that saw Francophone migrants as an instrument for catholicizing—and thus "saving"—the entire North American continent. The church then encouraged the establishment of national parishes, schools, convents, hospitals, and other institutions.

What has allowed this distinctive society to retain its identity for so long? Georges Thériault, in his sociological studies of Nashua, New Hampshire, gives three main reasons.[9]

First, the proximity of the motherland to the new country is of paramount importance. Unlike other immigrants, Franco-Americans crossed an unusually porous international border to get here, to a region, at least here in the North, that had always been part of their territory. In that sense, Franco-Americans can and do claim to be "at home" on nearly the entire continent. Visits to the mother country are simple. Ties are not broken forever. Many of the interviewees in *Amoskeag*, for example, were sent back to Quebec by their parents to live with a relative for a significant part of their childhood.

Secondly, the majority of Franco-Americans arrived here in waves—large groups that emigrated together, settled in the same part of the city, and worked at the same place for nearly the same wages. This provided a large support group, strengthened by proximity and similarity of interests. Only much later did upward mobility and scattering to the suburbs weaken the group. Although living conditions were often harsh, especially in some company-owned tenements, one's neighbors could be depended upon for help, entertainment, and support. In Vermont, with its mills to attract workers, two *Petits Canadas* developed: nearly all of Winooski and the Lakeside neighborhood of Burlington. Both communities are still heavily Franco-American.

The third element cited by Thériault as necessary to the support and preservation of a distinct ethnic group is the establishment of traditional and community institutions. This the Franco-Americans did with a vengeance, especially as naturalization became the norm. The church, after initial resistance and prodded by its French-Canadian flocks, began to send missionaries and finally to found parishes. The Catholic church had already established itself in New England, but its members were predominantly Irish and nothing about the Irish churches satisfied the Franco immigrants. They could not understand the homilies nor go to confession because of the language barrier. They missed their ritual, full of Gregorian chant. The financial burden imposed on Irish parishioners fell heavily on French workers, who occupied the lowest rungs on the economic ladder. They had contributed faithfully to their churches at home, but with a smaller percentage of their income and usually in kind rather than in money. Although nothing can be more autocratic than a certain type of French-Canadian priest, nevertheless the Francos found the

Irish priests even more dictatorial, especially as they were used to governing their own financial affairs, through a parish council called the *fabrique*.

Many of the most persuasive complaints of Franco-American Catholics came from the Burlington area. The Breton Bishop Louis de Goësbriand of Burlington pleaded the cause of the Franco-Burlingtonians with eloquence, and one of the most moving requests for French-speaking priests and other relief came from François Biron of Burlington, writing painfully and with what might be called "creative" spelling to transmit the requests of his fellow French Catholics to the bishop of Montreal.[10]

Fearful that the emigrants would be lost to Protestantism or atheism, and afraid that their children would be tainted by attending public schools, the Roman Catholic hierarchy encouraged the building of churches and schools throughout New England. Eventually Franco-American parochial schools outnumbered those of any other national group. These were often imposing and richly decorated, representing an impressive energy and financial sacrifice by low-wage laborers. The *Guide Officiel des Franco-Américains* of 1940, for instance, lists twenty-six parishes in Vermont with predominantly Franco populations and Franco priests.[11]

Schools were generally bilingual, and every subject, from composition and grammar to arithmetic, used moral lessons and adages to promote piety, strict morality, and adherence to the teachings of the Catholic church. Religion was always taught in French, for language and faith were inextricably tied in the messianic ideology. High schools, though less numerous, were common, and finally colleges such as Assumption (Worcester, Massachusetts), Rivier (Manchester, New Hampshire) and Saint Michael's (Colchester, Vermont) were founded to serve immigrant communities.

Nationalist (and thus also Catholic) organizations played a vital part in this infrastructure. Societies such as the Union Saint-Jean-Baptiste and the Dames de Saint-Anne promoted the use of French and the preservation of the culture, although all admitted that English was necessary—especially for men—in order to transact business outside the home. Fraternal organizations such as the Association Canado-Américaine began to sell their own insurance. Franco-Americans, in the cooperative spirit of their villages at home, brought with them a Québécois innovation: the credit union.

Communication among Franco-Americans was vital, and an astounding number of newspapers sprang up throughout the region. Nearly 250 were launched, some of which lasted only a short time but many of which only recently closed their doors (for example, *Le Travailleur* of Lowell, Massachusetts). In fact, in the 1920s, Franco-Americans in Rhode Island founded a newspaper (*La Sentinelle*), solely to air their grievances and arguments in a tragic conflict with their Irish bishop, a conflict that they lost and from which Francos never fully recovered, as it meant an end to the building of national parishes.

What were the reactions of the "Yankees" to this influx of foreign blood? They range from violence, intolerance, and bigotry to paternalistic stereotyping and sometimes sincere appreciation. An "invasion" by the descendants of the traditional enemies of the British in Europe, and Catholic to boot, was bound to bring out the worst in many Yankees. Stereotypes of the most uncomplimentary and contradictory kind were common coin: Francos were welcomed to Lowell, Massachusetts, as people who "though poor in purse" were "rich in honesty of purpose and genuine goodness of heart," who "when settled into work" became "excellent citizens, adding to the wealth of this city by their industry." But this was rare.[12]

Those who feared Catholics saw the immigrants from Quebec as totally in the thrall of their priests. Being of French descent, these new neighbors were said to have lower morals and did not like to send their children to school. They were fit only for manual labor but at the same time would leave work on a "whim," which, in fact, usually turned out to be a family emergency. Other observers saw French-Canadians as crafty peasants, good-humored, laughing and singing, but shrewd Norman bargainers. They were good workers because they were docile, while at the same time they liked to go their own way.

The most famous of the demeaning attacks on Franco-American character came from the Massachusetts Bureau of Statistics of Labor in its report of 1881:

> With some exceptions, the Canadian French are the Chinese of the Eastern States. They care nothing for our institutions, civil, political, or educational. They do not care to make a home among us, to dwell with us as citizens and so become a part of us . . . They are a horde of industrial invaders, not a stream of stable settlers . . . Rarely does one of them become naturalized. They will not send their children to school if they can help it, but endeavor to crowd into the mills at the earliest possible age. To do this they deceive about the age of their children with brazen effrontery . . .
>
> These people have one good trait. They are indefatigable workers and docile . . . To earn all they can and by no matter how many hours of toil, to live in the most beggarly way so that out of their earnings they may spend as little for living as possible, and to carry out of our country what they save: this is the aim of the Canadian French in our factory districts. Incidently, they must have some amusements; and so far as the males are concerned, drinking, smoking, and lounging constitute the sum of these.[13]

The report did not go unchallenged by Franco-Americans who pressured the Massachusetts government to hold hearings at which evidence was brought forth to refute such ideas. We can laugh or gasp at the sheer outrageousness of this report, but these attitudes, whether expressed privately or in chilling diatribes, such as the Rev. Calvin E. Amaron's 1891 tract, *Your Heritage; or, New England Threatened*, tended to justify violence.[14] No wonder the Know-Nothings and the Ku Klux Klan felt free to wreak violence upon Franco-Americans in the 1920s.

Moreover, some of these attitudes can still be found today, although more subtle and hidden. There persists, for example, a tradition in Vermont of writing poems featuring a good-natured, ignorant Franco-American, usually named Baptiste, who makes us laugh less at the stories he tells than at his fractured English. We look down on him but, of course, say that we admire Franco-Americans and that it's just good fun.

What has been the Franco-Americans' own image of themselves? It was often schizophrenic. Encouraged by their elite to remain "pure" and "simple" yet at the same time excluded from elite organizations and denied power, working-class Franco-Americans suffered from an inferiority complex while still feeling pride in their history and heritage. They loved their culture, but their elites seldom participated in typical activities, which were generally "hidden" within the family group. In fact, part of the so-called invisibility of Franco-Americans stems from their own successful efforts not to rock the boat and attract perhaps unwelcome or antagonistic attention.

The same schizophrenia applies to the French language as it is spoken in North America. Expressing themselves in a French that dates from before the great seventeenth-century "reformation" of the language in France, Franco-Americans are living history. Their language is salted with some earthy terms, which the French eventually banished from their tongue when they made it a beautiful latinate language. North-American French has much to offer "standard" French, and although now impoverished here in the U.S. through lack of schooling in the language, it is nevertheless not a dialect but grammatically identical to standard French.

The traditional elites point with pride to distinguished and accomplished Franco-Americans, and every people has a need for such heroes. From Frank Fontaine to Vermonter Rudy Vallée, Napoléon Lajoie, Robert Goulet, Will Durant, Jack (Jean-Louis) Kérouac and Grace Metalious (de Repentigny), there is a long list of Franco-Americans who have gained national recognition. Thus we shouldn't overemphasize the "inferiority complex" of the ordinary Francos, most of whom have considerable dignity and pride. Note also that many of the positive values of the Franco-American culture—humanity, priority of the family over other concerns, and sense of community and place—offer examples of what the rest of us often look for in this post-industrial society.

What is the present status of the culture in New England? With church-going reduced, with the mixing of cultures in the old national parishes, and with ambiguous questions on census questionnaires, it is difficult to estimate how many people have French as their mother tongue and how many of French-Canadian descent there really are. We know that language use is diminishing, but it is difficult to quantify. It is obvious that, without the communal living, with the rejection by many of traditional institutions, and under the leadership of a small group that has excluded "ordinary" people and rejected many of those institutions, we find a scattered, more Americanized, anglophone or vaguely bilingual group that is less homogeneous and less identifiable. Discrimination and stereotyping continue, and Franco-American schoolchildren have been made to believe that their forebears had nothing to do with New England history. The few bilingual education programs in Vermont have long since lost their federal funding, and a smaller number of Franco-Americans, compared to other Vermonters, go on to higher education or management jobs, according to a report prepared by the Vermont Advisory Committee to the United States Civil Rights Commission.[16]

There are positive signs, however, in new movements not tied to old institutions, the reform of some old institutions, the emergence of new leaders, and the development of new ties with French-speakers outside of New England. Many Francos now feel more comfortable investigating their heritage, accepting and rejecting whatever facets of the culture please or displease them. They are abandoning the idea that, without the French language, one does not "qualify" as a Franco-American, and they are producing Franco-American literature in English and French. The many people who trace their genealogies or who ask their grandparents to tell family stories are keeping their cultural identity alive. Pessimists say that the culture is in its death throes, but I like to think it is instead undergoing a sort of transformation from which it may well emerge stronger, better defined than it has been, and capable of becoming a positive force for those who have inherited it.

NOTES

1. John Gunther, *Inside U.S.A.* (New York: Harper, 1947), 493.

2. Jacques Ducharme, *The Shadows of the Trees. The Story of French-Canadians in New England* (New York: Harper, 1943), 8.

3. Ibid., 17.

4. Camille Lessard-Bissonnette, *Canuck* (Lewiston, Me.: Édition du Messager, 1936; reprinted by National Materials Development Center).

5. Horace Miner, *St. Denis: A French-Canadian Parish* (1939; reprint, Chicago: University of Chicago Press, 1963).

6. Gerard J. Brault, *The French-Canadian Heritage in New England* (Hanover, N.H.: University Press of New England, 1986).

7. Tamara K. Hareven and Randolph Langenbach, *Amoskeag: Life and Work in an American Factory-City* (New York: Pantheon Books, 1978).

8. Ralph Nading Hill, *The Winooski, Heartway of Vermont* in Rivers of America (New York: Rinehart, 1949), 255-258.

9. George Thériault, "The Franco-Americans of New England," in *A Franco-American Overview*, vol. 3 of New England, pt. 1 (Cambridge, Mass.: National Assessment and Dissemination Center for Bilingual/Bicultural Education, 1981). [Reprinted from a University of Toronto monograph of 1960, *Canadian Dualism: Studies of French-English Relations*], 22-24.

10. Robert G. Keenan and Rev. Francis R. Privé, eds., *History of St. Joseph Parish, Burlington, Vermont, 1830-1987* (Burlington, Vt.: St. Joseph Parish, 1988), 20.

11. *Guide Officiel des Franco-Américains* (Fall River, Mass.: A. A. Bélanger, 1940). This was an annual guide (c1915-1946) listing political, religious, and business leaders of the Franco-American community of each state and reporting on Franco-American societies and organizations.

12. *Twenty-Eighth Annual Report of the Ministry-at-Large* (Lowell, Mass.: 1872), 14-15, quoted by Francis H. Early in "The Settling-in Process: The Beginnings of Little Canada in Lowell, Massachusetts in the Late Nineteenth Century," in Claire Quintal, ed., *The Little Canadas of New England*, Proceedings of the Third Annual Conference of the French Institute (Worcester, Mass.: Assumption College, 1982), 28. A ministry was a local, interdenominational, charitable organization.

13. Massachusetts Bureau of Statistics of Labor, *Twelfth Annual Report*, 1881, 469.

14. Calvin E. Amaron, *Your Heritage; or, New England Threatened* (Springfield, Mass.: French Protestant College, 1891).

15. United States Commission on Civil Rights, Vermont Advisory Committee. *Franco-Americans in Vermont: A Civil Rights Perspective* [researched and authored by Peter Woolfson] (Washington, D.C.: The Commission, 1983).

Some Intolerant Vermonters

T. D. Seymour Bassett

I have five kinds of stories about intolerant Vermonters. These are stories about people or groups who looked down upon and to a greater or lesser degree acted to exclude from among their communities (1) religious dissenters from the Congregational establishment, (2) Roman Catholics, (3) pacifists, (4) communists, and, finally, (5) Indians, African-Americans, and other ethnic Americans. The intolerant Vermonters, like intolerant people in all states and nations, wanted to wipe out all individuals and groups that they believed defiled or debased the community.

In only a few instances has violence born of intolerance erupted in Vermont. More often the victims of intolerance have been deprived of their lives, work, or homes through the use of the legal system, and intolerant Vermonters have been scrupulous in the use of due process to attain their ends. In 1778 David Redding was hastily convicted of selling American arms and ammunition to the British. When an angry mob threatened to lynch Redding after the conviction was overturned because of a faulty procedure, Ethan Allen promised to get a proper conviction or hang for the crime himself. In 1953 Alex Novikoff lost his job at the University of Vermont when he defied first a congressional committee and then the governing body of the university and their due processes. In 1969 Reverend Johnson was forced to abandon his home in Irasburg after law enforcement officials, investigating a night-time assault on his property, accused him of an altogether different crime. Thus, in Vermont as elsewhere in our nation and around the globe, intolerance is a slowly working poison, mainly silent, and usually employing and corrupting the legal system to accomplish its unjust and inhumane ends.

CONGREGATIONAL CHURCHES VERSUS OTHER PROTESTANTS

The Congregational ideal, with medieval roots, envisioned everyone in town belonging to one church, going to one school system, living within walking distance of one meetinghouse where each year the people, all sharing the same basic beliefs, chose one set of magistrates to whom deference was due and who would keep deviants in line or expel them. So the Puritans exiled Anne Hutchinson and Roger Williams and hanged a few Quakers who would not stay exiled. As New England numbers increased and Puritans became unsure whether they had come to worship God or catch fish, they begrudged the bona fide Baptists and Quakers and Anglicans their own religious societies, but "Home Baptists," belonging to no church, had to support the "majority" faith unless they petitioned the town and received permission to direct their church tax to support their own denomination.

Pioneer Vermonters brought this multiple establishment with them and maintained it for thirty years. The Republic of Vermont also enacted a set of blue laws similar to Connecticut's: capital punishment for sex crimes, fines for traveling or picking berries on Sunday or absence from divine worship. Though usually unenforced, the blue laws stayed on the books, however, available like spotlights to catch anyone the authorities did not like. A young man might hesitate to become a Freewill Baptist lest he hurt his chances to clerk for the Congregational storekeeper. Joining the Congregational church might help him get a scholarship to college.

The Congregationalist-Federalists did not like Matthew Lyon, and the feeling was mutual. Lyon was not a deferential character. His behavior manifested the frontier philosophy that those who could get ahead, by hook or crook, should enjoy power and preach the freedom of anyone else to go and do likewise.[1] Lyon was formally an Episcopalian but basically a deist, like so many of the nation's founding fathers. Congregationalists opposed the Episcopalians in Connecticut where Lyon came from and even more so in Vermont, where they tried to divert the Episcopal glebe lands to school uses.

From the time of Vermont's first election of U.S. congressmen in 1791, Lyon was a contender, losing by a narrower margin each time until his victory in 1797. The bitter partisanship of the times, between pro-French Republicans (including Lyon) and pro-British Federalists, can be symbolized by Lyon's spitting in Congressman Roger Griswold's face for calling him a coward and Griswold's beating Lyon with his cane on the House floor. With the country near war with France when its attempt to bribe the American envoys became known, the Federalist-dominated Congress passed the Sedition Act, which severely penalized those who spoke or published against the government. It seems obvious to us today that this law violated freedom of speech and press, as members of Lyon's Republican Party believed. Yet it expressed the dominant eighteenth-century view that, once an election has been decided, further partisanship must stop. Many still hold this view in wartime, asserting that opposition to our country's war aids the enemy and is seditious.

Lyon, holding the new two-party concept of loyal opposition, started a new campaign organ to promote his re-election, *The Scourge of Aristocracy*, and continued his violent language against the administration of John Adams. Congressional immunity did not extend to treason. His Federalist enemies indicted and convicted him under the Sedition Act, *ex post facto*, for what he had written before the act was passed. Most of the jurymen were chosen from towns hostile to Lyon, who was denied any peremptory challenges of jurymen he felt would be prejudiced against him. And he was virtually deprived of defense counsel.

The sentence was a thousand-dollar fine plus the costs of the trial, four months' imprisonment, and continued confinement until he paid his fine. Instead of jailing him in Rutland County, where he was tried and where he lived, his enemy, U.S. Marshal Jabez Fitch took him under guard (as if he would flout justice by escaping) on a triumphal, two-day, forty-four-mile procession to and around Vergennes. Lyon was placed in a common cell with horse thieves, counterfeiters, and runaways, with one stinking "necessary," an open window, and no stove in the cold season. The Vergennes city council eventually supplied windowpanes, and Lyon's friends furnished a stove and writing materials, which at first had been withheld.

Filling his newspaper with Jeffersonian arguments, Lyon won an absolute majority over all other candidates in the December run-off election but could not go to Philadelphia to take his seat in Congress until the end of his prison term on Valentine's Day 1799. Marshall Jabez Fitch had another warrant to slap on Lyon the moment he stepped out of jail, but Lyon eluded the tag and took off by sleigh up frozen Otter Creek, his supporters cheering him on to Philadelphia. President Adams denied a petition of thousands of Vermonters to pardon him and remit his fine. But more important, the Federalist policy of silencing opposition had backfired.

The Congregationalists' animus against dissenters was expressed in political language in Lyon's case, but they did occasionally and openly persecute Baptists. In the 1780s enemies in disguise surrounded the house of Elder Elisha Rich of Clarendon, beat his cattle, and tore out his pulpit.[2] In 1795 a member of the Hartford Baptist church was jailed for not paying his church tax and not released until he paid it. He spent some fifty pounds suing to recover his money and failed. The next year Amasa Green of Bethel petitioned the general assembly to recover for the distraint (seizure and sale) of two oxen to pay for part of the Congregational minister's salary but got no satisfaction.[3]

In 1807 the general assembly abolished the multiple establishment and Vermont joined the American system of voluntarism. Henceforth each denomination had to support itself. However, there was lingering favoritism and bickering over the denominational use of the town house—built with tax money and contributions—for worship. In 1821 the Baptists of Westford asked to use the town house they had helped build. The Congregationalists replied that they could use the meetinghouse on any day but Sunday. So the Baptists and Methodists built a brick house of worship at the other end of the green.

PROTESTANTS VERSUS CATHOLICS

The tensions that developed when Irish fled the potato famine and *Canadiens* came south contained a number of non-religious ingredients. Their speech seemed strange to Vermonters even when the Irish spoke English instead of Gaelic. Both Yankee and foreign-born gathered for gossip after worship, but the Protestant Sunday atmosphere was better buttoned, more solemn. Furthermore, foreigners competed for jobs. Nathaniel Hawthorne, observing Irish immigrants in Burlington in the summer of 1835, wrote that they "elbow the native citizens entirely out of competition in . . . mere bodily labor."[4] The foreigners were accused of clannishness, that is, they preferred to be beholden to those familiar with their ways and not show forced deference to strangers.

The religious ingredient of nativism was the assumption that anyone who accepted the authority of the pope as supreme monarch of the Catholic church and the authority of the bishop in a region or diocese, could neither be democratic nor loyal to this country. Catholic monarchy in religion was incompatible with democracy in politics, while the Protestants' monarchy in business was compatible with democracy in politics.

The Irish welcomed the free entry afforded them by United States immigration policy, in contrast to New England's and New France's original policy of excluding heretics. Jeremiah O'Callaghan, the principal missionary priest in Vermont from 1828 to the establishment of the Diocese of Burlington in 1853, wrote about his favorable impression of America:

> See the happy effect produced by the sound policy of the people [of the United States]. There all tribes and nations, blacks and whites, Turks and Jews, Greeks and Arabs, [live] in perfect order; peace without interruption; though there is no standing army, every man, to the age of forty-five, a soldier, and every soldier a citizen, ready, on the first call, to die for the common welfare.[5]

Reports like this brought cheap Irish labor, a stream in the thirties and a flood in the forties. Builders of railroads welcomed the Irish, and when that work was done, so did the managers of mills and quarries.

This tide produced the first Vermont nativism. It took the form of Protestant jeremiads: we have erred and strayed; we need to revive our piety and faith. Protestants also promoted prohibition, blaming intemperance and resultant crime mainly on foreigners. They distributed the Protestant Bible and used it in the common schools. They offered Sunday schools in immigrant neighborhoods and tried to lengthen the period required before naturalization. But no recorded, overt, illegal harm, no damage to life, limb, or property, has come to light. The destruction by fire of St. Mary's Catholic Church in Burlington in May 1838 was widely believed to be arson committed by nativists, but that is not correct.

On the contrary, some employers let the visiting priest use their buildings and gave land for a church and cemetery. Domestic help had time off on holy days and Sundays, although employers invited them to their own Protestant churches and a few temporarily joined. Chauncey Brownell (1847-1938) told me that his father, who had a large farm in Williston from 1839, went to New York when he needed hired hands and picked them fresh off the wharf. After he had taught them how to farm the Vermont way and profited from their labor, they would go off on their own, and he would get more.

There appeared to be a symbiotic relationship between native bosses and immigrant labor.

The American or Know Nothing Party, a secret, anti-Catholic, antislavery, temperance group, was a threatening third force in 1855-56, dominating many town meetings and electing several legislators. It is hard to say whether Yankee intolerance was ethnic or religious. Ryland Fletcher, lieutenant governor, 1854-56, was a Know Nothing, rewarded with the governorship, 1856-58, a clear demonstration that the Republican syndrome included nativism.

The next eruption came after the Ku Klux Klan was revived. The KKK burned fiery crosses and drew crowds in several central Vermont towns for two or three years in the mid-1920s, and bills introduced in the Vermont legislature to penalize masks and disguises in public failed. Perhaps the Vermont congressional delegation's support for immigration restriction in 1924 was in part a response to this nativism.

PACIFISTS

The presence of Quakers in Danby and a few other towns in the 1770s was probably why Vermont law early provided for conscientious objectors. The state always intended to exact a *quid pro quo*, and when Friends refused to train with the militia, they were fined for not bearing their share of the expense or their goods were distrained to cover the fines. During the Civil War, Quaker elders advised their members who were drafted to pay the three-hundred-dollar commutation provided for in the draft law. Several from Danby served in the armed forces. Three Friends, Lindley Murray Macomber of Grand Isle, Peter Dakin of North Ferrisburg, and Cyrus Guernsey Pringle of Charlotte, refused commutation and were made to serve with the troops on the Potomac front. Refusing to bear arms, they were subjected to hazing by subordinate officers but were otherwise humanely treated until Quaker lobbyists got them furloughed for the duration.[6]

Democratic "Copperheads," who were not pacifists but were opposed to "Mr. Lincoln's War" to free the slaves, were subjected to more violations of their civil rights. A few young men of draft age studied in Montreal and others fled to Canada to avoid the draft. Democratic editor Hiram Atkins long displayed one of the brickbats thrown through the window of his Montpelier *Argus and Patriot*.

Conscientious objectors probably received their worst treatment during World War I. While University of Vermont super-patriots engineered the dismissal of Professor Anton Appelmann, because as a German he sympathized with the Kaiser, they also told Vermonter Francis Irons, a freshman who had worked for two years to earn tuition money, that he could not return to classes because he refused military training. Middlebury College, which had no such required training, accepted him. Baptist minister Clarence H. Waldron of Woodstock was tried, convicted, and sentenced to fifteen years for "causing insubordination, disloyalty, and refusal of duty in the military forces," according to Peter Jennison.[7]

COMMUNISTS

Vermonters have looked askance at communists who, except for most of the Marxian variety, have usually been pacifist. Before the Civil War, a sprinkling of community-seeking radicals said their sermons unhindered. When transient Dorrilites and Pilgrims wandered through the state, residents caricatured their flaws and let them pass. Individual Vermonters joined the Shakers and suffered some legal penalties. Orson S. Murray, editor of the Baptist *Vermont Telegraph*, and John A. Collins both went West to join communitarian settlements. John Orvis, an ex-Quaker from Addison County, toured Vermont in the 1840s as a missionary for Brook Farm and other Fourierist communities.

The only communistic settlement that took root in Vermont was in Putney, from 1838 to 1847. It was soon uprooted, however, by irate townspeople when they heard that the community was practicing "free love." John Humphrey Noyes, Putney Perfectionist leader, called it complex marriage, and their practice, Bible communism, traced to the Book of Acts, (2:44, 4:32) where the first Pentecostal Christians "had all things in common." Born of an elite Vermont family, trained for law or divinity at Dartmouth, Andover, and Yale, Noyes was swept into the evangelical revival and developed his own version of perfectionist theology. By 1837 he was convinced "when the will of God is done on earth as it is in heaven there will be no marriage."[8]

Hubbard Eastman, Putney Methodist minister, first attacked Noyes as a faith healer, and the charismatic Noyes had, in fact, experienced several successes as a healer. Then the practice of complex marriage, started in 1846 by mutual agreement of the members of the Putney Perfectionist church, leaked out to Eastman, who roused the town against this "house of assignation." Noyes, charged with adultery, was willing to go to jail for his beliefs, but at the warning by his brother-in-law, state senator Larkin G. Mead, that mob violence was impending, he chose another text to follow: "When they persecute you in one city, flee to another." (Matt. 10:23) He jumped bail and led his community to the recently evacuated Oneida Indian tract in New York State, where frontier tolerance allowed his community to flourish for a generation. Again, Vermonters had chosen the legal route plus a threat of violence to eliminate those they would not tolerate.

The most notorious case of anti-communist action in recent memory is that of Alex Novikoff, later a Nobel Prize-winning biochemist. Novikoff, a Young Communist in his college days, was dismissed from the University of Vermont after many hearings because he would not testify before a U.S. Senate committee.[9]

REDS, BLACKS, AND OTHER ETHNICS

The most damaging intolerance of ethnic Vermonters was shown against Indians and other non-white Americans. Dorothy Canfield Fisher is half right in the title of her chapter in *The Vermont Tradition* on Vermont's lack of Indian wars, "No Scalps, No Tomahawks, No Master Race."[10]

Vermonters fought Indians only as they were attached to imperial enemies, French and British. But the master race they did believe themselves to be. Hence they could look right through Indians as if they were not there. The pioneers could take the land because it was "no man's." John Moody, historian of the Abenaki, points to probable murders in Sheldon.[11] If Indians were decimated by white men's diseases because they had no immunity, that was the hand of God, not biological warfare. If Indians keep hanging around as if they belonged here, we'll give them a handout, buy their baskets, let them camp on our creek, but it is *our* land.

Antisemitism has religious, political, and ethnic facets. One Vermont example is the story Roger L. Amidon tells of Morris Cohen, junk man, who got along fine until the Ku Klux Klan came to Barnet and asked him to leave.[12] According to the statistics collected by the Anti-Defamation League, after Vermont's Public Accommodations Act of 1957, discrimination dropped sharply. Before that, advertisements for summer camps sometimes noted, "Gentile Clientele." The first Jew on the University of Vermont faculty was probably Russian-born Alexander Gershoy, appointed in 1923.

What I know about social cleavage in Burlington is spelled out in Elin Anderson's *We Americans; A Study of Social Cleavage in an American Town*, and in her working papers, stored with the Public Records Office in Middlesex.[13] Over two hundred sterilizations performed under the 1931 law (repealed in 1981) were certainly overt invasions of individual liberty in the interests of demographic health as the eugenicists understood it.

African-Americans have not flocked in large numbers to Vermont, Yankees say, because it is cold. Yes, in both mean temperature and social climate. We can point to Lemuel Haynes of West Rutland, leading Congregational preacher, or Freewill Baptist revivalist Charles Bowles of Huntington, and Alexander Twilight, Middlebury A.B., 1823, who ran an academy in the stone house he built in Brownington. A handful of Vermonters helped fugitive slaves to Vermont freedom, and a handful of Civil War veterans brought freedmen home with them, one of whom, George Washington Henderson, University of Vermont, 1877, became a distinguished educator. But the rest of the several hundred blacks recorded at each census, remained transient, poor, and looked down upon until past World War II. Were there racist overtones in the Woodstock boxing match between a local black and a French- Canadian on Fast Day 1868? Almost a century later, a Burlington Community Relations Council was formed to help African-Americans find housing, because they had a harder time than others. In the heightened consciousness of the 1960s, the University of Vermont's Kake Walk came under attack as a caricature of black culture and was finally abolished in 1969.

Gov. Philip Hoff has claimed that his 1968-1970 New York City-Vermont Youth Project, which mixed urban black with rural white youth, had more to do with his defeat for the U.S. Senate in 1970 than anything else, more even than his establishing the Vermont Civil Rights Commission and his handling of the Irasburg Affair.

Initiated by the governor's office in April 1968 in response to the findings of the National Advisory Committee on Civil Disorders and continued as a private non-profit venture after Hoff retired from office, the Youth Project of Vermont used educational sites for hastily funded and improvised humanistic, cross-cultural, and outdoor programs each summer, involving several hundred youths. "Rocky, traumatic, explosive," Director Benjamin Collins reported in 1969, but psychologist M. W. Perrine concluded, "an enormous success at the human level."[14] Support for this social experiment was too weak, funding dried up, and the instigators paid the price as the civil rights decade ended.

Two weeks after a black family moved to Irasburg in July 1968, an army sergeant on furlough, son of a prominent Glover businessman, shot up their house. State police soon identified him as prime suspect but, according to the blue ribbon board of inquiry, were delinquent in handling the case, embarking on a totally irrelevant attempt to pin an adultery charge on the victims. The board concluded that racial prejudice was involved: "The issue is . . . the safety of a man's home in . . . Vermont."[15] Public sentiment that year in the aftermath of the Robert Kennedy and Martin Luther King assassinations hurt Vermonters who prosecuted the so-called Irasburg case against the law-enforcement misconduct. This no doubt added to votes against Att. Gen. James Oakes in the ensuing Republican gubernatorial primary, as well as against Hoff in 1970.

CONCLUSION

Like other mortals with hatred of those whose different ways seem to threaten them, Vermonters of each majority have used social pressure, threats of violence, and the law to eliminate, put down, or inconvenience those they would not tolerate. Whether the differences among groups were as slight as those of brothers or as great as those between Indians and Europeans, intolerant behavior has been constant. When the whole population was mostly descended from the Puritans, the Congregationalists tried to eliminate non-Congregationalists. Frightened by the size of Catholic immigration, Protestants tried to revive their own flocks while nibbling at freedoms enjoyed by "aliens." Intolerance was most successful against the few lower-class, patronless Indians and blacks. People's selective vision did not see the Indians living on the lands they had taken; acceptance of a few educated blacks made them feel they were not penalizing the rest.

Yet people paid little heed to the minor threat of pacifists, who had status and patrons and removed only one pacifist, John Humphrey Noyes, because his Bible communism seemed to threaten their families and churches. "Socialist" and "communist" are still epithets voiced with fear and hatred by a minority of Vermonters, yet a plurality elected one avowed radical to Congress in 1990 and none has been burned alive.

Finally, I find it ironic that the eugenicists, basing their idea of the good society on health, regardless of race, color, creed, or previous condition, seemed to find "ethnics" more degenerate than others. Feeling sure they were right, they left all their records for another generation to use, with a different perspective. I commend them for that. As a lifelong collector of records revealing every persuasion, I see, as George Orwell did in his novel, *1984*, the destruction of our enemies' records or our friends' to hide what we think they did wrong as insidiously intolerant. Such efforts are perhaps the most common form of intolerance in Vermont.

NOTES

1. The Lyon story is based on Aleine Austin, *Matthew Lyon* (University Park, Pa.: Pennsylvania State University Press, 1980).

2. Henry Crocker, *History of the Baptists in Vermont* (Bellows Falls, Vt.: P. H. Gobie Press, 1913), 114.

3. William G. McLoughlin, *New England Dissent, 1630-1833: The Baptists and the Separation of Church and State* (Cambridge: Harvard University Press, 1971), 2:814, reports both cases.

4. Quoted in T. D. Seymour Bassett, ed., *Outsiders Inside Vermont: Three Centuries of Visitors' Viewpoints on the Green Mountain State* (Canaan, N.H.: Phoenix Publishing Co., 1967), 63.

5. Jeremiah O'Callaghan, *Usury*, 3rd ed. (London, 1828), 116.

6. See Cyrus Guernsey Pringle, *The Civil War Diary of Cyrus Pringle* (Wallingford, Pa.: Pendle Hill, Pendle Hill Pamphlet 122 with foreword by Heary J. Cadbury, 1918) (Lebanon, Pa.: Sowers Printing, 1962).

7. Peter Jennison, *The History of Woodstock, 1890-1983* (Woodstock, Vt.: Countryman Press for the Woodstock Foundation, 1985), 64n.

8. George W. Noyes, *The Religious Experience of John Humphrey Noyes* (New York: Macmillan, 1923), 3-5.

9. The Novikoff story is told by David R. Holmes in *Stalking the Academic Communist: Intellectual Freedom and the Firing of Alex Novikoff* (Hanover, N.H.: University Press of New England, 1989).

10. Dorothy Canfield Fisher, *Vermont Tradition* (Boston: Little, Brown, 1953), 17-31.

11. These charges are mentioned by Hiram R. Whitney in A. M. Hemenway, ed., *Vermont Historical Gazetteer* (Burlington: A. M. Hemenway, 1871), 2:371, 372, 376, and supported by oral tradition.

12. Roger L. Amidon, *Barnet Days* (Columbia, S.C.: R. L. Amidon, 1986, typescript in Vermont Historical Society), 5.

13. Elin Anderson, *We Americans; A Study of Social Cleavage in an American Town* (Cambridge: Harvard University Press, 1937; reprint, New York: Russell & Russell, 1967); Kevin Dann has used Anderson's materials effectively, for example, in his article "From Degeneration to Regeneration: The Eugenics Survey of Vermont, 1925-1936," *Vermont History* 59 (Winter 1991): 5-29.

14. Youth Project of Vermont, Inc., Sponsoring the New York City Vermont Youth Project, *Report and Evaluation* (n.p.: The Project, 1969), unpaged.

15. *Findings and Recommendations of Board of Inquiry Investigating the So-Called Irasburg Affair* [n.p., 1969], 30; see also the superb review in depth by Tom Slayton, "Cost of 'Irasburg Affair' Was State's Innocence," *Barre-Montpelier Times-Argus*, 16 July, 1978.

Our Patriotic Identity

Willard Sterne Randall

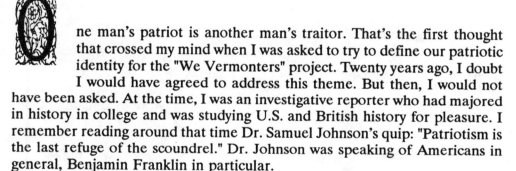ne man's patriot is another man's traitor. That's the first thought that crossed my mind when I was asked to try to define our patriotic identity for the "We Vermonters" project. Twenty years ago, I doubt I would have agreed to address this theme. But then, I would not have been asked. At the time, I was an investigative reporter who had majored in history in college and was studying U.S. and British history for pleasure. I remember reading around that time Dr. Samuel Johnson's quip: "Patriotism is the last refuge of the scoundrel." Dr. Johnson was speaking of Americans in general, Benjamin Franklin in particular.

Our identity is as much an open question as the notion of patriotism. So many of our traits as Vermonters depend on defining ourselves. Are we not a deeply schizophrenic people? Do we not believe as much in dissent as in any unanimous ideology of a *patria*, much less patriotism? Do we Vermonters not believe at least as much in extending sanctuary from war and in opposing bloodshed as we do in the patriotic bloodlettings that have punctuated our two hundred years of American history?

From the first days of the Revolution, Vermonters, what few there were and all of them recently arrived, believed in competing strenuously for a homeland. But often, their motives differed from those of citizens of neighboring states. From the opening moments of the Revolutionary War, Vermonters participated in the conquest—and the looting—of British forts: Ticonderoga, Amherst, St. John, Chambly. A few future Vermonters tried and failed, under Ethan Allen, to seize Montreal; others marched off to Quebec with Benedict Arnold and, like Roger Enos, thought better of it and settled close to the Vermont-Canadian frontier, one foot in and one foot out of this new land.[1] Vermonters like thirteen-year-old Pascal DeAngelis fought to defend their shores at the Battle of Valcour Bay in October 1776, buying the precious time that made possible the victory at Trenton hundreds of miles away.[2] Tom Paine spoke for their unsung bravery when he wrote lines first read in the snow the night before that pivotal Christmas attack: "These are the times that try men's souls . . . The summer soldier and the sunshine patriot will, in this hour, shrink from the service of his country, but he who stands it now deserves the love and trust of every man and woman."[3] Vermonters helped to provide the vital rear guard that slowed the British onslaught at Hubbardton in July 1777, and they critically weakened Gen. John Burgoyne's invaders again one month later at Bennington, to preserve this, their new homeland, from domination by the old.[4]

In adopting its first constitution in 1777, the independent state of Vermont embraced the most radical form of government in America, modeled on Benjamin Franklin's and Thomas Paine's Pennsylvania constitution. Based on John Locke's theory of a social contract, which arose from the state of nature that Vermont so clearly exemplified, Vermont's constitution of 1777 echoed the principles proclaimed in the Declaration of Independence, placing all power in the hands of the electorate.[5] But, by the summer of 1780, when Maj. Gen. Benedict Arnold at West Point was put in charge of Maj. Gen. Ethan Allen and Roger Enos and the Vermont militia, there were some Vermonters who were not so sure that they wanted to be part of the United States, even if it did survive, which still was far from certain.[6]

Indeed, by 1786, when Capt. Daniel Shays and other Revolutionary veterans sought sanctuary in Vermont after their taxpayers' rebellion in western Massachusetts was crushed, the United States seemed on the verge of dissolution. It was at this juncture that Ethan Allen wrote to Canadian Gov. Gen. Guy Carleton his possibly treasonous letter on January 12, 1787:

> I belong to this Republic, which is not connected with the United States of America. . . . It appears to me that nature has situated the inhabitants of these territories to be friends and neighbors . . . The animosities and confusions which are taking place in the United States forebodes their dissolution.[7]

The Union, reshaped by the counterrevolutionary Constitutional Convention of 1789, did survive, however. It welcomed Vermont into Congress Hall in Philadelphia in 1791, shortly before the United States Congress approved its Bill of Rights, which Vermonters already enjoyed through their own constitution.

In the early nineteenth century, Vermonters once again exhibited their split political personality as the Napoleonic Wars wracked so much of the world and divided the United States into pro- and anti-French factions. By this time, newspapers were proliferating throughout Vermont, most with strong political points of view. One of the more moderate, the Montpelier *Watchman*, thought war with England "inevitable" by March 1808, and considered President Jefferson's embargo on trade with Europe "unnecessary" and "destructive."[8] Vermont newspaper readers did not get to see official British estimates that their garrisons and civilians in Montreal and Quebec were receiving two-thirds of their beef and grain from northeastern New York and Vermont, but they certainly would not have been surprised by them: smuggling had become big business in Vermont. To its readers, the *Watchman* proclaimed that the embargo was

> a system which was to distress Great Britain, but has only distressed ourselves; which was to starve her subjects, but has actually driven our own citizens to beg for bread; which was to produce disorders and discontent in England, but has only produced them at home; which was only to destroy her revenue, but has actually ruined our own.[9]

More and more letters from readers condemning the embargo appeared in Vermont newspapers by 1811, when only a handful of Vermont papers continued to support the commercial quarantine. Vermonters had already developed a well-defined scepticism toward the federal government's policies.

Anthony Haswell, editor of the *Green Mountain Farmer*, published a travel diary he had kept during a trip around the state in 1811. Haswell started out supporting President Jefferson and the Democratic party's embargo but found that "the bench, the bar, the public seminary and the sacred desk" were largely opposed to the embargo and to war against England, which was being advocated by settlers on other American frontiers. As war loomed, the citizens of Rockingham refused to assist in the enlistment of soldiers. Poultney voted not to pay for them. Bennington protestors broke up a muster. There were widespread rumors that secret committees were being formed to plot secession from the Union.[10]

When the War of 1812 finally broke out, the Federalist governor, Martin Chittenden, dissented and resisted. Governor Chittenden refused to permit Vermont troops to defend the western side of Lake Champlain. His action in 1813 certainly suggested to the British that victory was within reach of its invading army. But in this war, Vermonters were to thwart their own governor and the British. In their own declaration of independence, the officers asserted that they now saw their cause as greater than Vermont's. They refused to come home until they had defended the Union.[11]

Yet, by 1814, when the British attack came down the west shore of Lake Champlain, even as Vermont-built ships helped Commodore McDonough defeat a British fleet at Plattsburgh, more than half of all Vermonters still opposed the war.[12] The British had shrewdly exploited Vermont's exports and anti-war sentiments when they chose to march down the New York side of the lake at least in part to avoid antagonizing Vermonters who, more than any other Americans, seemed to oppose "Mr. Madison's War." The *Green Mountain Farmer* seemed to sum up the majority of Vermonters' view of the War of 1812: "Disasters, defeats, disgrace and ruin and death."[13] All through the four-year embargo and ensuing war, Vermonters, especially those west of the Green Mountains, were caught between their natural trade with British Canada—they supplied timber, beef, grain, and potash to Canada and imported British manufactured goods in return—and their respect for the law. In 1808, for example, at the height of opposition to Jefferson's embargo, Cyrus B. Dean, the lookout on the potash smuggling ship *Black Snake*, was hanged for his part in an armed confrontation at the mouth of the Winooski River with a customs boat, the *Fly*, which left three federalized Rutland militiamen dead. After a sensationally publicized trial, more than ten thousand Vermonters (four times the town's population) trudged up Pearl Street in Burlington to watch Dean hanged. The uproar over his trial and execution helped bring down the Jeffersonian Republicans in Vermont and put a Federalist back into the governor's chair.[14]

During the three decades between the Revolution and the War of 1812, Vermont's population had more than tripled, but in the wake of the second war for American independence, the population declined and Vermont changed rapidly, its forests all but consumed to make potash and make way for wheat cultivation. Topsoil, too, had been depleted by runoff. But the state's natural resources still were far from exhausted. Fast rivers provided power to turn the wheels of mills along the Winooski, the Connecticut, and Otter Creek.

New immigrants came, many of them French-speaking, Roman Catholic refugees, thousands fleeing the failed French insurrection of 1837 in which they fought the British side-by-side with Vermont volunteers answering the Vermont legislature's offer to annex Quebec Province. Their arrival eventually led to nativist, anti-Catholic unrest. But religious controversy had been developing from the earliest days in Vermont, spawned by Congregationalist reaction to Ethan Allen's notorious deism.

From 1830, Vermont was swept by an unparalleled religious revival movement, the Second Great Awakening. Scores of new churches were built as a classless religious revolution rocked the traditional churches. So many itinerant evangelists seared the listeners with fire-and-brimstone sermons at the 42nd parallel running from the Erie Canal to the Atlantic—right through southern Vermont—that the path of the preachers became known as the "Burned Over District." Preachers such as Lyman Beecher and Charles Grandison Finney wrought thousands of spontaneous conversions with their egalitarian gospel. Wealth, birth, and social status would no longer determine salvation. Men and women were their own moral free agents. Sin was avoidable and voluntary. Every man and woman was responsible to reform home, workplace, community.

Vermonters embraced this long-lasting crusade and began to root out evils around them. Two main targets emerged: alcohol-drinking and slavery. As temperance and anti-slavery tracts and sermons poured into the state, Vermont laws as well as mores changed. In 1852, Vermont outlawed the sale of alcoholic beverages and kept prohibition on the books for half a century, long after most other states had repealed it. To be sure, Vermonters with a thirst must have been able to find a drink: there are records of citizens protesting the failure of local authorities to enforce the temperance laws.

At first, all industries but textiles seemed to avoid Vermont, because it was difficult to attract workers who could not have a drink. But recent research shows that mill owners influenced the passage of local laws banning drinking in the mills.[15] Investors who could cut down on lost time, accidents, and injuries had no trouble finding eager workers as immigration from Canada and Ireland surged in the 1840s and 1850s. It was not until 1902, however, that local option was allowed and towns could vote to be "wet" or "dry." Vermonters still remain split on the evils of Demon Rum: five towns—Athens, Baltimore, Holland, Maidstone and Weybridge—still remain dry.

Sermons and sermonizing not only brought about reforms, but spoken words bound Vermont to the Union even as they helped Vermont shape its own flinty identity. Ralph Waldo Emerson was one of those hardy lecturers who traveled widely in Vermont as he brought the ideas of the outside world to the remote green hills and trim white-painted towns of mid-nineteenth-century Vermont in a lyceum movement of which the "We Vermonters" lecture series was a vestige. Emerson understood the importance of reading and reflecting in solitude, and he spread his message from Grafton to Burlington. He had seen the mill cities and slums of midland England, the political mobocracy of Boston and New York:

> Voices which we hear in solitude, grow faint and inaudible as we enter the world. . . . Society everywhere is in conspiracy against every one of its members. The virtue in most request is conformity . . . A foolish consistency is the hobgoblin of little minds, adored by little statesmen.

As North and South railed at one another, Emerson worried about the American love of demagoguery: "Now we are a mob . . . We must go alone . . . I like the silent church before any preaching begins."

Emerson had come to admire Vermonters by the time of the Mexican War. Like his houseboy and protegé, Henry David Thoreau, he worried about "the majority of men" who were living lives of "quiet desperation." Emerson held up the sturdy Vermonter as a model to the world:

> If our young men miscarry in their first enterprises, they lose all heart. If the young merchant fails, men say he is *ruined*. . . . [but] A sturdy lad from New Hampshire or Vermont, who in turn tries all the professions, who *teams* it, farms it, peddles, keeps a school, preaches, edits a newspaper, goes to Congress, buys a township, and so forth, in successive years and always, like a cat, falls on his feet, is worth a hundred of these city dolls.[16]

Sermons, the weekly arrival of abolitionist newspapers from New York, and the passing around of sensational anti-slavery books fanned the hatred of the slave South. Vermonters read a lot: on average ninety percent of all New Englanders could read and write and stayed in school until seventeen, while only thirty percent of Southern whites were literate.[17] Vermonters were among the one million purchasers of the runaway bestseller *Uncle Tom's Cabin*, written by the daughter of a Great Awakening popular preacher in Vermont. Vermonters overwhelmingly saw slavery not only as evil but as the dangerous economic rival of free-soil farmers.

When the inevitable conflict came, Vermonters were the first to demonstrate their patriotic attachment to the Union. Vermont was the first state to offer troops to President Lincoln in 1861. In emergency session, the legislature pledged $500,000 to the cause, but when a member shouted, "Make it a million!" they did. No other state gave that much. Vermont's 315,000 people provided 35,000 soldiers. Five thousand were killed and another five thousand were disabled.

The fact that they often suffered and died horribly did not staunch the flow of volunteers from farm to battlefield. In one day, during the Battle of the Wilderness in northern Virginia, 1,100 Vermonters were shot or bayonetted, many of the wounded burning to death when dried leaves in the woods were ignited by muzzle-flashes and cannon fire. Their renown as fighting patriots spread in October 1864, as Vermonters bore the brunt of a Confederate counterattack up the Shenandoah Valley at a place called Cedar Creek. The Union general, Philip Sheridan, became immortalized in verse for his famous ride to rally his troops. The four hundred Vermonters shot that day are honored in the enormous painting by Julian Scott at the Vermont State House in Montpelier.[18]

But in every war that has touched Vermont and Vermonters, there have been the strong and sometimes overwhelming voices of dissent. Vermont has been a haven for people fleeing war from the time of the Loyalists and Quaker pacifists of the Revolution. Vermont was the first place to allow the return of the Loyalists after the Revolution and to elect them to office. In World War II, emigré Jews fleeing from Nazi persecution came to our green hills to go on working in peace and safety. John Lennon straddled the border anxiously at Derby Line during the Vietnam War, and more than one of the Chicago Seven eventually took up residency in Lyndonville. And in Vermont, that capstone of the anti-war movement, "the Freeze," was born and spread to join the peaceful and no less patriotic forces that have finally ended the Cold War.

As we entered our bicentennial year, the debate over war or peace was far from finished. We have and will continue to be shaped in our identity by that debate, by our belief, not as expressed by our neighbors from New Hampshire that the only way to live is to "live free or die," but, to live and let live. Vermonters, with Jefferson, believe that "the tree of liberty must be refreshed from time to time with the blood of patriots and tyrants."[19]

Like Ethan Allen, Ralph Waldo Emerson, and Thomas Jefferson, Vermont's form of patriotism is cranky, unpredictable, stubbornly independent, and, most of all, self-reliant.

NOTES

1. Willard S. Randall, *Benedict Arnold: Patriot and Traitor* (New York: Morrow, 1990), 212; 176-180.

2. C. M. Snyder, "With Benedict Arnold at Valcour Island: The Diary of Pascal DeAngelis," *Vermont History* 42 (Fall 1974): 195-200.

3. Thomas Paine, "The Crisis," in Henry Steele Commager and Richard B. Morris, *The Spirit of Seventy-Six* (Indianapolis: Bobbs-Merrill, 1958), 505.

4. Col. John A. Williams, *The Battle of Hubbardton: The American Rebels Stem the Tide* (Montpelier: Vermont Division for Historic Preservation, 1988) provides the best account of Revolutionary War fighting in Vermont.

5. Gary J. Aichele, "Making the Vermont Constitution: 1777-1824," in Michael Sherman, ed., *A More Perfect Union* (Montpelier: Vermont Historical Society, 1991), 2-34.

6. Don R. Gerlach, "The British Invasion of 1780 and 'A Character . . . Debased Beyond Description,'" *Bulletin of the Fort Ticonderoga Museum* 14 (1984): 311-321; H. Nicholas Muller, III, "Diplomacy of the Republic: The Haldimand Negotiations," in Frederic F. Van de Water, *The Reluctant Republic: Vermont, 1724-1791* (Taftsville, Vt.: Countryman Press, 1974), vii-x.

7. Quoted in the *New York Times*, 2 December 1990, I:37.

8. *Montpelier Watchman*, 11 March 1808.

9. Quoted in Edward Brynn, "Patterns of Dissent: Vermont Opposition to the War of 1812," *Vermont History* 40 (Winter 1972): 16-17.

10. Brynn, 110-111.

11. Ibid., 113; Paul S. Gillies, "Adjusting to Union: An Assessment of Statehood, 1791-1816," in Michael Sherman, ed., *A More Perfect Union*, 114.

12. Brynn, 115.

13. Ibid., 109.

14. Kate M. Kenny, "The *Black Snake* Affair: Implications for the Present," *Chittenden County Historical Society Bulletin* 22 (1987): 1-4.

15. See, for example, any history of St. Johnsbury.

16. Ralph Waldo Emerson, "Self Reliance," in Brooks Atkinson, ed., *The Selected Writings of Ralph Waldo Emerson* (New York: Modern Library, 1940), 162.

17. James M. McPherson, *Ordeal by Fire: The Civil War and Reconstruction* (New York: McGraw Hill, 1982), 24, table 25.

18. The author is indebted to Howard Coffin for material on Vermonters in the Civil War, which he generously provided in an interview in January 1991.

19. Thomas Jefferson to William S. Smith, 13 November 1787, *Works of Thomas Jefferson* (Washington, 1905) 5:320-1.

Rudyard Kipling, Vermonter

Robert E. Stanfield

*This paper is a fictionalized representation of Rudyard Kipling speaking to a modern Vermont audience about his experiences as a resident of Vermont during the 1890s. Material has been drawn from writings by Kipling and from writings about him. Statements in Kipling's own words appear below in **bold face**, and statements attributed to him are <u>underlined</u>. Other parts of this text were specifically created or adapted for this paper. Kipling materials are used with permission of Doubleday & Co., New York.*

I am pleased to return to Vermont for the first time since my wife and I left in 1896. I have some fond memories of the time I spent here and the people that I met here. The passing of almost a century has begun to ease a little the pain occasioned by some unhappy experiences. Since I was asked to comment on our departure from Vermont, I shall have a few words to say on the matter, but let me begin with some of the great hopes and expectations that Carrie and I had as we began our marriage in 1892.

Our wedding trip took us first to Canada, then to Japan, where my wife's maternal grandfather had once been an advisor on international law to the Emperor. **Back again, then, across the cold North Pacific, through Canada on the heels of the melting snows, and to the outskirts of a little New England town** [Dummerston] **where my wife's paternal grandfather (a Frenchman) had made his home and estate many years before. The country was large-boned, mountainous, wooded, and divided into farms of from fifty to two hundred barren acres. Roads, sketched in dirt, connected white, clap-boarded farmhouses, where the older members of the families made shift to hold down the eating mortgages. The younger folk had gone elsewhere. There were many abandoned houses too; some decaying where they stood; others already reduced to a stone chimney-stack or mere green dimples still held by an undefeated lilac bush.**[1]

This part of the country belongs by laws unknown to the United States, but which obtain all the world over, to the New England story and the ladies

who write it. You feel this in the air as soon as you see the white-painted wooden houses left out in the snow, the austere schoolhouse, and the people—the men of the farms, the women who work as hard as they with, it may be, less enjoyment of life—the other houses, well painted and quaintly roofed, that belong to Judge This, Lawyer That, and Banker Such an one; all powers in the metropolis of six thousand folk over there by the railway station. More acutely still, do you realise the atmosphere when you read in the local paper announcements of "chicken suppers" and "church sociables" to be given by such and such a denomination, sandwiched between paragraphs of genial and friendly interest, showing that the countryside live (and without slaying each other) on terms of terrifying intimacy.[2]

. . . On one small farm was a building known as the Bliss Cottage, generally inhabited by a hired man. . . . Its rent was ten dollars or two pounds a month.

We took it. We furnished it with a simplicity that foreran the hire-purchase system. We bought, second- or third-hand, a huge, hot-air stove which we installed in the cellar. We cut generous holes in our thin floors for its eight-inch tin pipes (why we were not burned in our beds each week of the winter I never can understand) and we were extraordinarily and self-centeredly content.[3]

When winter shut down and sleigh-bells rang all over the white world that tucked us in, we counted ourselves secure. . . . When our lead pipe froze, we would slip on our coon-skin coats and thaw it out with a lighted candle. There was no space in the attic bedroom for a cradle, so we decided that a trunk-tray would be just as good. We envied no one—not even when skunks wandered into our cellar and, knowing the nature of the beasts, we immobilised ourselves till it should please them to depart.

But our neighbours saw no humour in our proceedings. Here was a stranger of an unloved race, currently reported to 'make as much as a hundred dollars out of a ten-cent bottle of ink,' and who had 'pieces in the papers' about him, who had married a 'Balestier girl.' Did not her grandmother still live on the Balestier place, where 'old Balestier' instead of farming had built a large house, and there had dined late in special raiment, and drunk red wines after the custom of the French instead of decent whisky? And behold this Britisher, under pretext of having lost money, had settled his wife down 'right among her own folk' in the Bliss Cottage. It was not seemly on the face of it; so they watched as secretively as the New England or English peasant can, and what toleration they extended to the 'Britisher' was solely for the sake of 'the Balestier girl.'[4]

There is so much, so very much to write, if it were worth while about that queer little town by the railway station, with its life running, to all outward seeming, as smoothly as the hack-coupes on their sleigh mounting, and within disturbed by the hatred and troubles and jealousies that vex the minds of all but the gods.[5]

Not till much later did we realise the terrible things that 'folks thought of your doin's.' From their point of view they were right. Also, they were practical as the following will show.

One day a stranger drove up to the Bliss Cottage. The palaver opened thus:—

'Kiplin', ain't ye?'

That was admitted.

'Write, don't ye?'

That seemed accurate. (Long pause.)

'Thet bein' so, you've got to live to please folk, hain't ye?'

That indeed was the raw truth. He sat rigid in the buggy and went on.

'Thet bein' so, you've got to please to live, I reckon?'

It was true.

'Puttin' it thet way,' he pursued, 'we'll 'low thet, by and by, ye <u>can't</u> please. Sickness—accident—any darn thing. <u>Then</u>—what's liable to happen ye—both of ye?'

I began to see, and he to fumble in his breast pocket.

'Thet's where Life Insurance comes in. Naow, <u>I</u> represent,' etc., etc. It was beautiful salesmanship. The Company was reputable, and I effected my first American Insurance.[6]

Other visitors were not so tactful. Reporters came from papers in Boston, which I presume believed itself to be civilized, and demanded interviews. I told them I had nothing to say. 'If ye hevn't, guess we'll <u>make</u> ye say something.' So they went away and lied copiously, their orders being to 'get the story.' This was new to me at the time; but the Press had not got into its full free stride of later years.

My workroom in the Bliss Cottage was seven feet by eight, and from December to April the snow lay level with its window-sill. It chanced that I had written a tale about Indian Forestry work which included a boy who had been brought up by wolves. In the stillness, and suspense, of the winter of '92 some memory of the Masonic Lions of my childhood's magazine, and a phrase of [Rider] Haggard's *Nada the Lily*, combined with the echo of this tale. After blocking out the main idea in my head, the pen took charge, and I watched it begin to write stories about Mowgli and animals, which later grew into the *Jungle Books*.

Once launched there seemed no particular reason to stop, but I had learned to distinguish between the peremptory motions of my Daemon, and the 'carry-over' or induced electricity, which comes of what you might call mere 'frictional' writing. Two tales, I remember, I threw away and was better pleased with the remainder. More to the point, my Father thought well of the workmanship.

My first child and daughter was born in three foot of snow on the night of December 29th, 1892. Her Mother's birthday being the 31st and mine the 30th of the same month, we congratulated her on her sense of the fitness of things. . . . Her birth brought me into contact with the best friend I made in New England—Dr. [James] Conland.

It seemed that the Bliss Cottage might be getting a little congested, so, in the following spring, the Committee of Ways and Means [Carrie and I] "considered a field and bought it"—as much as ten whole acres—on a rocky hillside looking across a huge valley to Wantastiquet, the wooded mountain across the Connecticut River.

That summer there came out of Quebec Jean Pigeon with nine other *habitants* who put up a wooden shed for their own accommodation in what seemed twenty minutes, and then set to work to build us a house which we called "Naulahka."[*] Ninety feet was the length of it and thirty the width, on a high foundation of solid mortared rocks which gave us an airy and a skunk-proof basement. The rest was wood, shingled, roof and sides, with dull green hand-split shingles, and the windows were lavish and wide. . . . Those were opulent days, when timber was nothing regarded, the best of cabinet work could be had for little money.[7]

Horses were an integral part of our lives, for the Bliss Cottage was three miles from the little town, and half a mile from the house in building. Our permanent servitor was a big, philosophical black called Marcus Aurelius, who waited in the buggy as cars wait to-day, and when weary of standing up would carefully lie down and go to sleep between his shafts. After we had finished with him, we tied his reins short and sent him in charge of the buggy alone down the road to his stable-door, where he resumed his slumbers till someone came to undress him and put him to bed. There was a small mob of other horses about the landscape, including a meek old stallion with a permanently lame leg, who passed the evening of his days in a horse-power machine which cut wood for us.

I tried to give something of the fun and flavour of those days in a story called "A Walking Delegate" where all the characters are from horse-life.[8]

It would be hard to exaggerate the loneliness and sterility of life on the farms. The land was denuding itself of its accustomed inhabitants, and their places had not yet been taken by the wreckage of Eastern Europe or the wealthy city folk who later bought "pleasure farms." What might have become characters, powers and attributes perverted themselves in that desolation as cankered trees throw out branches akimbo, and strange faiths and cruelties, born of solitude to the edge of insanity, flourished like lichen on sick bark.[9]

In the little town where we shopped there was another atmosphere. Vermont was by tradition a 'Dry' State. For that reason, one found in almost every office the water-bottle and thick tooth-glass displayed openly, and in discreet cupboards or drawers the whisky bottle. Business was conducted and concluded with gulps of raw spirit, followed by a pledget of ice-cold water.

---

[*] Editors' note: The spelling of "Naulahka," in reference to both the name of a Kipling book and to his house, often causes confusion. The book, *The Naulahka, A Novel of East and West*, is spelled differently than Naulakha, the name of the house. See, for example, Hilton Brown, *Rudyard Kipling* (New York, Harper Brothers, 1945), 69. Charles E. Carrington's *Life of Rudyard Kipling* offers the same clarification and tells us "Naulakha, as the word should properly be spelt, was the Hindu word for nine 'lakhs' of rupees, and the name was applied in India to a fabulous jewel" (New York: Doubleday & Co., 1955), 140.

"Naulakha," Kipling's home in Dummerston. Photo by Lewis R. Brown, Brattleboro (1954). Courtesy of Vermont Historical Society, Montpelier, Vt. (F-TO-Dummerston). See editors' note regarding the spelling of "Naulakha."

Then, both parties chewed cloves, but whether to defeat the Law, which no one ever regarded, or to deceive their women-folk of whom they went in great fear . . . I do not know.

But a promising scheme for a Country Club had to be abandoned because many men who would by right belong to it could not be trusted with a full whisky bottle. On the farms, of course, men drank cider, of various strengths, and sometimes achieved almost maniacal forms of drunkenness. The whole business seemed to me as unwholesomely furtive and false as many aspects of American life at that time.

Administratively, there was unlimited and meticulous legality, with a multiplication of semi-judicial offices and titles; but of law-abidingness, or of any conception of what that implied, not a trace. Very little in business, transportation, or distribution, that I had to deal with, was sure, punctual, accurate, or organised.[10]

The political background of the land was monotonous. When the people looked, which was seldom, outside their own borders, England was still the dark and dreadful enemy to be feared and guarded against. The Irish, whose other creed is Hate; the history books in the Schools; the Orators; the eminent Senators; and above all the Press; saw to that.[11]

But how thoroughly the doctrine was exploited I did not realise till we visited Washington in '96, where I met Theodore Roosevelt, then Under Secretary . . . to the U.S. Navy. I liked him from the first and largely believed in him. He would come to our hotel, and thank God in a loud voice that he had not one drop of British blood in him.[12]

Meantime, our lives went on at the Bliss Cottage and, so soon as it was built, at Naulakha.[13]

I once indiscretely said to a Vermont farmer after his afternoon milking was done: "I envy you. Your day's work is finished. You can go in and wash up and sit right down at the table for supper. I've got to go home and put on evening clothes before I can dine."[14]

I had a yearning about me to tell tales of extended impropriety—not sexual or within hailing distance of it—but hard-bottomed unseemly yarns. I worked for a while on the lamentable history of a big fat Indian administrator who was, in the course of duty, shot in his ample back-side by a poisoned arrow, and his devoted subordinate sucked the wound to the destruction of his credit as an independent man for the rest of his days. One can't be serious always.[15]

Now even in the Bliss Cottage I had a vague notion of an Irish boy, born in India and mixed up with native life. I went as far as to make him the son of a private in an Irish Battalion, and christened him "Kim of the Rishti"—short, that is for Irish. This done, I felt like Mr. Micawber that I had as good as paid that I.O.U. on the future, and went after other things for some years.[16]

We went once or twice to Gloucester, Mass., on a summer visit, when I attended the annual Memorial Service to the men drowned or lost in the cod-fishing schooners fleet. Gloucester was then the metropolis of that industry.

Now Dr. Conland had served in that fleet when he was young. One thing leading to another, as happens in this world, I embarked on a little book which was called *Captains Courageous*. My part was the writing; his the details. This book took us (he rejoicing to escape from the dread respectability of our little town) to the shore-front, and the old T-wharf of Boston Harbour, and to queer meals in sailors' eating houses, where he renewed his youth among ex-shipmates or their kin.... And Conland took large cod and the appropriate knives with which they are prepared for the hold, and demonstrated anatomically and surgically so that I could make no mistake about treating them in print. Old tales, too, he dug up, and the lists of dead and gone schooners whom he had loved, and I revelled in profligate abundance of detail—not necessarily for publication but for the joy of it. And he sent me—may he be forgiven!—out on a pollock-fisher, which is ten times fouler than any cod-schooner, and I was immortally sick, even though they tried to revive me with a fragment of unfresh pollock.

... Yet the book was not all reporterage. I wanted to see if I could catch and hold something of a rather beautiful localised American atmosphere that was already beginning to fade. Thanks to Conland I came near to this.[17]

And so, in this unreal life, indoors and out, four years passed, and a good deal of verse and prose saw the light. Better than all, I had known a corner of the United States as a householder, which is the only way of getting at a country. Tourists may carry away impressions, but it is the seasonal detail of small things and doings (such as putting up fly-screens and stove-pipes, buying yeast-cakes and being lectured by your neighbours) that bite in the lines of mental pictures. They were an interesting folk, but behind their desperate activities lay always, it seemed to me, immense and unacknowledged boredom—the deadweight of material things passionately worked up into Gods, that only bored their worshippers more and worse and longer.... So far as I was concerned, I felt the atmosphere was to some extent hostile. The idea seemed to be that I was "making money" out of America—witness the new house and the horses—and was not sufficiently grateful for my privileges. My visits to England and the talk there persuaded me that the English scene might be shifting to some new developments, which would be worth watching. ... [Carrie and I] came to the conclusion that Naulakha, desirable as it was, meant only 'a house' and not '<u>The</u> House' of our dreams. So we loosed hold and, with another small daughter, born in the early spring snows and beautifully tanned in a sumptuous upper verandah, we took ship for England, after clearing up all our accounts.[18]

Mr. Frederic Van de Water has said that what I have just told you is an "odd patchwork" that "leaps completely over one of the most violent passages" in my life.[19] Let me break silence after so many years and tell you of events that occurred at the time we decided to leave Vermont.

May 1896 began happily enough. The students of Yale University had established a Kipling Club, and on May 1 they invited me to attend their first banquet at Heublin's Cafe in New Haven. I had to decline their invitation, but I did send them a poem to be read at the dinner:

> **Attend ye lasses av swate Parnasses**
> **An' wipe my burnin' tears away**
> **For I'm declinin' a chanst o' dinin'**
> **Wid the bhoys of Yale on the fourteenth May.**   and so on[20]

Between their invitation to me on May 1 and the dinner on May 14, there occurred some circumstances that robbed me of the very time for writing that I had wanted to preserve. It began with an encounter that I had on the Pine Hill road in Dummerston on May 6th.[21] Mr. Frederic Van de Water, in a book that he called *Rudyard Kipling's Vermont Feud*, claims[22] that this incident was what I had in mind when I told you that **"I felt the atmosphere was to some extent hostile."**[23]

Since I myself have never written of the matter, I shall rely on the reports of the press at the time. You can judge the public mood from this report on the front page of your very own *Burlington Daily Free Press* on Monday, May 11, 1896:

> BRATTLEBORO, Vt. May 10 - Beatty Balestier, brother-in-law of Rudyard Kipling, the dollar a word man, and author of those creepy stories of Indian life, has threatened Kipling with death, and thereby placed Rudyard in fear of such "Americanism." Balestier is a jovial man, open hearted, likes a good time, and generally gets it, much to his sister's (Mrs. Kipling) displeasure.
> Recently Balestier got into financial difficulties, and Kipling, with brotherly kindness, offered to straighten out his affairs if he would look to the better things of life. This proposal galled Balestier's pride and high words were indulged in, open hatred being the outcome. This found vent in a quarrel a short time ago. It is customary for Kipling to come to Brattleboro quite often to do trading, he making his appearance in stylish "rigouts" with a "poker" coachman. Rudyard sees the light in golf pants, Tuxedo coat, a farmer's shirt without a neck cloth, striped stockings, and congress shoes.
> While on the road to town the other day he met Balestier. Dark blue words weighed the air and Kipling claims that Balestier threatened his life. To satisfy the ends of justice, Balestier was brought before Judge Newton yesterday afternoon [that would be Saturday, May 9]. Kipling was present, but was fearful of newspapermen and notoriety. A short hearing was held with the result that Balestier was held in $300 bail for hearing Tuesday morning.[24]

You see now that the press had finally **got into its full free stride of later years.** I regret having to rely on the errors, distortions, and insults of these newspaper reports, but they are closer to the truth than some books and articles that have relied on interviews and conversations with my assailant.

The court hearing of Tuesday, May 12, was mistakenly reported as a trial by the Burlington and Rutland papers in front-page articles on Wednesday. I was the only witness called to testify, and I was questioned by the attorneys for nearly five hours. The hearing ended at five o'clock in the evening, with Justice Newton imposing a bail of $400 to assure the defendant's appearance before the grand jury in September, and a peace bond of $400 as well. The *New York Times* of the same date carried on its first page its own report of the hearing, again not without significant error. It misspelled the name of my wife's family, and its description of the incident on the road placed me in a carriage and my assailant on a bicycle.

Notwithstanding the shortcomings that I find in these press reports, this is what those newspapers relate that I said in court:

I had been on my way to the village on my bicycle the preceding Wednesday, when I was accosted. My attacker said: "See here, I want to speak with you."[25] He was wild and ungovernable, wishing me to retract certain stories he claimed I had circulated.[26] I replied: "If you have anything to say, say it to my counsel." Thereupon, he assailed me with a flood of profanity and abuse, threatening to blow my brains out, and calling me all manner of vile names.[27] He said: "This is no case for lawyers. If you don't retract, I'll blow your soul out of you." He then called me a liar, thief, cheat, and coward.[28]

The whole incident occupied but three or four minutes, after which I continued on my way to town. I was struck by his excited appearance and was in fear of my life.[29] I thought him insane, and that he would commit murder under similar circumstances. I confess, however, that I knew him to be dangerous only when under the influence of liquour.[30]

I had settled in Brattleboro mainly to help this man in fulfillment of a promise that I made to his brother Wolcott. The good feeling between him and myself had ceased about a year earlier. I had furnished work for him and helped him to money which he paid months afterwards and at such times and in about such manner as he pleased. I denied circulating any stories derogatory to him, although some of the townspeople had asked me if I were not supporting him or something of the kind, but this I told them I had not done, within a year past.

I profoundly regretted that these circumstances had compelled the course that I had pursued. This was the first time I ever had my life threatened and I did not know just what was etiquette under the circumstances. I did not feel secure in Vermont and the only thing for me to do to protect my family and myself, so far as I could see was to leave the place and possibly the country.[31]

Indeed, Carrie, the children, and I did leave the town, the state, and the country in late August, returning to England to live. There was a brief time some three years later when I considered returning to Vermont, but it was quite evident that my brother-in-law would not let the matter rest.[32]

That is all that I want to say about the matter now. It was a painful occasion because it made a public event out of a family quarrel. I make this final appeal to you:

> If I have given you delight
>   By aught that I have done,
> Let me lie quiet in that night,
>   Which shall be yours anon:
>
> And for the little, little span
>   The dead are borne in mind,
> Seek not to question other than
>   The books I leave behind.[33]

NOTES

1. Rudyard Kipling, *Something of Myself—For My Friends Known and Unknown* (Garden City, N.Y.: Doubleday, Doran, 1937), 118-119.

2. Rudyard Kipling, *Letters of Travel: 1892-1913* (Garden City, N.Y.: Doubleday, Page & Co., 1920), 7-8.

3. Kipling, *Something of Myself*, 119.

4. Ibid., 120-121.

5. Kipling, *Letters of Travel*, 15.

6. Kipling, *Something of Myself*, 121-122.

7. Ibid., 122-125.

8. Ibid., 125-126.

9. Ibid., 127.

10. Ibid., 128-129.

11. Ibid., 130.

12. Ibid., 131.

13. Ibid., 134.

14. Frederic F. Van de Water, *Rudyard Kipling's Vermont Feud* (Rutland, Vt.: Academy Books, 1981; originally published New York: Reynal and Hitchcock, 1937), 40.

15. 2nd Earl of Birkenhead, Frederick Winston Furneaux Smith, *Rudyard Kipling* (New York: Random House, 1978), 154.

16. Kipling, *Something of Myself*, 147-148.

17. Ibid., 138-140.

18. Ibid., 141-142.

19. Van de Water, 17.

20. Birkenhead, 163.

21. Van de Water, 18.

22. Ibid., 17.

23. Kipling, *Something of Myself*, 142.

24. *Burlington Daily Free Press*, 11 May 1896, 1:3.

25. *Burlington Daily Free Press*, 13 May 1896, 1:8; *Rutland Daily Herald*, 13 May 1896, 1:1.

26. *The New York Times*, 13 May 1896, 1:2.

27. *Burlington Daily Free Press*, 13 May 1896, 1:8.

28. *The New York Times*, 13 May 1896, 1:2.

29. *Burlington Daily Free Press*, 13 May 1896, 1:8.

30. *The New York Times*, 13 May 1896, 1:8.

31. *Burlington Daily Free Press*, 13 May 1896, 1:8.

32. Van de Water, 115-117.

33. Rudyard Kipling, *Collected Verse: Definitive Edition* (New York: Doubleday Anchor, 1989), 836.

Dorothy Canfield Fisher's

Vermont Tradition

Ida H. Washington

 y the time she wrote *Vermont Tradition*, Dorothy Canfield Fisher was well-known, not only in Vermont but nationally and internationally as well, as the author of best-selling novels, a popular children's book, non-fiction works on education and social problems, and literally hundreds of articles and short stories. She wrote her novels and short stories as Dorothy Canfield, and her non-fiction (on which her husband John Fisher sometimes collaborated) under her married name, Dorothy Canfield Fisher. Her first novel, *Gunhild*, was published in 1907. Even before that numerous short stories had appeared in popular magazines, so many in fact that for a while some of them appeared under a pseudonym, "Stanley Crenshawe," so that there could be two stories by the same author in the same issue. Her last major work, *Vermont Tradition*, was published in 1953, when she was seventy-four years old.

Like many of the most effective spokesmen for Vermont, from Ethan Allen to Robert Frost, Dorothy Canfield Fisher was a Vermonter by choice, not by birth. She was born February 17, 1879, in the university town of Lawrence, Kansas, where her father was a professor at the state university.

Although she was not a Vermont native, her family on both sides was very much a Vermont family, and contained within it the love-hate dichotomy that divides the people who "come from Vermont." Her educator father, James Hulme Canfield, was openly proud of his Vermont heritage and fond of saying that he "had lived in Vermont since 1763,"[1] the date when his ancestors had traveled north from Connecticut to settle in the southwestern Vermont town of Arlington. In his Green Mountain background he found values that formed a strong basis for his own life. At the other end of the family table sat Flavia Camp Canfield, Dorothy's mother, an artist. Flavia's mother was a Rutland girl, her father an adventurer who died in California prospecting for gold. Flavia told her daughter that Vermont imposed a heavy burden of old-fashioned restrictions on personal freedom. She was glad to escape from Vermont.

With an older brother, Jim, Dorothy grew up in the midst of controversy about Vermont. As a child, she cut her intellectual teeth on questions that are just as relevant today. They continued with her and appear again and again in articles, short stories, and longer works of fiction and non-fiction throughout a lifetime of writing.

Practical experience supplemented the theoretical family discussions of what it means to be a Vermonter, for from early childhood Dorothy was sent back east to spend summer vacations with her father's elderly relatives in Arlington. There she roamed the Vermont hills on a part-Morgan horse her uncle gave her, visited with neighbors, and listened eagerly to the talk of the old people around her.

The pattern of winter in Kansas and summer in Vermont was broken when, at the age of eleven, Dorothy spent a winter in Paris, where her mother went to study art. Dorothy was placed in a Catholic girls' school, a sink-or-swim experience for her, since she knew no French. Fortunately it turned out that she had exceptional language ability; before long she had made friends among her classmates and became her mother's interpreter in the foreign culture. When Dorothy and her mother returned to the United States, the Canfields moved to Lincoln, where Professor Canfield had become chancellor of the University of Nebraska. There Dorothy attended high school and became a good friend of Willa Cather, who was an undergraduate at the university. After four years, James Canfield moved on to become president of Ohio State University in Columbus, and Dorothy completed her undergraduate studies there. The year of her graduation, her father moved again, this time to New York to be Librarian of Columbia University, where Dorothy began graduate studies, which led to a Ph.D. degree in French in 1904.

Through all these years of moving about, of winters in Kansas, Nebraska, Ohio, and Europe, Dorothy Canfield kept returning to Vermont in the summer. Then, when Dorothy and John Fisher were married in New York, in 1907, they decided to settle in Vermont, a move made possible by a wedding gift of one of the ancestral Canfield properties in Arlington. Vermont continued to be their home from that time until Dorothy's death in 1958, and John's a year later.

Their New York friends were horrified by the Fishers' move. They said what so many of us have heard so often: "What will you do up there—so far from people?" In the introduction to her first collection of short stories, *Hillsboro People*, Dorothy gave them her answer: that it is only in the small community that you really get to know people. She wrote:

> City dwellers make money, make reputations (good and bad), make museums and subways, make charitable institutions, make with a hysteric rapidity, like excited spiders, more and yet more complications in the mazy labyrinths of their lives, but they never make each others' acquaintances . . . and that is all that is worth doing in the world.[2]

Dorothy wrote these words in 1915. It was twenty-three years later, near the close of her long and distinguished literary career, that Roger Scaife, vice president of the publishing firm of Little, Brown and Company, suggested that she write a book about Vermont in which, as he put it, she should "convey her love for the State."[3] He had in mind what we sometimes call a "coffee table book," which would combine the words of a well-known author with pictures by a prominent artist. He arranged for the artist N. C. Wyeth to do the illustrations. Though Dorothy was very much interested, and even signed a contract for the book, in 1938 she was very busy. Her last novel, *Seasoned Timber*, was nearing completion, and she was still a member of the Book-of-the-Month Club board, a position that required extensive reading of new book manuscripts. The book about Vermont was shoved aside. Then came World War II, with years of anxiety about French friends, and the tragic death of Dorothy's only son, who was killed in action in the spring of 1945.

In December 1946, when Dorothy expressed interest in working on the Vermont book again, she found the publisher still patiently waiting—almost nine years after she had signed a contract to write it. N. C. Wyeth had died in 1945, and the illustrator was now to be Norman Rockwell, for a while a neighbor of the Fishers in Arlington. The editor as well had changed by the time Dorothy really started work on the book in 1950, the year she resigned from the Book-of-the-Month Club board. She wrote to her new editor, Ned Bradford, "I find before me more free time than for the last quarter of a century, for writing. And the Vermont book will be one of the first things I take up."[4]

It was now twelve years since Roger Scaife had first approached Dorothy to write the book. Then she had exclaimed, "If only I were ten years younger!"[5] A year later, she wrote to an historian in January 1951, "I am beginning work on a book to be called 'Vermont Tradition.'"[6] In March of that year she began to realize what an enormous problem she was grappling with and wrote, "I really want the book to be read, and to make a really readable book out of historical material takes plenty of heart's blood from the author."[7] Dorothy was now seventy-two years old. For the next two years she worked steadily, putting into the project all her waning strength. She called on her friend, the poet and political activist Sarah Cleghorn, for help in editing the manuscript. Her husband John made suggestions, which she gratefully acknowledged. Others took on the onerous tasks of searching out detailed historical information. In February 1953 the bulky manuscript was finally delivered to the publisher.

With the book went a letter to Ned Bradford, in which Dorothy exclaimed:

> What an absorbing piece of work this has been! I've worn myself out, physically, with the intent focussing on it of all my faculties for so long; the financial cost has been rather ruinous, as I have had to pay for much more research, historical and economic, than I had dreamed of; and as for the never-ending cost of typing a long book, the pages of which have been

revised as many times as this book—the less said the better. And yet—I wish I could reach Mr. Scaife and thank him for pushing me into this by main force and persistence. I don't regret all this expenditure of time, money and vitality.[8]

Vermont Tradition has the subtitle *The Biography of an Outlook on Life*. It is about history, but it is not a history book in the usual sense of that term. In the introduction, Dorothy describes the difference between her book and other historical accounts, saying:

A biographer, about to write a man's life, looks intently at the record of external events of that life, asking himself, 'How did those facts influence what the man became and did?' That's the way I hope to look at Vermont history. I am setting myself to write the biography of a community. Not its history, but the influence of that history, through the ups and downs of nearly two centuries, on the development of a community's personality.[9]

Thus she starts *Vermont Tradition* from the premise that the mature character of a community, like that of a person, is the result of a series of formative experiences. "The only way to understand people is to know them," she writes. "And to know them you need to live with them. So let's start back at the beginning, and share the lives of the men and women who have made Vermont what it is."[10]

It is Dorothy Canfield the novelist who takes over from Dorothy Canfield Fisher the historian to bring her account to life and take us into the day-to-day experience of our Vermont ancestors. To collect historical information about the early years of the state of Vermont and its subsequent development, Dorothy uses scholarly sources. But when she has digested this material and has made from it an outline for her story, she does not recite a series of facts within a framework of trends in the usual manner of history books. Instead she clothes her facts in stories about people and uses historical incidents to develop regional traits of character in the same way her novels use childhood incident to create adult personality.

Through her novelist's eye we accompany an early settler who comes north alone to build a cabin, and then shares it with an Indian family while he spends the winter trapping for furs and waiting for his wife and children to join him in the spring. We delight in the symbolism of interracial harmony, as the Indian baby toddles back and forth in the warm cabin over the line dividing the possessions of white man and red.

We make the journey north again with later settlers from Connecticut and Massachusetts, among them Dorothy's own great-great-grandmother, who insisted on pushing on until they came to a stream of soft water in which to wash her fine homespun linens, getting down from her horse with a piece of soap and a handkerchief to test every brook they crossed. We smile with understanding at the optimism of young couples setting out from crowded home conditions to found homesteads of their own, disregarding hardships in the exhilaration of independence. Dorothy reminds us repeatedly that the first settlers of Vermont were not very religious or straitlaced, but fun-loving young people who enjoyed living and rejoiced in coping with the problems and challenges of the wilderness.

They were the raw material out of which Vermont was to be formed: vigorous settlers, proud to be creating homes of their own. They set out from southern New England towns with the blessings of family and friends left behind, and in the years that followed they generally kept in friendly contact across the miles. Dorothy tells us they were not penniless refugees nor political exiles, but simply young families seeking their own identity, as young families continue to do today.

It was what happened to these optimistic settlers after they reached Vermont that changed and shaped them into a uniquely different group and made them what Vermonters are today. The book *Vermont Tradition* calls attention to the two characteristics Dorothy Canfield Fisher feels are the most important elements in the Vermont character. The first is a belief that every person has a right to live his own life in his own way, with only the most elemental requirement of cooperation with the community, and its corollary, a respect for individual human beings based on qualities of character independent of wealth, titles, or other external matters. The second is an ability to persist and endure in basic convictions in the face of personal problems and economic and social changes as sudden and unpredictable as the Vermont weather. The historical events that played the greatest role in developing these traits and molding the early settlers and their descendants into what they are in our times came early, in the pre-1791 struggle to achieve a recognized identity as a state and the alternating prosperity and poverty of the first half of the 1800s. The Civil War and its aftermath put these traits to a fiery test of strength, from which Vermonters emerged into the challenges of the twentieth century.

What did the dispute between Vermont and New York really mean for the families settling into homes of their own throughout the area we now call Vermont? To find the answer, Dorothy went back to the historical records. These turned out to be a singularly amorphous mass of documentary detail. As Dorothy struggled through them, she searched with her novelist's eye for signs of living, breathing human experience. In her own words:

> I set myself to see what those learned words meant in human lives, to translate, as best I could, into straightforward, man-to-man meanings, each of the cautiously qualified statements of scholars, the "provided thats" of accurate lawyer language. The effort was worthwhile. From those legal words (which I have been obliged to look up in the dictionary, one by one), from those literal citations quoted by historians, from official reports made by governors and lieutenant governors to eighteenth-century London, there rose before my eyes a vivid picture of human beings.[11]

To transmit that picture to her readers, she turned to fiction, creating the story of a western Connecticut boy out hunting squirrels, who wanders across the border into New York State and visits with tenant farmers there. Then, as if her scholar's conscience bothers her, she defends her story, saying:

> You don't believe a word of what you have just been reading, do you? It does sound incredible, as though a fiction-writer, temporarily acting as historian, had slid off from the dry, papery crackle of documents, into the never-never land of imagination. Nevertheless, every single detail of that conversation is backed by some statement of that period, written or printed, some memoir, letter, deed, diary, official report, will or lease.[12]

In an appendix at the end of the book, she includes a summary of the facts on which her fictional account is based.

What did the Connecticut boy see in New York? He saw farmers who were the victims of a class system, denied a chance to move out of circumstances as primitive as those endured by medieval European serfs, totally dependent on the whim of a powerful landlord and his friends. Illiteracy was general, for there were no public schools for tenant farmers. There was no recourse from unfair treatment or oppressive renting conditions, for the courts were controlled by the oppressors. Self-esteem was low among the tenant farmers of the Hudson Valley, for they had no voice at all in their own affairs. It was no wonder that the settlers who came to Vermont from western Connecticut and Massachusetts vigorously rejected all attempts by New York landowners to lay claim to the property they held under New Hampshire grants. Only on the eastern edge of Vermont, settled by southern New Englanders who lived far from the New York border, was there any acquiescence to New York jurisdiction over Vermont lands.

It was not the isolated and occasional conflicts with New York authorities, however, that Dorothy saw as the most important building blocks in Vermont character, but instead the long years, a full twenty of them, during which there was no certainty that the New York landowners would not appear with the full force of the law behind them to seize properties and evict landholders. It was the relentless fear that improvements to land, additions to houses, new mills on the streams would then serve not to improve the lot of the farmers and builders, but to enrich the already wealthy estate owners, that toughened the spirit of resistance in Vermont. In the light of such uncertainty, could a thoughtful, prudent, conscientious father of a family take the risk of adding the room much needed by his growing family, setting up a mill on his stream to saw the boards, cutting the trees and clearing the land for his raw materials?

Dorothy reminds us that these young settlers "lived all their adult lives in what psychologists tell us is harder on human nerves than actual and immediate physical danger—in suspense."[13] Living a whole generation long in uncertainty, yet going ahead courageously, clearing, milling, and building as though the future were assured, is the experience that she feels made the difference for the future.[14]

The force that motivated these ordinary men and women was not, Dorothy points out, primarily the desire for wealth, but a matter of principle. More specifically, the conflict was between New York and New England principles, between the idea that one class of people deserves to control another and the belief that all men should have a voice in their own affairs. As Ethan Allen put it colorfully for his fellow citizens, the Vermonters were ready "to eat mouse-meat" before they would become vassals of the wealthy New Yorkers.[15]

If the first formative problems for Vermonters were those of human dignity, the next were economic. The small independent farm was only partially self-sufficient. In an increasingly cash-oriented society, money was needed for everything from shoe buckles to stoves and implements. To supply that need, there had to be a cash crop. The first generally successful cash crop in Vermont was potash, or lye, an essential element in the early manufacture of soap. It was produced in amazing quantities in Vermont, as settlers cut and burned trees and made lye from the ashes. In 1791, a thousand tons left Vermont, most of it going to England to be used in the manufacture of wool. To the settlers the supply of trees appeared endless, and thus they looked forward to a steady and inexhaustible source of money. But with the perversity that fate visits on men's plans, the market for potash dried up and vanished completely in the first third of the nineteenth century, when a soap-making process was discovered that used cheap, readily available deposits of salts.

It was just about the time when the market for potash collapsed that Merino sheep were imported into Vermont. Again, some Vermonters enjoyed great prosperity, followed after a few years by sudden loss, when the great sheep-raising areas of the west were opened up. As you travel through rural Addison County today, you will pass many large brick houses, some with white columns along the front and fanlights over the front doors, testimony to the prosperity of nineteenth-century Vermont sheep raisers.

What happened to Vermonters in this quick alternation of prosperity and poverty? How did those who had become wealthy endure when they were suddenly as poor or poorer than their neighbors? These were questions Dorothy wanted to answer. She knew the disastrous social consequences of sudden loss of employment and income in other parts of the country; loss of friends, suddenly terminated courtships, mental anguish, and even suicide. Was it the same or different in Vermont? She found the most satisfactory answer in talking to her old family physician, Dr. Russell, whose father and grandfather had been sheep farmers. In her words:

"How did your older generation stand the big comedown when the bottom dropped out of the market?" I asked. The doctor answered equably, "Well, I never heard they took it as a comedown. They hadn't ever set up to be better than their neighbors just because they made money out of sheep."[16]

Dorothy fills out her picture of the Vermont tradition by generalizing:

Those men and women of Vermont were not by nature more unworldly than anybody else. If they did not suffer anguish over the loss of fortune, if the personalities of their sons and daughters were not warped by that loss, was it because according to their tradition—the Vermont tradition—an impressive inventory of capital (pleasant and reassuring though it doubtless was) did not raise its possessors in any marked, publicly acknowledged degree above those less wealthy? It could not establish them in a conspicuously superior class in a society so democratic—or, for people who see it that way, so boorishly crude and primitive—that no fixed social hierarchy exists. Consequently to them the loss of money meant no more than the loss of the material objects it might have brought, not the loss of pride or   position or gratified vanity.[17]

Having to adjust to the violent economic fluctuations of the early nineteenth century did something to Vermont character, just as forced adjustment has always changed and shaped personality. One of the basic secondary traits of Vermonters, doubtless reinforced by those years of boom and bust, is thrift, a plain, drab, unromantic quality, but one that provides insulation against economic disaster—and also enables Vermonters to give material backing to their convictions. These convictions were sorely tested in the Civil War.

Historians can find many causes for the Civil War, but for the plain farmers of Vermont, there was only one important cause—to free the slaves. Every Vermonter knows that the Vermont constitution was the first to include a prohibition of adult slavery, and for years the "underground railway" path of escape for runaway slaves bound for Canada went north through Vermont valleys. There was no question of where Vermont sympathies lay.

It is also a matter of historical record that the emergency session of the Vermont legislature voted on April 24, 1861, a sum in support of the war that was 110 percent of the largest tax amount ever raised in the state, an enormous amount made possible only by the habit of thrift of its citizens, who could bring out from savings accounts, sugar bowls, and packets under mattresses the money required to fight for the basic human freedoms they believed in.

The monetary costs of the Civil War were heavy, but the costs in human life were much greater. Of every two Vermonters of military age, one served in the Union army. In proportion to its population the number of Vermont soldiers killed in battle was second only to the casualties of New Hampshire.

When the war ended the future looked bleak. Many young men had been lost in battle. Others had packed up and moved west. Farms were abandoned, or bought by immigrants who had different languages and customs. Again people drew on inner resources to adapt to change, and again those who remained in the state held on and waited for what the future would bring.

As Dorothy wrote, "A good deal of what older Vermonters who survived the Civil War foresaw in dismay did, factually, come to pass. But it did not mean what they assumed it would mean."[18] The prophets of doom foresaw ruin from the remaining financial burdens of the conflict, but fourteen years after the end of the war every penny of war debt had been paid. Vermonters were not wealthy, but they had self-respect that no wealth could buy.

It was feared that emigration would drain Vermont of its lifeblood. Many young people did indeed pack up and go away from Vermont to other places to find their own way, even as their ancestors had moved from southern New England north. But with the Vermont tradition of freedom for individuals to act, to use the folk phrase, "as they felt to," such migration could go on with less stress on all sides than in some societies, and with improvements in transportation, distance no longer meant total separation. The foreign immigrants, whose strange languages and ways seemed so threatening to the older people, had children who attended the free public schools, another benefit of the Vermont tradition, and soon they were indistinguishable from other young Vermonters.

Dorothy winds up her long account of the development of the Vermont tradition with biographical sketches of several Vermonters, who seem to her to embody the spirit of Vermont in their various fields. These are Justin Morrill, Warren Austin, John Dewey, and Robert Frost, contributors, respectively, to public education, international peace, educational philosophy, and literature. Among Vermont's human resources Dorothy finds, however, "no famous painter, or sculptor, or actor, no multimillionaire, no mighty captain of industry, no glamorous beauty, no master of the abstract like Einstein, no adept manipulator of national politics, no famous organizer of the armies of wage-earners." As she says, "Peaches and pomegranates do not, you see, grow on apple trees, but apples do."[19]

NOTES

1. Ida H. Washington, *Dorothy Canfield Fisher, A Biography* (Shelburne, Vt.: New England Press, 1982), 3.

2. Dorothy Canfield, *Hillsboro People* (New York: Henry Holt and Company, 1915), 6.

3. Letter of June 23, 1938. Special Collections, Bailey/Howe Library, University of Vermont.

4. Letter of February 3, 1950. Special Collections, UVM.

5. Letter of June 23, 1938. Special Collections, UVM.

6. Letter to Dr. Irving Mark, January 8, 1951. Special Collections, UVM.

7. Letter to Ned Bradford, March 9, 1951. Special Collections, UVM.

8. Letter of February 19, 1953. Special Collections, UVM.

9. Dorothy Canfield Fisher, *Vermont Tradition* (Boston: Little, Brown and Company, 1953), 6.

10. Ibid., 13.

11. Ibid., 57.

12. Ibid., 70.

13. Ibid., 121.

14. Ibid., 121.

15. Ibid., 127.

16. Ibid., 206-207.

17. Ibid., 207.

18. Ibid., 251.

19. Ibid., 392.

Private Lives:

Vermonters at Work and at Home

Connell B. Gallagher

uch has been written about Vermont and the stark, independent, self-reliant figures who have peopled its landscape. Vermonters enjoy a reputation for hardiness, perhaps because the state is small, sparsely populated and physically isolated, and because the climate is harsh. Vermont clung to its agricultural roots even as America became more urban and industrialized after the Civil War, and it still retains many traditional rural values. The 1990 census confirmed that Vermont is the second most rural state in the nation, next to Idaho.

Ethan Allen, Calvin Coolidge, Robert Frost, George Aiken, Dorothy Canfield Fisher, and even Robert Stafford, the quintessential Vermonter out-of-place among the big spenders and glitz of Washington, D.C., come to mind as typical Vermonters. These were leaders who trace their roots to the portraits penned by Norman Rockwell in those famous *Saturday Evening Post* covers of the nineteen-twenties, thirties, forties and fifties. Yet history shows that these Vermonters and others were not really so far out-of-step with national trends, the 1936 presidential election not withstanding.[1] Some of them were the chief architects of national public policy. Justin Smith Morrill wrote the Land Grant College Act of 1862, which was responsible for the creation of the great state universities; General Oliver O. Howard directed the Freedman's Bureau after the Civil War; George Aiken built the St. Lawrence Seaway and brought millions of Americans cheap public power for a generation; and Dorothy Canfield Fisher tended wounded World War I soldiers in France while she guided young novelists like Willa Cather to national fame.

History is multifaceted and to understand it we must come at it from a number of different vantage points. Traditional sources such as books, articles, and newspaper accounts serve to introduce topics to us, but to really understand we must dig deeper and come to grips with the actual record left by our forebears, the primary sources. Anthropologists, for example, uncover the prehistory of Vermont by excavating the earth and photographing it using infrared and other techniques to see below the surface. Historic preservation specialists study buildings to see how Vermonters chose to express themselves in their living and working environments, and oral history helps us acquire historical information when there are no written records available or fleshes out and enhances incomplete records. Paintings and other visual materials tell us how Vermonters have portrayed each other, and a "public" record exists in courts and in the archives of state and local government.

But what of the everyday lives of ordinary Vermonters? How did we spend our days? Who were our friends and how did we relate to them? What did we buy and use, and what were those everyday issues that each of us faced with regularity? Those great leaders mentioned earlier were all somebody's neighbor, and they all shared similar values, as is so wonderfully portrayed in the photographs of Clara Sipprell published in her book *Moment of Light*.[2]

The archival, and more particularly the manuscript, record helps us see Vermonters at work and play in their normal environment. We get to see those unknown Vermonters whose names appear in the census and on the index cards in the Vermont Vital Records Office.[3] Diaries and letters are the two most common forms of manuscript that come to mind when we want to find out what it was like to be alive back then. Diaries reveal the tedium of the day-to-day life of the farmer who consistently recorded the weather and chores, but no more, each day. They show us the aspirations of a young girl to teach school, or to marry and raise a family. And they record the quiet words spoken around a campfire on the night before a terrible battle. Erastus Root, 1789-1829, a medical student in Burlington in 1815 provides a vivid description of the diary as a historical record in the opening of his own journal:

> New objects, circumstances and situations; new ideas, emotions and passions blended together according to their different shades and order of succession, and producing fantasies, hopes and fears in endless variety, render human life the most variegated as well as the most fleeting scene with which we are acquainted in the whole circle of nature. As the power of language is unable to arrest & describe the mixed emotions of the mind at the moment they pass, so it is fitted far less to recall them at pleasure. But if we cannot clothe in language and mark down the various sentiments and feelings that occupy our minds in different times and situations, it is in our power, in some measure, to make up for this deficiency by recording the objects that occasioned them; And the diaries in which these are comprehended afford, at least to him who takes the trouble of making them, a very curious and interesting subject of both entertainment and improvement.[4]

With the rise and popularity of social history a host of studies using diaries and private letters have given us insights into courtship and marriage in the nineteenth century, French-Canadian immigration, the first women graduates of the University of Vermont, the foreign missionary movement, and other topics in Vermont social history. This work is difficult and time-consuming. It is much easier to read a text or a monograph on Vermont or American history in which some scholar has preselected and boiled down the evidence to suit his or her own purpose. It is hard to read hundreds of pages of a diary with no beginning, middle, or end. The persons mentioned are strangers with only first names, and it is not easy to trace the relationships among them. But, with patience, the picture comes into focus and often the student becomes a committed manuscript researcher choosing facts and figures to support an original thesis.

Diaries present a private and thus candid description of a person's life and thoughts. Though many diaries, such as the one written by Erastus Root, were meant for public consumption, they are usually written strictly for the eyes of the diarist, and the pages are filled without risk of exposure. Many diaries were not meant to be read by scholars and students in a public library, and the diarist would blush to know that they are here. I have found, however, that diaries lose this sense of secrecy over time and become more like novels based on real people's lives. Dorothy Canfield Fisher's 1923 diary presents the author's life as a whirlwind of travel and lectures, but Fisher did not donate diaries with her papers in 1959, probably because she felt that the content was too personal. The Bailey/Howe Library received them from Fisher's grand-daughter in 1988, and now what may have seemed private to Fisher simply serves to enhance the other papers in the Dorothy Canfield Fisher collection.[5]

Letters and diaries are usually considered primary sources because they tend to be written close to the events they describe, leaving the author little time to embellish the story. It seems, for example, that Ethan Allen penned his famous letter announcing the capture of Fort Ticonderoga almost immediately after the event. In it he writes to the Committee of Correspondence in Albany that he and Benedict Arnold "Took the Garrison Prisoners without Bloodshed or any opposition." It was only later that Allen would report that he said, to a trouserless Captain Delaplace, that he took the fort "In the name of the Great Jehovah and the Continental Congress."[6]

In general then, letters and diaries are considered very good evidence of events they describe. People do, however, lie to each other in letters and it is not that unusual for them to lie to themselves in diaries. All evidence needs to be corroborated with at least one additional source, and the context and purpose of each document needs to be examined. The first few pages of any diary are worth studying, particularly those in the first volume, for often the diarist, like Root, will explain his reason for keeping it. Some diaries present simple observations, others contain reflections, and still others aim to instruct. Burlington resident and photographer Alvaro Adsit wrote his diary in the form of a letter to his son in 1920 to warn him not to make the same mistakes made by the father.[7] Manchester poet Sarah Cleghorn begins her delightful 1907 diary with the following:

The rules which I mean to observe in this volume are only two:
1. Not to attempt making up news when too far behind . . .

> This is not an encyclopedia of our family's doings, but a random crossection of my own life and thoughts at 31. 2. To forbear conventional compliments, doing justice to others, like the "darling" and "dear" inserted in the old lady's diary before each mention of [the deceased] Maria. If I made a third rule, it would be that I would use moderation, and limit the pages I allowed myself to cover late at night! But I am apt in these mature years, to go to bed early.[8]

Personal records help flesh out what we already know about Vermont's history. There are relatively few documents preserved from the eighteenth century in Vermont, and these tend to be primarily legal papers relating to land and property transfer, other business records, and military papers. Some business papers describe household articles bought and sold, and thus shed light on life on the frontier. Vermont was sparsely populated at this time, and every effort had to be expended for survival. Transportation was poor, mail almost nonexistent, and the literacy level was low. This is the world of our friend Erastus Root, who on Friday November 10, 1815, set off from Burlington to Westford to help Dr. John Pomeroy with an amputation:

> Fine and pleasant morning. The medical students with Dr. Pomeroy started by 6 o'clock this morning to perform the aforsaid operation. Our journey, 18 miles in length lay thro' a rocky rough country. Mud and water were not all the difficulties we had to encountre, stones & sticks & roots of trees were passed over, and tho' four of us hired a waggon and driver & gave one dollar each, we had to walk half the way. We did not arrive there until two o'clock.[9]

As the nineteenth century moved along, villages began to grow and a society emerged, at first around the church and later around the business district. Literacy expanded, people became more active in the community, and they exchanged ideas. Diaries became more common in this atmosphere, as did the keeping of commonplace books.

By mid-century, children were beginning to leave home to work in the mills and factories, so we begin to see letters home that describe urban conditions, and letters written back to keep the distant member informed of family activities and events. Julia Dutton, for example, left her home in Essex Center at age fourteen in 1845 to work in Massachusetts at a cotton mill. Dutton's letters describe her homesickness and the unpleasantness of mill life, but we also learn that her boardinghouse became a second home with the landlady a surrogate mother, and that Julia was active in the church choir and the missionary sewing circle. She never returned to Vermont, but there is evidence that her mother joined her in Massachusetts years later when Julia was married with a family.[10]

The nineteenth century is the age of family papers, and the collections begin to grow in volume and complexity as the century moves on. Photographs start to appear after 1850, so we get an idea of the way people looked and dressed. A little later we see dwellings, first outside and then indoors, and their domestic furnishings and decorations. Among the most shocking for the modern researcher are the photographs of deceased persons, particularly children, which are common in nineteenth-century family collections.[11] As society becomes more educated and paper-based, family collections expand to include scrapbooks, albums of amateur photographs, bills, receipts, cancelled checks, bankbooks, tax returns, ration books, greeting cards, stock certificates, and other papers besides letters and diaries. By 1940, family collections begin to thin, mainly because of the telephone, and journal keeping almost disappears. The UVM Special Collections has received some family collections from the post-1940 period, but not many. We have the Irene Allen papers from Westford, for example, and the Anton Hansen papers from Halifax.

How will we continue to document individuals and family with the paucity of records being saved? Will we have to depend on the archives of TV sit-coms and movies such as *Ordinary People* or *When Harry Met Sally*? Certainly we will have a good visual record because of modern photography, and oral history will be important. The printed record will show a great interest in psychology, and I imagine that historians will be able to use published case studies to examine personal values. Somehow it seems that the records will be less personalized. The vast files of government social agencies will become more and more important for those interested in finding out what life was like in post-World War II America.

Some of you may still be asking why we need to have all the little personal dramas to understand historical events, so let me conclude with one last story. It's a letter from an unnamed woman who lived in Fair Haven to President Franklin Roosevelt in June of 1934:

> . . . We have certainly seen some hard days. we have been to bed a good many night with out nothing to eat. some days all we would have is blackberries. I would go and pick Black Berries last summer and we would eat them for dinner then my oldest boy 9 years old would take care of the smallest children while I and the next one to him eight years old would go and pitch on hay for mr. Ferguson. When my baby girl was born last December I didn't have a thing to put on her I wropt her up in one of my dresses until the Doctor got a few things for her. that is the way we are getting use. We didn't get only two quilts and one blanket that you sent out for the poor. and there is one person not far from here has got so many blankets she has got them stored away. . . . I am not complainin for it don't do any good, but it makes me feel bad. when some gets all they want and others can't. I know a party that has got a radio and spends some of his money for beer. We don't have no pleasure of any kind . . . and also tell us what we will do about the house I hate to lose it when I have seven little children and no place to go.[12]

NOTES

1. The Democratic landslide in 1936 carried every state for Franklin D. Roosevelt except Vermont and Maine. See Gorton Carruth and Associates, eds., *The Encyclopedia of American Facts and Dates* (New York: Crowell, 2d ed. 1959), 510.

2. Clara E. Sipprell, *Moment of Light* (New York: John Day Co., 1966).

3. The Vermont Vital Records Office is a subdivision of the Vermont Public Records Division.

4. "A Journal of the Most Remarkable Proceedings, Studies & Observations Kept by Erastus Root." 1815, 1-2. Small bound manuscript, Special Collections, Bailey/Howe Library, University of Vermont.

5. The Dorothy Canfield Fisher papers are housed in Special Collections, Bailey/Howe Library, University of Vermont.

6. See Charles A. Jellison, *Ethan Allen: Frontier Rebel* (Syracuse University Press, 1969), 118, for a discussion of what Allen actually said on the occasion.

7. Alvaro Adsit to his son Robert J. Adsit, St. Petersburg, Florida, December 10, 1920. Adsit Family papers, folder 1, Special Collections, Bailey/Howe Library, University of Vermont.

8. Sarah N. Cleghorn Diary, 1907, Sept. 21, 1-3. Sarah N. Cleghorn papers, box 23, folder 5, Special Collections, Bailey/Howe Library, University of Vermont.

9. Root Journal, 38. Dr. John Pomeroy, 1764-1844, came to Burlington in 1792 and was one of the first physicians to settle there. He was the moving force in the University of Vermont Medical College until his retirement in 1822. There is a small collection of Pomeroy family papers in the Special Collections, Bailey/Howe Library, University of Vermont.

10. For a good description of Dutton's experiences see Betsy Beattie, "From the Mountains to the Mills: Julia Ann Dutton and the Changing New England Society." Paper completed for History 283, December 1980. Vermont History Student Papers, Special Collections, Bailey/Howe Library, University of Vermont.

11. See Michael Lesy, *Wisconsin Death Trip* (New York: Pantheon Books, 1973) and the more recent *Sleeping Beauty: Memorial Photography in America* by Stanley B. Burns (Altadena, Calif.: Twelvetrees Press, 1991) for a description of this practice in the nineteenth century.

12. Letter from Mrs. A. J. F., Fair Haven, Vermont, to President Franklin D. Roosevelt, Federal Emergency Relief Administration Central Files, box 4. Quoted in Robert S. McElvaine, ed., *Down and Out in the Great Depression* (Chapel Hill: University of North Carolina Press, 1983).

The Roadside History of Vermont

Peter S. Jennison

nce upon a time, just after the Second World War, when people from away began to buy up hill farms that had been abandoned during the Depression, a potential purchaser asked the real estate broker in Londonderry if the "old Chapman place" had a view. "Well, yes," the broker allowed, somewhat grudgingly, "from the front porch you can see the tops of the Bakers' silos, and from the back porch you can see the roof of the Deckers' big barn, and from the upstairs windows you can just about see the steeple of the Congo church, but beyond them, there ain't nothin' but mountains."

And once upon an earlier time, in June 1770, Ethan Allen thundered his immortal maxim, "Sir, the gods of the hills are not the gods of the valleys." What did the impulsive Ethan have in mind? Ethan's cryptic remark was meant as a warning to James Duane, the New York Attorney General, when the New York Supreme Court cancelled the rights of all settlers in the New Hampshire Grants in favor of New York land jobbers. Righteously indignant at the aristocratic flatlanders of the Hudson Valley (Chief Justice Robert Livingston held patents to 35,000 acres of the disputed territory, a fact that might have tainted his judiciousness), Ethan was pressed to explain his pronouncement. "If you will accompany me to the hill of Bennington, the sense will be made clear." To this exchange can probably be attributed the derisive epithet, "flatland politics" so often applied to late twentieth-century immigrants who become burrs under the saddle of local and state political complacency.

The influence of geography on history has become a scholarly field that I approach gingerly, not as a professional historian, but more as a journalist intrigued by the past and present interplay of our natural, cultural, and psychological landscapes, as observed along the roadside. Let me try to "read our land," to identify ways in which it has shaped our character. And, since history is also biography, let's also look at a few of the characters who conserved and enhanced our natural environment and others who reshaped or rearranged it. This fascinating game is still being played out in the land-use arena at the proposed Pyramid Mall in Williston, on Killington Mountain, and in a score of other skirmishes between "developers" and "conservationists."

The siren song of land caused our eighteenth-century ancestors to venture into our countryside—some impelled by a true pioneering spirit, others by the vision of profits in land speculation. Whatever their motives, they and their descendants left their imprints on the landscape, humanizing the wilderness by clearing the forests for homesteads, crude roads, and primitive industries. Just as they rearranged the landscape, the geography of Vermont affected their attitudes and actions.

For most of our two hundred years of statehood, we have tended to take the land for granted and adjust to it, as we do to the weather. The Green Mountains have dominated nearly every aspect of our history as a state, and, until the railroads crawled through the gaps from Brattleboro to Rutland and from White River Junction to Burlington in the 1850s, followed by paved roads in the 1920s, almost literally divided us.

"The Green Mountains were a challenge to Vermonters from the beginning," Storrs Lee writes in *The Green Mountains of Vermont.*

> The ridge extending down the middle of the state formed a barrier that everyone had to reckon with. It was an obstruction to commerce, a hindrance to communication, a formidable obstacle to the gregarious . . . Much of the stubbornness with which Vermonters allegedly are endowed, much of the plodding patience and durability come from their experience in outwitting mountains . . . They provided a perspective—something to look up to and something to look down from. The barrier was there to conquer or be conquered.[1]

In what came to be called "The Mountain Rule," the mountains, indeed, distorted our political landscape for 170 years after the initial East-West struggle for supremacy. Under this rule, which was informally conceived but rigidly observed until 1944, statewide offices were apportioned between eastern and western Vermont. One Senate seat, for example, belonged to the East, the other to the West. Where there was only one position—such as the governorship—it was rotated: a governor from the East was always followed by one from the West, and so on.

According to Frank Bryan writing in *Yankee Politics in Rural Vermont,* our topography has helped "to perpetuate ruralism as the essential social condition." The growth of the state was defined by "the homestead and the hamlet. Nearly everywhere a hill lies across the path of togetherness."[2] The ex-urban gentry who have moved to Vermont in recent years are willing to pay dearly for ruralism because there's so little of it left elsewhere. At the same time, ruralism has honed "a special community ethic . . . bonds of communal spirit that are very likely matched by few other states."

"Rocky fields and angled visions have caused Vermonters to think with a hillside mentality," Charles Morrissey wrote in *Vermont: A Bicentennial History.*[3] "Their world is tilted in ways they take for granted. . . . Hillside living

instills an awareness of the need to comply with the natural shape of things."
Nonetheless, Vermonters have never been passive inhabitants of the land. For
more than a century we exploited our land, cutting and burning eighty percent
of our forests, clearing them for farms, using and exporting the timber, grazing
thousands of sheep who vacuumed the slopes. Now, about seventy-six percent
of our woodlands has been restored, divided somewhat unequally among state
and national forests and the big paper companies. We used our waterways for
transportation and waste disposal.

Alongside this attitude of using and conquering the land has grown,
somewhat more slowly and against greater odds, a Vermont tradition of
respecting and protecting the land. The conservation movement evolved
gradually, pioneered by our versatile countryman, George Perkins Marsh,
whose remarkable career spanned the nineteenth century from 1801 to 1882.
Distinguished scholar, linguist, Congressman, and diplomat, Marsh was the
prodigy who sounded the first serious warning of the consequences of our
profligate ways in his book *Man and Nature*, published in 1864, and based on
his observations of the landscape in Vermont, Europe, and the Middle East.
Its theme was majestically simple: "Man is everywhere a disturbing agent.
Wherever he plants his foot, the harmonies of nature are turned to discords."
To restore a balance of nature, both morality and science are needed: a feeling
of responsibility toward future generations and a thorough knowledge of the
terrain, soils, climate, and vegetation of the continents.

Woodstock, where Marsh was born into one of the most influential
families in the state, may now be the town many Vermonters love to hate, but
it encapsulates Vermont's most enduring linkage of environmental conservation—what might be called the Marsh-Billings-Rockefeller connection.
Frederick Billings bought the Marsh homestead on the lower slope of Mount
Tom in 1869, after making a fortune as a land-claims lawyer in San Francisco.
He twice remodeled the house into a Queen Anne style mansion, and,
following Marsh's precepts, reforested the hills around his estate. Julia Billings
wrote of her husband:

> He was led to consider forestry by reading the writings of Geo.
> P. Marsh regarding climatic changes induced by devastation of
> the forests; and he thought the farmers should be taught to see
> the importance of preserving their woodlands. He found out
> what trees were best adapted to the climate and then set them
> out by the hundreds or thousands. His example has caused
> many farmers there to plant trees on the barren hillsides and
> has therefore proved very valuable.[4]

When Marsh died, Billings purchased his 12,000-volume library and
retained H. H. Richardson to build a proper home for it at the University of
Vermont. As president of the Northern Pacific, Billings had demonstrated his
loyalty to Marsh's principles by planting trees and shrubs along the railroad's
right of way.

When Billings' granddaughter, Mary French, married Laurance S. Rockefeller in 1934 in Woodstock, Marsh's heritage became the keystone of their continuing efforts to preserve the historic core of the village around a non-polluting resort complex, which serves as the generator of Woodstock's economic livelihood. Their acquisition of several thousand surrounding acres of greenspace provides a buffer against overdevelopment.

An appreciation of Marsh's philosophy influenced Rockefeller's career in the conservation movement. "Preserving an ecological balance wherever man lives, both for his survival on the one hand, and for his general health, well-being and enjoyment of life" was a national priority, Rockefeller believed, according to his associate H. Frederik Smith in an unpublished biography. "Conservation and recreation: nature and people—there lay his consuming interests" from the middle 1940s, leading to his involvement with national and state parks, chairmanship of the first National Outdoor Recreation Resources Commission in 1958, and, later, presidential appointments to conservation posts.[5] This continuum has had lasting by-products: the forestry of the late Richard Brett, one of the founders and first president of the Vermont Natural Resources Council in 1964; the Vermont Institute of Natural Science; and the Vermont Land Trust, which began as the Ottauquechee Land Trust.

On the western side of the mountains, one discovers another example in Joseph Battell. We don't know for sure that Battell ever read *Man and Nature*. He didn't need to. Visitors associate Middlebury with the college, Robert Frost, and Bread Loaf, not realizing that the summer School of English and Writers' Conference are living memorials to Battell, the remarkable, cantankerous Bread Loaf innkeeper and newspaper publisher. He did not re-shape the landscape, he collected it, becoming a one-man land trust. Soon after purchasing the Bread Loaf farm in the 1860s, he saw a woodchopper slashing into a nearby timber lot. It occurred to him, Storrs Lee writes, that one day the thousands of acres he could see from the inn porch might meet the same fate.

> His friends were paying ten thousand dollars for paintings to hang on their walls. Why not buy the subject instead of the reproduction and preserve it for all time? Wallet in hand, he advanced to the woodlot and purchased it on the spot. Then with a dream of preserving the wealth of Bread Loaf scenery for posterity he began purchasing wild lands at fifty, twenty-five, even ten cents an acre . . . until he owned more territory than any other individual in Vermont.

As editor and publisher of the *Middlebury Register* for thirty years and a breeder of Morgans, he waged war against the dawning of the automotive age. Indeed, the automobile's conquest of the state was not consolidated fully until the interstate highways forever ended its insularity in the 1960s. Vermont's maverick opposition to the automobile was dramatized in the early years of the New Deal when promoters of tourism and conservationists squared off in a noisy argument over the Green Mountain Parkway. The issue symbolized a deeper philosophical and political test of strength between the proud defenders of states' rights and the pragmatists who welcomed federal funding to temper the chill winds of the Depression. It was also the first real battle of wills between advocates of growth and development and defenders of the environment.

Road builders have always been visionaries, and William J. Wilgus of Ascutney was no exception. He might have become Vermont's Robert Moses if his master plan for a 260-mile scenic skyline drive along the western crest of the mountains from Massachusetts to Canada had prevailed, reshaping our natural and socioeconomic landscape for all time. The Roosevelt administration offered eighteen million dollars in WPA funds for the project; after three years of divisive, often xenophobic, public debate between 1933 and 1936, the proposal was rejected three times by the legislature. One key vote in the senate to approve it was allegedly defeated when an opponent declared, "If God had wanted a parkway through them mountains, He'd of put one there." Finally, legislators gave up and called for a referendum for Town Meeting Day, 1936: the initiative lost, 42,000 to 30,000—a victory of "angled vision" over "flatland politics."

Although state government has often been identified as the enemy by both developers and conservationists, two land-shapers who left their finger-prints and footprints nearly everywhere we look, Perry Merrill and Deane Davis, made their mark by working with and through our political institutions. Under State Forester Merrill's direction, the Civilian Conservation Corps, in twenty-nine camp locations between 1933 and 1941 (more units per population than in any other state), built one hundred miles of forest and park roads, and created more than twenty camping and recreational areas, which have since become our chain of exceptional state parks. The CCC also developed the ski trails and other facilities at Mount Mansfield and Smugglers' Notch, the impetus for the dramatic growth of the state's ski industry, which has had such an impact not only on our principal mountain tops but the economic landscape as well.

The consequences of this impact on such overwhelmed towns as Dover became the genesis of the landmark Act 250 controls championed by Gov. Deane Davis. "As I studied the development in Windham County," Davis recalled years after he won a victory for planned growth with the passage of Act 250 in 1970, "I realized that the so-called second homes before too long turned out to be first homes and when they are first homes, there are children in the home, schools have to be taken care of, roads have got to be built to them and they were building $200,000 houses on dirt roads up on the mountain where the soil was fragile."[6]

In Shelburne, we find another land-shaper, Dr. W. Seward Webb, who, in the 1890s with his wife Lila Vanderbilt, assembled and rearranged the 3,000-acre landscape of Shelburne Farms into an outstanding, private country estate on the grandest Anglo-American scale. Although it is now dedicated to public uses as an educational and traveler center, it retains the hallmarks of America's foremost landscape shapers, Frederick Law Olmsted and Gifford Pinchot. To Pinchot, the turn-of-the-century founder of the U.S. Forest Service, conservation meant the wise use and management of natural resources to achieve the greatest good for the greatest number of people for the longest period of time.[7] Dr. Webb's intentions were more hedonistic, but he nevertheless bequeathed us a significant landmark of enlightened self-interest, one that is being adaptively preserved by his descendants.

Contrast Shelburne with what might be called a residential theme park, Quechee Lakes, where the landscape was reshaped to create lakes, golf courses, and second-home condominiums. This 6,000-acre planned suburban community, a colony for transplanted upper-income refugees from megalopolis, was artfully superimposed on a balding, superannuated mill village like a glossy permed wig. The original plan in 1969 respected the natural setting, but since then a palisade of condos has permanently ruined a ridge line. The silver lining here is that now esthetics have become a criterion in Act 250 proceedings, and several towns have adopted ridge-line restrictions on building.

Architecture reveals our cultural landscape. It's often said that the reason we have such a distinguished architectural showcase in our vintage villages and along our main but non-interstate travel highways is that we couldn't afford to tear down the past. There have been monumental exceptions, of course: too many of the Victorian mansions built by our mini-robber barons have been razed; and most of the grand Central Vermont depot in St. Albans was torn down before adaptive preservation became economically feasible in many places. In *Vermont Landscape Images*, however, Sheafe Satterthwaite argues that we have not, on the whole, asserted the special order to give man-made space a permanent character in the landscape. He holds that the landscape is very malleable: "It can be shaped to meet men's needs, and if those needs should change, the site or edifice or activity can be modified or deserted."[8]

True enough, but I still submit that, largely through enlightened self-interest—and sometimes seemingly through benign neglect—we have preserved more of the architectural heritage of our cultural landscape than we have abandoned or mutilated, despite the invasion of the mallers and the condo-maniacs. The perfect example of town planning gone awry—too little and too late—is Manchester, where the graceful past, exemplified by the Equinox House and other buildings around the village green, now collide in culture shock with discount emporia filled with designer labels. Dorset, Grafton, and Woodstock remind us that it takes a lot of money to prevent the future.

Each generation of Vermonters, it seems, must refight the battles of its ancestors under slightly different rules. In the 1990s we are choosing up sides again, with higher stakes, over Act 200. One team, the Citizens for Property Rights is using Act 200 as whipping boy for its accumulated resentments of "flatland politics." Eloquent, but to my mind misguided spokespersons such as Sen. John McClaughry, for example, contend that Act 200 is "a great engine of confiscation of private rights and town independence."[9] Others have alleged that the law prevents landholders from giving five acres to a son or daughter, or painting one's house blue. These are fabrications. Far from erasing local control over land use, the law helps us insure that land-use decisions will not be made by out-of-state developers. One could argue that those opponents of

Act 200 who see the legislation as a contest between rugged individuals and state control have left out the middle term: community self-determination.

On the Burlington waterfront, where public and private interests tangle in an intramural wrestling match, we can hear echoes of some prescient advice from Lord Bryce, the British historian and ambassador, speaking in 1909 at the Tercentenary Celebration of the Discovery of Lake Champlain. He warned us to preserve the environment of this "Switzerland of North America":

> Save your woods. . . . Do not permit any unsightly buildings to deform beautiful scenery which is a joy to those who visit you. Preserve the purity of your streams and lakes. . . . Keep open the summits of your mountains. Let no man debar you from free access to the top of your mountains and from the pleasure of wandering along their sides. . . . Keep open for the enjoyment of all of the people, for the humblest of the people, as well as for those who can enjoy villas and yachts of their own, the beauties with which Providence has blessed you.[10]

Finally, what do we learn from reading our land? The benchmarks can serve to illuminate some of the causes and symptoms of our present schizoid tendencies. We are becoming as confused as our forebears about our identity. They had to cope with shifting claims to the wilderness they penetrated. We tend to confuse ourselves with conflicting concepts, patterns, and stages of growth management. A part of us yearns to deflect the tide of change, to pretend that we are not, really, within a day's drive of some thirty-five million people who can make us a theme park playground whether we like it or not. Another part of us craves the short-term, but ultimately self-defeating, economic fix that comes from strip development and condomania.

We are as surrounded by perils as our ancestors were. Lurking on the banks of the Connecticut River in Vernon is Vermont Yankee, the ultimate malignant rearranger, not just of the landscape, but of our entire immediate environment. We have yet to deal decisively with what will happen to its hazardous remains when it is decommissioned. Nor is the so-called Federal Super-Fund being adequately deployed to clean up several toxic waste sites in the state. In fact, we seem powerless to prevent hazardous materials from being smuggled across our borders and dumped.

We are not alone, of course, in dealing with our share of the international crisis in solid waste disposal. We may take the lead in banning fluorocarbons and disposable diapers, but you can bank on the not-in-my-backyard syndrome to hobble such efforts as Act 78, which requires that towns recycle, reuse, or reduce their waste streams and participate in solid waste districts. Some towns are opting out of solid waste districts before they are even formed.

Even Act 250 is under attack. Despite the fact that only thirty-five or so of some five thousand applications for development permits have been denied, the act is accused of being a great barrier to economic development in Vermont. One inequity looms large: the developers and mall builders have virtually unlimited funds to appeal an adverse district commission ruling, while an underfunded regional commission either gives up or incurs a budget deficit. And in this increasingly litigious society, individuals and planning commissions run the risk of being sued by the developers, as a group of individual objectors was a few years ago in West Windsor by the Ascutney Mountain Resort. That particular suit was withdrawn, but the specter of astronomical legal fees has a chilling effect on public-spirited citizens who don't want to see their rural communities snapped up and transformed before their eyes.

In the long run, I am convinced, protective historic preservation and environmental conservation will prevail. Public and private agencies, such as the State Environmental Board, the Vermont Natural Resources Council, the Preservation Trust of Vermont, and the Vermont Land Trust, are in place and performing effectively. As Tom Slayton has written, "In the decade between 1968 and 1978, the State of Vermont built a protective structure of environmental law unsurpassed in the United States."[11] In her last year as governor, Madeleine Kunin proposed a 300 million dollar Third Century Trust to fund environmental protection, and fifty million dollars for the Vermont Housing and Conservation Trust Fund to preserve open space and construct affordable housing.

In the stagnant economy of the early 1990s, we cannot afford such appropriations, but the vision will persist. Moreover, it is clear that as a society we have crossed a psychological threshold in our attitudes about the land. Our schoolchildren are encouraged to be ecologically aware through the Vermont Institute of Natural Science's ELF (Environmental Learning for the Future) program in at least thirty-two towns and its "Waste Away" program teaches the virtues of recycling. Local and regional planning commissions are shaping ways to preclude the kind of haphazard growth that trashes our rural countryside.

Fortunately, responsible stewardship is alive and well, because, this time around, we cannot retreat to the mountains and invoke the thunderous gods to repel the rapacious land-guzzlers and mallers from Boston, Hartford, and Albany. If this be "flatland politics," make the most of it.

NOTES

1. W. Storrs Lee, *The Green Mountains of Vermont* (New York: Henry Holt, 1955), 9.

2. Frank M. Bryan, *Yankee Politics in Rural Vermont* (Hanover, N.H.: University of New England Press, 1974), 5ff.

3. Charles T. Morrissey, *Vermont: A Bicentennial History* (New York: W. W. Norton, 1981), 5.

4. Jane Curtis, Peter Jennison, and Frank Lieberman, *Frederick Billings: Vermonter, Pioneer Lawyer, Business Man, Conservationist* (Woodstock, Vt.: Woodstock Foundation, 1986), 70.

5. M. Frederik Smith, *Notes on the Life and Times of John D. Rockefeller's 3rd Grandson* (unpublished), 368 ff.

6. William Doyle, *The Vermont Political Tradition* (Barre, Vt.: Northlight Studio Press, 1984), 210.

7. Samuel N. Stokes with A. Elizabeth Watson. *Saving America's Countryside: A Guide to Rural Conservation* (Baltimore: Johns Hopkins University Press, 1989), 2.

8. William C. Lipke and Philip N. Grime, eds., *Vermont Landscape Images* (Burlington, Vt.: Robert Hull Fleming Museum, 1976), 28.

9. *Vermont Standard*, Woodstock, Vt., 23 Feb., 1989.

10. Peter S. Jennison, *The Roadside History of Vermont* (Missoula, Mont.: Mountain Press, 1989), 68-69.

11. *Vermont Environmental Report* (Montpelier, Vt.: Natural Resources Council, Fall 1989), 12.

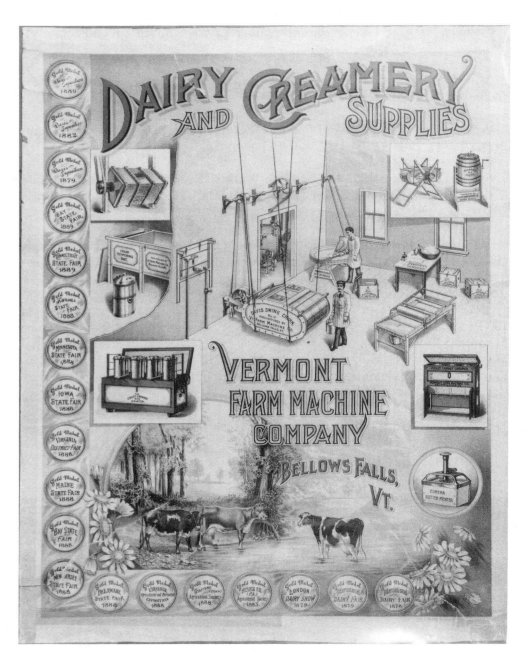

"Dairy and Creamery Supplies, Vermont Farm Machinery Company, Bellows Falls, Vt." (1899?) Courtesy of the Vermont Historical Society, Montpelier, Vt. (Broadside B 637 B41d).

MAKING A LIVING

The Evolution of Economic Identity

Jennie G. Versteeg

This paper will provide an overview of Vermont's economic evolution since statehood and connect developments in Vermont with broader national and international trends. To put this discussion into a coherent framework, I will first discuss the last two hundred years of economic history in terms of manageable chronological segments—eras of roughly fifty years each. This division was proposed in a 1935 article by Russian economist Nicolai Kondratieff, who identified what we now call "long-waves" in economic history, in contrast to the eight to ten year ups and downs of the business cycle. Although he noted a relationship between the waves and various wars, Kondratieff offered no particular explanation for the long cycles he described.[1]

Starting from a low around 1790, the Kondratieff waves reveal peaks in economic activity about 1825, 1873, 1913, and 1966, and troughs in 1848, 1894, the 1930s, and the present. The exact turning points, of course, depend somewhat on whether one looks at European or North American developments, or whether one measures movements in the level of prices or of output. Regardless of the variables, however, the general pattern of the long waves is inescapable.[2]

The common explanation for these cycles is given in terms of technological evolution. Upswings result from the adoption of a new technology and the capital expenditure that its widespread introduction requires. It takes time for the implementation of a series of related innovations to occur and for linkages to develop throughout the economy, but eventually saturation occurs and spending and activity drop off.

THE FIRST WAVE

Starting a narrative at the point of Vermont statehood in 1791 means coming in at the beginning of a global Kondratieff upswing. Alexander Hamilton had launched public debate on the nature of government economic policy making; the First Bank of the United States had just been chartered; and the New York Stock Exchange was about to be founded. The U.S. Patent Office had granted its first patent in 1790 to Samuel Hopkins, a native of Pittsford, Vermont, then living in Philadelphia, for an improved method of potash production. The first commercial marble quarry in America had been opened in Dorset in 1785, and copper mining was about to begin in Vershire. Justin Morgan was soon to bring his colt back from Massachusetts to start a new breed, and in 1793 Bennington's John Norton would open his pottery kiln, while the nation's first steamboat, invented by Samuel Morey, navigated the waters of the Connecticut River, and Burlington's first brick house, owned by Dr. John Pomeroy, was being built on Battery and King Streets. Jay's Treaty of 1796 would open Canadian markets to American goods, and in the 1790s James Wilson of Bradford, Vermont, set out to perfect a globe that could be inexpensively made and widely marketed. At the moment of statehood, therefore, Vermont was part of not only national but international economic life.

All of these were signs of the 1790 to 1825 Kondratieff upswing, the Industrial Revolution that brought profound transformation of economic and social life. Until this time descriptions of Vermont society emphasized land holdings and dealings, with wheat, corn, and livestock being the media of exchange. Although the entrepreneurial zeal of some of the Allen clan, especially Levi Allen, is legendary, and miscellaneous manufacturing was going on in many parts of Vermont, land was still the basis of the social and economic structure of society. Ethan and Ira Allen's emphasis on land deals through the Onion River Land Company demonstrates this with symbolic clarity. Even so, some people had begun to depend on non-land income for their prosperity. Take, for example, Stephen Fay of Catamount Tavern fame. Innkeepers in those days had cash and served as local bankers. Fay lent money at six percent interest and was one link to a new era.[3]

Manufacturing was about to come to the fore, with the use of new tools, new technology, and new ways of organizing work. We see this most clearly perhaps in Eli Whitney's demonstration of the productivity of what becomes known as the "American system," the use of interchangeable parts. In Vermont, facilities like paper and grist mills marked a new industrial beginning. Textiles, initially in the form of fulling and carding mills, soon became an important part of this activity.

In Vermont, as elsewhere, industrialization had an uneven impact and led to increased income inequalities. Vermont's first Poor Law, passed in 1797, and then its poorhouses reflected the public response to an increase in visible poverty. Burlington, for example, got its first poorhouse in 1816, starting a 150-year tradition.[4]

Once steam technology was in general use, investment activity slowed. Consequently the period from 1825 to roughly 1850 was one of downswing. The 1820s, for example, brought the end of an iron boom in Vergennes, as the Champlain and Erie canals caused trade patterns to shift.

Not all the new industrial efforts died after 1825, of course. Tariff protection and the canals stimulated some new companies, as did the first influx of European immigrants to Vermont. Thaddeus Fairbanks obtained a patent in 1826 for manufacturing cast-iron plows; and in 1830 he invented his famous platform scale. The precursor to Vermont's machine tool industry was started in 1829.[5] But in many ways the pace of change slowed. It was a transition period.

THE SECOND WAVE

Following English usage, the second upswing may be referred to as the "Victorian Boom." Lasting from 1848 to 1873, it coincided with the increase in commerce made possible by railroads and steamboats, as well as the exploitation of coal and manufacture of steel, much of which was underwritten by British capital. This was a period of dramatically increased use of machinery and automation, going hand in hand with the spread of wage labor. The dominant economic system of competitive capitalism experienced regular cycles of prosperity and downturn.

Millions were inspired by the rags-to-riches stories of Horatio Alger; Social Darwinism justified policies of exploitation and commercial imperialism; and there was a generally favorable attitude toward business enterprise.[6] However, this was also a time of speculative investment manias and financial crashes, such as that of 1869. One participant was Brattleboro's Jim Fisk, who helped churn out thousands of dollars worth of bad railroad stock before his death in an 1872 duel.

The coming of the railroad, of course, was crucial in many ways. Three Vermont railways had been chartered in 1835, but no rails laid for ten years.[7] Then a flurry of railroad construction integrated Vermont into the national market around 1850. Following the Civil War the railroad "gave new impetus to western settlement, fostered urbanization, and caused a securities market boom; its raw material needs promoted the rise of the steel industry; and it created the first real corporate managerial structure."[8] Railroad construction also brought deplorable working conditions and even before the railroad was finished, Vermont experienced its first railroad strike in 1846, called by Irish immigrants working on the Central Vermont Railroad.[9]

Consider the railroad's impact on the marble industry. Before the railroads, blocks of marble had to be dragged out of quarries by oxen to navigable waters, loaded onto barges and floated to and through the Champlain and Erie canals to go westward. If their destination was an eastern seaboard city, they traveled via Lake Champlain and the St. Lawrence River. The industry was revolutionized by the coming of the railroad in 1849, and new quarrying and finishing firms in the Rutland area followed.[10] The railroad also made possible a boom in talc.[11]

Nationally, the period 1874 to 1893 was one of downswing and readjustment to overaccumulation of capital and the end of the railroad boom. While Vermont remained the leading marble producing state from 1880 to 1930, the formative years had passed.[12] The fact that the boom in granite was just beginning was due to the late arrival of the railroad in Barre. Roadbeds were laid in 1875, growth took off, and between 1880 and 1890 Barre's population jumped dramatically as immigrant Italian, Scottish, French, Spanish, and Scandinavian stone workers arrived.[13]

Another natural resource industry that flourished in this period was the Vermont copper industry, located in the Vershire area. Ely Smith, a former New York furniture maker, was president of the Vermont Copper Mining Company from 1865 to 1883. As western open pit mines came into production, Vermont's copper mines peaked in 1880, supplying about three-fifths of America's copper output. But that was before greed caught up with the mines.[14]

Ely Smith's successor, Ely Ely-Goddard loved parties and fancy clothes and was said to light his cigars with dollar bills. Once he took over, management changed, production slowed, and back pay mounted. The so-called Ely War followed in 1883 and about seven hundred strikers shared what was left of the company's assets of just four thousand dollars. National Guardsmen, called out to maintain peace, proved sympathetic to the strikers.[15] Shortly thereafter the first enduring Vermont labor unions were formed: in 1885 the South Ryegate Branch of the Granite Cutters' National Union, followed by the Barre branch in 1886.[16] Public sentiment was swinging away from the excesses of unbridled enterprise, and by the 1880s the public and Congress were ready for at least some constraints provided by the Sherman Antitrust Act of 1890, drafted under direction of Senator George Edmunds of Vermont.

THE THIRD WAVE

The third Kondratieff expansion, roughly between 1894 and 1913, is labeled the "Imperialist Boom," because of the extent of overseas involvement by major powers. It followed commercial application of gas and electrical energy, leading to electric mass transportation and the use of alternating current in industry. Manufacturing changed as flow-line assembly processes were introduced, large-scale enterprises, such as John D. Rockefeller's Standard Oil, became more important, finance capital became more dominant, and large mergers occurred. Banks were very much involved in industrial interests, financial overaccumulation occurred, there were protracted industrial crises, and the United States acquired an overseas empire in the Spanish-American war, urged on by Vermont's own Redfield Proctor, who was a U.S. senator from 1891 to 1908.

Scientific management was born, United States manufacturing strength was reaching a peak, and as early as 1890 there was worry about an excessive trade surplus and the need for foreign markets if the U.S. "were not to be stifled in its own excess production." In 1893 the National Association of Manufacturers was formed to "help open up new markets in Latin America."[17] Vermont cheese manufacturers were among those seeking overseas sales. Early in the twentieth century the United States invaded Panama and Nicaragua for the first time, and followed up with other incursions later, including those ordered by Vermont-born Calvin Coolidge. The cult of the national flag began, and Europeans began complaining about the invasion of American manufactured goods.[18] By 1914 manufactured and semi-manufactured goods made up forty-eight percent of United States exports, compared with just sixteen percent in 1866.[19]

In Vermont, Springfield's machine tool industry boom rode this wave, starting when James Hartness introduced his turret lathe in 1889. By 1913, the U.S. exported 12.2 million dollars worth of machine tools to Europe, and early in the 1900s Jones and Lamson opened its own London office.[20] In contrast, in 1989 the U.S. machine tool industry as a whole experienced a 1.3 billion dollar trade deficit, with Vermont's machine tool industry sharing the decline.[21] By around 1900 the Springfield machine tool industry employed about two hundred women, and changes in women's employment patterns were taking place in other areas of the economy as well, for example, with the advent of typewriters.

One dark side of this period was the extent of child labor in this country. "As early as 1880 . . . one million children between the ages of ten and fifteen years were gainfully employed . . . by 1910 it reached a high of almost two million."[22] In reaction, a State Federation of Labor was formed in Vermont in 1903, which lobbied for women's and children's labor restrictions, and factory health and safety inspection. As part of progressive era legislation, a 1904 Vermont law prohibited any child under twelve from work in any mill, factory, or workshop.[23] "By 1914, thirty-five states had made it illegal to employ children under fourteen years old, and limited the work day to eight hours for those under sixteen . . . By the 1930s, child labor was beginning to disappear."[24] Still, of course, the problem has not totally gone away and, in fact, has drawn considerable recent attention and may be on the increase.[25]

Though it could be and is argued that the true automotive revolution came after World War II when automation was first specifically designed into Ford Motors plants in Detroit,[26] the automobile revolution in many ways belongs in this third big wave of innovations. In 1893 the first American-built gasoline car was in operation; by 1900 there were eight thousand autos in the country; by 1905 the U.S. was the largest car manufacturer. Low-cost mass market production was perfected by Henry Ford, who introduced his Model T in 1908; also in 1908 General Motors was founded and then transformed by the so-called Sloan revolution in corporate management.[27]

The automotive excitement lasted until the 1920s, by which time Vermont had its first auto dealers like Burlington's Fitzpatrick's GMC (established 1915), Shearer Chevrolet (1929), and Middlebury's Foster (1924). The automobile epitomized the 1900 to 1920 transformation to mass production in this country and its coming was a "watershed" event.[28] Small independent auto producers, however, could not compete in an auto industry increasingly characterized by mergers and bigness. Thus, for example, though Karl Martin of Bennington crafted the first of his WASPS in time for the 1920 New York Automobile Salon, his production halted in 1925.[29] In the 1920s there were many industries in which only the big survived.

As everyone knows, despite the spread of mass consumption in the turbulent twenties, the expansion ended and the depression of the 1930s followed. These were hard times. But, among other things, CCC work in Vermont during the depression helped lay the groundwork for post-World War

II ski tourism expansion. In 1934 the first ski tow in the U.S. was built in Woodstock, and in 1937 the Bromley and Pico Peak areas were created.

THE FOURTH WAVE

The fourth long-wave of expansion came after World War II, lasting till about 1966. It involved, first of all, an explosion in automobile ownership and the construction of the interstate highway system, which dramatically "changed the location of Vermont with respect to the rest of New England."[30]

Major technological changes included the use of plastics derived from petrochemicals, expansion of air transport, and the birth of the electronics industry and others, all aided by development that had occurred during the war. Thanks to George Aiken, Vermont's expansion was helped by the St. Lawrence Seaway and the hydropower projects connected with it, which brought electricity to power Vermont's post-World War II economic expansion. Of course, other new forms of energy, like nuclear power from Vermont Yankee in Vernon, have also played an important role in Vermont.

By now the economy was in the phase referred to as advanced capitalism: an internationalization of productive capital had occurred and inflation had apparently become permanent, though business cycles had become more shallow. The computer industry emerged and began to alter business information flows. While in 1955 there were fewer than one thousand computers in the United States, by 1966 there were thirty thousand.[31] This was a genuinely new departure, as automation took on its modern meaning and IBM came to Vermont.

A FIFTH WAVE?

Looking ahead now, we expect that after the transition period and sluggishness, which has characterized advanced economies since the mid-1970s or so, a new growth phase will emerge. Based again on new technologies, the "new industrial revolution," the "information age," or whatever we will finally come to call it, will see the real takeoff and maturation of biotechnology and the mass market proliferation of a vast new range of products made possible, for example, by computer chip technology. If this new phase truly warrants the "revolution" label, it will bring changes "in the whole manner of our life" as profound as those brought by mass production, the railways, electricity, or the automobile.[32] Think, for example, of the potential impact of gene splicing or of the yet unrealized potential of the home computer to revolutionize life styles.

SPECIFIC SECTORS

Taking a closer look now at some specific aspects of the economy, one might ask how the broad patterns showed up in specific sectors like manufacturing, services, and agriculture. In 1850 fifty-three percent of the economically active population nationwide was still involved in agriculture, with thirty percent involved in personal services, and just fourteen percent in manufacturing. By 1980 this was dramatically different, with about five percent in agriculture, more than sixty percent in services, including government services and tourism, and twenty-six percent in manufacturing.[33]

Let us look first at some aspects of manufacturing, then look briefly at services, and conclude with agriculture. The discussion of manufacturing will emphasize forest products and textiles. In 1850 they were the largest two manufacturing activities in the state, with twenty-nine percent and five percent of the manufacturing total respectively. Despite the emergence of machines and machine tools, textiles and lumber/wood remained the leaders at the turn of the century, though by then textiles about equalled lumber and wood in importance, as textiles grew and lumber shrank.[34] By 1982 things had changed dramatically. There was more diversity in manufacturing and electrical equipment, a category that includes the computer components produced at IBM, and Digital Equipment, for example, had grown to be the leading manufacturing activity.

Textiles

Textiles have formed the backbone of industrial revolutions all over the world. This industry, in Vermont and elsewhere, has gone through the phases of technological change and growth corresponding to the first three Kondratieff cycles.

First, leading up to and concurrent with the industrial revolution itself, the 1700s saw a series of inventions culminating in Eli Whitney's 1794 development of the cotton gin. Each innovation complemented or built on others, generating a cumulative effect. The rapid and enormous expansion of textile activity in the U.S. after 1794 was closely associated with the emergence of the factory system in general.[35] Social changes came with this. For example, "as early as 1822, a majority of textile workers in the country were women, and in the textile factory women workers became a permanent aspect of textile production, albeit often only for local production and for selected stages of the process like carding and fulling."[36]

An early example of adoption of the latest technology was the mill built by David Page on the Otter Creek in Middlebury in 1811. The mill was equipped with twenty power looms, "among the first in the United States."[37] By the 1820s, many local mills had a surplus of production that was bartered or sold outside their immediate areas. From Louis Steponaitis's 1975 master's thesis on the development, diffusion, and decline of the industry in Vermont, we can trace periods of upswing alternating with periods of decline or at least consolidation.[38] After 1829 we see decline and sluggishness through 1859. Consolidation marked the end for the smallest and least efficient mills.

The second phase of expansion, during the Victorian Boom, was characterized by increased automation in more integrated factories, while technological changes included the introduction in 1842 of the Bigelow carpet loom and introduction of pattern weaving on Jacquard looms. Elias Howe's sewing machines were introduced in 1845 and upright rotary knitting machines in 1855, which led, for example, to the founding of the Winooski Knitting Mill in 1860. All these innovations were associated with greater capital intensity in production and a larger scale of operation. The railroads, of course, took the output off to market.

Wage labor continued to spread as the normal way of making a living, and as labor shortages hit the Massachusetts mills by the 1840s Vermont farm girls were recruited for work in Lowell and elsewhere. The letters of Mary Paul and others tell us of the hours, pay, and experiences of these Vermont girls and others, but experiences were similar, for example, in the Middlebury mills.[39]

Another burst of expansion occurred late in the 1800s as new looms came into use and in the 1890s with the introduction of automatic bobbin changers. One person now could tend many more machines, with intensive division of labor and a flow line assembly process. These developments stimulated mass consumption of purchased apparel, and the industry reached maturity by about 1920 as the new processes spread. Spinoff industries ranged from potato starch factories to bobbin mills like those in East Corinth, Vermont, and elsewhere.[40]

The whole structure of the industry changed, as mills now had to grow or fail. There were sixty mills in Vermont in 1870, but just forty-three in 1889. In the 1885-1890 period Vermont saw the "greatest 5 year loss of the 19th century,"[41] but woolen mills with more than one hundred employees went from four in the 1880s to ten in the 1890s. A regional concentration also emerged with six giants in Windsor County and three in the Winooski area: Burlington Woolen Company, Colchester Mills, and Winooski Worsted. These three had interlocking ties and finally merged in 1900, right in the middle of what is labelled the first great merger movement in American history. The resulting American Woolen Company operated until the 1950s.[42]

One major reason why Vermont mills flourished was because wages here were far lower than elsewhere.[43] Fortunately or unfortunately for New England, however, over the long haul low wages were not enough to prevent decline of the textile industry after 1880 when automatic humidifiers for cotton factories negated the advantage of New England's climate. These were a major reason for the movement of industry to the south, closer to the source of raw materials.[44]

Meanwhile labor organized and after passage of the Wagner Act, union organizers got a pro-union vote at American Woolen Mills in 1937.[45] What followed was the heyday of union activity in the 1940s and 1950s, including formation of labor schools in the 1940s.[46] At the time the American Woolen Mill closed in the 1950s union wages there were much above those of non-union textile workers elsewhere in Vermont.[47]

Forest Products

Forest products have held their own better and now rank second in manufacturing importance in the state. These products were important for Vermont as early as the eighteenth century, when potash and lumber were major Vermont exports to Canada—even during the embargo of 1808 and War of 1812.[48] Also, as early as 1794, a Fair Haven, Vermont, paper mill was the first in the country to use wood in papermaking.[49]

Technological progress helped sustain the industry, as the waterwheel and single-sash saws of the first sawmills gave way in early decades of the nineteenth century to steam and mechanized lumber manufacture. After a brief decline, railroad building and a growing American urban construction market set off a second wave of growth in the middle decades. The Burlington and Newport lumber booms were part of this period's change, as railroads made it feasible to send lumber and finished wood products to Boston and other markets. This was the era of the Burlington lumber barons, and by 1889 there were one thousand people at work in the planing and other mills on Burlington's waterfront.[50] Vermont's first millionaire was a lumber baron from Danby, Silas Griffith, who mass-produced charcoal for the emerging steel foundries, which turned out rails and wire for the new telegraph and telephone lines.[51]

Completion of rail lines, the Dingley tariff of the 1890s, and growth of western lumbering brought an end to this era. Imports to Burlington, for example, which totalled 158 million board feet of lumber in 1897, dropped to about one-third of that in 1898. Nonetheless, the turn-of-the-century prosperity stimulated production of a diversity of products such as Venetian blinds, screen doors, and wooden refrigerators, which were manufactured in Burlington well into the 1900s.

In the post-World War II expansion, trucks replaced horses, and the logging camp lifestyle changed from seasonal isolation to year-round commuting. The story goes on into the new industrial revolution, with the introduction of computers, electron-microscope analysis of wood fibres, and microwave drying of lumber. Exports continue at the rate of about twenty million board feet of logs a year, but the output now goes to markets in Asia.[52] Furniture making and other wood products manufacturing continue, and the fourth largest manufacturing employer in the state is Ethan Allen, Inc., operating in four locations.[53] As is the case for agriculture, diversity and innovation characterize many successful small and medium-size enterprises in this industry. Hockey sticks, bowls, bobbins, baskets, musical instruments, clothespins, and Scrabble tiles are among the countless wood products manufactured in the state. Some involve home-grown companies; some involve divisions of large national and international firms. Altogether the industry provides employment to more than eight thousand Vermonters, not including those in support activities.

Services

As noted before, the services sector of the Vermont economy is now large. Tourism, of course, is a big part of that, ranking second only to manufacturing in dollars generated. Geographer Hal Meeks estimates that at least fifteen towns in present-day Vermont are almost completely dominated by summer property.[54] About one million skiers come to Vermont a year, but in July and August alone Vermont also sees about 1.2 million visitors. During the last week in September and the first few in October 800,000 people come to enjoy the foliage display, and the "fiscal impact of Vermont's fall foliage season is judged to be from $75 to $80 million."[55]

Vermont, of course, has always had many other service activities as well. These range from health services, which now employ about sixteen thousand Vermonters, to educational services, which employ about twenty-seven thousand, and financial services, like those of the Woodstock National Bank, Vermont's oldest bank, which started in 1849. Other economic activities in the service category include retailing, and—one of the largest—state government.

Agriculture

Finally, agriculture is closely associated with Vermont identity. When we think of agriculture in Vermont these days we often think of a general long-term declining area of economic activity. We already saw that while in 1850 more than fifty percent of Vermont employment was in agriculture, now it is five percent or less. But this sector, too, went through long waves of development.

The first phase of farming from 1760 to about 1830 was one of "all around farming."[56] Wheat kept the grist mills going and sheep raising gave impetus to fulling and carding mills. The nature of wool growing and cloth production changed from a part-time family activity to "a major cash crop and a significant industry," under the influence of events such as the embargo of 1808, War of 1812, tariff protection, and climate changes. The growing domestic demand for wool fostered a sheep boom in Vermont.[57]

By 1840, the height of wool mania, Vermont's economic shifts had accelerated integration into the national and international market economy. However, they also made Vermont more vulnerable to depressions and to changes in government policies like tariff cuts in the 1840s. Partly because of these factors, and because of the westward shift of activity made possible by canals and railroads, the sheep bubble burst, and by 1848 flocks were being sold for hides and meat. In 1849 there had been more than 1.6 million sheep in Vermont, but by 1850 only about 500,000 remained and the best rams had been sold to western breeders. This boom-bust pattern was to be repeated with other products, for example, hops, as railroads put Vermont farmers in competition with those on new, rich farmlands of the west.[58] Western farmers were aided, of course, by Rutland-born John Deere, who invented the "plow that broke the plains" and thus contributed to decline of the state's agriculture.

Livestock production followed a similar pattern of rapid rise and decline, with sheep and swine production dropping dramatically in the 1800s, for example, and with only cows and the increase in dairying surviving into the twentieth century. Mid-nineteenth century development in Vermont agriculture then is a story of the transition to dairying, made possible by the railroads.

Philip Elwert identified the years 1840-1870 as ones of "reorganization and new direction" in Vermont agriculture, with gradual adoption of dairy cheese production. Here, too, rapid transportation linked Vermont to national markets. Centralized processing plants, like the first Vermont cheese factory in Wells River (1854), started up around mid-century. Increases in sophistication of technology and larger scale cooperative processing became a trend. "By 1900, more than half of the state's forty million pounds of butter was made in centralized creameries."[59] As Vermont entered the twentieth century, new technological and economic changes once again affected agriculture. "Now the object of farming is not primarily to make a living, but it is to make money. To this end it is to be conducted on the same business basis as any other producing industry."[60]

By 1900 the benefits of scientific experiments at state agricultural colleges could be seen; and the county agent system came of age during World War I. More productive purebred stock replaced native livestock.[61] "By 1920 the conditions, institutions, and technology of modern Vermont agriculture were finally in place,"[62] and dairy was king. Cabot Farmers' Cooperative Creamery, started in 1919, today benefits four hundred Vermont farming families with its production of about fourteen million pounds of cheddar a year. Now, however, outreach and marketing, not production, seem foremost, even with or perhaps especially because of the difficulties Cabot is experiencing in the 1990s.[63]

Since World War II dairying has maintained its preeminent position in Vermont agriculture, accounting for eighty percent of agricultural receipts in the 1980s. Tank trucks and other innovations have boosted productivity and there is a trend toward bigness. As late as 1950 a herd of ten cows was economically viable, but by 1980 a sixty-cow herd was considered necessary.

On the other hand, a downward trend in the number of dairy farms continues and 192 farms took advantage of the whole-herd buyout in 1986. But though dairying seems to take an economic beating, 1989, for example, was overall a good year for Vermont dairy farmers. Vermont milk continues to be attractive and Vermont farmers continue to be competitive in New England.[64] Among others using the milk are more than a dozen ice cream makers in Vermont with flavors ranging from Malletts Bay Mud (Cream of Vermont) to Vermont Cider (Nicole's Sorbet, Inc., of Granville) and, despite some pollution concerns, many towns sought to benefit from the expansion of Ben & Jerry's Homemade, Inc., before St. Albans won out in March 1991.

We are seeing the new industrial revolution take hold in agriculture, as we argue the desirability of bovine growth hormone use and genetic engineering of animals, but Vermont is also in the forefront of organic farming. While many traditional Vermont products continue to do well, we also see new farms representing a greater diversity of output and food-product enterprises proliferate. Among livestock, for example, not only have sheep made a comeback, but we now have domestic herds of deer, goats, and llamas. Even though *real* Vermonters may not be milking those goats, someone is.

Vermont producers are creative in their production and exports. The Vermont Sheep Creamery of Underhill sells Vermont sheep's milk yoghurt and in Barre the Vermont Butter and Cheese Company markets fashionable, fresh goat-milk cheeses. Vermont Country Lamb in Orwell sent some twenty-six thousand pounds of paté, sausage, and smoked meat to France last year.[65] Not only do we have a total value of apple production in Vermont reaching about $7.7 million a year, but we make wine from apples. Not only does Vermont produce about forty-five percent of the nation's total maple syrup output, we have companies that make sugaring equipment for the whole industry, and Vermonters now also sell bottled, carbonated sap water.[66] While the McKenzie Packing Company continues to produce its traditional pork products, Vermonters now also export bovine embryos made possible by the technology of the new industrial revolution. Vermont's agricultural interests may be vastly smaller than in the 1800s, but perhaps in the coming years we will achieve the balance that has always eluded us.

A CONCLUDING NOTE

Peter Jennison has written that Vermont jumped from an essentially agrarian to a semi-technological society, untouched by the processes and changes of the industrial revolution.[67] In contrast, my argument has been that Vermont in one way or another has been touched by all the major trends in the global economy.

The real question, though, is: Now what? It seems clear that despite our entry into the information age or space age, or whatever it is going to be, we are not truly at the end of the era of the cow. Our identity may become connected to new economic activities as time goes by, but it also transcends economics and connects strongly to what we value. And we value the cow.

Stephen Terry in his *Rutland Herald* series on "The Hoff Era" in the late 1960s commented that "the cow, during the Hoff years, was dropped as the symbol of Vermont culture."[68] He was, of course, referring to the decline in rural political power after reapportionment, but I think he is probably wrong in terms of culture and Vermont identity. A state that promotes Woody Jackson cow T-shirts, and other such merchandise cannot afford to let go of its cows.

The problem is that we have a multiplicity of cow images competing for our loyalty. So what kind of cow reflects our values and should symbolize Vermont as we are poised for a new age? Will we choose the wholesome Holstein calves that make the rounds of fairs, or the cow-print boxer shorts at regional shopping centers? Perhaps this is the economic counterpart of the Vermont schizophrenia that Bill Mares discusses in his paper earlier in this volume.

At the same time we see that "there are two Vermonts," according to the report of the Governor's Commission on Vermont's Economic Future, "one [is] affluent and healthy . . . the envy of most Americans. The other Vermont is peopled by those who have missed the prosperity train . . . their prospects are narrow."[69] Whether struggling through a temporary business downturn or retooling for major shifts in technology, we do well to remember how at various times in our past many among us have suffered from the state's lack of economic diversity, even as others reaped the benefits of Vermont's participation in national and international trends. When the next economic growth cycle takes off will just a few of us be jumping on another economic bandwagon for another short ride, or can we bring both Vermonts along on a new wave of general prosperity?

NOTES

1. Nicolai D. Kondratieff, "Long Waves in Economic Life," *The Review of Economic Statistics 17* (1935).

2. A simple overview may be found, for example, in Herman Kahn, *The Coming Boom* (New York: Simon & Shuster, 1982), 36.

3. John Page, "The Economic Structure of Society in Revolutionary Bennington," *Vermont History* 49 (Spring 1981): 69 ff.

4. Steven R. Hoffbeck, "Remember the Poor," *Vermont History* 57 (Fall 1989): 226, 228, 227. See also Darlene Young, "The Poor Auction," *The Green Mountain Trading Post*, 23 September 1987. In 1838, during the tenure of Vermont's first native-born governor, Silas Jenison, imprisonment for debt became illegal.

5. This was the National Hydraulic Company in Windsor. See Wayne Broehl, *Precision Valley: The Machine Tool Companies of Springfield* (New York: Arno Press, 1976).

6. See, for example, Carl Degler, *Out of Our Past: The Forces that Shaped Modern America* (New York: Harper and Row, 1984), 211-213. The attitude is manifested in the 1863-64 National Bank Acts, for example, while the Contract Labor Law of 1864-68 facilitated importation of foreign skilled labor.

7. These were the Vermont Central, the Rutland, and the Connecticut and Passumpsic railroads.

8. Peter Drucker, quoted in William Greenleaf, ed., *American Development Since 1860* (Columbia, S.C.: University of South Carolina Press, 1968), 10. For a discussion of the coming of the railroad see, for example, T. D. Seymour Bassett, "500 Miles of Trouble and Excitement: Vermont Railroads, 1848-1861," in H. N. Muller, III and Samuel B. Hand, eds., *In A State of Nature: Readings in Vermont History* (Montpelier: Vermont Historical Society, 1985), 160-173.

9. See, for example, Gene Sessions's article on railroad workers in this volume.

10. Best known of the marble entrepreneurs was Redfield Proctor who became governor and then a U.S. senator. His Vermont Marble Company was "the largest single marble company in the world." See Peter Jennison, *Roadside History of Vermont* (Missoula, Mont.: Mountain Press Publishing, 1989), 182. Percival Clement took a different approach and became one of the state's railroad barons by selling his family's marble company. He used the proceeds to start a bank and bought control of the Rutland Railroad in 1882. See Jennison, 39.

11. William Viehman, "I Built a Vermont Talc Railway," *Vermont History* 48 (Spring 1980): 69-76.

12. Harold A. Meeks, *Vermont's Land and Resources* (Shelburne: New England Press, 1986), 106-120.

13. As population grew from 2,060 in 1880 to 6,812 in 1890, Barre experienced the largest rise in one decade ever recorded for a Vermont town. See Richard Hathaway's paper, "The Granite Workers of Barre, 1880-1940," in this collection.

14. Collamer Abbott, *Green Mountain Copper* (Randolph, Vt.: Published by the author, 1973). See also Abbott's "The Folklore of the Ely Copper Mine," *Vermont History News* 36 (March-April 1985), "Copperas--Humble But Useful," *Vermont History News* 37 (November/December 1986), and R. H. Hubbard & C. Abbott, "Pills, Pukes and Poultices and A Doctor's Account of the Ely Copper Riots," *Vermont History* 52 (Spring 1984): 77-78.

15. Abbott, *Green Mountain Copper*, 19-24.

16. J. D. Grant, "And at its first feeble cry the employers took alarm." *Vermont History News*, November/December 1983, 107-113. "Important Dates in Vermont Labor History," compiled by the Vermont Labor History Society, indicates that this was preceded by two short-lived unions in other industries: in 1869 Local 77 of the Cigar Makers Union, and in 1874 International Typographical Union Local 171, both in Burlington.

17. Degler, 506, 507.

18. Degler, 504.

19. Greenleaf, 35.

20. Broehl, 78. In 1894 E. R. Fellows followed Hartness with a gear-cutting facility in Springfield, and in 1909 the Bryant & Bryant Chucking Grinder Co. was founded.

21. Until 1978 the machine tool trade balance had been positive. Linda Novello, "Trade Watch: Machine Tools," *North American International Business* (June 1990): 44.

22. Degler, 387.

23. W. A. Flint, *The Progressive Movement in Vermont* (Washington, D.C.: American Council on Public Affairs, 1941), 75-76.

24. Karen Lane, "The Bitter Cry of the Children," *Green Mountaineer*, Fall 1988, 6-10. Lane focuses especially on cotton mills, using photographs by Lewis Henry Hine who did work for the National Child Labor Committee formed in 1904.

25. See, for example, Michael Tighe, "Vt. Firms Draw Child-Labor Fines," *Burlington Free Press*, 16 March 1990, 1B, 7B.

26. Greenleaf, 19. As a result, by 1959 engine blocks took 14 1/2 minutes to machine versus nine hours in 1949.

27. See, for example, Greenleaf, 17.

28. See Samuel B. Hand, "Potholes and Watersheds: Perspectives on 1920-1960," in J. Versteeg, ed., *Lake Champlain: Reflections on Our Past* (Burlington, Vt.: University of Vermont, 1989), 21-32.

29. Jennison, 20.

30. Harold A. Meeks, *Time and Change in Vermont: A Human Geography* (Chester, Conn.: Globe Pequot Press, 1986), 298.

31. Greenleaf, 172, 181. In 1955 about twelve large corporations had data processing machines installed.

32. Howard Rosenbrock, et al., "A New Industrial Revolution?" in J. Sheth and A. Eshgi, *Global Macroeconomic Perspectives* (Cincinnati: South-Western Publishing, 1990). "A substantial body of thought holds that U.S. manufacturing will fare considerably better over the next 10 or so years than it has in the past 10 years." Katharine L. Bradbury and Lynn E. Browne, "New England Approaches the 1990s," *New England Economic Review* (Jan./Feb. 1988): 41.

33. Data from Meeks, *Time and Change*, 300.

34. Meeks, *Time and Change*, 304.

35. See Jonathan Prude, "The Social System of Early New England Textile Mills: A Case Study, 1812-40," in Herbert G. Gutman and Donald H. Bell, *The New England Working Class and the New Labor History* (Urbana and Chicago: University of Illinois Press, 1987), 91.

36. Louis Steponaitis, "The Textile Industry in Vermont, 1790-1973" (University of Vermont, M.A. thesis, 1975), 28, 29.

37. See Andrea Torello, "Middlebury's Mill Girls," "Vermont Women's History Network Newsletter," March 1990.

38. Steponaitis's key points are included in Meeks's book *Time and Change*. See, for example, Meeks's overview of Bennington, "Vermont's most significant early textile center," 195-196.

39. Thomas Dublin, ed., *Farm to Factory: Women's Letters, 1830-1860*. See also Katherine Paterson's novel for young readers, *Lyddie* (New York: Lodestar Books, 1991), based on research in primary sources, and Deborah Clifford's "Vermont 'Mill Girls'" in this volume.

40. Potato starch was used for sizing of the warp threads, thickening of dyes, and treating of final cloth. This market died around 1875 when starch was imported from Europe and textile methods changed. Katherine Blaisdell, *Over the River and Through the Years*, Book Four (Bradford, Vt.: *The Journal Opinion*, 1982), 236. Bobbins were produced in Vermont from the 1870s until the late 1960s. Blaisdell, 210-216.

41. Steponaitis, 79, 90.

42. Steponaitis, 92; See Steponaitis for a full chronology of the mills in Winooski.

43. Labor costs per spindle in Vermont were $2.90, in Massachusetts $4.45, and in the south $4.50 in 1890. See Meeks, *Time and Change*, 198.

44. In 1915, fully sixty percent of cotton manufacture in the United States was carried on in the South. Degler, 277.

45. The first labor union came to Winooski in the 1920s, though without much community support. It was voted out in the Depression, though in 1934 "employees of the American Woolen Mill became the first in the country to achieve one hundred percent participation" in an AFL Labor Day walkout. Richard M. Judd, *The New Deal in Vermont: Its Impact and Aftermath* (New York: Garland Publishing, 1979), 150.

46. The organizers included such Edmundite priests as Fr. Edmund "Jimmie" Hamel and Fr. Lorenzo D'Agostino from Saint Michael's College, and others.

47. American Woolen was acquired by a major conglomerate, Textron Industries, which closed all of its New England mills, including those in such places as Manchester, New Hampshire, Lawrence and Falls River, Massachusetts, and others.

48. H. N. Muller, III, "Smuggling into Canada: How the Champlain Valley Defied Jefferson's Embargo," *Vermont History* 38 (Winter 1970): 5-21.

49. Meeks, 265. Bellows Falls was once Vermont's and the nation's principal paper mill center. Jennison, 110.

50. See, for example, Jennie Versteeg, "Aspects of the Vermont-Canada Forest Products Relation," *Vermont History* 58 (Summer 1990): 164-178; William G. Gove, "Burlington: The Former Lumber Capital," *Northern Logger and Timber Processor* 19 (May 1971), and "The Forest Industries of Lake Memphremagog," *Northern Logger and Timber Processor* 23 (March 1975).

51. Yvonne Daley, "Silas Griffith's Legacy," *Vermont Life*, Winter 1986, 8-13.

52. 1988 Annual Report of the Georgia Pacific Corporation; "Microwave Drying of Sawn Timber," *World Wood*, February 1988, 20; Koreans alone received close to one million board feet of Vermont hard maple, out of the twenty-nine million board feet of maple logs produced. See "State's Timber Going Out of Vermont," *Burlington Free Press*, 4 July 1988, 1B.

53. "Wood Products: Manufacturing a Home-grown Natural Resource," *Vermont Life*, Autumn 1986, 37-40.

54. Meeks, *Time and Change*, 229.

55. Nancy G. Boardman, "Foliage Facts and Figures," *Vermont Magazine*, September/October 1989, 47-48. Nevertheless there are complaints. See, for example, "Tourist income not growing quickly enough for some," *Burlington Free Press*, 22 January 1990, Business Monday 7, 31.

56. Philip Elwert, "All Around Robinson's Barn: A Social History of the Vermont Farm," *Vermont History News* 36 (Nov/Dec 1985): 125 ff.

57. Philip Elwert, "Lots More Sheep Than People: A Review of the Sheep Industry in Vermont," *Vermont History News* 35 (May/June 1984): 60-63. See also, for example, J. Versteeg, "Counting Sheep and Other Worldly Goods," in *Lake Champlain: Reflections on Our Past*; and David Demeritt, "Climate, Cropping and Society in Vermont, 1820-1850," *Vermont History* 59 (Summer 1991): 133-165.

58. At peak, Vermont produced more than eight percent of all hops in the nation. Thomas Rumney, "The Hops Boom in Nineteenth Century Vermont," *Vermont History* 56 (Winter 1988): 36-41.

59. Elwert, "All Around Robinson's Barn," 133.

60. Degler, 354, quoting the 1904 *Cornell Countryman*.

61. For example, by 1909 a formal Morgan horse registry was established by Col. Joseph Battell of Middlebury, *The Morgan Horse and Register*. See Jack McKnight, *Vermont Life*, Autumn 1986, 51-53.

62. Elwert, "All Around Robinson's Barn," 137.

63. In 1990 alone, Cabot won contracts with, among others, United Airlines, General Mills' Olive Gardens restaurant chain, Wendy's Restaurants, etc. See, for example, Kathryn Van Sant, "Cabot Lands New Airline Market," *Burlington Free Press*, 8 June 1990, 8D; Eloise Hedbor, "Area Wendy's to Market Cabot Burger," *Burlington Free Press*, 28 July 1990, 6A; Eloise Hedbor, "Cabot Sharp Cheddar Slices Through National Competitors," *Burlington Free Press*, 25 November 1989.

64. The year 1989 was "the decade's best for the average Northeast dairy farmer. . . ." Kathryn Van Sant, "Northeast Dairy Farmers Saw Higher Profits in '89," *Burlington Free Press*, 19 May 1990, 8c.

65. "Vermont Exports," 20 June 1988, *Burlington Free Press*.

66. Susan Callahan, "North River Winery Puts Vt. Wines on the Map," *Burlington Free Press*, 23 June 1990, 2D; Betty Ann C. Lockhart, *The Maple Sugaring Story*, Vermont Maple Production Board. Charlotte: Perceptions, Inc., 1990, 2; Susan Callahan, "Perrier, Move Over: Vintner Puts Vt.'s Finest in a Bottle," *Burlington Free Press*, 7 July 1990.

67. Jennison, 5.

68. Stephen Terry, "The Hoff Era," part 7, *Rutland Herald*, 1 January, 1969, reprinted as "History of the Hoff Years, 1963-1969" (privately printed, 1990), 55.

69. State of Vermont, "Report of the Governor's Commission on Vermont's Future: Guidelines for Growth" (Montpelier, 1988).

Agriculture and the Good Society:

The Image of Rural Vermont

David A. Donath

sk a prospective visitor or a third grader from the Midwest, "What is Vermont like?" You'll get a predictable answer: "Vermont is a rural place. It has lots of farms with black and white cows. It has green mountains and hilly fields, red barns, white farmhouses, and neat white churches with steeples." This popular image of Vermont is rooted in truth, mythology, and marketing. According to the federal census, Vermont is as rural a place as you can find in the United States. Through most of the last century, Vermont was predominantly a dairy state. For most of this century Vermont has occupied a special place in the imagination of Americans and its rural charms have lured visitors from downcountry.

Woody Jackson's pop-art images of Vermont Holstein cows are popular icons of rural America. Jackson's cows decorate T-shirts and Ben & Jerry's ice cream trucks from coast to coast. His Vermont cows have even found a niche in Wisconsin, a state that ought to have plenty of its own bovine icons.

Starting right after the Second World War, *Vermont Life Magazine* popularized a picturesque image of a beckoning Vermont. Arguably the most successful state promotional publication in the country, the magazine etched the pictorial image of Vermont into the national consciousness. *Vermont Life* is only the latest in a sequence of state-sponsored publications that date back to the early decades of the twentieth century, each seeking to define and market Vermont's image.

"Real" Vermonters may joke at the stereotypes and the oversimplifications inherent in the popular image of Vermont, but it is a fact that rural Vermont can delight the eyes of "woodchucks" and "flatlanders" alike. The popular image is based on kernels of truisms and truths. *Vermont Life* no longer avoids photographs including automobiles and snowmobiles, but its images are still rural and beautiful.

How did the Vermont of image and reality get to look the way it does? Ethan Allen did not have much to do with it, nor did Ira Allen, nor did Thomas Chittenden—neither did the Revolutionary War, the War of 1812, the Mexican War, nor the Civil War. Rather, it was agriculture and the ways of life of Vermont farm families that shaped Vermont's characteristic rural landscape.

It is important to remember that landscapes and built environments are dynamic things. Change is among their principal characteristics. Up close, changes are almost imperceptible, but over time changes give character to places and mark the relationships of humans with the land. Gradual forces of change produced the rural Vermont that we value today; they continue to alter Vermont, glacially and inexorably.

For more than two hundred years, the evolving landscape of rural Vermont has mirrored its agricultural history. Vermont bears the physical imprint of its particular mode of agriculture—family-based farming—and of the ways of life of her farm families. The essential elements that shaped Vermont as we know it today were in place by the last decade of the 1800s—from about the Civil War onward.

In living memory, Vermont has been a dairy state—but it has not always been so. Just as dairying in Vermont had its heyday in the first half of the twentieth century and now feels hard times, other modes of agriculture waxed and waned through earlier periods of Vermont's history. Through the nineteenth century the state struggled to find a place in a broadening commercial marketplace.

Between the time that Vermont was first settled in the 1760s and about 1820, most Vermont farms were comparatively self-sufficient, but they also sold or bartered what they could in order to purchase those things they could not grow or make. Historians continue to debate the extent to which American farm families were self-sufficient and argue about when self-sufficiency gave way to a capitalist or market orientation. There probably never was a time when Vermont farm families could be called purely self- sufficient. Over time, however, farm families tended gradually to become more market oriented.

Through the nineteenth century, America was transformed by the industrial and commercial revolutions, and farm families felt a gradually increasing demand for manufactured goods and non-native commodities. An acceptable standard of living, or "a competency," included a growing proportion of purchased items. Farmers used the expression "competent freehold" to mean ownership of a farm large and productive enough to support a family at an acceptable standard of living.

As the century progressed, the standard of an acceptable "competency" steadily increased. Rather than producing what they needed and doing without what they could not produce, more and more families bought what they wanted. The need for purchasing power demanded greater amounts of farm produce for exchange and for cash sale. The need to raise cash crops prompted increasing specialization both on the farm and elsewhere.

Throughout the nineteenth century, Vermont farm families increasingly accommodated themselves to, and became part of, a burgeoning market economy. The history of Vermont agriculture is a story of the interaction of forces of change and impulses of tradition, played out in a limiting natural environment.

When Vermont was first settled in the late eighteenth century, some promoters heralded the new territory as a breadbasket for coastal New England. Jacob Bayley and John Hazen, who settled the twin towns of Newbury, Vermont, and Haverhill, New Hampshire, respectively, believed that their fertile Connecticut River intervale would become an entrepôt, shipping wheat and lumber down river to markets in Massachusetts, Connecticut, and New York City. Ethan and Ira Allen had a similar vision of Champlain Valley commerce with Canada.

Although some early settlers made agricultural and mercantile fortunes, by the 1820s it was clear that Vermont was no breadbasket. The nation looked westward. Vermont, with its thin, rocky soils and short, unpredictable growing seasons, often proved a distant second choice when compared with the fertile prairies of the Upper Midwest.

Moreover, by the 1820s, Vermont was largely filled up with farms. Vermont agriculture began to face increasing competition from the west at a time when there was little suitable new land here to be brought into cultivation. For a family farm that had achieved its "competent freehold," subdivision promised economic disaster. For the children of Vermont farmers, opportunity increasingly meant emigration.

Just to maintain their "competency," Vermont farmers had to change and adapt their modes of agriculture. Extensive cereal crops proved unsuited to Vermont. They exhausted the already thin soils and the fungal rusts and blasts that destroyed crops only hastened the inevitable. In Illinois and Iowa, emigrant Vermonters and others found black prairie soil more than eight feet deep. The wide expanses of the Midwest would prove vastly better suited to field-crop agriculture, particularly with the coming of mechanization.

But Vermont farmers found that livestock, especially sheep, could thrive on their rocky soils and hilly terrain. For several decades, through the middle of the nineteenth century, the production of wool fiber for mills, both in Vermont and in southern New England, was a mainstay of Vermont agriculture. The story of how Consul William Jarvis spirited breeding flocks of Merino sheep out of Portugal in 1811 is almost the stuff of legends. Europe quickly lost its monopoly on fine Merino fleece and wrinkly-type Vermont Merinos came to dominate North American wool production.

For several decades, the raising of sheep and the production of lumber and wood by-products seemed to complement one another. Prior to white settlement, Vermont had been almost entirely covered with forest. By the Civil Way, two-thirds of the state's acreage had been cut, and many denuded hillsides were turned into sheep pasture. Sheep will graze successfully where other animals cannot. Hill farmers raised sheep on acreage that was marginal at best.

The era of sheep and wool production peaked in Vermont in the late 1830s. In 1840, Vermont had 1,681,819 sheep, or nearly six sheep for every human. Mills for processing the clip were numerous in every county except in Essex and Orleans in the northeast. By 1850, however, sheep were statistically in decline in Vermont. Vermont could not raise sheep as economically as the West, and by mid-century, the railroad made the West easily accessible to eastern markets and mills. Vermont remained a well-known producer of Merinos for a few more decades, but increasingly, Vermont farms produced fine breeding stock destined for the West, rather than fleece for manufacture.[1]

By 1850 dairying had grown as important as sheep raising in Vermont agriculture. Adjusted for the fact that a cow needs about five times the feed and pasturage as a sheep, the size of Vermont's herd in 1850 was equivalent to the size of its flock. Thereafter, sheep raising continued to decline, and Vermont increasingly became a dairy state. Dairy products are perishable, whereas wool is not. Therefore, once the railroad connected Vermont with coastal population centers, Vermont dairying found a secure commercial niche. At the same time that the railroad hastened the demise of Vermont wool production, it encouraged the rise of dairying.

The history of Vermont's ability to market its cheese, butter, and finally its fluid milk is related to improvements in transportation, refrigeration, hygiene, and processing of the product. With the rise of Vermont dairying came the advent of science as well as commercial and governmental regulation of Vermont farming. This is an important story that must be left for others to tell while we focus on how dairying reshaped rural life and the Vermont landscape.

Dairying demands intensive work on the part of the farm family, and if the family is not large, it demands hired help. To succeed commercially, dairying demands 365 days of work per year—seven days a week, with milking done before sunup and again twelve hours later, and chores often after sundown.

Vermont's transition to dairying was uneven. Some farmers chose not to rearrange their farms, work rhythms, and lives, and gave up farming rather than become dairy farmers. The keeping of the family cow had often been a female occupation, whereas field work was most often done by males. Some farmers found the prospect of becoming dairymen unappealing. A shortage of cheap farm labor discouraged others from taking up dairy farming. Nonetheless, dairying ultimately became the mainstay of Vermont agriculture.

Dairying also had a profound impact on the rural landscape. Most significantly, it affected the amount of land in cultivation and pasturage. Dairy cows require a higher quality and quantity of feed and forage than sheep. Marginal farmland on which Merinos had thrived proved unable to support dairy cows. The economics of commercial dairying, its labor and capital requirements, and the demand for ever increasing productivity, encouraged larger, better quality farms.

Over time, many marginal, upland farms were abandoned, reverting to second-growth timber. Farmers who adopted dairying increasingly turned their marginal acreage back to woodlot. Much of this acreage should never have been farmed in the first place. Stripped of its forest cover, upland pastures eroded rapidly and caused flooding and silting downstream. With nearly three-quarters of its landscape stripped of forest by the mid-nineteenth century, Vermont was headed for environmental trouble.

In the second half of the 1800s, some Vermonters gained a growing awareness of the environmental consequences of unwise land use. George Perkins Marsh, originally of Woodstock, wrote about the problem in *Man and Nature*. Marsh argued that just as human action had damaged the environment, enlightened land use could repair it. Today, Marsh is regarded among America's first ecological thinkers.[2]

Just as the transition from sheep raising to dairying helped to reforest Vermont's upland pastures by encouraging the abandonment of marginal acreage, today the decline of dairying in many parts of Vermont is resulting in unwanted second growth on pasture land, and a small resurgence of sheep raising and mixed animal husbandry is helping to keep pastures open.

A mix of open fields and forested hills is characteristic of the Vermont image. The mix, however, has changed dramatically. A century ago, more than two-thirds of the land was open; today more than two-thirds is forested. The continued loss of open lands has implications not only for agriculture, but also for tourism and second-home development. Open spaces are esthetically important. For every excellent Vermont view, there is a field in the foreground. Consider the difference between the open I-89 vistas in Vermont and the forested views along the same highway in New Hampshire.

Fields and viewsheds are not the only artifacts of dairying that have helped to characterize the Vermont landscape. With dairying came the need for new and specialized farm buildings—most notably large dairy barns and silos. The sophistication of Vermont's dairy barns and silos reflects the significant capital investments needed to engage in dairying for market. The modernization of barns, with milking parlors, milk rooms, and bulk tanks, reflects the technological specialization of dairying as well as governmental regulation and demands for hygiene. The evolution of silos—needed to store field crops for winter feed—also reflects the impact of science, technology, and capital on the farm.

The efficient design of dairy barns, using gravity to help move feed and by-products, and their location close to the farmhouse reflect the complexity and labor intensity of dairying. On the eastern side of the state, barns often were connected to the farm house in a form that follows the children's rhyme, "Big house, little house, back house, barn . . ." The connected farmstead form became common from Maine to eastern Vermont, beginning in the mid-nineteenth century. It reflects some of the ways that farmers organized their farm buildings, both by moving them and building new ones. They did so to improve the efficiency of their farms, both in actuality and in appearance.[3]

This spirit of improvement was also reflected in the ways that farm families "prettified" their farmsteads. During the late nineteenth century when white became a standardized farmhouse color, the red barn became ubiquitous. Dooryards were enclosed in neat fences. The improved farmstead became an advertisement to the world, to the neighborhood, and to the farm family itself that it was progressive and that it was going to succeed. This pride was psychologically important to the farm families of northern New England who repeatedly found it difficult to compete with western agriculturists, and who had witnessed the steady emigration of many of their children to the West and to industrial cities.

The late nineteenth century was an era of improvement as well as change for farm families. The contemporary watchwords "progress" and "improvement" implied adopting scientific techniques and new technologies, taking advice from agricultural journals and the newly formed experiment stations, participating in agricultural societies, entering prize cows in fairs, sending children to the new agricultural college at the university, and perfecting farming practices to improve both the quality and the quantity of produce.

In Vermont, the progressive age of agricultural improvement coincided with the rise of market dairying. Commercial dairying was, itself, made possible by progress in science, technology, and transportation. However, within the progressive drive for improvement were sown the seeds of the downfall of family-based dairy farming. The pursuit of ever greater productivity has become like a cat chasing its tail. As each cow produces larger and larger amounts of milk, fewer and fewer cows are required. As milk becomes over-abundant, its value as a commodity drops. As dairy farms became unable to earn enough to maintain a family's "competency," they disappeared. And following them, inexorably, the landscape they created is fading before our eyes, to be reshaped for other uses in the late twentieth century.

NOTES

1. For a geographic and economic analysis of the transition from sheep raising to dairying in Vermont, see Harold A. Meeks, *Time and Change in Vermont: A Human Geography* (Chester, Conn.: Globe Pequot Press, 1986).

2. George Perkins Marsh, *Man and Nature; or, Physical Geography as Modified by Human Action* (New York: Scribner's, 1864).

3. See Thomas C. Hubka, *Big House, Little House, Back House, Barn: The Connected Farm Buildings of New England* (Hanover, N.H.: University Press of New England, 1984).

Vermont "Mill Girls"

Deborah P. Clifford

n advertisement in the Middlebury *National Standard* for 1 October 1817 reads as follows: "Wanted immediately a number of good women weavers. Apply to David Page, Middlebury." Page was the owner of the stone cotton mill on the east side of the Otter Creek. Earlier that year he had commissioned Joseph Gordon of Scotland to build twenty power looms for what was then the very latest model in textile factories, a fully integrated factory in which all the processes of cloth manufacture, including spinning and weaving, took place under one roof.[1]

By the mid-1820s Middlebury was one of three burgeoning textile centers in Vermont (the other two were Bennington and Windsor). But Page's cotton mill was still the largest in the state. According to an article in the *Standard*, thanks to an impressive capital outlay of $100,000, the mill in 1826 boasted all the latest in machinery and equipment. One hundred and thirty employees worked in the factory, which contained eighty power looms and produced ten thousand yards of cloth a week. The newspaper also claimed that this up-to-date factory was the only one in the country lit by gas.[2]

Page's enlarged cotton mill not only employed the latest technology, but also engaged a new kind of labor force to run its new machinery: young unmarried women. In September 1826, an advertisement appeared in the *Standard* calling for "15 to 20 young women or misses from 13 to 15 years old" to work in the Middlebury cotton factory and promised "Constant employment and good wages."[3]

Women had been the chief producers of cloth in this country since colonial times, but they had traditionally made it in their own homes. Then, beginning with the founding of the first fully integrated textile mill in Waltham, Massachusetts, in 1814—Page's cotton mill is reputed to have been the second—factory production began to compete with, and displace, household manufacture. When the textile mills in Lowell were built in the 1820s, they sought as their principal labor force the daughters of New England farmers. To attract these young women, the mill owners offered good wages and built boardinghouses where their employees could be carefully supervised.

Young girls by the thousands responded to this call for employment. By 1845 there were reportedly twelve hundred Vermont women working in the mills of Lowell alone, and thousands more were employed in other textile centers in Massachusetts, Rhode Island, Connecticut, and New Hampshire. In an era of upward mobility, factory work appealed to young women intent on bettering their lot in life. The pay was better than for any other occupation open to women. In 1835 the average "mill girl" earned $3.15 a week with $1.25 taken out for room and board. By contrast a domestic worker in Vermont earned as little as one dollar a week.[4]

Mill work also provided young women from the farms of New England with an unprecedented opportunity for independence. Like the young men who went west in the early nineteenth century, women who chose mill work were also able to leave home and seek their fortunes elsewhere. The only difference was that for most of the young farm women who left home for the textile mills, factory work was only a temporary occupation. Few stayed for more than two or three years. Many returned home to live. Others found husbands in the mill towns where they worked. Still others found employment elsewhere.

Thanks to the scholarship of Thomas Dublin, whose two books, *Farm to Factory* and *Women at Work*, discuss the experiences of women workers in the Lowell textile mills, the story of Vermont women who emigrated to the factories in southern New England is a familiar one.[5] Less well known is the story of those women who chose to remain nearer home and work in one of the many small mill towns scattered throughout the Green Mountain State.

Unfortunately, little information survives on conditions for the employees of Middlebury's cotton mills—in the 1830s, for a brief time, there were three such mills. The little we do know tells us that women in Page's mill far outnumbered men until 1860. There is even a tantalizing editorial in the *Middlebury People's Press* for 1843 that describes twenty or thirty female operatives in Page's cotton mill striking for higher wages. The editor of the paper apparently had little sympathy with the workers. Like Josiah Bounderby in Charles Dickens's novel *Hard Times*, he insisted they were better off than their employers. "People must reflect," he patronizingly suggested, "not so much upon the quantity of money they receive, as what amount of the comforts of life it will pay for."[6]

No further mention of the strike appeared in the local press. Nor are there any extant records telling us how long the strike lasted or how effective it was. We do know that by the 1840s the cotton textile boom in Vermont was over. We also know that in that decade deteriorating working conditions and falling wages had prompted considerable labor agitation in Lowell, and this may have influenced Vermont millworkers. Thomas Dublin points out that "working in the mills created bonds among women and provided them with a solidarity that later played a major part in the growth of collective protest."[7]

Sometime in the late 1830s Rebecca Ford, the daughter of Asa Ford of Granville, crossed over the mountain pass dividing the White River Valley from the Champlain Valley and went to work in one of Middlebury's three woolen mills. With the sheep boom of the late thirties and forties, woolen textile factories had proliferated in mill towns throughout Vermont, employing women primarily as weavers. Rebecca Ford was in her late twenties when she first arrived in Middlebury, and she was soon followed by her younger sister Caroline. The two worked on and off there for more than a decade. A time book from Davenport and Turner's woolen mill shows that Caroline's employment there ended in 1849 (when she was thirty-four), and Rebecca's in 1851 (when she was forty-one).[8] This was much longer than the average Lowell textile worker. The Ford sisters were also a good deal older than most of the Lowell operatives; neither of them apparently married and thus had to continue earning their own living.

Both sisters spent most of their working years as weavers in Davenport and Turner's woolen factory, located in what is now the Frog Hollow Craft Center. While the two seemed generally satisfied with their work, there were occasional complaints. In one letter home Rebecca moans that she is getting tired of working all the time to pay for her board. But when, in April 1843, her mill closes down for a week, she longs to go back to work claiming that "I have got most tired of doing nothing and paying my board in the bargain."[9]

Although Rebecca and Caroline Ford earned wages comparable to those paid to the operatives in Lowell—during a good month twelve to fourteen dollars——frequent slowdowns and shutdowns may have brought their average earnings below those of their sisters in the larger manufacturing centers of New England. When spring floods brought work to a halt in 1843, Caroline took off for Lowell, presumably in the hope of finding steadier employment.

When the factories were operating, the day was long. The records from one Middlebury woolen mill in the 1840s show that hours were 6:00 a.m. to 7:00 p.m. in summer, and 7:00 a.m. to 7:30 p.m. in winter.[10] Although these hours strike us today as unreasonable, for someone used to laboring in the fields or the farmhouse from sun-up to sun-down a lengthy working day was taken for granted. What did not seem normal to the rural people who went to work in the mills was the kind of discipline required of them. Unlike the farmer, whose labor was task oriented and varied with the seasons, the mill operative of the early nineteenth century had to learn to "punch a time clock" summer as well as winter. A "mill girl," particularly one working in a large urban textile factory, had to learn to arrive promptly at work, to follow orders precisely, and to work with a steady intensity.

One advantage of working in a rural mill may have been the more relaxed atmosphere. A millworker of the 1850s provides us with this description of the lack of discipline in a Brattleboro factory. "Every person living near the mill went out between meals for a lunch or anything they wanted. . . . We read books, wrote letters, crocheted, etc. We did not ask permission to stay at home for a day or two. We would ask him (the supervisor) if we wanted to stay out a week or two."[11]

Whether discipline was this relaxed at Davenport and Turner's woolen mill in Middlebury, we do not know. But for Caroline and Rebecca Ford periods of intense labor alternated with periods of respite. Sometimes the entire factory would close down for the day. At other times the women would be given the day off. In common with factory operatives elsewhere in New England the sisters took extended leaves of absence—without pay, of course—to visit their families.

An unsolved mystery in the Ford sisters' letters is the reference to what they call "black work." In the summer of 1843 Rebecca Ford writes Caroline, who is then working in Lowell, that she "had black work last week," adding that "the way we look I was a caution to white folks to keep out of such black work."[12]

Both sisters left Middlebury to work in the Lowell mills for short periods, but in the end they returned to Vermont. Caroline's departure in the spring of 1843 coincided with the spring flood mentioned earlier when the mills all closed down. Presumably she hoped to get steadier employment in Lowell. We do not know why Rebecca went to Lowell nor why the two returned to work in Middlebury. In the end the less demanding nature of work in a rural mill may have appealed to them. Davenport and Turner's mill was also small and intimate. In 1850 it had a total of fifty employees. If employment there was not as dependable as elsewhere, at least the two women were known, so when work was available it was presumably given to them.

Middlebury also had the advantage of being nearer home, and close ties with their families were important for the Ford sisters as they were for most "mill girls." "I think of you all verry often," Rebecca writes her family in November 1838, "an wish I could Jest step in set down have a chat with you aet some homany an milk." She longs to have her sister Caroline join her and writes home assuring Caroline that she can stay in the same boardinghouse and share a pew at the Methodist church.[13]

Religion may have been another influence tying the Ford sisters to Middlebury. According to Rebecca, the Methodist church there had an "up and coming" preacher. Beginning on 1 January 1843 a "protracted meeting," or revival, was sponsored by the Methodists. According to Rebecca, it lasted for twelve weeks, and she mentions that Caroline was among the 250 converts. Caroline herself describes a Sabbath school parade in the summer of 1842, when children and young people representing the various denominations in town marched from what is now the Middlebury Inn through the college grounds to the local academy. There they formed a gathering of "token friendship and love."[14] Labor historian David Zonderman has observed the close resemblance between this elaborate procession and the political and labor rallies of the 1830s and 1840s. He points out that the organization of specific groups into marching units, the waving of banners, and the final convocation "also characterized protest demonstrations in industrial cities like Lowell, raising the intriguing possibility that women workers from various communities may have re-appropriated the structure of such processions for use in their public demonstrations regarding wages and working conditions."[15]

By the 1850s, young Yankee farm women were no longer the principal work force in the big textile mills of New England. Better opportunities beckoned them to urban centers and the West. By this time teachers were earning higher wages than factory workers and mill jobs were now more likely to be taken by recent immigrants from Ireland and Canada.[16] Wages and working conditions in the mills deteriorated as the century progressed. Here in Vermont weaving jobs grew scarcer as the number of mills steadily declined. Although wool was manufactured in Middlebury until the late 1880s, by 1871 there was only one firm in town. Middlebury's distance from markets and from adequate transportation routes became more and more of a handicap as the textile business itself grew more competitive and the margin of profit for the owners of the mills shrank markedly. By the early twentieth century only the largest and most prosperous of the woolen mills in the state had survived. None was in Middlebury. Rebecca Ford was still working at Davenport and Turner's in 1851 and might have stayed on if the mill had not shut down for three years.

The letters of Caroline and Rebecca Ford open a window into what was once a dark and unexplored corner of Vermont's history. But we still know very little about the many young native Vermont women who, in the years between 1820 and 1850, chose to stay closer to home and work in the state's many textile mills.

NOTES

1. I am chiefly indebted to the collections of the Sheldon Museum in Middlebury for this paper. The Sheldon's Research Center boasts a complete run of local newspapers and an extensive manuscript collection, which includes several time books from the woolen mills in town. These books list the hours and pay of each worker. Here also are the letters of Caroline and Rebecca Ford, two young women who were employed in the town's woolen mills in the 1820s and 1830s.

2. *Middlebury National Standard*, 30 October 1827, 2.

3. Ibid., 26 September 1826, 3.

4. [Rebecca Ford?] to [Asa Ford], 15 November 1838, Ford Family Papers, Sheldon Museum, Middlebury, Vt.

5. Thomas Dublin, *Farm to Factory: Women's Letters, 1830-1860* (New York: Columbia University Press, 1981); *Women at Work: The Transformation of Work and Community in Lowell, Massachusetts, 1826-1870* (New York: Columbia University Press, 1979).

6. *Middlebury People's Press*, 17 May 1843, 3.

7. Dublin, *Women at Work*, 13. See also Katherine Paterson's novel for young readers, *Lyddie* (New York: Lodestar Books, 1991), which tells a story of a

Vermont girl's experience in a Lowell mill and relies heavily on Dublin's books and other sources related to the Lowell mills.

8. Time Books, Spaulding Mill, Davenport and Nash Papers, Sheldon Museum, Middlebury, Vt. I am grateful to David A. Zonderman's article, "From Mill Village to Industrial City: Letters from Vermont Factory Operatives," *Labor History* (Spring 1986): 265-284, for pointing out significant aspects of the Ford Letters.

9. Rebecca Ford to Asa Ford [n.d.], Ford Papers; Rebecca Ford to Mrs. Asa Ford, Jr., 29 April 1843, Ford Papers.

10. Insurance Survey, #501, Woolen Manufactory, Middlebury, Vermont, Elisha Brewster Papers, vol. 2, 1 December 1843, Sheldon Museum.

11. "Recollections of a Millworker" (Brattleboro, Vt. c. 1859).

12. Rebecca Ford to Caroline Ford, 10 July 1843, Ford Papers.

13. [Rebecca Ford?] to Asa Ford, 15 November 1838, Ford Papers; Rebecca Ford to Sally K. Ford, 1 June 1840, Ford Papers.

14. Rebecca Ford to Sally Ford, 6 August 1839, Ford Papers; Rebecca Ford to Mrs. Asa Ford, Jr., 29 April 1843, Ford Papers; Caroline Ford to Asa Ford, 1 August 1842, Ford Papers.

15. Zonderman, 269.

16. Dublin, *Women at Work*, 138.

The Granite Workers of Barre, 1880-1940

Richard O. Hathaway

he history of the granite workers of Barre commands interest for several reasons. First, the strikingly diverse population of the city allows us to appraise the validity of the "melting pot" versus "mixing bowl" interpretations of the workings of immigration, assimilation, and retained ethnic identity over several generations. Second, we can ask whether the experience of the granite workers in the quarries and the finishing sheds validates the thesis that many scholars of labor history have proposed: Did these laborers lose status, shifting from relatively autonomous artisans to industrial workers during the late nineteenth and early twentieth centuries? Finally, as another index of the changing status of granite workers, we can analyze the persistent struggles for worker health and safety in both the quarries and the sheds. Especially poignant was the awful prevalence of silicosis/tuberculosis among workers. Until the belated advent of effective suction devices in the late 1930s finally put an end to that work-related plague, it carried off a disproportionately high number of granite workers, especially from 1910 through 1940.

This paper will focus on the "artisan into worker" thesis and on issues of health and safety. It will also comment on the large question of whether the granite workers' experience suggests that Vermont enjoyed a special status during this nation's urban-industrial revolution. Was Vermont a significant "exception" in possessing a peculiar history, different from the experience, say, of New Hampshire or Massachusetts? In their provocative look at Vermont, for example, Frank Bryan and John McClaughry suggest that Vermont was lucky in having "leap-frogged" over the most glaring aspects of the urban-industrial revolution.[1] Other variants of this theory of Vermont exceptionalism can be found in such examples as Rowland Robinson's cautionary *Vermont: A Study of Independence* (1892), Charles Morrissey's wonderfully idiosyncratic *Vermont: A Bicentennial History* (1981), William Doyle's *The Vermont Political Tradition and Those Who Helped Make It* (3rd edition, 1990), and countless

Fourth of July orations that celebrate the myriad ways that Vermont remains (as the theory goes) a state apart.[2]

Without discounting the merit and appeal of these overviews of the Vermont experience, it may be helpful to examine a generous slice of Barre history to test these hypotheses with a healthy dose of empiricism. In particular, what does an examination of the conditions of work demonstrate about who controlled the production process in the granite industry during the period 1880-1940? Was this process defined basically by the laborers, operating in a labor-intensive, essentially decentralized industry? Or was the granite industry increasingly controlled by a small number of firms in a capital-intensive industry that gradually took from the workers their control of the day-to-day conditions of labor?[3] Before suggesting answers to these critical questions, we will view the conditions of the industry during two key periods: from 1880 to 1910 and from 1910 to 1940.

Had a Barre resident of the early nineteenth century revisited that town after 1880, he or she would have been astonished. After remaining a village of 2,000 through the early 1870s, Barre's population increased dramatically. By the mid-1880s, it was over 4,000; by 1890, nearly 7,000; by 1900, some 8,500, and by 1910, Barre exceeded 11,000 persons, seemingly destined to become within a few years Vermont's leading metropolis.[4] These heady anticipations proved excessive, yet Barre of the late nineteenth century exhibited most of the attributes of a "boom-town." These included incomplete town planning, a lagging infrastructure of schools, roads, and building regulations, land speculation, and burgeoning neighborhoods only partially served with city services. While city leaders made commendable efforts to catch up as Barre made its transition from village to city, much remained to be done.[5]

Observer George Ellsworth Hooker has left a compelling view of conditions of life, employment, and social conditions on Millstone Hill in the fall of 1895. His descriptions offer fascinating glimpses of everyday life as Barre became one of the leading granite centers of North America. While Hooker focuses upon the quarrying aspects of the industry, he also touches upon the intricate patterns of work manifest in the industry at large. The hill itself was the workplace of some six hundred men, and the living quarters, crude and isolated as they were, of some two thousand persons. Rather than focus upon the business aspects of the quarry district, Hooker touches upon the topics of life in the boardinghouses, the strenuous aspects of work, difficulties in securing homes, the negative effects of land speculation upon the community, rent abuses, and the "lack of sanitary, intellectual, recreative institutions."[6]

Development was rapid in both the quarrying branch of the industry on Millstone Hill and the finishing branch in Barre Village. The industry was stimulated by the arrival of the railroad in Barre in 1875. By the late 1880s the "sky route" railroad had reached the summit of Millstone Hill, allowing the locomotive to replace the ox teams and horse trains that had previously hauled the heavy granite stone down to the finishing sheds. Some forty quarries extracted stone used mainly for monumental work. The granite's even texture meant that "Shafts forty or fifty feet long are absolutely free, over their entire length, from spot or cloud."[7] Hooker's description of the techniques of quarrying powerfully underlines the labor-intensive nature of this demanding work, involving an intricate sequence of test blasting, stripping the ledge of soil, erecting a derrick (originally powered by men turning a crank, then by horse power, finally by steam engine), deciphering how the granite was to be cleaved, and then using blasting, hedge holes, and/or channeling to secure the blocks of stone.[8]

While certain functions in the granite industry had been mechanized by the 1890s, many tasks still depended upon hard manual work, ranging from the labor of the paving-stone cutter to the intricate work of carving designs on the monumental stones in the finishing sheds. Workers could generally afford the tools needed to accomplish their craft tasks, indicating that even at this stage of the industrial revolution and the mechanization of the work process, the industry employed individual artisans for many of its key tasks. As Paul Demers stresses in his insightful study of the industry, "the processing of raw materials took place near the site of extraction. Barre was therefore something of an anomaly for Vermont. An industry employing highly skilled workers in a complete production process was something almost unknown in the state."[9]

It is not surprising, then, to learn that at the turn of the century, some ninety percent of the laborers in the industry were members of one of fifteen local unions. In 1907, 1,750 workers belonged to the granite cutters' union alone. Demers concludes that during this period, labor "was not a commodity; labor was a way of life."[10] Indeed, by 1900 Barre had become a classic instance of a working-class city, with the great majority of its laborers members of one or another of the generally strong unions in the locality. Membership figures for the Barre branch of the craft-organized Granite Cutters' International Association indicate the strengths of this key union from the period 1901 through 1910.[11]

Granite Cutters' International Association

Year	Membership
1901	1331
1902	1356
1903	1371
1904	1374
1905	1521
1906	1511
1907	1750
1908	1750
1909	1750
1910	1750

Source: P. Demers, "Labor and the Social Relations of the Granite Industry in Barre" (B.A. thesis, Goddard College, 1974), 108.

The cutters were part of the fledgling American Federation of Labor, during a period when corporate and federal government forces often joined to beat back unionizing efforts and when the environment was often hostile for labor.[12] Whatever its limits in inclusiveness and ambition, at least workers organized to struggle together as workers and demonstrated a willingness to, if necessary, use the strike as an instrument of class aspiration.

Far from being a depressed and passive proletariat, Barre's granite workers labored in a highly structured and complicated system. They arranged work hierarchically, with the economic rewards for each job carefully defined in ways indirectly derived from medieval guild traditions. Whether the workers were originally Scots from the Aberdeen district of Scotland, Irish, French-Canadians, Yankee, or (especially after 1900) Italians from northern towns, this young and vigorous laboring force remained mindful of the special skills they brought to the work station and jealously guarded their rights.[13]

Hooker notes that of the six hundred men employed on Millstone Hill in 1895 in the "busy half of the year," between twenty-five and one hundred were paving cutters, and about seventy were blacksmiths, steam drill men, engineers, and foremen. The remainder were quarrymen, paid from $1.75 to $2.25 per day. Steam drill operators got $2.50, "blacksmiths $2.75, paving cutters by the piece, from $2.50 to $5.00 per day." Engineers received $50.00 to $60.00 monthly, whereas foremen got from $90.00 to $150.00 per month.[14] As Peter Liveright reminds us, overall those who carved, dressed, and lettered the granite employed the most sophisticated skills, followed by polishers, tool sharpeners, and then those who possessed semi- and unskilled capabilities such as lumpers and boxers, grouters, tool-grinders, derrickmen, machinists, power plant engineers, firemen, etc. Quarry work thus employed far more workers who were semi-skilled or unskilled in nature.[15]

Even by 1895, we can see the beginnings of a carefully defined hierarchy of status in these pay differences. The great majority of workers, however, received relatively equal pay. On the other hand, workers who were injured received little recompense. Even the theoretical right to litigate was more illusion than reality. The delays and high costs of litigation meant that, as a local engineer declared, "unless he's a stayer and got money, [the plaintiff] might jest as well git out."[16]

Hooker also reports that quarriers from Maine contrasted "the easy pace there with the uninterrupted and rapid movement here." He graphically describes the work scene:

> The heavy, eight-pound sledge, swung with both hands while
> the drill is held by a third man, falls about 40 times per minute,
> and the 3 1/2 pound hammer, swung with one hand while the
> drill is held with the other, averages double that rate. Shifting
> drills, driving wedges, hitching chains, vary the exercise, but the
> physical expenditure of energy in the nine hour day is heavy.[17]

The labor force varied according to the season and available work. Winter, for example, brought some out-migration to lumbering camps. Paving cutters, "an especially unstable class," followed the contracts, making frequent moves, even as far as from Maine to Georgia and back. Their relatively high wages suffered attrition in these comings and goings.[18]

Ethnic diversity within the labor force, even before the massive inflow of northern Italians after the late 1890s, sometimes compromised efforts to work in tandem for particular goals of the labor movement. Despite the amalgam of four main groups in 1895 (Scots, French Canadians, Irish, and native Yankees), however, and the religious diversity evident in such a mix, the stridency evident elsewhere during the 1890s by the organization of the anti-Catholic, nativist American Protective Association did not exist in Barre. Perhaps the considerable number of Catholics, together with frequent contacts at work, over boardinghouse tables, in the unions, and in the schools, dampened overt conflicts and suspicions.[19]

Merchants extended liberal credit terms to the workers, with settlements made on a monthly basis. Hooker downplays the assumption of the more sedate residents of Barre that Millstone Hill must have been "a terrible place":

> True, many of the refinements of life are absent. Men go to the table in their short sleeves. They disfigure a hall floor pretty badly at an entertainment. They swear in a most senseless manner . . . sometimes gamble, and oft times get drunk. On the other hand, it is, as elsewhere, the minority who thus grossly discredit local life and defy the better judgment of the community.

Besides, Hooker approvingly notes that

> General conditions are improving in that the boarding house is steadily yielding to the fireside. About one-half of the men in the district are married. Of the more than two hundred houses, at least two-fifths are owned by the occupants. Comfortable homes and normal family circles are increasing in number.[20]

If this pattern obtained for the district beyond the immediate reach of the greater amenities of Barre city proper, we can assume that comparable events were occurring in Barre itself, although both hill and city dwellers experienced the decidedly mixed blessing of living in an unfinished boom town.

Overall, given the strength of the union movement in the period ending in 1910, the granite workers could be cautiously optimistic that they could defend and preserve their status in the workplace. Powerful and proud unions, a steadily increasing work force, and overall prosperity in the granite industry helped subdue the fissures that could have reasonably been expected to split a community marked by numerous ethnic divisions. They moderated the worst exactions of the urban-industrial revolution in this formative period in the community's life.

In 1910, a writer in the *Granite Cutters' Journal* waxed euphoric, declaring that "history is being made. Progress is visible in every direction. Evolution is duly and truly performing its function."[21] Certainly, from a technical perspective, the granite industry had many reasons to celebrate. The use of more sophisticated tools resulted in markedly increased efficiencies. The work force was growing and membership in the Barre branch of the Granite Cutters' International Association exceeded two thousand by 1915.[22] Barre itself was a bustling, cosmopolitan, feisty community beginning to boast of an infrastructure of schools, municipal facilities, and other community resources that marked its own evolution from the improvised and rough-hewn boom-town of two decades earlier.

Yet, in a striking reversal of historical trends, by the early 1920s, the situation of the Barre granite workers had profoundly changed. Membership in the cutters' union declined to just over one thousand in the twenties. Beyond this, in the aftermath of the war and the "Red Scare" that followed it, the granite manufacturers mounted a vigorous campaign to curb the power of the union movement with their so-called "American Plan." This scheme envisaged non-union "open shops" and was designed to maximize the owners' ability to establish the basic conditions of employment. These anti-union initiatives came at a time when granite as a building and monumental material was suffering vastly increased competition. Finally, in a lethal counterpoint to the workers' loss of status, the increasing incidence of silicosis/tuberculosis underlined the severity of the workers' predicament during the period 1910 through 1940.[23]

As the use of high-powered pneumatic tools increased after 1900, so did the incidence of dust and disease. Plug drills, the "bumper," pneumatic chisels, jackhammers, layner drills, and sand blasting equipment were some of the technological innovations that not only compromised the intricate craft traditions of the individual artisan, but accentuated a health crisis in both quarry and shed. As early as 1904 the conservative head of the Granite Cutters' Union noted that

> These sheds are splendidly equipped with all known appliances
> facilitating the output of granite, but they are generally lacking
> in one thing, mainly a means of ventilating dust which is
> produced in the course of granite cutting.[24]

For a time, woefully incomplete remedies within the sheds were accompanied by warnings that workers should not focus solely on the quarry owners as bearing responsibility for the high incidence of tuberculosis in Barre, and that "there must be the personal attention of each man to himself and his manner of living."[25] Unfortunately for those who offered such well-intentioned advice, the clearest correlation was that evident between increased illness and the increase in dust-creating pneumatic tools.

Ironically, the very attributes of granite that made it a highly polishable stone produced, as part of the quarrying and finishing processes, tiny shards of silica. These invaded the lungs "like microscopic razor blades." As one worker declared, the sufferer could end up "drowning in his own blood." Nor were such early devices as "Spencerian Throat and Lung Shields" adequate to fend off the deadly results of the dust-impregnated workplace.[26] By 1921, eighty-six percent of all granite cutter deaths were the result of silicosis-tuberculosis. In 1937, an astonishingly high forty-five percent of the workers endured some stage of silicosis.[27]

In addition to this primary threat were the more traditional risk factors such as rockslides, faulty explosions, dropped stones, falls, and the like. The workers also confronted problems of seasonal unemployment as well as the increasing mechanization of the industry. Even when a rudimentary workmen's compensation bill was passed just before American intervention in World War I, it was difficult to collect significant damages. Indeed, it was not until 1951 that the state of Vermont finally passed legislation allowing compensation for the crippling disease of silicosis/ tuberculosis.[28]

Beyond this, the Great Depression brought dramatic declines in monumental stone sales in the United States; they fell from $15,848,000 in 1929 to only $7,456,000 by 1931. In 1932, wages were cut fifteen percent, accompanied by underemployment and outright layoffs. A campaign in 1933 to organize open shops and address the wage issue resulted in worker setbacks comparable to 1922-23. Not until 1941 were the unions able to secure an organizational status within the industry at all comparable to their pre-1914 situation.[29]

Grim health statistics do not begin to communicate the devastation of the silicosis epidemic among the granite workers. Barre resident Pace Nicolino vividly recalled granite cutters walking to their homes after their day's work looking like white ghosts, covered from head to toe with granite dust.[30] Former Mayor Cornelius Granai, who had visited the granite sheds as a youth, distinctly remembered the workers' black spit on the workplace floors.[31] A stonecutter from Viggiu, Italy, was especially eloquent in his recollections:

> I have gone to work in the morning and after a little while in the shed I couldn't recognize my own body. It was covered from head to toe with dust. Of course we had to breathe that dust in. That is what does it. We give our whole strength, our hearing, our hands, our sight, the eyes, everything we possess to the business. We give our lives, our family, we give everything we have and love, and then what do we get out of it? Just a little money.[32]

Present-day scholar and poet Verbena Pastor powerfully suggests the ironies that pervade this period of history for the stonecutters in her moving poem, "Alberto P." She portrays a granite worker, an artisan from Monza, Italy, who works in the sheds. He was warned before leaving Monza to avoid the "houses" of dubious repute else he be killed when young by "an illness that begins with S." Pastor's poem continues:

Donato Colletti, Brusa Monument, Hope Cemetery, Barre, Vt. 1937. Photograph by Karen Lane.

Didn't pay heed to the cough
and short breath (it was cold,
this wasn't Monza), and in the dust
of the sheds I worked on, snatching
images of angels and round-kneed victories
being polished, thinking of the "houses"
and how I kept away from illness.
In three years my lungs were sagging pouches
packed with the chips of angels, the sprinkle
of Celtic crosses
and others' tombstones.
My own grave was inside.[33]

Some stonecutters died in their thirties, more in their forties, and frequently in their early fifties. Certain Barre streets became known as *la strada della vedove*—the street of widows. Women struggled to survive and to protect their children by opening their homes to boarders. They sometimes resorted to selling *grappa*, a homemade liquor. Many families urgently encouraged their children to select trades that would take them away from the sheds.[34]

The awful persistence and extent of silicosis/tuberculosis puts into poignant perspective the critical questions concerning the status of the granite workers. Put most boldly, were these workers with respect to health issues reduced to the status of proletarians? Were they doomed to be acted upon, rather than retaining a degree of autonomy through which they could truly shape the conditions of their employment? David Seager forcefully claims that "regardless of pay or self-image, workers are always merely raw material in the production equation for capitalists, and hence interchangeable (to varying degrees, of course)." Therefore, "the workers were commodities whether they realized it or not."[35] Conversely, to Paul Demers, "The wage earners of Barre were not degraded proletarians. Compared with other areas, the work week was shorter, the pay better, and the living conditions were more healthful." Indeed, Demers concludes that "the most conspicuous vices of industrial society were not present in Barre."[36]

Certainly, especially in the years before 1917, Barre was a highly organized community where "labor was a way of life." The unions had often been successful in structuring the work in ways that affirmed the many strengths of a proud artisanal tradition. Seager himself notes that "the workers were not only passive and helpless pawns to be used or totally controlled by the bosses."[37] Unions worked persistently for shorter hours, better working conditions, and higher wages. Why then did it take nearly forty years to substantially resolve key safety and health issues, when most aspects of the problems were identified before World War I?

No simple answer will suffice. A key factor, of course, was the breakneck pace of technological change. The careful, incremental nature of negotiations over the work process simply did not keep up with the accelerating pace of technical innovations in the industry. Both quarrying and finishing processes were modified markedly and continuously. Even as management encouraged healthier working conditions, new machines were introduced offering greater profit to an increasingly cost-conscious industry. The unions themselves sometimes focused on higher wages rather than health conditions in an increasingly competitive economic environment. Dust and increased profits seemed locked in a deadly embrace, with the vulnerable granite worker as victim in this lethal relationship.[38]

Even when the unions were in their ascendency before 1917, there was a lag between the introduction of technology and efforts to counter its negative effects. This lag was accentuated given the relative decline of union strength in the chastening aftermath of the early 1920s owners' campaign to implement the "American Plan." It was no accident, then, that a more inclusive resolution of the dust issue awaited a reinvigorated union movement in the mid-1930s, given the more friendly environment for labor organization that occurred after 1935 passage of the Wagner Act during the New Deal. Moreover, the medical profession had identified the causes of the stoneworkers' plight by the 1930s, adding its considerable weight in encouraging a proper response. At long last, after belated, piecemeal actions, the terrible linkage between work and premature death would be broken, as effective suction devices became nearly universal between 1936 and 1939.[39]

What do these oscillations in the history of the granite workers of Barre teach us? Does granite industry experience suggest that the overall theme of transition from relatively autonomous artisan to owner-controlled worker also typified the stone trades? Evidence indicates that even powerful unions could do little more than slow the pace at which craft unions were forced to yield greater control of the production process to owners. It is also true that the industry had become increasingly centralized since 1880, although there remained a significant number of relatively small-scale operations. Generally, however, the need for increased capital investment made widespread ownership increasingly difficult as the twentieth century progressed.

Yet these developments did not transpire without exceptional efforts by the workers to mitigate the more lethal aspects of the trade. Even in the 1920s, when half the firms were non-union open shops, the unions pressed for and established the general standards of work conditions that persisted well into the century, as what historian Bruce Laurie has termed "prudential unionism" survived despite assaults from both owners and government during the formative stages of union growth in the late nineteenth and early twentieth centuries.[40] Until the heightened attacks on unions in the early 1920s, they had been able to protect their workers' right to organize, increase wages, define working conditions, and at least partially mitigate the multiple impacts flowing from new technology.

It is provocative to speculate upon what might have happened had there been no world war from 1914 to 1918 and no "Red Scare" following that conflict. Seen in retrospect, the disruptions of the war and the anti-radical agitations that followed from 1919 through the early 1920s are critical to understanding the granite workers' decline in status. Shifting currents within the granite industry and technological innovation also compromised worker initiatives, but the "Red Scare" and anti-foreigner impulses in the 1920s also provided cover for sometimes virulent anti-union efforts in Barre, as they did throughout the country. Given these challenges, it is surprising that the unions fared as well as they did. Despite occasional ethnically based cleavages within the work force, the unions retained a foundation upon which they could rebuild in the far friendlier environment of the mid-1930s and after.

It would be misleading to portray owners as simply exploitive capitalists, seeking to turn their workers into underpaid proletarians. The long tradition of many owners having formerly worked alongside their fellows in the quarries and sheds surely mitigated many of the raw aspects of worker-owner conflicts. Then, too, the workers were not mere victims of cupidity and rampant technology; they were ultimately successful in enhancing their work environment, acting as a critical force in achieving proper suction devices by 1940. Two generations of workers had paid a terrible price, but the prospect for dignified and non-lethal employment was at last at hand. The bittersweet impact of advanced technology necessitated constant vigilance, but eventually the balance tipped towards increased health and safety.[41]

While approaching the issues from differing perspectives, both Seager and Demers offer us insight into the production process, and the relative responsibilities of owners and workers to make this process work without severe mortality rates. Seager suggests the dangers in turning workers into mere commodities; Demers affirms the resiliency of the workers' organizations even when sorely pressed. The granite workers fared no worse than comparable groups over the same period. Despite their relative loss of control over the work process as compared to the pre-1917 context, workers' initiatives, medical evidence, owner acquiescence, and creative negotiations had resolved a critical aspect of worker health and safety. Many struggles remained, but at least the most persistent lethal threat to the labor force had been virtually eliminated.

Finally, does this survey of the experiences of the Barre granite workers affirm those who claim that Vermont was spared the worst exactions of the urban-industrial revolution? It would scarcely seem so, given the twin realities of diminished artisanal autonomy and the high mortality inflicted upon workers by silicosis/tuberculosis. If there is compelling evidence to sustain the hypothesis of Vermont's being an exception to the negative aspects of urban-industrialism, it is not to be found in workers' experiences in Barre from 1880-1940.

NOTES

1. See Frank Bryan and John McClaughry, *The Vermont Papers: Recreating Democracy on a Human Scale* (Chelsea, Vt.: Chelsea Green Publishing Co., 1989), especially pages 26-44. See also my review of this stimulating book in *North by Northeast* (June 1989), 28.

2. Rowland E. Robinson, *Vermont: A Study of Independence* (Boston: Houghton Mifflin and Co., 1892). See also the reprint with introduction to the new edition by Paul A. Eschholz (Rutland, Vt.: Charles E. Tuttle Co., 1975). Also Charles T. Morrissey, *Vermont: A Bicentennial History* (New York: W. W. Norton and Co., 1981); William Doyle, *The Vermont Political Tradition and Those Who Helped Make It*, 3rd ed. (Barre, Vt.: Northlight Studio Press, 1990). I suggest other ways to view Vermont history in my essay, "Vermonters: A Yankee Kingdom?" *Vermont Life* 44 (Spring, 1990): 26-27.

3. A splendid overview concerning these and similar questions is provided by Leon Fink, "Industrial America's Rank and File: Recent Trends in American Labor History," *Social Education* 46 (February 1982): 92-99. Reprint: Education Department of the AFL-CIO.

4. See H. Nicholas Muller, III and Samuel B. Hand, eds., *In A State of Nature: Readings in Vermont History*, 2d ed. (Montpelier, Vt.: Vermont Historical Society, 1982), especially Appendix B, 403-404.

5. See Paul Demers's thoughtful and important study "Labor and the Social Relations of the Granite Industry in Barre" (B.A. thesis, Goddard College, 1974), 1-4. This thesis is one of the key works concerning Barre history.

6. George Ellsworth Hooker, "Labor and Life at the Barre Granite Quarries: A Brief Survey of Social Conditions on Millstone Hill, Barre, Vermont in the Autumn of 1895" (Typescript at the Aldrich Public Library, Barre, Vt., November 1895).

7. Demers, 2-5; Hooker, 1-2.

8. Hooker, 2-3.

9. Demers, 3.

10. Demers, 15.

11. As cited in Demers, 108. See also Otto Johnson, "The Labor Situation in the Granite Industry in the Barre District, Vermont" (Ph.D. diss., American University, 1928), 370-A. Membership figures vary according to the month the tabulation occurred.

12. Demers, 10. See also the significant study by Bruce Laurie, *Artisans into Workers: Labor in Nineteenth-Century America* (New York: Farrar, Straus and Giroux, 1989), which exceeds the usual qualities of a synthesis and introduces the concept of "prudential unionism" in evaluating the origins and policies of the American Federation of Labor. See especially pages 176-210.

13. Demers, 10-15.

14. Hooker, 4.

15. Peter Liveright, "Unionism and Labor Relations in the Granite Industry, Barre, Vermont" (B.A. thesis, Goddard College, 1943), 5.

16. Hooker, 5.

17. Ibid.

18. Ibid., 6.

19. Ibid.

20. Ibid., 8, 9.

21. Quoted in Richard Hathaway, "Men Against Stone: Work, Technology, and Health in the Granite Industry," in Gene Sessions, ed., *Celebrating a Century of Granite Art* (Barre and Montpelier, T. W. Wood Art Gallery at the Vermont College Arts Center and the Barre Museum at the Aldrich Public Library, 1989), 19-20.

22. Demers, 108.

23. Ibid.; Liveright, 23-26; Hathaway, "Men Against Stone," 20-21.

24. As quoted in David Seager, "Technology and Health in the Granite Industry in Barre, Vermont, 1880-1940" (M.A. thesis, State University of New York at Binghamton, 1989), 32. See also Albert E. Russell, et al., "The Health of Workers in Dusty Trades, II: Exposure to Silicosis Dust (Granite Industry)," U.S. Public Health Bulletin No. 187 (Washington, D.C.: USGPO, 1929); Wendy Richardson, "The Curse of Our Trade: Occupational Disease in a Vermont Granite Town," *Vermont History* 60 (Winter 1992): 5-28.

25. *Barre Daily Times*, 10 February 1905, 1; see also Seager, 32-33.

26. Seager, 30-31.

27. Demers, 53-54.

28. Seager, 28; Liveright, 71.

29. Roby Colodny, "Labor in Barre: 1900-1941," in *Vermont's Untold History* (Burlington, Vt.: Public Occurrence, 1976), 14-17; Liveright, 29-35.

30. Pace Nicolino. Interview, July 25, 1972, Vermont Historical Society.

31. Notes from interview with Mayor Cornelius Granai, undated (probably 1975). Ben Collins papers. Aldrich Public Library, Barre, Vermont.

32. Anthony Tonelli (fictitious name), as quoted in Ann Banks, ed., *First-Person America* (New York: Vintage Books, 1981), 105.

33. The poem appears in its entirety in Jill C. Lessard, ed., *25% Rag: Short Stories and Poems by Northern New England Writers* (Woodstock, Vt.: Elm Tree Press, 1989), 14-15.

34. Hathaway, 21; Mari Tomasi, "The Italian Story in Vermont," *Vermont History* 28 (January 1960): especially 81-83. See also the ground-breaking article by Maria Susanna Garroni, "Coal Mine, Farm and Quarry Frontiers: The Different Americas of Italian Immigrant Women," *Storia Nordamerica* 5 (1988): 115-136.

35. As quoted in Hathaway, "Men Against Stone," 19; see also David Seager to Richard Hathaway, personal correspondence, 31 May, 1989.

36. As quoted in Hathaway, "Men Against Stone," 19.

37. David Seager to Richard Hathaway, personal correspondence, 31 May 1989.

38. Hathaway, 19-20.

39. Ibid., 20-22.

40. Laurie, 176-210.

41. Hathaway, 22-23.

Vermont's Nineteenth Century Railroad Workers

Gene Sessions

Much has been written about the politics of the state's railroads, their economic impact on communities, and the financial dealings of their leaders. Handsome pictorial publications have focused on individual roads. Almost nothing, however, has been written about the experience of the mainly anonymous workingmen whose labor actually kept the industry running. Railroad employees were the first Vermonters to work in large numbers for what would later be thought of as big, impersonal corporations, but little is known of those early Vermont industrial laborers.

Compared to other eastern states, Vermont came late to railroading. The first run by a steam-powered train in the United States occurred in 1830, and in the next ten years about three thousand miles of track was laid, most of it in the northeast. Vermont's first railroad construction did not begin until 1846. In that year, the Vermont Central Railroad (later renamed the Central Vermont) started building a route diagonally across the state from White River Junction on the Connecticut River to Essex Junction near the shores of Lake Champlain. In 1847, the Rutland Railroad began building up the western side of the state from Bellows Falls to Burlington. Also in the late 1840s, the Connecticut and Passumpsic Rivers Railroad began construction on a route up the east side, from White River Junction through St. Johnsbury and Newport to the Canadian border. Other minor roads undertook construction projects through the end of the 1890s. In the process, St. Albans, Rutland, and St. Johnsbury, three towns located at busy rail junctions, emerged as major centers of railroad activity. Together they employed approximately half the state's rail work force. By 1900, almost 1,100 miles had been built in Vermont and little additional track was laid thereafter with the exception of short spur lines to lumber camps and quarries.

Early track construction projects created the first demand for railroad workers. Local men and nearby farmers provided a source for those first rail-laying crews. The Woodstock Railroad, for example, recruited workers locally by plastering fences with posters calling for five hundred laborers and promising "good pay and steady employment."[1] To a large extent, however, Vermont's railroads were built by immigrants. Irish newcomers, pushed across the Atlantic by the potato famine of the 1840s, entered Vermont by way of Canadian ports in time to join work crews being assembled for the great Vermont Central and Rutland Railroad construction projects. Employed by labor contractors holding leases from railroad companies to construct the roads, the Irish laborers earned fifty cents a day and board for ten hours of work.[2] In the 1870s, French-Canadians "were imported for labor" on the St. Johnsbury and Lake Champlain line, and during the 1890s Italian immigrants brought in from New York City provided the labor for construction of the Wilmington Railroad while other Italian immigrants laid the rails for the Bristol Railroad.[3] When these construction projects were completed many workers—native and newcomer—sought more permanent railroad jobs in towns located along the tracks.

The size of the state's railroad work force as it emerged in the late nineteenth century is difficult to ascertain. In 1850, the U.S. Census identified a total of 163 men as railroad employees in the state; by 1900 the census totals had climbed to 3,182.[4] These numbers, however, did not include the many railroad laborers, sometimes identified by census takers simply as "laborers" or "day laborers," who filled the railroads' lower ranks and who were sometimes long-term railroad employees. In the mid-1860s, payrolls of the Vermont Central Railroad, alone, stood at approximately twelve hundred workers, yet the 1860 Census showed only 881 rail workers statewide, and only 1,592 in 1870.[5] These limitations of the census data and the absence of complete payroll sheets or other forms of employment information suggest a need for caution in discussing railroad employment totals.

Mid-nineteenth century Vermont enterprises such as farming, quarrying, or milling involved relatively small numbers of individuals performing essentially similar tasks. The new railroads, however, required large numbers of workers with highly diverse skills. In the earliest days, the rail companies filled many of the most crucial positions from the existing local transportation concerns. Thus, the Vermont Central Railroad drew on "stage drivers and other employees of the old turnpike companies" to fill jobs for engineers, conductors, and station agents. According to one account, those early train crews "were rather a happy-go-lucky lot."[6] Nevertheless, relatively rapidly in those first years, railroad employment became highly specialized and the positions of locomotive engineer, fireman, brakeman, and conductor came to be occupied by trained, responsible, and experienced men. This was the case as well for the craftsmen in the engine and repair shops: the carpenters, machinists, and painters who built the engines, repaired the cars, and constructed the sometimes massive Vermont railroad bridges. Walter Licht, in his excellent 1983 study, *Working on the Railroad*, states that it was common for early railroad companies to recruit engineers and firemen from the pool of machinists and machinists' apprentices in the machine shops where the new locomotives were built and that early brakemen were drawn from the collection of young men, including farmers' sons, in the local casual labor force.[7]

Of all railroad labor, the railmen commanded the highest pay. These were the workers who actually rode the rails rather than toiled in the shops or yard, and whose jobs required the greatest skill and experience. Engineers and conductors led in wages, followed by firemen, who worked directly under engineers, and brakemen, who were under the supervision of conductors. Generalizations about annual wages are difficult, however, because systems of payment were not consistent or uniform. Rather than straight salary, payment was by day, or by the trip, or by the number of miles on a trip, or by the total miles in a month, or by some combination of these methods.

An example of the complexity was the Central Vermont Railroad's pay system. Edward Kirkland relates that main line passenger conductors, northern division, "were paid $75 a month for a mileage of 3,000-4,000, $85 for 4,000-5,000, and $97 for 5,000-6,000, while for all miles in excess of 6,000 they received 2 cents a mile. Conductors on branch runs were paid $55 to $65 a month. Conductors on through freights received 2.75 cents per mile south of St. Albans, and from St. Albans to Montreal $1.85 a trip; overtime began after seven hours on joint runs; conductors on way freights were paid $65 to $70 per month."[8]

The compensation for conductors and engineers, along with their positions of responsibility, placed them among the highest paid and most respected of Victorian America's work force. These "knights of the road" were among the most prosperous workers in Vermont in the 1870s, 1880s, and 1890s, with a standard of living similar to that of shopkeepers and clerks.[9] Daniel Willard recalls of his boyhood in central Vermont in the 1870s that "a locomotive engineer had a status in any community that placed him, if he behaved himself, on a level with the best men of the town."[10]

Conductors, too, "oozed respectability." Charles George, a conductor on Vermont's Western Railroad, recalled that he and his fellow conductors adopted a distinctive bearing and wardrobe, complete with topcoats and silk hats. They also drew satisfaction from each other's company, spending leisure time together and arranging social gatherings with conductors from other Vermont and New England railroads.[11] Perhaps it was their propensity for style and fashion that earned early conductors a reputation as "arrogant and dandies."[12]

The shophands and yardmen also received, according to their skills and responsibilities, earnings above that of average nineteenth-century workers. Ticket office clerks earned a higher wage than machinists, and machinists more than baggage men or station agents, although of this group only machinists were paid per diem wages. The rest received monthly salaries.[13] By the end of the century, a day's work for most yardmen had been stabilized at ten to eleven hours. Shop hands also enjoyed a certain regularity in their employment that was unavailable to workers at a lower grade of railroad tasks.

As with the railmen, Vermont communities also held in high regard the most skilled of the shop hands. In the 1850s, when Northfield briefly reigned as the state's railroad capital, editors of the town's two newspapers agreed that the community's shop hands were men of "high . . . character" and that "as a class" Northfield had "no better citizens."[14]

The lowest ranks of railroad employment were occupied by unskilled workers—those section hands, yard laborers, and station hands who made up the mass of the industry's general labor force. They represented the largest single category of railroad employment and had the least job security. Their jobs were often intermittent or seasonal, their tasks physically demanding, and their wages low. In the 1860s the Vermont Central paid its section men one dollar per day, or twelve cents below the average wage for ordinary day laborers in the state at that time.[15] Daniel Willard claims to have been paid ninety cents per day as a Central Vermont section hand in the late 1870s.[16] To get by, consequently, workers in railroad towns sometimes took on more than one job with the rail company. An example is Northfield's John McCarthy who at the time of his accidental death was holding down positions as janitor at the railroad station, flagman at the village crossing, and handyman at the freight office.[17]

Most of Vermont's unskilled railroad laborers and trackmen were not farmers' sons. This is true despite the notable example of Daniel Willard, who at age eighteen left behind the drudgery of work on his father's North Hartland farm to take a trackman's job on the nearby Central Vermont Railroad. In Northfield, few sons of farmers or other non-blue collar fathers entered railroad employment at all. The sons of native Vermont fathers did occupy positions at every level of the railroad job structure and they tended to dominate those trades requiring greatest responsibility, but the lower ranks were filled in large numbers by immigrants and their sons, primarily from Ireland, French Canada, and Italy. In 1870 in St. Albans, immigrants and their sons held less than fifteen percent of positions above the unskilled level, but occupied three-fourths of the jobs as railroad laborers, section hands, and watchmen. In the same year, in the rail towns of St. Johnsbury, Rutland, and Northfield, foreign-born workers and their sons represented only twelve percent of conductors, sixteen percent of engineers, and eleven percent of firemen.[18]

Railroading at all ranks was essentially a young man's sphere. Workers in their twenties and thirties made up the bulk of the state's railroad work force, and few men continued to work beyond age fifty. Railroading was also sometimes a family affair, especially in the larger railroad centers, with fathers and numerous sons all working the rails. In fact, the Connecticut and Passumpsic's superintendent sought to hire the sons of employees, believing them potentially more reliable and industrious than laborers not so deeply rooted in the community.[19]

New England railroad companies, nevertheless, experienced high worker turnover at all levels. This was especially true from the 1840s through the 1860s when only half of all workers stayed on the job longer than six months, with yard and track laborers most transient.[20] This high rate of labor mobility was at least partly a reflection of the high residential movement of the population as a whole. Analysis of U.S. Census data shows that three-fourths of Irish workers living in Northfield in 1850, 1860, and 1870 did not remain in town long enough to appear on more than one census, and that native-born workers were only slightly less transient.[21]

The prospect of promotion or movement upward to better paying jobs and higher status conditioned the focus of many workers who made long-term commitments to the railroads.[22] For engineers and conductors, the elite of the railroad labor community, however, the desire to go beyond their already proud positions was often limited. Thus, Northfield engineers Robert Gregg and George Randall and conductor Elbridge Pierce, all of whom achieved their ranks by their mid-thirties, continued in those jobs contentedly through three decades, all the while accumulating savings for a comfortable old age.[23] For semi-skilled and other skilled positions, beginning in the 1860s, promotion from within the ranks became settled company practice. The moves from fireman to engineer, achieved by Northfield's Lewis F. Henry,[24] or from machinist to engineer by William L. Hurlbert[25] were characteristic promotional patterns for career railroaders in skilled positions.

Upward movement proved least likely for those numerous workers at railroad's lowest ranks. Daniel Willard, the farmer's son who moved from trackman to fireman to engineer, and ultimately to the presidency of the Baltimore and Ohio Railroad, was certainly unrepresentative. Somewhat more characteristic of mobility from the bottom ranks was the Central Vermont's Thomas O'Grady, who, over a long career, made the modest advancement from common laborer to head of a section gang, and eventually to the semi-skilled position of switchman at the Northfield yard.[26] Perhaps most typical was the inability to move out of unskilled posts at all, as seen in the careers of three long-time Northfield railroad workers. Patrick Cannon, son of Irish immigrants, became a "railroad laborer" on the Vermont Central at age sixteen in 1850; when he retired forty years later he was still doing pick and shovel work as a trackman.[27] John McGrath, also the son of Irish immigrants, grew up in a modest house beside the Vermont Central tracks in Northfield. He began working for the railroad at age eighteen in 1874 and remained a "railroad laborer" for forty-five years.[28] Robert Paine, Irish-born, of North-field, spent his entire working life of almost thirty years as a railroad "day laborer."[29]

For some railroaders, mobility involved physical movement to another town in Vermont for better opportunity. William Mulcahey was typical of many in the Northfield area who relocated to St. Albans when the Vermont Central's managers transferred the railroad's main operations there in the 1850s and 1860s. Mulcahey retired from the road after forty years and returned to Northfield to die.[30] Other Vermont railroaders, seeking better prospects, removed themselves from Vermont altogether. The *Northfield News*, the *Rutland Herald*, and other newspapers in the late 1870s and 1880s regularly reported the departure of local men for railroad jobs in the west.

For others, railroading represented only one part of a worklife marked by occupational changes. Simeon Curtis of Northfield had worked variously as a merchant, blacksmith, and foundryman before finally taking employment with the Vermont Central.[31] More striking, perhaps, is the downward mobility of men such as Moses Johnston, who in his early forties achieved the rank of railroad brakeman, accumulating assets of almost a thousand dollars, but by his early fifties was occupied as a peddler with resources of less than four hundred dollars.[32]

Above the unskilled ranks, a number of benefits occasionally were available to railroad employees in addition to their relatively high wages. The Vermont Central provided some company-built lodging for its workers. Along Central Street in Northfield, paralleling the tracks, the company constructed ten multifamily dwellings of identical architecture. Arranged five on each side of the street, facing each other and known as the "company houses," they apparently provided accommodations primarily to the families of engineers and conductors. Charles Paine, the Vermont Central's first president, gave to the town's large Irish-Catholic community, mostly railroad employees, land for Northfield's first Catholic church and also land for a Catholic cemetery.[33] In the 1850s, the Vermont Central and the Connecticut and Passumpsic Rivers Railroad established libraries for their employees. The Vermont Central's library, located in the depot at Northfield, was used by employees who were willing to buy stock in the library for three dollars each. Begun as a collection of six hundred volumes, it had grown to fifteen hundred volumes several years after its move to St. Albans.[34]

The fringe benefits of railroad employment for workers were more than balanced by numerous disadvantages. Under the railroad companies' complex pay systems, many of even the most skilled and experienced railmen led lives of relative instability, vulnerable to the vagaries of seasonal freight demands, unpredictable weather patterns, and railroad traffic schedules often dictated in far distant locales. Their work, one contemporary said, "imperils their lives with almost every duty they perform."[35] The risk was high that legs, arms, hands, or fingers might be crushed, or lives lost, in carrying out ordinary railroad tasks. Faulty road-bed construction, washouts, stone slides, crude technology (such as the link-and-pin coupler), mechanical failure, snow drifts, and human error were constant threats to their safety. Railroad men were, as one observer stated, "a maimed lot."[36]

Accidents were commonplace. By the end of the century, two or three thousand railroad workers were being killed per year nationally, and seven to ten thousand injured. Railroad companies, placing most of the responsibility for the deaths and injuries on worker carelessness, drew up employee handbooks elaborating precise duties and standards of conduct for each job. One of the few American railroads to resort to the use of fines as part of its railway discipline system was the Rutland Road which in its "Book of Rules" required the "withholding of pay" from negligent employees.[37] More serious efforts to improve railroad safety—such as the introduction of air brakes and the automatic car coupler—did not come until after Congress passed the Railroad Safety Appliance Act in 1893.

The hazards of their trades prompted rail workers to organize mutual aid societies. These national railway organizations emerged along craft lines, offering at least a partial solution to the prohibitive expense of commercial insurance for men in their kind of work. For some Vermont railroaders the societies' impact was measurable. Thus, workers such as Charles McCarty, a long-time Central Vermont freight conductor forced to retire because of ill health, could be "substantially aided" during long illness by the Order of Railroad Conductors.[38] They also provided significant fraternal functions. Railroader John C. Hurley's bonds with the Order of Railroad Conductors was so strong that he arranged for the monument over his grave in Northfield's old Catholic cemetery to display a carved passenger train accompanied by the initials "O.R.C."[39] These craft-based brotherhoods did not often collaborate nationally with each other. Not until late in the century did they gradually begin to use their organizations in a direct way to influence immediate economic situations through collective bargaining.

Initiative for forming the brotherhoods did not come from New England railroaders, but by 1900 the four largest associations, involving locomotive engineers, conductors, firemen, and trainmen, all had gained a footing in the region. Railway managers in Vermont, as in the rest of the country, responded with hostility. During a membership drive in the late 1870s, Harley Folsom, superintendent of the Connecticut and Passumpsic Rivers Railroad, bluntly warned engineers on his road not to join the Brotherhood of Locomotive Engineers. Many of his employees joined anyway, including Daniel Willard, the future railroad president.[40]

By 1900, the growth era of Vermont's railroad industry was at an end. For the industry's workers in the state, the half-century after 1850 was a transition step. Not enough is known yet concerning their working and personal lives, or the actions of their employers, to draw conclusions about the changes experienced by labor in the new industry. We know enough, however, to conclude that for these nineteenth century Vermont workers, the self-paced rhythms, informal relationships, local control, and limits of scale characteristic of much pre-industrial and early industrial Vermont employment were no longer a reality.

NOTES

1. Edgar T. Mead, Jr., *Over the Hills to Woodstock: The Saga of the Woodstock Railroad* (Brattleboro, Vt.: Stephen Greene Press, 1967), 8.

2. Ellen C. Hill and Marilyn S. Blackwell, *Across the Onion: A History of East Montpelier, Vermont, 1781-1981* (East Montpelier, Vt.: East Montpelier Historical Society, 1983), 165.

3. John S. Kendall, *History of the St. Johnsbury and Lake Champlain Railroad* (Barnet, Vt., 1975), 6; Bernard R. Carman, *Hoot Toot and Whistle: The Story of the Hoosac Tunnel & Wilmington Railroad* (Brattleboro, Vt.: Stephen Greene Press, 1963), 7; William Gove, "Thirty-Eight Years With the Same Locomotive: The Saga of the Bristol Railroad," typescript, n. d., Vermont Historical Society, MSC-204, 17.

4. U.S. Census, Seventh Census, 1850, Twelfth Census, 1900.

5. Charles Spooner Forbes, "History of the Vermont Central-Central Vermont Railway System, 1843-1932," *The Vermonter* 37 (1932): 244; Burlington *Times*, 24 March 1866; U.S. Census, Eighth Census, 1860, Ninth Census, 1870.

6. Theodore Graham Lewis, ed., *History of Waterbury, Vermont, 1763-1915* (Waterbury, Vt.: Harry C. Whitehill, 1915), 89-90.

7. Walter Licht, *Working for the Railroad: The Organization of Work in the Nineteenth Century* (Princeton, N.J.: Princeton University Press, 1983), 41-43.

8. Edward Chase Kirkland, *Men, Cities, and Transportation, A Study in New England History* (Cambridge: Harvard University Press, 1948) 2: 406.

9. Leon Fink, *Workingmen's Democracy: The Knights of Labor and American Politics* (Urbana, Ill.: University of Illinois Press, 1983), 72.

10. Edward Hungerford, *Daniel Willard Rides the Line* (New York: G. P. Putnam's Sons, 1938), 44.

11. Licht, 234.

12. Kirkland, 2: 403.

13. Forbes, 244.

14. *Star of Vermont* (Northfield), 22 March 1856.

15. Forbes, 244.

16. Hungerford, 30.

17. Gene Sessions, "'Years of Struggle': The Irish in the Village of Northfield, 1845-1900," *Vermont History* 55 (Spring 1987): 77.

18. U.S. Census, Manuscript Schedule I, Ninth Census, 1870, for St. Albans, St. Johnsbury, Rutland, and Northfield.

19. Licht, 52.

20. Licht, 73.

21. Sessions, "'Years of Struggle,'" 72.

22. In *Working for the Railroad*, 160, Walter Licht concludes from a study of the account books of two non-Vermont railroads that only about seven percent of the companies' workers, to 1877, achieved any upward occupational mobility.

23. U.S. Census, Manuscript Schedule I, Seventh Census, 1850, Eighth Census, 1860, Ninth Census, 1870, Tenth Census, 1880, for Northfield.

24. U.S. Census, Manuscript Schedule I, Eighth Census, 1860, Ninth Census, 1870, for Northfield.

25. U.S. Census, Manuscript Schedule I, Seventh Census, 1850, and Eighth Census, 1860, for Northfield.

26. Northfield *News*, 11 September 1894.

27. Northfield *News*, 1 July 1913; U.S. Census, Manuscript Schedule I, Seventh Census, 1850, Ninth Census, 1870, Tenth Census, 1880, for Northfield.

28. Northfield *News*, 24 February 1920; U.S. Census, Manuscript Schedule I, Tenth Census, 1880, Twelfth Census, 1900, for Northfield.

29. Northfield *News*, 24 June 1880; U.S. Census Manuscript Schedule I, Seventh Census, 1850, Eighth Census, 1860, Ninth Census, 1870, Tenth Census, 1880, for Northfield.

30. *Northfield News*, 22 June 1915.

31. U.S. Census, Manuscript Schedule I, Seventh Census, 1850, Eighth Census, 1860, Ninth Census, 1870, Tenth Census, 1880, for Northfield.

32. U.S. Census, Manuscript Schedule I, Ninth Census, 1870, Tenth Census, 1880, for Northfield.

33. Maxine McNamara, *Roman Catholicism in Northfield, Vermont, 1856-1977* (Barre, Vt.: Northlight Studio Press, 1977), 6.

34. *Vermont Christian Messenger* (Northfield), 16 January 1856; L. L. Dutcher, *The History of St. Albans, Vt.* (St. Albans, Vt.: Stephen E. Royce, 1872), 330.

35. Alfred D. Chandler, ed., *The Railroads: The Nation's First Big Business* (New York: Harcourt, Brace & World, 1965), 133.

36. Hungerford, 59.

37. Licht, 118.

38. *Northfield News*, 21 July 1908.

39. *Northfield in the Bicentennial Year, 1976* (Northfield, Vt.: Bicentennial Committee, 1976), 26.

40. Hungerford, 57-58. Despite Vermont and New England railroaders' participation in the brotherhoods, they were little involved in the great national railroad strife of 1877 and the 1890s.

Rails, Trails, and Automobiles:
Tourism in Vermont

Michael Sherman

ere are two views of how Vermonters think about tourists and tourism:

> Vermont's development as a recreational region affords the most promising opportunity for business growth in the state at the present time, and as far as can be foreseen, for a considerable period in the future. The beauty and variety of our scenery, our proximity to great urban centers of population, our situation in the midst of America's principal vacation region, constitute advantages of great potential value. If industrial growth is retarded, if agricultural problems are difficult of solution, the recreational field offers a wonderful opportunity if we are wise enough to establish and maintain high standards of genuine hospitality and wise and consistent policies of protection of our scenic assets.[1]

> Thelma Jordan walked over to a car parked beside her orchard one day and looked at it. The driver said, "Hello. Can we take this road back to the city?" "Don't know why not," Thelma said. "You've taken 'most everything else."[2]

There is a dramatic and durable contrast between these two passages, one a quote from the 1931 report of the Vermont Commission on Country Life and the other one of a host of tourist jokes we have all heard and told. Together they are indicative of the ambivalent attitude of Vermonters toward tourism and tourists. Since the late eighteenth century, when the first mineral spring was exploited, tourism has been both the goose that lays the golden egg and a tapeworm growing out of control and destroying what is most vital and distinctive about Vermont.

According to information from the U.S. Travel Data Council, tourism is currently the third most important economic activity in Vermont, accounting for twenty percent of the state's economy. Vermont ranks third in the nation in its dependence on tourism. For 1989 the Agency for Development and Community Affairs reported visitors spending of some $1.65 billion, and the industry employs about 30,000 people as a year-round average—approximately five percent of the state's population.[3] Yet tourism presents problems. Although industry spokespersons assert that tourism generated $92 million in state and local taxes in fiscal year 1990 and that the rooms and meals tax now generates twice the revenue of state corporate taxes, many people argue that its contribution to the local tax base does not compensate for the demands tourism makes on community services.

Tourism is unreliable, and can be seriously affected by weather conditions, ecology (a plague of mosquitoes), or global politics (a shortage of petroleum). It is also subject to fads and fashion. For example, Vermont was not popular in the mid- to late-nineteenth century, became popular again in the early twentieth century, enjoyed a ski boom in the 1960s, but suffered as the western states developed their ski tourism. And tourism puts stress on the environment, an issue that has become increasingly important.

Vermont's tourist industry is old—it dates back to early in the nineteenth century—and has been shaped by influences as diverse as changes in transportation, esthetics, and public policy.[4]

TRANSPORTATION

Getting to and through Vermont has not always been easy. Indeed the state's geography and topography have presented some formidable barriers. The transportation history of the state, therefore, is an important part of any analysis of the Vermont tourist industry.

Canal building, steamships, the railroad, the automobile, and, to a lesser degree, air transportation have each in turn opened up Vermont to new and larger populations of tourists. We can begin to recreate the expansion of travel and tourism by listening to the accounts of travelers dealing with the purely physical aspects of touring to and in Vermont.

In 1836 G. C. Burnap, a Vermont native who had moved to New York City, took a hasty business trip back to his home state by boat and stagecoach. He described some of the physical conditions of his trip in a letter to his sister:

> August 31, on board the boat DeWitt Clinton
> . . . On a clear night there is almost as much disparity in the *deck* and *cabin* of a steam boat as in the brightness of Elysium and the shades of Cerebrus. To be stowed away in a close cabin, *perfumed* by the respiration of some 200 bipeds—laid up on a shelf, where, if frightful dreams or nightmare should give you a sudden impulse to rise, your head comes in contact with something much more *substantial* than either of these

charms—is like sleeping in the *table* drawer in the kitchen, over the steam of the dinner pot.

Sept. 3, from Burlington to Montpelier—a pleasant ride—good road and the best line of stages I have found anywhere.[5]

Burnap was uncommonly fortunate in his stagecoach ride. Not all stage travelers in Vermont enjoyed such an easy trip. Here, for example, are the comments of Addison Bancroft of Philadelphia, who traveled by stage from Boston to Montpelier on his way to Cabot:

. . . 33 stages (6 horses each) all crowded inside and out. The roads were very bad, was obliged to walk the Horses most of the way afternoon and night. I rode outside untill nearly dark when I had a chance to get inside [S]oon after it commenced to rain and continued untill 2 in the morning. Of course, the outside got a complete soaking. Such roads and such a shaking I never had before. . . . It was very dark and rainy and although the horses walked we were tossed about like a ship at sea. There were in the stage 3 Gentlemen—2 of them were stage sick and vomiting most of the night, 3 Vermont girls going home, 1 woman with 2 children, 1 delicate woman from Nashua.

By the time Addison Bancroft returned to Philadelphia he had used every form of transportation available in his day: horse and wagon, horseback, foot, stage, steamboat, canal boat, and railroad. Of his trip to Vermont Addison notes wryly, "If anyone wishes to visit Vermont I advise them to wait untill the RailRoad is made, which will probably be next Summer."[6]

In 1849 the railroad did arrive. But despite some improvement in comfort, and dramatically increased speed, train travel was not always easy or convenient. The history of railroads in Vermont has been summarized by Tom Bassett and by Hal Meeks.[7] For my purposes, it is important to note first that while railroads played a major role in opening up tourism in Vermont, they also failed to serve passengers or freight customers as well as they might have. This is evident in some of the nicknames given to the various railroad lines in their own day—"The Slow, Jerky, and Long Coming" for the St. Johnsbury and Lake Champlain; "the Old and Late Coming" for the Ogdensburg and Lake Champlain; the "Hold Tight and Worry" for the Hoosac Tunnel and Wilmington; and "36 Miles of Trouble" for the West River Railroad. Perhaps the most famous complaint about Vermont railroads is the lament of frustrated traveler Hon. Edward S. Phelps in his "The Lay of the Lost Traveler," a sample verse of which captures the general sentiment of the time:

Here Boston waits for Ogdensburg
And Ogdensburg for Montreal,
And late New York tarrieth

And Saratoga hindereth all!
From far Atlantic's wave swept bays
To Mississippi's turbid tide
All accidents, mishaps, delays,
Are gathered here and multiplied!
Oh! fellow man, avoid this spot
As you would plague or Peter Funk shun!
And I hope in hell his soul may dwell
Who first invented Essex Junction.[8]

Familiar tales of the failure of railroads should not obscure the fact that trains ushered in the first great age of Vermont tourism and that the railroad companies that built the tracks also promoted, and in some cases owned, the resort hotels their trains served. At the same time, of course, the routes of the railroad determined to a great extent where tourism developed.

To increase passenger traffic, railroads began publishing guidebooks that described their routes, suggested side trips, and listed accommodations. They practically created the image of Vermont as a haven from the moral and physical evils and the hectic pace of urban America. These guidebooks are among our earliest sources for seeing what some grand tourist hotels looked like and give us information about a wide variety of accommodations, attractions, and activities for tourists.

We sometimes fail to consider that railroads also connected people *within* Vermont in a more reliable manner than was possible before 1849. As the railroads grew, they began promoting not only out-of-state tourism but also in-state tourism. Announcements of day excursions combining rail and boat, trains for special occasions, group excursions, and other promotional broadsides show us that the railroad played an important role in creating statewide consciousness by connecting formerly remote communities. An excellent example was Dewey Day in Montpelier on October 12, 1899. The culmination of a nationwide tour made possible by the railroads, Admiral George Dewey's return to his native state was a triumph of nationalism and an event which, in itself, helped strengthen national identity. In Vermont a special train, provided by Dr. William S. Webb of Shelburne, carried Dewey from North Bennington to Montpelier. The Central Vermont Railroad built thirteen special tracks and a temporary station in Montpelier to handle trains bringing an estimated forty thousand visitors to the celebration.

The automobile brought the next and probably the most important change in travel and tourism, not only to Vermont but nationally. Beginning early in the twentieth century the automobile began to break down the communal nature of travel, connected in a more consistent and relentless way urban and rural societies, completed the democratization of travel and tourism by creating demand for a wide variety of tourist accommodations and options, and, by removing many of the physical barriers between people and communities, hastened the homogenization of American culture and the breakdown of regionalism.[9]

Before the automobile, people traveled mostly in groups and mostly as strangers to each other. As the letters of Burnap and Bancroft show, travel was a communal experience and created the conditions for fellowship, often through adversity. Automobile travel, especially in the early years, had its hazards, but rarely did one travel in the company of strangers or with as many people as were jammed into coaches, ships, or railway cars. Much early automobile travel was done as family excursions. Consequently travelers rarely met each other or shared their experiences with others on the road.

On the other hand, automobile travel completed the democratizing of tourism. In the early years of the twentieth century auto excursions were chauffeur-driven affairs. Burlington's Jarvis limousine company in 1915 advertised several chauffeured trips in Vermont, ranging from an afternoon to five days duration.[10] Then Henry Ford's mass marketing of automobiles changed things beginning in 1908, with the low cost, standardized, and easy-to-repair Model T. Ford sold fifteen million Model T's between 1908 and 1928 and put the automobile within reach of a broad range of social and economic groups. As automobiles became more common, touring became a self-guided adventure.

Hotels and inns, recognizing the trend and seeing ways to capitalize on it, began providing their visitors with self-guided motor tours of surrounding towns and villages. People who could not easily afford the expense of a month-long or season-long stay at a grand tourist hotel could, in their autos, take trips of shorter duration and alter or improvise their travel plans in a way that travel by steamship or rail discouraged. One other consequence of the popularity of the automobile was the appearance of the gas and service station as an important and ubiquitous architectural feature.[11]

Most important, the automobile allowed travelers easy access to more and more remote areas than boats, railroads, even stagecoach. The automobile, in fact, finally freed tourists from all itineraries other than those of their own making. If a road was passable at all an automobile soon found its way down it, bringing tourists into contact with a wider cross-section of the population. Conversely it also put residents of even the most remote communities in contact with an increasingly broad cross-section of travelers. The social, economic, and cultural consequences of this wider contact between tourists and residents were of particular interest to the committee that wrote the chapter on tourism for the Rural Life Commission in 1931.

As increasing numbers of tourists penetrated rural areas and left the beaten paths of spas, mountain houses, railroad hotels, and pre-planned itineraries, they demanded and consequently helped create new kinds of accommodations. Farms and private homes in villages and along back roads took in guests, expanding contact between tourists and residents of Vermont. Dorothy Canfield Fisher's 1932 play, *Tourists Accommodated*, is evidence of the powerful effect on the lives of Vermonters of this new form of enterprise and the often intense contact with a wider world that came with it.[12]

In the play, the Lymans—a farm couple faced with difficulty in meeting tax payments, their older daughter, Lucy, aching to attend the Normal School but unable to raise the money for tuition, a restless young son, Phillip, with a yen to travel, and two younger children—decide to open their home to tourists.

A parade of archetypal tourists passes through their home. These include snooty urbanites; penny pinchers; French-Canadians unable to speak English and therefore rather badly treated; "good" city tourists who appreciate the healthy, vigorous outdoor life of a Vermont farm; and a wandering artist who settles for a free room in the hayloft and philsophizes on the beauty of Vermont's landscape. There is a clear programmatic, even propagandistic purpose to the play's simple, even one-dimensional characters and dialogue. It is easy to know who are the good folks and who are not. The play extols the virtues of industrious Vermont farm families, their simple good nature, the deviousness of city folk who wander into the bucolic landscape and uncomplicated rural life and who are, we are meant to be satisfied to note, defeated by it.

Just how well any of this fits with the reality of rural families who, in fact, operated guesthouses is difficult to tell. We lack diaries and other documentation for learning about their experiences, which suggests the need for some oral history work before memories of this era of tourism are lost to us. Clearly, however, automobile tourism had a dramatic effect on families who began coming in contact with a diverse tourist population driving through their communities.

One final aspect of automobile tourism was its public policy implications as development of more and better roads became increasingly important from the 1920s. Vermont, like the rest of the nation, although a generation later, got caught up in the good-roads movement and was embroiled in debates about financing road improvement. Perhaps the best- known controversy over road building in Vermont was the debate over the Green Mountain Parkway. Proposed in 1933 by Col. William J. Wilgus, former chief engineer of the New York Central Railroad and later author of the book, *The Role of Transportation in the Development of Vermont* (1945), the Green Mountain Parkway was to have been a scenic road through the mountains, which would follow the model of Virginia's Skyline Drive. The parkway held out the lure of federal funding, jobs in the midst of the Great Depression, and the promise of greatly increased tourist traffic.[13]

The proposal deeply divided Vermont's political and cultural leaders. In the legislature, the bill authorizing state spending for the parkway was first defeated by the House on March 27, 1935, passed in the Senate on April 3, then passed in a special session of the House in the fall of 1935 subject to approval by Vermont citizens in a special referendum. The issue was hotly debated and on March 3, 1936, Vermonters voted down the parkway 42,318 to 30,897. This was, of course, not the last word on road development in Vermont, but merely the opening episode in a series of debates on super-highway building. Twenty years after the defeat of the Green Mountain Parkway, in 1957, work began on Vermont sections of the Interstate Highway System. The first stretch, eleven miles of I-91 in southeast Vermont, opened in 1961. By 1967 more than 125 miles of I-89 and I-91 had been built, and in 1982 the last link, I-93 between St. Johnsbury and the New Hampshire border, completed the project. The interstate highway has been a major stage in the transportation revolution affecting Vermont tourism.[14] With accessibility to major metropolitan areas assured year round, Vermont's tourist economy went into high gear in the 1960s and 1970s.

TOURING

Knowing how tourists have made their way to Vermont does not tell us why they came. The travelers' letters I have quoted were accounts of people with family in Vermont but who traveled here on business. Indeed, many early travelers and visitors appear to have combined pleasure with business. Vermont's earliest tourist attractions, however, were its mineral springs and mountains.

As Louise Roomet has written, "Vermont's earliest resorts were literally watering holes." Clarendon was the site of the first commercial mineral spring, found in 1776 and already booming in 1798. By 1835 the hotel at Clarendon Springs received five hundred guests each year, many of whom stayed for the entire season. Throughout the first half of the nineteenth century many more mineral springs were discovered, exploited as tourist sites, and transformed into fashionable and costly spas with elegant hotels.[15] Hal Meeks found 115 springs in the Beers county atlases of Vermont (1869-1878) and sixteen more in other sources for a total of 131 documented mineral spring sites by the 1880s. "At one time or another," Meeks writes, "probably thirty-two spring locations supported hotels. Some, such as Clarendon, Sheldon, Guilford, Highgate, and Middletown, were large and diverse recreation spas with bowling [greens], croquet lawns, bottling works, and livery stables. Others, such as Wheelock, Plainfield, Waterville, Barre, and Hartland, were much smaller."[16] With only a few exceptions, the most successful mineral spring hotels were located on or within five miles of a railway, making them easily accessible. Extensive advertising helped draw visitors from great distances and into the 1850s Vermont mineral springs were very popular with visitors from the South. The more elegant hotels created a summertime high society in Vermont that poet John Godfrey Saxe satirized in his poem, "The Song of Saratoga," written at Highgate Springs in 1868.

> In short, as it goes in the world—
> They eat, and they drink and they sleep;
> They talk, and they walk, and they woo;
> They sigh, and they ride, and they dance—
> (With other unspeakable things);
> They pray, and they play, and they pay—
> And that's what they do at the Springs.[17]

Vermont's city hotels and mountain houses also experienced a boom in the mid-nineteenth century, partly as a result of railroad building and partly because they provided visitors access to scenic attractions, genteel recreation, and an unhurried life. Many hotels maintained roads to the summits of nearby mountains and provided coach service to transport visitors. Montpelier's Pavilion Hotel, for example, advertised "pleasant drives and places of Interest about Montpelier," including Middlesex Narrows, Williamstown Springs, Berlin Lake, Owl's Head, and the summit of Mt. Hunger. The hotel cut and maintained a road up Mt. Hunger and ran a stagecoach for guests. In July 1866 Ovid Duke Oberlin of Pennsylvania wrote about a trip up Mt. Mansfield that originated from the Waterbury Hotel.

> The thundering gong told the hour of six and that breakfast was fast preparing, that the inmates of the Waterbury Hotel could acquire an early start for Mount Mansfield—the all absorbing topic discussed among strangers gathered in from all sections—from the Hills of France, the lowlands of Scotland and England and from all parts of our great beloved union—all verging on towards old Mansfield. . . . Soon another gong is sounded and the morning meal is dispensed with and the coach for Mansfield is at the door, which in five minutes is filled to overflowing with emigrees to the mountain and fishing ground. After long and laborious driving we at last reach the foot of the lofty hill. Horses are soon obtained and a few more minutes of time behold us ascending the rugged cliff. Peril is thick on every side, but the noble steed of the mountain, for long years trained to his post, bears safely his precious burden to the top.[18]

Vermont enjoyed a brisk tourist trade of mountain sightseers until the 1870s when the search for the sublime came to dominate esthetic sensibility and drove tourists to the Adirondacks in New York and the White Mountains in New Hampshire. Tourism in Vermont fell off as tourists searched elsewhere for natural beauty. The last quarter of the century also saw tourists going in search of historical sites, most often and importantly those associated with the American Revolution. Vermont's appeal to tourists declined abruptly and precipitously in the 1880s and 1890s, so that by 1900 the state had lost most of its wealthy tourist clientele and its reputation as a fashionable destination declined.[19]

At the same time, however, Vermont began attracting a new clientele. As a growing middle class discovered the charms of pastoral scenery and pursued recreations such as fishing, golf, canoeing, hiking, and skiing, Vermont became an attractive destination and refuge for these city dwellers. Twentieth-century tourism in Vermont has been driven by the quest for a tamed outdoors, with recreational as well as scenic possibilities, nostalgia for America's agrarian roots, and a search for a remnant of the largely imagined golden age of simple pre-industrial virtues.

EMBRACING TOURISM

How have Vermonters and Vermont institutions responded to the challenges and opportunities of tourism? There is no single response, of course, and while some Vermonters have resented the influx of tourists with their somewhat alien and unsympathetic attitudes toward the rural or not-yet-urbanized culture of the state, others embraced tourism as an economic and social panacea.

In his essay for Abby Hemenway's *Vermont Historical Gazetteer* in 1867, Matthew H. Buckham, later to become president of the University of Vermont, expressed his disdain for visits from wealthy "city cousins." "[W]hen they come with their long baggage trains of trunks and band-boxes and take possession of a country village . . . importing into industrious communities [the habit of] doing nothing and doing it elegantly, they . . . demoralize the whole tone of society, and turn respectable villages into the likenesses of Connecticut and New Jersey."[20] That attitude, of course, has survived in words like "flatlanders" and "leaf-peepers," in bumper stickers that welcome people to Vermont and remind them to go home, and in the many jokes told at tourists' and travelers' expense. As recently as October 1990 the Vermont Chamber of Commerce urged Vermonters to be polite to tourists and warned that continued prosperity in the tourist industry depends on it.[21] But since the late nineteenth century there has been another, more positive theme of welcoming tourism and tourists. That response deserves study for its pragmatic approach to solving a variety of problems in Vermont.

In the 1880s the legislature recognized the potential for tourism to solve some of Vermont's economic ills. As early as 1890 the state Board of Agriculture began advertising the availability of abandoned farms and touting their attractiveness and appropriateness as second homes for Buckham's despised "city cousins."[22] In his 1890 inaugural address, Gov. Carroll S. Page noted that "New Hampshire is solving the problem of deserted farms by attracting from the large cities those who would make their summer homes upon her hillsides. Vermont may well follow her example . . ."[23] Two years later, in his farewell address, Page noted that among "the wealthy residents of the large cities . . . there is a growing demand for village homes and small farms which promises to turn backward the tide of decadence in real estate values which has afflicted us for a quarter of a century."[24]

Together with the railroads, the state government promoted tourism and the purchase of unused lands through booklets and annual publications listing available properties. In 1911 Vermont created a Publicity Department, the nation's first state agency to promote tourism. Operating under the Secretary of State, the department received a modest allocation of five thousand dollars for the 1911 biennium, increased to ten thousand dollars in 1913, held at about that level until 1922, with slow increases thereafter.

The Publicity Department emphasized the sale of summer homes and took over the task of publishing the annual list of available properties. Writing in 1934, H. H. Chadwick, director of what was by then called the Vermont Bureau of Publicity, elaborated on Page's rationale for encouraging land sales. "[P]eople thus attracted to Vermont become part-time residents, tax-payers, and usually good missionaries who bring their friends to the state. Much of the property thus used was of little agricultural value or was forest land."[25] By 1934 the bureau was publishing seventeen booklets for wide distribution out-of-state. Three were revised annually: "Where to Stop When in Vermont,"

"Vermont Cottages, Camps, and Furnished Homes for Rent," and "Vermont Farms and Summer Homes for Sale."

By this time the railroads had cut back on their efforts to promote Vermont. They were replaced by the Vermont Chamber of Commerce, whose driving force was James P. Taylor, and by a comprehensive proposal for social reform: the Vermont Commission on Country Life's 1931 book-length report, *Rural Vermont: A Program for the Future by Two Hundred Vermonters*.

The Country Life Commission, organized in 1928, had its roots in the 1925 eugenics survey. Both were promoted by Prof. H. F. Perkins of the University of Vermont; both grew out of a concern about the growing complacency of Vermonters, their isolation, and their long decline "below the level expected of Vermonters."[26] The commission, like the survey, sought to apply "scientific planning" to solve the problems of Vermont, which they saw as being also the problems of American culture. The commissioners saw the possibilities of a symbiotic relationship between rural and urban culture and values. While they focussed on solving economic and material problems in Vermont, they returned constantly to the need to reinvigorate Vermont and national cultural life by asserting and reinforcing "traditional" values of rural life.

Tourism and summer residents played an obvious if not central part in this program, and the commission devoted an entire chapter to the promises and pitfalls of tourism.[27] The commissioners noted with alarm the declining prosperity of Vermont towns, the stagnation of the state's economy, especially in agriculture, and the abundance of otherwise useless property. They acknowledged the burgeoning success of summer camps for boys and girls—drawing a clientele from wealthy urban families in New England and New York—and the dramatic growth of tourist homes that boosted income for farm families, and—here is a revealing point—provided a cultural and social leavening for Vermont's rural communities. One section of the chapter on summer residents, entitled "Effect Upon Families Who Keep Tourists" quotes "at random" some reports collected by the committee:

> The family enjoys meeting cultured people.
> Helpful farm ideas are obtained from visiting farmers from other states.
> Tourists help the children to overcome their "greenness" and shyness, and they learn about different parts of the country from the tourists.
> Tourists help the whole community. Since they began to come, a community club has been organized, street lights have been installed, and a schoolhouse has been built.
> We get hints as to clothing and manners from guests and learn how other people live and what they do.
> The tourists are as good as a school for the boys and Mr. S.
> Taking tourists affords a pleasant break in the monotony of farm work.[28]

With evidence such as this to bolster their argument for a strong tourist industry, the commissioners made sixteen recommendations. Among them were extending the work of the Publicity Bureau, continuing highway and road improvement, encouraging farmers to develop summer camps and cottages, developing recreational facilities, setting up a licensing bureau, having the Agricultural Extension Service give courses on the care and feeding of tourists, and operating more information bureaus at gateway points to Vermont. Acknowledging the persistence of attitudes like Matthew Buckham's, the commission members instructed Vermonters to be "friendly, cordial and hospitable but neither servile or fawning nor narrow, intolerant, [or] suspicious." Finally, in a passage that presages the tension that we find in current debates about how to develop tourism, the committee recommended an approach to the tourist industry that "respects and preserves the natural beauty of the state."[29]

The Country Life Commission was the first of many groups to take a long look at Vermont's future. In 1944 Governor William Wills created a Governor's Postwar Planning Committee for Vermont. Two pages of its report discussed recreational development, including tourism. The committee noted that in 1937 forty-three percent of the total summer travel on Vermont's main roads was by out-of-state tourists and that the introduction of winter sport tourism in the 1930s had begun to make Vermont a four-season attraction "even during the war winters [and] despite the transportation difficulties." Sounding now familiar notes, the committee warned that further success in tourism "depends upon the attitude of Vermonters" and that Vermonters must be careful to "maintain the state's reputation for non-commercial exploitation in a commercial sense."[30]

The committee's recommendations included publications for the tourist market on Vermont's history, geography, agriculture, industry, and attractions; additional attention to publicity—more advertising, opening a promotional office in New York City, and establishing a state magazine (*Vermont Life* was finally established for such a purpose in 1947); employing disabled veterans at gateway and community information booths; state acquisition of lake frontage; new construction projects for the state fish and game service; encouraging winter sports; and "reducing or eliminating stream pollution by a) requiring new industries to provide for the disposal of waste to avoid pollution and b) assisting municipalities in developing plans for the disposal of domestic sewage."[31]

When state government looked at tourism again, during the administration of Gov. Philip Hoff, tourism had taken on major economic significance. The 1964 report of the State Planning Office gave 1946 to 1962 statistics that validated the postwar planning committee's predictions. A steady upward trend led to an estimate that some 3,750,000 tourists came to Vermont in 1962. "These tourists averaged to spend $36.00 each. The estimated total economic impact on the state for 1962 was $135,000,000."[32]

Today, tourism and travel continue to be major economic contributors. The state has taken a much more active and costly role in promoting tourism, although there are many who argue that one percent of the general fund budget for economic development is not nearly enough and that the state has taken a limited view of tourist possibilities. But as tourism has expanded, some issues that received casual attention in the past have come into higher relief. For example, the call for simultaneous development and environmental preservation that earlier generations saw as complementary efforts to promote tourism and preserve Vermont's natural attractions, we now consider contradictions and mutually exclusive choices.

Perhaps no person represents more clearly the ambiguous goals and results of tourist promotion than James P. Taylor. Taylor had a long career in Vermont—as an educator, outdoorsman, and promoter of tourism, outdoor recreation, and environmental protection. His promotional activities point dramatically to the issues, contradictions, and hopes that continue to hold the attention of Vermont citizens and government.

In 1916 Taylor sketched a rough map of a footpath through the Green Mountains from Massachusetts to Canada. Although he enlisted the aid of others in realizing his plan, Taylor is generally credited as the father of Vermont's Long Trail, a founder of the Green Mountain Club, and the man who sold the idea of Vermont's outdoors to Vermonters. He accomplished these goals by shifting the scene of his activities from the classroom—he had previously taught at Saxton's River Academy—to the work of commerce and politics.

For thirty-seven years Taylor worked as a promoter of Vermont, first through the Greater Vermont Association, and after 1922 through its successor organization, the State Chamber of Commerce. His voluminous files, now at the Vermont Historical Society, show him engaged in promoting tourism, paved roads, road beautification, winter sports, golf, wilderness activities, Vermont products, and real estate sales. To our minds, perhaps, this is a contradictory set of issues and in her 1985 article on the Green Mountain Club in *Vermont History News*, Reidun Nuquist quotes unnamed historians who characterized Taylor as "a slightly shabby, slightly disreputable chamber of commerce huckster, . . . amiable schemer, . . . compulsive promoter, . . . mercurial and most unvermonterish grand champion of Vermont." For Taylor, however, as for many of his contemporaries, there was apparently a continuity and harmony in pressing forward with the Long Trail and encouraging the ski industry, promoting paved roads, summer homes, and clean water.[33]

Taylor died in 1949, an outdoorsman to the end. At the time he was involved in projects to clean up pollution in Vermont's lakes and streams. He never retreated from his position as an advocate for developing year-round tourism in Vermont. His is a mixed legacy, which has its echoes in the 1931 report of the Country Life Commission, the 1960s campaigns to make Vermont "the beckoning country," and Act 250, the centerpiece of Vermont's environmental policy, passed in 1970.

The arguments that still rage around Act 250 demonstrate the ambiguous significance of our long history of tourism and tourist promotion. Its proponents interpret Act 250 as an effort to put the brakes on what by 1970 had become a too successful campaign to sell Vermont as a tourist haven. Its opponents interpret the legislation as a short-sighted policy that will kill

Vermont's economic future by cutting off tourism and tourist-related development. For those who lament the decline of our traditional, although somewhat exaggerated agricultural base, tourism—now including summer homes and ski condominiums as well as summer camps, bed-and-breakfasts, and fancy hotels—has been the Vermont equivalent of the sorcerer's apprentice. It is a magic that works too well.[34]

After more than a century of trying to discover the formula that would set tourism going, bring prosperity to the state, and solve a myriad of economic and social problems, we now find ourselves wondering how we can fine-tune the industry. There is broad agreement that we do not wish to lose the natural resources that support tourism and make it possible. At the same time, however, we see in every debate about tourism strong and sometimes bitter disagreement about how we will prevent Vermont's dependence on people and money from out of state from destroying our economic independence and, most of all, our identity as Vermonters.

NOTES

1. Vermont Commission on Country Life, *Rural Vermont. A Program for the Future by Two Hundred Vermonters* (Burlington: Free Press Publishing Company, 1931), 117.

2. Keith M. Jennison, *Green Mountains and Rock Ribs* (New York: Harcourt Brace and Co., 1954), 64-66.

3. Vermont Public Radio, "Switchboard"; program on Vermont's tourism industry, October 17, 1990, guests: Candy Moot, Gene Cenci, Sen. Douglas Racine; Nancy Crowe, "Tourism: Spending Dollars to Make Dollars," *Burlington Free Press*, 25 January 1988, 24-26; Nancy G. Boardman, "Foliage Facts and Figures," *Vermont Magazine* (September/October 1989), 47-48.

4. For an excellent survey of the themes, history, resources, and research that remains to be done on tourism in Vermont and elsewhere in New England, see T. D. Seymour Bassett, "Documenting Recreation and Tourism in New England," *American Archivist* 50 (Fall 1987): 550-569.

5. G. C. Burnap to his sister, Anna Pierce. New York, September 12, 1836. Vermont Historical Society (VHS), manuscript collection, MISC. #201.

6. Addison Bancroft to his mother. Philadelphia, August 25, 1847. VHS manuscript collection.

7. T. D. Seymour Bassett, "500 Miles of Trouble and Excitement: Vermont's Railroads, 1848-61," *Vermont History* 49 (Summer 1981): 133-154; reprinted in H. Nicholas Muller, III and Samuel B. Hand, eds., *In a State of Nature: Readings in Vermont History*, 2d ed. (Montpelier: Vermont Historical Society, 1982), 160-173. Harold A. Meeks, *Time and Change in Vermont: A Human Geography* (Chester, Conn.: Globe Pequot Press, 1986), 106-139.

8. The full poem is reprinted in Muller and Hand, 206-207.

9. Michael Berger, *The Devil Wagon in God's Country: The Automobile and Social Change in Rural America, 1893-1929* (Hamden, Conn.: Archon Books, 1979); John A. Jakle, *The Tourist: Travel in Twentieth-Century North America* (Lincoln, Neb.: University of Nebraska Press, 1985).

10. Jarvis Palace Garage [Burlington, Vt.], *Jarvis Auto Tours: Sightseeing Journey to Historic and Picturesque Places in Vermont* (Burlington: Hays Advertising Agency, 1915) in VHS pamphlet collection.

11. Chester H. Liebs, *Main Street to Miracle Mile: American Roadside Architecture* (Boston: Little, Brown, 1985).

12. Dorothy Canfield Fisher, *Tourists Accommodated. Some Scenes from Present-day Summer Life in Vermont* (New York: Harcourt, Brace and Co., 1934).

13. Frank Bryan, *Yankee Politics in Rural Vermont* (Hanover, N.H.: University Press of New England, 1974), 202-233; Richard M. Judd, *The New Deal in Vermont, Its Impact and Aftermath* (New York: Garland Publishers, 1979), 85-88; William Storrs Lee, *The Green Mountains of Vermont* (New York: Holt, 1955), 156-158.

14. Kevin O'Connor, "25 Years Later: The Impact of the Interstate," *Vermont Sunday Magazine, Sunday Rutland Herald and Sunday Times Argus*, 7 December 1989, 4-5, 14-16. See also Benjamin L. Huffman, et al., *Getting Around Vermont. A Study of Twenty Years of Highway Building in Vermont, with Respect to Economics, Automotive Travel, Community Patterns, and the Future* (Burlington, Vt.: The Environmental Program, University of Vermont, 1974).

15. Louise Roomet, "Vermont as a Resort Area in the Nineteenth Century," *Vermont History* 44 (Winter 1976): 1-13.

16. Meeks, *Time and Change in Vermont*, 144.

17. Ibid., 155.

18. "Servicetownship in Vermont," journal entry, July [24 ?], 1866. VHS manuscript collection.

19. Andrea Rebek, "The Selling of Vermont: From Agriculture to Tourism," *Vermont History* 44 (Winter 1976): 14-27 (reprinted in Muller and Hand, 273-282); David Strauss, "Towards a Consumer Culture: 'Adirondack Murray' and the Wilderness Vacation," *American Quarterly* 39 (Summer 1987): 270-287.

20. Matthew H. Buckham, "Burlington as a Place to Live In," in Abby Maria Hemenway, ed., *The Vermont Historical Gazetteer: A Magazine Embracing a History of Each Town, Civil, Ecclesiastical, Biographical, and Military* (Burlington, Vt.: Miss A. M. Hemenway, 1867), I:723-724.

21. Andrea Zentz, "Vermont Rakes in Dollars From Fall Tourists," *Burlington Free Press*, 22 October 1990, 1A *et seq.*

22. For a summary of Vermont state government efforts to promote tourism see D. Gregory Sanford, "When Beckoning Began," *Vermont News and Views*, September 1986.

23. Inaugural speech, Carroll S. Page, October 2, 1890, in *Journal of the Senate of the State of Vermont*, Biennial Session, 1890, 342.

24. Farewell speech, Carroll S. Page, October 6, 1892, in *Journal of the Senate of the State of Vermont*, Biennial Session, 1892, 354.

25. H. H. Chadwick, "Vermont Bureau of Publicity, Its History, Expenditures, Organization and Activities" (1934), manuscript and published pamphlet in VHS, James P. Taylor Papers, DOC T-10, folder marked "Publicity."

26. *Rural Vermont*, 2.

27. Ibid., Chapter VIII, "Summer Residents and Tourists," 117-133.

28. Ibid., 124-125.

29. Ibid., 129-133.

30. *A Summary Report from the Governor's Postwar Planning Committee for Vermont* (1944), "Recreational Development," 36-37.

31. Ibid.

32. *State Planning in Vermont* (Montpelier: State Planning Office, January 1964), 16-17.

33. Reidun Nuquist, "The Founding of the Green Mountain Club, 1910," *Vermont History News* 36 (May-June, 1985): 60-65; Vrest Orton, "Mr. Vermont," *Vermont Life* 4 (Summer 1950): 49-51. Taylor's papers are in the manuscript collection of the VHS, DOC T-1 through 13.

34. Fay Cambell Kaynor, "The Golden Era of Private Summer Camps," *Vermont History News* 41 (May-June 1990): 46-50; Peter S. Jennison, *Vermont on $500 a Day (More or Less)* (Woodstock, Vt.: Countryman Press, 1987). See especially Jennison's introduction, with its discussion of the "gentrification" of Vermont and Vermont tourism and the author's concerns for the future of the Vermont landscape and environment.

Spreading the News:

Newspaper Reporting in Vermont

Nicholas Monsarrat

Vermont newspaper reporters have recorded their state's history for almost as long as Vermont has been a state. However, very few reporters have done much historical writing about themselves or their work. That leaves me with a particularly difficult task. Newspaper reporting in Vermont, as Weston Cate, the former head of the Vermont Historical Society, has said, represents one of numerous holes that still exist in Vermont history books. Most Vermont reporters seem to have written about almost everybody but themselves.

This may not be as ironic as it seems. Getting into reporting can be, for many reporters, a subtle act of concealment. The reasoning goes something like this: "I'm basically a shy person, but by becoming a reporter I can gain access to the most dramatic events and people in life and live vicariously through them, without having to reveal myself." I will confess to being one of those people, at least I was in the beginning. In my twenty years of reporting and editing in Vermont, I have also met many others who seem the same way.

Fortunately, however, I have also found a few who have written something about their work or the work of others. I have also personally seen or heard much about Vermont reporting and reporters as a newspaperman myself. In August of 1991 publisher Robert Mitchell of the *Rutland Herald*, published an updated history of the *Herald* for the bicentennial of Vermont statehood.[1] As Vermont's senior journalist, Mitchell is able to fill in many historical gaps and I am indebted to him and to the *Herald's* news clip files.

What I will try to do in this paper is piece together a general picture of Vermont reporting from what I have been able to read, hear, or personally experience. It is a necessarily incomplete picture, but I hope an accurate one as far as I can paint it for you. Vermont newspaper history includes, I think, four distinct stages: (1) the "we don't need local news" stage; (2) the expansion of news phase; (3) the advocacy journalism stage; (4) the "let's be balanced and fair" stage.

THE "WE DON'T NEED LOCAL NEWS" STAGE

This was the period between Vermont's earliest days as an organized state in the late 1700s and just before the trains came to Vermont in the mid-1800s. The first newspaper published in Vermont, the *Dresden, Vt., Mercury* (1779), was not even located in Vermont once the Vermont-New Hampshire boundaries had been redrawn. Dresden, Vermont, later reverted to New Hampshire and became Hanover.[2]

The Vermont newspapers of those earliest days had more editors than reporters, because the publishers did not see local news as a necessity and thus did not need local reporters to write it. The publishers believed, probably rightly, that Vermont towns were so small, and their gossip mills so fast and reliable, that any local news that a reporter might write about in his weekly newspaper (the normal frequency then) would surely be out-of-date, and thus not news at all, by the time it had reached the street. Instead, the newspapers mostly reprinted national and international news from the more metropolitan-oriented newspapers to the south, such as the *Boston Evening Post* and the *Connecticut Courant* (which is now the *Hartford Courant* and the oldest newspaper in the United States still in continuous publication). They also included literary fiction and anecdotes as well as advertising.

The *Rutland Herald* of 17 October, 1820, for example, looked like this: there were four pages for a total of twenty columns. A little over six of those twenty columns were devoted to advertising, two for the publisher's own store. There were nine columns of reprints from London newspapers, a column of French news, more than two columns of Gov. Skinner's inaugural address at Montpelier, and a column and a half on the second Rutland County agricultural fair, where the publisher's best bull calf won a ten dollar prize. There was also a column and a half of poetry, but no editorial content whatsoever produced by *Herald* writers themselves.

A few years before, the *Herald* had reported on the current legislative session. However, it merely noted that the session had just concluded. It never said what the legislature had actually done.

It also was not unusual in those early days for newspaper publishers to take active roles in the political campaigns of politicians. One former *Herald* publisher, William Fay, is credited with reviving the Whig Party in Vermont. Another, Percival Wood Clement, was not shy about using the *Herald* to promote his own ideas and political ambitions. He ran for governor of Vermont in 1902 and 1906, and in 1918 when he finally won the office.[3]

This blurring of political-journalistic lines intensified in the late 1800s and early 1900s as some Vermont newspapers began to gain influence, and some publishers, editors, and even a few reporters saw nothing wrong with mixing their journalistic work with moonlighting for one political candidate or another. As late as 1928, *Herald* City Editor Robert St. John worked from 5 p.m. until 2 a.m. at the *Herald*, then moonlighted for pay at Republican headquarters for a variety of GOP political causes from 8 a.m. until 5 p.m.[4]

The Expansion of News Phase

The picture changed to a large degree with the arrival of the train and the telegraph, making modern newspapers possible in Vermont.

The trains brought wider and more frequent distribution of newspapers. The advent of the telegraph at virtually the same time made foreign, national, and regional news more accessible to Vermont newsrooms. Both developments provided the seeds for the growth and expansion of Vermont newspapers, including the *Burlington Free Press*, which became Vermont's first daily newspaper in 1848. By 1861, the weekly *Rutland Herald* (founded in 1794, and now the oldest family-owned newspaper in the United States) was considering the same move, spurred on by the advent of the Civil War. It became a daily in 1861 and, like many other papers of the time, began to place increasing emphasis on the local news that earlier Vermont newspapers had shunned.

Local news in those days did not always mean what it means today. In many cases, it meant publishing brief accounts of what local people were doing—personals columns. Usually what these local newsmakers were doing wasn't news at all by modern standards: visiting their children in another town; hosting a friend for tea; holding a community supper for a local cause. But it was news that was widely read because it contained the names of neighbors. As late as the 1960s, when most Vermont newspapers began phasing out the personals, it was "news" still loyally read by many older Vermonters.

I remember well when we began phasing out the local correspondents at the *Barre-Montpelier Times Argus*, people who had been producing this kind of personal news for years. It wasn't easy. A lot of feelings were hurt. There was criticism that we were getting too big for our britches. Since then, I have also often wondered how much of our understanding of Vermont's smaller towns has suffered because we no longer have those local correspondents to keep us informed of such personal, intimate things. At best, the change has probably been a mixed blessing. A few weekly papers, like the *Herald* of Randolph, have maintained the personals tradition.

In the 1920s, the competition for very personal "local" news was fierce. At one point, the *Rutland Herald* was so put out by an upstart competitor, the *Rutland News*, hiring more "personals" reporters than it had, that it began lifting the personals from the *News* that its own reporters had failed to get. This fattened its already considerable list of personals at the *Rutland News's* expense. The *News*, however, fought back. It proceeded to invent a fictitious person, insert him into its personals as a frequent man-about-town, then eventually exposed the *Herald*'s use of the phony personal by admitting the man did not exist. Alas, for the *News*, the hoax backfired. As Robert St. John chronicled in 1953 in his book, *This Was My World*: "Rutland did not like such tricks. Imputing moral turpitude to the aged and respectable *Herald* brought the same reaction from Vermonters as a man might have if someone were to cast doubt publicly on the morals of his favorite maiden aunt."[5]

Discretion could also be the better part of valor in those days. St. John remembers the night Will Rogers came to Rutland, and, at the Knights of Pythias, made the mistake of poking fun at Calvin Coolidge's intelligence. St.

John said this about that awful moment: "Never did any joke by any comedian on any stage on any circuit in the world fall so flat. There was not a smile, not a titter. Every face in the room froze as if suddenly hit by an arctic blast." That was one story, St. John said, "I did have sense enough not to print."[6]

Much the same problem confronted *Herald* publisher Bob Mitchell in the 1930s, when he was a reporter covering the administration of then-governor George Aiken. Much like President Franklin Roosevelt, Gov. Aiken would frequently invite reporters into his office to talk informally. At one point, he gave Mitchell the state budget to review prior to its public release, asking him to check for errors. Mitchell found a sizable one, but kept the news in confidence until Aiken was ready to release the corrected budget, then reported it.

It was a time when collegial rapport between reporter and politician was more the rule than the exception. That would change radically in the more confrontational 1960s and 1970s, when reporters and politicians became more like adversaries than allies.

In the one hundred years after the train and telegraph reached Vermont rapid technological changes also occurred at many newspapers, spurring more local and regional reporting. Printing and transmission of news became increasingly rapid, while the need also grew for reporters to understand and report increasingly complex issues facing their readers. Hand-set type gave way to machine-set linotype. Telegraph transmission of news gave way to teletype. Teletype and linotype were then replaced by far more rapid electronic typesetting and transmission in the 1960s, and now through even faster and less expensive desk-top publishing. Along with the "personals" was now far more coverage of local and regional hard-news events.

Through all the changes, reporters had to keep pace and adapt. They had to know more about more things, and they had to report the news much faster.

ADVOCACY JOURNALISM STAGE

The third stage arrived in Vermont in the 1960s with the advent of advocacy journalism.

It was a reporting style whose beginnings are often linked to the Watergate scandal, but it was actually well under way in Vermont and other places by the mid-1960s due in part to the civil rights movement. In Vermont, it was practiced by an increasing number of reporters, who believed that newspapers should be instruments of change and reform, and some editors who were willing to give them room to pursue various causes.

The *Free Press*'s top reporter of that era, Victor Maerki, later went on to become a senior legislative aide for former U.S. Senator Robert Stafford. As a Vermont State House reporter in the early 1960s, he believed down to his toenails that the job of the journalist was to "afflict the comfortable and comfort the afflicted," and he taught reporters who worked for him to follow his lead and act on it. I didn't work for or against Maerki, but I had many a fight with him on the telephone as a reporter. This was usually because even after he went into public relations work, he was always testing reporters to see if they knew anything, or at least enough to make them worthy of his time and information. Talking to him was always a learning experience.

Mavis Doyle was probably the best-known graduate of the Maerki school of journalism. She worked first for the *Times Argus*, then for the *Free Press*, then for the *Herald*, and was admired, feared, and occasionally detested by politicians wherever she worked, as was Maerki in his reporting days. Reporting in the 1960s and early 1970s, Mavis was most widely known for her encyclopedic memory of where many of the bones of Vermont state government were buried, and, secondly, for having the sources willing to tell her where many of the other bones were buried.

Her competitive spirit and keen instinct for news were so well refined that those of us who worked with her had to worry as much about her beating us to a story as we did about the competition getting ahead of us. One day, late in a legislative session in the early 1970s, a prominent state senator suddenly left the Senate in the middle of a hot debate and I decided to follow him. I found him in an unannounced meeting of a Senate committee, quietly attempting to attach an amendment to a flood-plain bill. The amendment would have removed all electric cooperatives in the state from the jurisdiction of the state Public Service Board. Since the senator also happened to represent the co-operatives as their legal counsel, and the amendment had no relationship to the environmental bill at hand, I knew I was onto something big.

Somehow, however, Mavis had learned of the move before it had even begun to happen, had already rushed over to ask the governor what he was going to do about such a travesty of justice, and had heard him promise that such an amendment would never see the light of day. She not only already had the story, she had more of the story than I did, and it was happening right under my nose.

Those were the days when we didn't think twice about reporting whatever we could overhear and later confirm about secret meetings going on behind closed doors: listening at keyholes, staking out hotels where candidates for top state jobs were being secretly interviewed, and routinely working fourteen hours a day, because that was what we thought it would take to get more stories than the competition. State House reporters then, unlike now, covered most major actions of committees, including many of the debates in those committees, in addition to most floor action dealing with most bills. Rarely was there a time when reporters from the dailies were not sitting in on House or Senate Appropriations Committee deliberations on the budget, usually reporting something about what those important committees had done each day until final passage of the spending bill.

The hours were grueling, the pay was modest (about $250 per week for the best reporters in the early 1970s), but the influence of the State House reporters was considerable, usually because they knew more about what was going on each day than most of the legislators themselves. Lawmakers had to read all the dailies just to learn what they themselves had actually done the day before. Not to read about it could put a lawmaker at a distinct disadvantage, particularly if the story he failed to read included news that his own pet bill was in trouble.

There were problems with this sort of aggressive, advocacy journalism, however. The use of unnamed sources in the reporting of controversial stories was more prevalent than it is today. That led to the public perception that along with our aggressiveness might be coming unfairness and bias. Because more sources were not identified, fairness could not be so easily judged.

We ended up with more in-depth reporting, but it was less balanced in some cases, because we tended to see things in rather black versus white, good guy versus bad guy terms. At least, that has been my perception as I have re-evaluated some of my own stories from those days. They weren't incorrect, and the sources did exist, but the stories were more one-sided than would be tolerated today. Readers, I suspect, had to do more filtering out of our real or perceived biases as they read these stories.

Out of this era came some notable alumni. Among them, in addition to Maerki and Doyle, were former *Rutland Herald* State House reporter Anthony Marro, a Pulitzer prize winner at Long Island's *Newsday* and now one of *Newsday's* top editors; former *Herald* State House reporter Stephen Terry, who went on to become an influential aide to Sen. George Aiken; Jane Mayer, White House reporter for the *Wall Street Journal*; Colin Nickerson, a Vermont-born reporter for the *Herald*, whose beats for the *Boston Globe* have included the front lines during the Persian Gulf War and a Pulitzer prize for his reporting on world hunger; and Robert Sherman, a former reporter for the *Herald* and *Times Argus*, who became an investigative reporter for Jack Anderson before returning to Vermont.

THE "LET'S BE BALANCED AND FAIR" STAGE

Advocacy journalism has given way to the stage we are in now: the "let's be balanced and fair" stage. Part of this, I think, is a result of today's somewhat different editing and reporting problems, as well as basic economics.

This change has been a mixed blessing. The good news is, there seems to be less personal bias of reporters in the news stories you read today. There are far fewer unidentified sources. The stories are more balanced, but it also seems that there is less passion, less sense of outrage about genuine injustice, and less willingness on the part of reporters to spend the time it takes to go after a complicated story and report it thoroughly.

Many Vermont newspaper editors today, like their counterparts elsewhere, are trying to tell more stories in fewer words because they have less space to waste and a more diverse readership. They must do more things for more readers, avoiding heavy emphasis on any one subject like government coverage, for example. They are also under intense pressure to attract and hold the attention of readers who are increasingly drawn to more visual, "easy" television.

At the same time, newspaper publishers, editors, and reporters are under pressure to hold down costly overtime, which when used effectively helps a newspaper be more than just a nine-to-five operation. Less overtime can mean less in-depth coverage and already explains, in part, why even the important money committees of the Vermont legislature are not given the extensive, daily coverage now that they once were. On the one hand, many readers probably did not read that daily coverage when it was there. On the other, because legislators did read and often heed it, the newspapers had more influence on day-to-day legislative actions when those committees were being extensively reported on. In turn, the Vermont public was probably better served. There was a greater likelihood in the days of advocacy journalism that bad public policy in the making could be challenged and then corrected sooner.

CONCLUSION

In conclusion, I think newspaper reporting in Vermont over the past ten years has tended to become more diverse, serious, and fair than it was, but also more superficial, less passionate, and less interesting. I am also worried that Vermont newspaper work is increasingly an ordinary nine-to-five business rather than a profession with a unique responsibility to serve the public interest and expose injustice. It is becoming more subject to outside economic forces that, increasingly, seem to be out of the control of even publishers. As a result, newspapers cannot be as responsive to the news judgments, diverse personalities, and good-faith crusading of reporters, editors, and publishers who run them. At least three things are to blame: a volatile economy, a shift to out-of-state chain ownership and financial control of many Vermont newspapers, and a media market that is increasingly fragmented and in competition for the same advertising dollar.

With the latest recession taking a toll on almost all newspapers, I think the balance has been shifting still further away from thorough, aggressive, in depth, and inevitably costly news coverage, toward more superficiality and basic survival—just getting out the newspaper. This may correct itself as the economy once again improves. The state and its newspapers have been through hard economic times before. However, it's an imbalance that journalists and readers alike need to watch, lest newspapers become merely poor imitations of television, and, at the worst extreme, vulnerable to pressure from advertisers unwise enough to try to dictate editorial policy by exploiting newspapers' financial weaknesses.

It seems to me that's the real bottom line today for Vermont newspapers.

NOTES

1. "Episodes from Herald History," special insert *Rutland Herald*, 18 August 1991.

2. John P. Clement, "Rutland Herald Serves Areas for 100 Years," *The Herald Centennial Issue*, 29 April 1961, 1.

3. John P. Clement, "Rutland Herald and Other Early Vermont Newspaper History," *The Herald Bicentennial Issue*, 6 September 1961, 4.

4. Robert St. John, *This Was My World* (Garden City, N.Y.: Doubleday & Company, 1953), 231.

5. St. John, 210.

6. St. John, 213.

Daguerreotype of Second Vermont Statehouse, 1837-1857. Courtesy Vermont Historical Society, Montpelier, Vt. (FG-2).

GOVERNING VERMONT

Inventing Constitutions:

The Vermont Constitution and

the Print Revolution of the Eighteenth Century

Patrick H. Hutton

The Vermont constitution of 1777 is an embodiment of the broad democratic revolution of the late eighteenth century that swept across the Western world. The historian Robert Palmer speaks of the era as the age of the democratic revolution, stressing parallels between the events that transpired on either side of the Atlantic, but particularly in France and the American colonies. The Vermont constitution, therefore, invites comparison not only with its American counterparts but also with those in western Europe during this era.

In the making of democratic revolutions, constitutions gave form and substance to the vision of the revolutionaries. They enshrined democratic principles; established governmental and judicial procedures; and guaranteed individual rights. So there are good reasons for comparing constitutions. The Vermont constitution of 1777 may have provided the covenant of what was only a tiny and remote community of tenuous legal standing, but it exemplifies a much larger process working change throughout the Western world.[1]

Equally important, the state constitutions of the 1770s were the first written constitutions of the democratic revolution. They were drafted at the urging of the Continental Congress, whose delegates were preparing to declare American independence from Britain in May 1776.[2] They served as prototypes for the more famous documents written a decade later—the American constitution of 1787 and the French constitutions of 1791 and 1793. The Vermont constitution gave expression to the most advanced republican thought of the age. The French constitution of the Year III (1793), the most radical document of the French Revolution, goes no further. The Vermont constitution, moreover, had a genealogy within an illustrious constitutional tradition. It was modeled on the Pennsylvania constitution of 1776, in whose drafting Benjamin Franklin had a role, and that in turn was modeled on the Frame of Government granted by William Penn in 1682 under the authority of King Charles II of England. As a preface to state papers concerning Vermont's founding compiled a century later (1873), the editor, E. P. Walton, stressed this point.[3]

The constitutions of the eighteenth century typically set two tasks: the establishment of machinery of government and the protection of individual liberties.[4] In both respects, the Vermont constitution of 1777 was a highly progressive document. It established universal manhood suffrage and opened public office to all eligible voters. It provided for a unicameral legislature, to be elected annually by the towns of Vermont, with two representatives for the larger towns, one for the smaller.[5] All sessions were to be open to the public, and the decisions of this assembly were to be printed weekly.[6] It outlined the executive powers of a governor, lieutenant governor, and an executive council.[7] As a unique feature, the constitution established a Council of Censors that would review legislation to insure that it did not violate the principles of the constitution.[8] It guaranteed individual liberties in such measure that jurists are today returning to its provisions to protect individual liberties insufficiently guaranteed by the federal bill of rights.[9] Particularly noteworthy was the abolition of adult slavery. This was no "glittering generality," as it was in the American constitution, for in 1786 the Vermont General Assembly passed a law prohibiting the sale and transportation of blacks out of the state.[10]

In its content, the Vermont constitution of 1777 gave expression to a political revolution that was liberal in its recourse to law and its concerns for the protection of liberties, republican in its conceptions of community, and democratic in the procedures it established for political participation. It was amended several times over the following two decades, principally in 1787 and again in 1793, and it has been amended several times since. The principal change in 1787 was designed to insure the separation of governmental powers. The 1793 modifications were minor in form and procedure and concerned a short residency requirement, legislative control of revenues, and measures to prevent conflicts of interest.[11]

All of this is well known and provides the context in which the Vermont constitution is typically discussed. Instead what I wish to examine here is the Vermont constitution in the context of a different sort of eighteenth-century revolution—the print revolution or, more precisely, the cultural revolution made possible by the ever more pervasive use of print as a medium of communication and public discourse.[12] This is a way of looking at the meaning of the broader intellectual movement of the late eighteenth century known as the Enlightenment. Typically the Enlightenment is discussed in terms of its leading ideas and values, notably the practical applications of natural science or the political theories of philosophers and statesmen. But from the vantage point of the print revolution, the Enlightenment concerned a new way of organizing and presenting knowledge.

THE PRINT REVOLUTION

Print culture enhanced the cognitive capacity for generalization by literate people. The culture of the Western world until the eighteenth century was still primarily a manuscript culture heavily dependent on oral transmission. Most people learned by hearing rather than seeing the word. The move from a manuscript to a print culture between the fifteenth and the eighteenth centuries shifted the focus of communication from voices to be heard to surfaces to be seen. It marked an entry into more abstract understanding. The encoding of knowledge for visual communication promoted a desire for clear, distinct ideas and a more schematic presentation of knowledge.[13] The characteristic text usually cited to illustrate this cultural change is the encyclopedia, which classified knowledge according to an alphabetic arrangement, displacing the mnemonic designs upon which manuscript culture had relied.[14] But one might as easily cite constitutions, for they organized the principles of community in an abstract way, and they documented them in a clear, concise manner. As today's students of rhetoric would phrase it, knowledge in the eighteenth century was being textualized into a print culture.

The print revolution fostered a new mode of political discourse, which described politics in more nearly universal terms than ever before. It also made possible a new political culture, "the republic of letters," shared and shaped by the collaboration of an emerging literate class of those who wrote to be published and an increasingly sophisticated and entrepreneurial artisan class of printers who published what the literati wrote.[15] The printing press gave writers the power to publicize their ideas in unprecedented ways. Historians have also recognized that in some essential ways the new print culture reorganized the relationships between knowledge and power.[16]

Historians studying the Enlightenment have been drawn to the topic of print culture by their awareness of the profound cultural changes attending our current communications revolution. Sensing that print culture was historically conditioned and from the vantage point of today's electronic culture increasingly dated, historians have become curious about how it came into being and how it left its imprint upon the culture of the eighteenth and nineteenth centuries.

The Vermont experience provides us with an excellent case study of these changes and tendencies in eighteenth-century culture. In this respect it is important to note that the Vermont constitution was a printed document. When it was drafted in 1777, there was no printing press in Vermont, and so the Council of Safety (the provisional government) sent Ira Allen as its representative to the printers Watson and Goodwin in Hartford, Connecticut, to have the document printed. So grateful was Allen for Watson's services that he described him as "remarkable for his humanity, and anxious for the safety of his country" in his willingness to devote his press to the cause.[17] As a means of publicizing its pronouncements, access to a printing press was obviously of preeminent importance to the early Vermont assemblies.

Recourse to the printer predates the constitutional convention in Windsor. As early as 1772, Ethan Allen had turned to the Hartford printers to publish the New Hampshire Grants' defiance of the claims of New York upon their territory.[18] Given the urgency of the issues, however, frequent travel to Hartford was a vexing inconvenience. Hiring an official Vermont printer, therefore, became a top priority of the first legislative assembly in 1778.[19] Eventually three printers worked for the Vermont government during the late 1770s and early 1780s.

We might ask then whether Vermont was in fact an "invention" of print culture. The constitution, its revisions, and the laws passed by the legislature during the era of Vermont's quest for independence were printed documents in contrast to the records of the proceedings of the legislature, which remained in manuscript form until the nineteenth century. They stand out in the political discourse of the era as points of reference in an emerging print culture.

THE BROADER CONTEXT

The significance of constitution writing as a manifestation of the growing power and influence of print culture must be appreciated within two broad contexts: the deep roots of constitutional history in oral tradition, and what scholars have recently characterized as the making of the "republic of letters" in late eighteenth-century America.

I have referred to the state constitutions of the 1770s as the first written constitutions. By this I mean that they were the first written constitutions within the context of print culture. There were written constitutional documents dating at least from the seventeenth century on which these newer ones were to some extent modeled. Before them, there is the unwritten English constitutional tradition and even principles of Roman law to which they owe some debt. To understand the significance of eighteenth-century constitutions as printed documents, one must understand their relationship to this heritage.

The problem of written constitutions and the print revolution raises the question of the earlier relationship between written constitutions and legal customs that emerged out of oral tradition. It is not simply a matter of uncovering the provisions of eighteenth-century constitutions in seventeenth century models or even in the common law. It concerns the way in which law is conceived in a manuscript culture. Scholars emphasize that manuscript culture remains closely bound to the protocols of oral tradition. The constitutional documents drafted within such a culture served a different function and therefore were interpreted differently. The question of the relationship of law to oral tradition is only beginning to be examined by historians.[20]

However, their work to date does permit some generalizations. First, until the eighteenth century, written law was subordinate to unwritten tradition. The law was grounded in custom, procedures, and rights fashioned in a time beyond memory. The power of the law was sanctified by the fact that its origins were unknowable. Law had been conveyed to posterity through the repetition of precedent as it was remembered. Certainly customary law was modified over time. But because the presence of the law was continually invoked, such changes passed unnoticed. Thus the law might change even as it was described as being of such remote origin as to be changeless. Law was immersed in living memory, so the past was of interest only insofar as it continued to live in the present. In this sense, time immemorial means living in time, not a remote and changeless past.[21]

Second, the interjection of written documents into such a milieu from the late Middle Ages until the early eighteenth century modified the interpretation of the law, but in limited ways. The documents on which claims to legal authority were based were manuscripts to which very few people had access. Because they were not easily consulted, interpretation of the law continued to be a matter of personal, or at best corporate prerogative, rather than a public function. Judgments made under such conditions were not really being measured against a fixed standard. The boundary between law openly disclosed and law hidden in tradition remained undefined. In ancient Rome, the official bearers of the law chanted its provisions long after these had been written on wooden tablets.[22] In the Western legal tradition, jurists learned to recite maxims based upon oral formulae that were easily and accurately remembered. They continued to follow this practice as late as the early nineteenth century.[23]

Third, the claims made in such documents were of a particular nature. The origins of the constitutional tradition that culminates in the printed constitutions of the eighteenth century began in the defense of particular rights in medieval and early modern England. These rights were defined as the specific privileges of groups, not as the universal rights of autonomous individuals, as they were to be redefined by the constitutions of the eighteenth century.[24]

Fourth, the power to govern in traditional European society was thought of in personal terms. In medieval political theory, the king had rights, as did the corporate interests of the realm. When in the sixteenth century the notion of sovereignty became a constitutional issue—the power to exercise authority in the name of the realm—the personal element remained prominent in its definition. Even though kings ceased to speak of their powers in terms of rights and spoke instead of their sovereignty, they continued to conceive of governance in personal terms. Thus, despite the significant advance toward the modern state accomplished over the course of the seventeenth century, kings defined their absolute powers as personal ones.[25] The charters that the English kings granted to the American colonies, for example, prominently retained the proprietary element.[26] For a manuscript culture—in which the written word always embodies the signature of a human hand—personalism was inherent in the political process.[27] My point is that the constitutions of the late eighteenth century, which eliminated personalism from the definition of rights and powers, confirmed the advance into a more abstract order of political understanding.

That more abstract order is what cultural historians are today calling the republic of letters of the eighteenth century. This is the second broad context for establishing the significance of the new culture that came into being with the printed word. It was this print culture that enabled the new republic to be textualized as an imaginary discourse long before it was institutionalized in revolutionary regimes.[28] The republic was invented by those who publicized it through the printed word. To understand how, we must consider such topics as the books and pamphlets that were published, the people who produced them (the printers as well as the writers), and the people who read these published works.

The history of the book and its impact on eighteenth-century culture is currently a lively topic among historians.[29] Their main point is that the coming of the printed word signaled the creation of a culture of texts. Viewed archaeologically, the text was the leading artifact of this culture. In American history, we are able to consider this argument in depth, thanks to research by bibliographers that considerably predates the current interest in the cultural effects of the print medium. I am referring especially to the bibliography of American imprints compiled by Charles Evans in the early twentieth century and since elaborated by a number of successors. Evans inventoried the entire corpus of printed work in America from colonial beginnings through the revolutionary era, that is from 1639 to 1800. His work is an extraordinary resource, even with its occasional lacunae and errors.[30] We might say that Evans's bibliography launched a genre of historical studies, since institutionalized under auspices of the American Antiquarian Society, which has supported research and publication that has extended, refined, and interpreted his project. There is a study of Vermont imprints before 1800 by Elizabeth Cooley, who extracted Vermont publications from Evans's twelve-volume corpus.[31] It has more recently been corrected and augmented by Marcus McCorison, who carried the project forward to 1820.[32]

These studies of American imprints enable us to establish with some confidence the nature of books being published and to interpret changing publishing interests over the course of the colonial era. Evans himself described the larger trends for the early period. In the seventeenth century, most of what was published was devotional literature. Sermons of eminent preachers were the most frequent items on the list, followed closely by theological works, destined for the edification of ministers. Political proclamations and legal pronouncements were also important.[33] Over the course of the eighteenth century, the relative prominence of religious as opposed to political tracts began to reverse itself. On a much smaller scale, books about travel and history began to appear. But reading material was for the most part serious, and the notion of reading for pleasure emerged very slowly during this period. The novel, conceived as a form of reading for the cultivation of the affective self, was only beginning to acquire a readership by the end of the eighteenth century.[34] Arthur Berthold, a student of Evans's inventory, notes 8,760 printed works in the American colonies between 1639 and 1763. (Many more, of course, were imported, and the press is another matter altogether.) Of these, 1,381, or sixteen percent, were sermons. Add the array of other theological writings and the figure jumps to 3,262 (thirty-seven percent). The total for law and politics is 2,275 (twenty-five percent).[35]

One thing is certain to anyone who studies these data. The eighteenth century was the age in which print as a medium of communication expanded most dramatically. Even though the printing press was invented in the fifteenth century, the eighteenth century was the age of the print revolution. Fewer than ten percent of the imprints that Berthold analyzes date from the seventeenth century, while more books were published from 1739 to 1763 (4,747 or fifty-four percent) than in the entire first century of publishing in the colonies.[36]

We must also examine the entire publishing business if we wish to understand the cultural implications of the print revolution. We are not dealing merely with the *philosophes*—the great political writers of the age, such as Thomas Jefferson or even Thomas Paine. We are concerned about a spectrum of literary types from highly literate philosophers to lowly and often unlettered printers and their helpers. The pioneering study on the subject is by an historian of France, Robert Darnton, who makes much of an intermediary figure, the hack writer. These were the writers of what was in that day called Grub Street, and which we might call a prototype of the bohemias of the nineteenth century. They eked out an existence on the periphery of the republic of letters by ghost writing, drafting political pamphlets, or, worse, writing what passed as the pornography of the day—scandalous accounts of the foibles and human frailties of the high and mighty. Darnton characterizes these writings as the "low life of literature," a counterpoint to the refined writing of the high Enlightenment with which most of us are more familiar.[37] American studies of this underside of the republic of letters are just beginning to appear.[38] They suggest that it had a corresponding role in the American colonial experience, discrediting the old ways of conducting politics and desacralizing the role of kings and privileged people, even if few such pamphlets made their way into print in America.

In the republic of letters, printers also assumed a new historical importance, for they occupied a mediating position. There were a few who doubled as *philosophes*. For that reason, Benjamin Franklin is today gaining new attention among the historians of print culture.[39] But Vermont's own Alden and Judah Spooner, the first printers hired by the Vermont government, are probably more representative of the profession. Technicians more than inventors, artisans more often than entrepreneurs, they nonetheless played the instrumental role in bringing the republic of letters into being. Printing may have been a primitive technology, and the printing trade a relatively humble calling, but in the making of eighteenth-century political culture, printers played a role analogous to the television producers of the late twentieth century. The printers were the image makers of their day; no one discounted their importance, least of all Vermont's founding fathers.

Finally, there is the issue of the reading public. The figures on those who could read by the late eighteenth century are impressive. David Hall, a student of literacy in early America, contends that in New England nearly all males and two-thirds of the females could read.[40] Reading permitted vicarious participation by the literate public in the republic of letters that was being invented.[41]

Toward Republican Discourse

How do we bring together these two contexts—the heritage of the unwritten constitutional tradition and the cultural effects of the new culture of print—to shed light on the ties between the Vermont constitution and the print revolution? My thesis is that the Republic of Vermont was born in the political imagination of the republic of letters. Republican discourse publicized its possibilities. The constitution of 1777 gave the discourse a textual form. Republican rhetoric was a universalizing discourse. Concepts such as the nation, the state, and the people were extracted from the particular, concrete settings in which they had been considered in manuscript culture to become the more generalized, abstract vocabulary of a new political code. Indeed, one might say that one of the most important features of the democratic revolution of the eighteenth century was the invention of this code.[42] As the key to the code, the constitution became the ultimate reference for republican discourse. For the republic of letters, the state of nature so frequently invoked by political theorists of the day was not some long-lost primitive past but rather the more immediate customary society before it was reconstituted in printed texts.

The Vermont constitution of 1777, moreover, was an impersonal reference, in contrast to the personalism of the traditional political world. It was a document without signatures. In this respect, it invites comparison with the Declaration of Independence, written in the previous year, which was a manuscript and, of course, famous for its signatures. Jacques Derrida, today's leading authority on linguistic deconstruction, has remarked that the signatures on the American Declaration of Independence signify this transition from manuscript to print culture. The Declaration was a half-way house, revealing how the determination of its framers to sever ties with old authorities was coupled to their reluctance to relinquish personalism.[43]

During the Revolutionary era, Vermont was a contested territory. Long known as the New Hampshire Grants, it was claimed by both New Hampshire and New York, and was saved from such absorption by the willingness of its inhabitants to fight for independence.[44] But the fight for independence was also a fight for an identity. Vermonters were by no means unified in their political allegiances. Land tenure was a burning issue. The leaders of the party seeking independence were wealthy men, many of them real estate speculators who had much to lose if the wrong side won. Printing political proclamations helped solidify support for independence and gave Vermont an identity at the same time. In this respect, Vermont was the only state without a specific colonial past, and the only one without its own colonial charter that tied it to a particular political tradition. As historian Peter Onuf has argued, Vermont was the only state that literally constituted itself anew, and the capacity of its leaders to use a written constitution to impress its claims is indisputably a factor in the success of their venture.[45] The capacity to mobilize the people through the printed word was an important weapon in this struggle. The Vermont constitution of 1777 may never have been ratified by the people of Vermont. But in a way it invented them by textualizing their political experience.

Herein lies the significance of the print revolution as a context for the appreciation of the Vermont constitution. Studying the cultural implications of the print revolution of the eighteenth century enables us to understand how we came to textualize our identity as a community and how the constitution is the representation of that identity. The constitution was an icon of republican discourse. By this I mean that it was not a sacred doctrine embodying original intentions of the framers that posterity would be obliged to obey slavishly. Rather it was a reference point for a new way of talking about politics. As such, it invented a new beginning and empowered society to reshape itself in the future.[46] Because it was conceived as a beginning, the constitution has since become a commemorative document. Accordingly there has been a tendency to idealize it, as the conditions under which it was invented have faded from living memory. But as a document that established our identity as a state and as a republic, it is one into which we continue to look to see ourselves. In that sense it is much like a mirror. The image of ourselves that we see is only as good as our current discourse.[47]

Has the electronic revolution changed the way we understand this icon of a print culture? So far, I don't think so. But understanding more of the reality of the rhetorical conditions under which it was invented, we have become more sensitive to other ways of imagining community, and that has set higher expectations about our capacity to realize the imperatives for democracy that our constitution has enshrined.[48]

NOTES

1. R. R. Palmer, *The Age of the Democratic Revolution* (Princeton: Princeton University Press, 1959) 1:213-82.

2. Resolution of the Continental Congress, 15 May 1776, republished in Marshall True and William Doyle, eds., *Vermont and the New Nation* (Hyde Park: Vermont Council on the Humanities, 1985), 33.

3. E. P. Walton, "Introduction," in *Records of the Council of Safety and Governor and Council of the State of Vermont*, ed. E. P. Walton (Montpelier: J. & J. Poland, 1873), 83-89. See also Nathaniel Hendricks, "The Experiment in Vermont Constitutional Government," *Vermont History* 34 (January 1966): 63-65; John N. Schaeffer, "A Comparison of the First Constitutions of Vermont and Pennsylvania," *Vermont History* 43 (Winter 1975): 33-43.

4. See Patrick H. Hutton, "The Print Revolution of the Eighteenth Century and the Drafting of Written Constitutions," *Vermont History* 56 (Summer 1988): 159-60.

5. *Constitution of the State of Vermont* (1777), Ch. 1 (Declaration of the Rights of the Inhabitants), Article 8; Ch. 2 (Frame of Government), Sections 6, 7, and 8.

6. Ibid., Ch. 2, Sections 12, 13, and 14.

7. Ibid., Ch. 2, Sections 3, 17, and 18.

8. Ibid., Ch. 2, Section 44. This council was abolished in 1870.

9. Ibid., Ch. 1. On judicial interpretation of the sphere of rights protected by the Vermont constitution vis-à-vis the United States Constitution, see *State v. Jewett*, 146 Vt. 221 (1985), and Thomas L. Hayes, "Clio in the Courtroom," *Vermont History* 56 (Summer 1988): 147-53.

10. *Constitution of the State of Vermont*, Ch. 1, Article 1. See Walton, ed., *Records of the Council of Safety*, 92 n. 1.

11. *Constitution of the State of Vermont Established July 9, 1793*, ed., James H. Douglas (1987), 3-25.

12. On the print revolution, see especially Robert Darnton and Daniel Roche, eds., *Revolution in Print: The Press in France, 1775-1800* (Berkeley: University of California Press, 1989); Elizabeth L. Eisenstein, *The Printing Revolution in Early Modern Europe* (Cambridge: Cambridge University Press, 1983); Lucien Febvre and Henri-Jean Martin, *The Coming of the Book: The Impact of Printing, 1450-1800*, trans. David Gerard (London: N. Lyons Books, 1976); Marshall McLuhan, *The Gutenberg Galaxy; The Making of Typographic Man* (Toronto: Toronto University Press, 1962).

13. Walter J. Ong, *Orality and Literacy* (London: Methuen, 1982), 117-23, 130-35.

14. Robert Darnton, *The Great Cat Massacre and Other Episodes in French Cultural History* (New York: Basic Books, 1984), 191-213.

15. Michael Warner, *The Letters of the Republic; Publication and the Public Sphere in Eighteenth-Century America* (Cambridge: Harvard University Press, 1990), 1-71.

16. See, for example, Peter Gay, *Voltaire's Politics: The Poet as Realist* (New York: Random House, 1965), 18-32; and Michel Foucault, "Truth and Power," in *Power/Knowledge; Selected Interviews and Other Writings, 1972-1977*, ed. Colin Gordon (New York: Random House, 1980), 109-33.

17. Two copies of the original document still exist, one in the Vermont State Library, the other in the Vermont Historical Society. In 1977 a limited edition of a facsimile was reprinted as *The Original Constitution of the State of Vermont, 1777: A Facsimile* (Montpelier: Vermont Historical Society, 1977), 1-24. The quote by Allen is taken from its introduction.

18. John Spargo, "Early Vermont Printers and Printing," *Proceedings of the Vermont Historical Society*, N.S. 10 (1942): 215.

19. Journal of the General Assembly, State of Vermont, meeting at Manchester, 27 October 1779, as quoted in Elizabeth F. Cooley, "An Introductory Essay on the History of Printing in Vermont," in *Vermont Imprints Before 1800*, ed. Elizabeth F. Cooley (Montpelier: Vermont Historical Society, 1937), xii.

20. Donald R. Kelley, "'Second Nature': The Idea of Custom in European Law, Society, and Culture," in *The Transmission of Culture in Early Modern Europe*, ed. Anthony Grafton et al. (Philadelphia: University of Pennsylvania Press, 1990), 131-72.

21. J. G. A. Pocock, *Politics, Language and Time; Essays on Political Thought and History* (London: Methuen, 1972), 237-38.

22. Donald R. Kelley, "Vico's Road: From Philology to Jurisprudence and Back," in *Giambattista Vico's Science of Humanity*, ed. Giorgio Tagliacozzo, et al. (Baltimore: Johns Hopkins University Press, 1976), 22.

23. Donald R. Kelley, *The Human Measure; Social Thought in the Western Legal Tradition* (Cambridge: Harvard University Press, 1990), 106-08, 172, 201.

24. C. B. A. Behrens, *The Ancien Regime* (New York: Harcourt, Brace & World, 1967), 46-62, 96-102.

25. Ibid.

26. Andrew C. McLaughlin, *The Foundations of American Constitutionalism* (New York: New York University Press, 1932), 3-61; Forrest McDonald, *Novus Ordo Seculorum: The Intellectual Origins of the American Revolution* (Lawrence: University of Kansas Press, 1985), 1-55.

27. Jonathan Goldberg, *Writing Matter* (Stanford: Stanford University Press, 1990), 233-78.

28. Warner, *Letters of the Republic*, 4-5.

29. See Roger Chartier, *The Cultural Uses of Print in Early Modern France*, trans. Lydia G. Cochrane (Princeton: Princeton University Press, 1987), 110-264.

30. Charles Evans, ed., *American Bibliography, 1639-1820*, 12 vols. (Chicago: Blakely Press, 1903-31).

31. Cooley, *Vermont Imprints Before 1800*.

32. Marcus A. McCorison, ed., *Vermont Imprints, 1778-1820; A Checklist of Books, Pamphlets, and Broadsides* (Worcester: American Antiquarian Society, 1963).

33. Evans, *American Bibliography*, 2: vi-xiii; 3: vii-xii; 4: vii-xvi.

34. Darnton, *Great Cat Massacre*, 215-56.

35. Arthur Benedict Berthold, *American Colonial Printing as Determined by Contemporary Cultural Forces, 1639-1763* (New York: Burt Franklin, 1934), 19-77, 86.

36. Ibid., 86.

37. Robert Darnton, *The Literary Underground of the Old Regime* (Cambridge: Harvard University Press, 1982), 17-40.

38. The study by Michael Warner, *The Republic of Letters*, is particularly important in this respect.

39. Ibid., 73-96.

40. David Hall, "The Uses of Literacy in New England, 1600-1850," in *Printing and Society in Early America*, ed. William Joyce, et al. (Worcester: American Antiquarian Society, 1983), 1-47.

41. William J. Gilmore, *Reading Becomes a Necessity of Life; Material and Cultural Life in Rural New England, 1780-1835* (Knoxville: University of Tennessee Press, 1989).

42. Warner, *Letters of the Republic*, 97-117; François Furet, *Interpreting the French Revolution*, trans. Elborg Forster (Cambridge: Cambridge University Press, 1986), 46-61, 193.

43. Warner, *Letters of the Republic*, 103-06; Jacques Derrida, *Otobiographies* (Paris: Éditions Galilée, 1984), 13-32.

44. Gary J. Aichele, "Making the Vermont Constitution," *Vermont History* 56 (Summer 1988): 166-90, provides a narrative of the events attending the making of the Vermont constitution. Peter S. Onuf, "State-Making in Revolutionary America: Independent Vermont as a Case Study," *Journal of American History* 67 (March 1981): 797-815, and *The Origins of the Federal Republic* (Philadelphia: University of Pennsylvania Press, 1983), 103-145, are authoritative accounts of the problems of state-making by way of a short-lived republic.

45. Onuf, *Origins of the Federal Republic*, 144-45.

46. Michael Kammen, *A Machine That Would Go of Itself: The Constitution in American Culture* (New York: Knopf, 1986), 18; William E. Nelson, *Ameri-*

canization of the Common Law; The Impact of Legal Change on Massachusetts Society, 1760-1830 (Cambridge: Harvard University Press, 1975), 90.

47. See Albert Furtwangler, *American Silhouettes; Rhetorical Identities of the Founders* (New Haven: Yale University Press, 1987), 157-63.

48. See Benedict Anderson, *Imagined Communities; Reflections on the Origins and Spread of Nationalism* (London: Verso Editions, 1983).

Biennial Government?

Eric L. Davis

Vermont is one of only three states in which the governor and other constitutional officers are elected for terms of two years.[1] The 1991-92 legislature is considering an amendment to the Vermont constitution that would extend the terms of these officers to four years. In this paper, I will outline the procedure for amending the Vermont constitution, discuss the major arguments for and against the four-year term, and address some of the implications of the four-year term issue for the process of constitution-making in Vermont.

AMENDING THE VERMONT CONSTITUTION

Extending the terms of state officers from two to four years would require an amendment to Chapter II, Section 43 of the Vermont constitution, which establishes the terms of the statewide constitutional officers—the governor, lieutenant governor, treasurer, secretary of state, and auditor of accounts—at two years. The procedures for amending the Vermont constitution are specified in Chapter II, Section 72 of the document. Vermont's constitution is one of the most difficult to amend in the entire country. Amendments to the Vermont constitution must originate in the general assembly, and they may be proposed no more frequently than every fourth year. The 1991-92 biennial session of the general assembly was one in which action on constitutional amendments could be initiated. An amendment must be introduced in the Senate, where it is referred either to the Government Operations Committee or to the Judiciary Committee, depending on its subject matter. If the amendment is reported by the committee back to the Senate floor, a two-thirds vote of the full Senate is necessary to send the amendment to the House for further consideration. If a majority of the House concurs in the Senate proposal of amendment, the amendment will be considered again by the next biennial session of the general assembly. In the second biennium, a simple majority vote in favor of the amendment is needed in both the Senate and the

House. If the amendment is approved by such majorities, it is then referred to a direct vote of the people at the next general election.[2] To become part of the constitution, the amendment must be approved by a majority of the freemen voting thereon.[3]

Thus, for the four-year term to become part of the constitution of Vermont, the amendment would have to receive a two-thirds majority in the Senate and a simple majority in the House in the 1991-92 biennium, a simple majority in both the Senate and the House in the 1993-94 biennium, and a majority of the votes cast on the amendment at the November 1994 general election. An amendment providing for the four-year term was approved by the Senate in 1991. The vote in the Senate was 20-10 in favor of the amendment, the bare minimum two-thirds vote required by the constitution. Since the amendment was not approved by the House during the 1992 legislative session, the amendment process will have to start over again during the 1995-96 biennium.

THE FOUR-YEAR TERM

The four-year term for governor is a feature of the constitutions of forty-seven of the fifty American states. Other than Vermont, only New Hampshire and Rhode Island still have two-year terms. The four-year term for an American chief executive was first established in 1787, for the president of the United States, and was adopted by nearly half the states for their constitutional officers in the nineteenth century. The table below shows the number of states establishing the four-year term during four periods of American history.

States Adopting Four-year Gubernatorial Terms

Before 1850	6 states
1850-1900	15 states
1900-1950	8 states
Since 1950	18 states

Most of the states originally had two-year terms for governor.[4] The governor's term in many of the southern states was extended from two to four years in the post-Civil War years, when those states wrote new constitutions as part of Reconstruction.[5] Many of the northeastern, midwestern, and western states established a four-year term in the 1950s, 1960s, or 1970s, frequently as part of general revisions of their state constitutions.[6] A proposed constitutional amendment to extend the term of Vermont's governor and other officers to four years was rejected by the voters at March 1974 town meetings. I will discuss the history of this attempt at constitutional revision later in this paper, but many of the arguments made then in support of or in opposition to the four-year term are still relevant.

Arguments in Favor of the Four-Year Term
(1) *Better Planning and Program Execution*

The reason most frequently offered for extending the governor's term to four years is that it would permit better planning and execution of state programs. Because Vermont operates on a July 1 to June 30 fiscal year, a newly elected governor is not really able to make his or her mark on state government until the beginning of the first fiscal year for which he or she is responsible for preparing and implementing the state budget. This occurs six months into a governor's two-year term. By the time the governor's new programs have been in place for only one year, the governor is just four months away from the next election. A four-year term would give the administration more time both to plan and execute programs. There would not be the pressure to present the legislature with new programs (be they program expansions or budget retrenchments) at the very beginning of the biennial session, because the four-year governor would also have the second and third legislative sessions of his or her term as times to present new programs that could be in place before the end of the term.

Similarly, the four-year term would give the administration more time to learn from experience in implementing programs, because there would not be the pressure to achieve results in two years. Improved implementation could lead to improved delivery of state services, as programs could be adjusted to achieve their intended consequences and avoid unintended ones.

(2) *Improved Budgeting*

Another argument for a longer gubernatorial term is that it would lead to better state budgeting. With a four-year term, there would be less pressure to eliminate a deficit or spend a surplus than there is when gubernatorial elections are every second year. Assuming that governors want to go into elections with the state budget as close to balance as possible, the four-year term would damp down the large year-to-year fluctuations in taxing and spending policy produced by biennial elections. Budgets that change less from year to year are more likely to result in state spending and revenues growing at about the same percentage as the overall economy, adjusted for inflation, an outcome that some consider desirable on economic grounds.

(3) *Making Service More Attractive*

The proponents of the four-year term believe that governors would find it easier to attract top-quality men and women to appointed positions in their administrations if the length of term were doubled. People who have innovative ideas need time to convince the legislature and the bureaucracy that their plans are worth implementing. In the complex environment of today's state government, two years may not be enough time for such people to conceive and carry out their plans. Additionally, many people who accept appointed state positions are men and women who are successful in the private and non-profit sectors and must take pay cuts to accept state jobs. The four-year term, by providing greater job security to potential agency heads, might make more people willing to consider accepting appointed state positions, thus reducing the amount of relatively unproductive start-up time that occurs when there is a transition in an agency's appointed leadership.

Arguments Against the Four-Year Term

(1) *Vermont Politics as Citizen Politics*

One of the most frequently heard arguments against the four-year term is that it would mark another change in the nature of Vermont politics away from a polity based on small towns and close contact between citizens and elected officials, and toward a polity marked by centralized and bureaucratized state government.[7] Those who make this argument often tie the two-year term to other unique features of state government in Vermont—the citizen legislature, lay members of the judiciary (assistant judges), and town meeting. Many of these features of Vermont government have been changing in recent years—the legislature has become more professional, the side judges' ability to rule on questions of law has been substantially reduced, and the town meeting has lost much of its autonomy as the state has imposed more and more mandates on the towns—so those who take this position see retention of the two-year term as a last line of defense of traditional Vermont government.

(2) *Mistrust and Desire for Small Government*

Other defenders of the two-year term justify it on grounds not so unique to Vermont. They argue that the two-year term forces candidates for governor and other state offices to get out and around the state every second year, thus keeping in close contact with the people. With the state's population growing, and the media playing an increasingly important role in the state's politics, this direct contact between officials and citizens is considered crucial to preventing the government's losing touch with the citizens. The two-year term is also defended as a way of keeping public officeholders from getting too far ahead of public opinion. The fact that the next election is never more than two years away will put "the fear of the people" into the elected officials.

(3) *There is a De Facto Four-Year Term Already*

Another reason for keeping the two-year term in place is that, in practice, we already have at least a four-year term for governor in Vermont. The last Vermont governor to be defeated after a single two-year term was F. Ray Keyser in 1962. Since then, turnover in the governorship has come only when the incumbent governor has voluntarily left office, or has died in office. The voters of Vermont may be generally willing to give the governor the benefit of the doubt, and to return him or her to office even if he or she was not able within two years to accomplish all of the goals talked about during the last campaign. In this view, the two-year term serves as a useful check on the governor, and protection for the voters, since if the voters make a bad choice and elect someone to the office who turns out to be a disaster, they can remove that person from office after just two years.

Similarly, those who take this position note that governors frequently keep their appointed staff and agency heads with them for more than one term (other than in positions such as press secretary, where burnout and high turnover seem endemic to the job), and that the two-year term has not been an impediment to attracting high quality persons to state positions in recent years. Whether or not the governor can attract the best people to his or her administration depends much more on the governor's policy agenda than on the length of term of the office.

(4) *Imbalance of Power*

A final argument against the four-year term is that it would lead to an increase in the power of the executive branch, without a corresponding increase in the power of the legislative branch. Under this view, a governor serving a four-year term would be able to claim a "mandate" from the voters and use this to exert pressure on the legislature to pass his or her programs. Legislators would find it difficult to resist a governor who made such claims, especially a governor who was skilled in presenting his or her claims on television. Additionally, with a four-year term, the voters might take out their frustrations on the governor by voting against legislative candidates of his or her party in the midterm elections. This argument about the balance of legislative-executive power would likely be made with more vehemence should the general assembly submit to the voters not only an amendment to extend the governor's term to four years, but also an amendment that would give the governor the item veto on appropriations bills.

It is worth noting that in thirty-eight of the forty-seven states with four-year terms for governor, one or both houses of the legislature serve for four years.[8] None of the New England states has any legislators elected for four-year terms. Increasing the terms of one house of the legislature to four years would be a strong counterweight to the increase in executive power resulting from a four-year term for governor. There is no groundswell of support for four-year legislative terms in Vermont. Besides, such terms would be difficult to implement in our current multi-member legislative districts, since half the seats in a chamber whose members are elected for four-year terms are usually up for election every second year.

Campaign Spending and the Four-Year Term

There has been justified concern about the increasing costs of statewide political campaigns in Vermont in recent years. Candidates for governor now routinely raise and spend between $300,000 and $600,000 every two years. However, the decision on the proper length of the governor's term should be independent of consideration of campaign finance reform. Moving to a four-year term for governor may lead to higher campaign spending every fourth year than is now the case every second year, as the stakes in the governor's race are seen as more important. The spending on a four-year race would be much less than the combined spending over two election cycles for two two-year races. In any case, the way for the general assembly to address the problem of rising campaign costs is to pass legislation on that subject, not to address the problem indirectly through changing the length of the governor's term.

Campaign finance is an area of policy where unintended consequences of decisions are frequently apparent. One unintended consequence of moving to a four-year term, which the legislature may want to anticipate, is that in the election years when there are no statewide offices on the ballot, spending on legislative campaigns may increase as legislative candidates and party organizations turn for campaign dollars to those interest groups and political action committees that have traditionally been big donors to gubernatorial campaigns.

THE 1971-1974 EFFORTS AT AMENDMENT

The four-year term amendment that was rejected by the voters in March 1974 was part of a larger package of revisions to the Vermont constitution considered and debated between 1971 and 1974. These constitutional revisions were placed on the legislative agenda by a constitutional commission, which had been established by the legislature in 1968. At the time, the process of constitutional amendment could begin only every tenth year. (This ten-year restriction was known as the "time-lock.") The commission, which consisted of eleven members appointed through a bipartisan method, was given two years to study the Vermont constitution and make specific proposals of amendment to the 1971 legislative session. The commission was chaired by John Burgess (R.-Brattleboro), who was House Speaker from 1969-70 and lieutenant governor in 1971-72.

The constitutional commission submitted its final report to the general assembly on January 5, 1971. The report recommended a wide range of amendments including, in addition to the four-year term for governor, lieutenant governor, and attorney general, appointment of the secretary of state and treasurer by the governor, election of the auditor of accounts by the general assembly, lowering the voting age to eighteen, reform of the judicial system, and several possible changes in the process of amending the constitution, including elimination of the "time-lock" and allowing the voters to call a constitutional convention by petition.[9]

The four-year term was one of the least controversial recommendations of the commission. As finally approved by the 1971-1972 legislature, the amendment provided for the governor, lieutenant governor, attorney general, secretary of state, treasurer, and auditor of accounts to be elected for terms of four years, beginning in 1974. The legislature did not adopt the changes in the method of selection for the secretary of state, treasurer, and auditor of accounts that had been proposed by the constitutional commission, although the amendment did add the attorney general to the list of constitutional officers.[10]

The lack of controversy surrounding the four-year term proposal was reflected in the margins of victory on the key votes by which it was approved by the legislature in 1971. In the Senate, the key vote was on a motion to recommit the proposal, which was defeated on a 5 to 24 roll call.[11] The House adopted the operative language of the four-year term proposal by a division vote of 97 to 48.[12] Debate on the four-year term issue in 1971 appears to have been perfunctory. In the Senate, Sen. Russell Niquette (D.-Chittenden-Grand Isle), floor manager for the proposal on behalf of the Judiciary Committee, said that the four-year term was the most popular amendment of several proposals before his committee, and he noted that no one had appeared at the public hearings of the constitutional commission to speak against the proposal.[13] The majorities in favor of the four-year term in the 1973 legislative session were even greater than they had been in 1971: 25-3 in the Senate, and 120-22 in the House.[14]

Having received the necessary legislative majorities in 1971 and 1973, the proposed constitutional amendment was prepared for submission to the voters at the March 1974 town meetings. In addition to a four-year term for statewide officeholders, Proposal 1 (as it was known) also included a provision, which received very little attention from both the public and the press, changing the method of electing statewide officers when no candidate received a majority of the votes cast at the general election. Instead of the procedure specified in the constitution, which called for the legislature to elect the governor, lieutenant governor, and treasurer from the top three candidates, if no one received a majority at the polls, the amendment would have established a run-off election procedure, with the two top finishers for any state office in those races where no candidate received a majority at the polls running off in a special statewide election to be held on the second Tuesday after the first Monday in December.[15]

Proposal 1 was one of five proposed constitutional amendments that went to the voters in March 1974. The other amendments were designed to (1) shorten the length of the "time-lock" forbidding consideration of constitutional amendments from ten years to four years; (2) reform the judicial system by, among other things, establishing a unified court system, extending the terms of assistant judges, sheriffs, and state's attorneys from two to four years, requiring the governor to fill judicial vacancies from a list of names submitted by a judicial nominating commission, and mandating the retirement of judges at age seventy; (3) bring the Vermont constitution into conformity with the United States constitution by establishing a voting age of eighteen; and (4) bring the provisions of the Vermont constitution regarding apportionment of the House and Senate into conformity with federal constitutional requirements. All of the amendments, except Proposal 1, were approved by the voters on March 5, 1974. The four-year term amendment was defeated by a margin of 41,457 (52.3 percent) to 37,773 (47.7 percent).[16]

Why did Proposal 1 lose? First, it was voted on in a year when the public mood was to check executive power, not to increase the terms of executive officials. The March 1974 vote occurred as the Watergate investigations were reaching a climax. Just four days before the vote on Proposal 1, seven senior officials of the Nixon administration, including H. R. Haldeman, John Ehrlichman, and John Mitchell, were indicted by a federal grand jury in Washington on Watergate-related charges. Some of the same town meetings that voted on the four-year term also passed resolutions calling for the impeachment of President Nixon.[17]

Even without the Watergate connection, there were other reasons for the defeat of Proposal 1 in 1974. The amendment was poorly drafted in several respects. The proposed runoff election for governor when no candidate received a majority of the vote at the November general election was a scheme fraught with unintended consequences. Also, the amendment would have gone into effect immediately, with the governor elected in November 1974 being the first one to serve for a four-year term. Thus, some voters responded to the amendment in terms of their opinions on the incumbent governor, Democrat Thomas Salmon. Finally, there was no organized campaign in favor of the amendment. Civic groups such as the League of Women Voters, as well as important interest groups such as business, labor, and the education community, did not take a stand on the amendment. In the absence of a pro-four-year term campaign, with a poorly drafted amendment, and in the Watergate year, it is not surprising that Proposal 1 was defeated by the voters.

THE FOUR-YEAR TERM ISSUE SINCE 1974

One of the constitutional amendments approved in 1974 was the one reducing the "time-lock" from ten to four years, and making the consideration of constitutional amendments in order in the 1975-76 biennium, and every fourth year thereafter. Since 1975, the four-year term amendment has been introduced in the Senate every fourth year, with the following results:

1975-76: Amendment calling for election of governor, lieutenant governor, attorney general, secretary of state, and treasurer (but not the auditor of accounts, who was removed from the list of elected state officers on a 20-10 roll call) for four-year terms beginning in 1978 rejected in the Senate on a 19-11 roll call, the necessary two-thirds vote not having been attained.[18]

1979-80: Amendment calling for election of governor, lieutenant governor, secretary of state, treasurer, and auditor of accounts for four-year terms beginning in 1986 rejected in the Senate on a 12-17 roll call.[19]

1983-84: Amendment introduced calling for election of all state officers, including attorney general, as well as senators and representatives, for four-year terms beginning in 1988. Amendment referred to Senate Government Operations Committee, and no further action was taken.[20]

1987-88: Amendment calling for election of governor, lieutenant governor, secretary of state, treasurer, and auditor of accounts for four-year terms beginning in 1994 rejected by the Senate on a 17-12 roll call, the necessary two-thirds vote not having been attained.[21]

1991-92: Amendment calling for election of governor, lieutenant governor, secretary of state, treasurer, and auditor of accounts for four-year terms beginning in 1998 passed by the Senate on a 20-10 roll call.

The four-year term amendment approved by the Senate in 1991 provides for the longer term to commence with the governor and other state officers elected in 1998. Most states with four-year gubernatorial terms have their elections for statewide offices in the presidential off-years (thirty-two states) or in odd-numbered years (six states). Only nine states elect their governor for four years coincident with presidential terms. The amendment introduced in the 1991-92 biennium would, if it receives the necessary legislative approvals, come before the voters for ratification in 1994. If approved, the four-year term could theoretically begin with the 1996 election. There are sound policy reasons for delaying the effective date until 1998. First, the longer the time between discussion of the amendment and its effective date, the less likely the debate on the merits of the amendment will be associated with consideration of its effects on current officeholders. Second, having the gubernatorial election in the off-years insures that the governor's race will not be overwhelmed by the media attention devoted to the presidential race, and that gubernatorial candidates will not be elected on the coattails of their party's presidential candidates. Finally, if the presidential and gubernatorial elections coincide, turnout in the off-year elections, when state legislators, the U.S. representative, and, in two out of three off-years, one of the U.S. senators, will be elected could be very small. While turnout in an off-year gubernatorial election is likely to be lower than in the preceding presidential election, a closely contested gubernatorial race will draw voters to the polls in great numbers. Additionally, voter turnout in Vermont tends to be high to begin with, because of the ease of registering to vote in the state, and the relatively late checklist deadline of seventeen days before the election.

The amendment approved by the Senate in 1991 does not provide for any limit in the number of consecutive terms that a governor may serve. Of the forty-seven states with four-year gubernatorial terms, three have a one-term limit, twenty-six have a two-term limit (either an absolute two-term limit or a limit of two consecutive terms), and eighteen have no limits.[22] The usual practice is for whatever term limit there may be to apply to the office of governor, but not to the other state constitutional offices.

If the legislature decides to propose four-year terms, the provisions of the amendment regarding re-eligibility should be given close attention. There are three questions that must be considered: (1) Should there be any limits on re-eligibility in the constitution, or should the voters be trusted to decide when someone has served long enough in state office? (2) Should the limits on re-eligibility for statewide constitutional offices be connected with limits on re-eligibility for members of the general assembly? (3) Should there be a limit on re-eligibility for the statewide offices other than governor? Do the same considerations that may appropriately limit a governor to eight or twelve years in office also apply to offices such as secretary of state, treasurer, and auditor of accounts? In considering these questions, it would be wise to remember that the number of years established in the constitution as a limit on gubernatorial service often becomes the "expected" or "normal" length of service of a governor.

THE FOUR-YEAR TERM AND THE VERMONT CONSTITUTION

The four-year term issue has been discussed in the Vermont political community since the time Philip Hoff was governor, nearly thirty years ago. Yet, in spite of the regular attention the issue has received, the voters have had a chance to speak their mind on the issue only once, in 1974, and the amendment has been rejected by the general assembly more frequently than it has been approved. At one level, the regular discussion but lack of action on extending the terms may mean that the critics of biennial government are concentrated in the state's political community. The most ardent supporters of the four-year term have been former governors Madeleine Kunin and Richard Snelling. Outside of the fifth floor of the Pavilion Building, the press corps, senior officials of state agencies, and some statehouse observers, the four-year term may have very little support among the Vermont public at large. Extending the terms of state officials may very well be a change in the Vermont political system that the voters do not want pushed on them by the state's top elected and unelected officials. Indeed, there is a strong national movement to limit the terms of legislators and other elected officials. The voters of California, Oklahoma, and Colorado have amended their states' constitutions to place limits on the number of consecutive terms members of their legislatures may serve, and there is a growing groundswell of support for a twelve-year limit on the service of members of the United States Senate and House of Representatives. If Vermont were to extend the term of its statewide officers from two to four years in the 1990s, the Green Mountain State would once again be showing that it often does not follow national political trends.

The caution in amending the Vermont constitution shown by a reluctance of the legislature and the electorate to adopt the four-year term is consistent with other constitutional developments in the state's history. Vermont's first constitution provided for a unicameral, or one-house, state legislature. A bicameral, or two-house, system was first proposed in 1792, but the first Senate was not seated until 1836. The first constitution provided for a system of representation based on the rule of one representative per town, regardless of the town's population. Proposals to move toward a population-based apportionment of legislative seats were made as early as 1785, but the one-member-per-town system remained in place until the federal courts declared it unconstitutional in 1964. And the two-year term did not become part of the state constitution until 1870, even though it had been first suggested late in the eighteenth century. Amending the state constitution has always been a slow process in Vermont, and the fate of the four-year term proposal is no different from that of other major changes in the structure of state government which have been proposed over the past two centuries.

Vermont's constitution, as I noted in the beginning of this essay, is the most difficult to amend of all the fifty states.[23] Furthermore, constitutional amendments can originate only in the legislature; there is no provision for constitutional amendment by popular initiative. Nor is there a provision for the legislature to call a constitutional convention, either on its own motion or in response to popular petition. Considering the difficult process of amending the constitution in Vermont, it is no surprise that this state's constitution is the shortest state constitution in the United States.

Some states, especially those that permit constitutional amendments by means of the popular initiative, have constitutions that are relatively easy to amend. However, those states, such as California, whose voters have frequently amended their constitutions, may have state governments that are unable to respond to the increasingly heavy policy demands being placed on the states in the 1990s. The Vermont constitution is relatively immune from short-term popular political demands, yet, through its ability to endure and adapt over two centuries, it has led to a state in which the level of popular participation and governmental responsiveness to citizen concerns is arguably the highest in the country.

NOTES

1. New Hampshire and Rhode Island are the other two states with two-year terms for state officers.

2. Until 1982, the vote of the people on proposed constitutional amendments was held on Town Meeting Day. Since 1986, the vote of the people has been held as part of the November general election.

3. The phrase "a majority of the freemen voting thereon" means that for the constitutional amendment to be approved, the number of "yes" votes must exceed the number of "no" votes and blanks. In other words, blanks on constitutional amendment questions are the equivalent of "no" votes.

4. The three states that currently have two-year terms were among the last to move from one-year terms to two-year terms. The two-year term was established in Vermont in 1870, in New Hampshire in 1877, and Rhode Island in 1911.

5. For example, the four-year term was established in 1868 in North Carolina and South Carolina, 1869 in Mississippi and Virginia, and 1883 in Georgia.

6. Among the states establishing a four-year term during this period were Arizona (1970), Colorado (1966), Connecticut (1950), Kansas (1974), Maine (1958), Maryland (1950), Massachusetts (1966), Michigan (1966), Minnesota (1958), Montana (1972), Nebraska (1974), New Jersey (1947), North Dakota (1964), Ohio (1958), South Dakota (1974), and Wisconsin (1980). The Council of State Governments, a research organization for state governments, was especially active in promoting constitutional revision during this period. For a review of the council's work on this issue, see Albert L. Sturm, *Modernizing State Constitutions, 1966-1972* (Lexington, Ky.: Council of State Governments, 1973).

7. For a strong defense of small-polity government in Vermont, see Frank Bryan and John McClaughry, *The Vermont Papers: Recreating Democracy on a Human Scale* (Chelsea, Vt.: Chelsea Green Publishing Co., 1989).

8. In four states, both houses serve for four years. Nebraska has a unicameral legislature elected for four years. In thirty-three states, the house of representatives is elected for two years, and the senate for four years. Council of State Governments, *The Book of the States*, 1990-91 edition (Lexington, Ky: 1988), 123.

9. "Time-Lock Splits Team," *Rutland Herald*, 19 January 1971, 16, and "Legislators Main Audience at Hearing on Constitutional Reform," *Rutland Herald*, 20 January 1971, 16.

10. The attorney general was then, and remains today, a statutorily created office. See 3 V.S.A. § 151 et seq.

11. *Journal of the Senate*, January 22, 1971, 42-44.

12. *Journal of the House of Representatives*, April 16, 1971, 603-605.

13. "4-Year Terms Voted," *Rutland Herald*, 23 January 1971, 8.

14. *Journal of the Senate*, April 4, 1973, 354. *Journal of the House of Representatives*, April 11, 1973, 658-659.

15. The full text of Proposal 1 is in *Journal of the Senate*, April 4, 1973, 353-354.

16. "Amendment Final Tally," *Rutland Herald*, 7 March 1974, 16.

17. "Town Meeting Results," Ibid., 12.

18. *Journal of the Senate*, March 18, 1976, 336-339.

19. *Journal of the Senate*, April 14, 1980, 521.

20. *Journal of the Senate*, January 19, 1983, 48-49.

21. *Journal of the Senate*, January 26, 1988, 73-77.

22. *The Book of the States*, 62-63.

23. For information on state constitutional amendments, see *The Book of the States*, 42-45.

Challenges Facing Vermont Women in Government

Vi Luginbuhl

he challenge for women in Vermont is to take over the government and run it for the next two hundred years. It is our turn. Isn't that equal opportunity?

A number of men in politics suggested that I address the great strides women have made in Vermont. We currently constitute one-third of the House membership and just over one-fifth of the Senate membership. We have elected a woman governor and now have a woman supreme court justice. Over a period of two hundred years, Vermont has had two women lieutenant governors and one woman speaker of the house.

Yes, I thought, we have made some progress, because for most of our two hundred year "herstory," we had no political power. But it is too easy to overstate how far we have come. Even now, the positions of power too often escape us. Women may experience no more barriers than men in getting elected to the general assembly, but once there, we have not been very successful at gaining leadership roles, holding them, and climbing to higher positions. While I jest about taking over for the next two hundred years, I think it quite reasonable to expect parity. By that I mean that when it is as common for women to be elected governor, lieutenant governor, congresswoman, speaker of the house, president pro tem of the senate, and attorney general as it is now for men, and when the supreme court appointments are at least half women, we will have achieved true equality in the political arena. That is our challenge and our opportunity.

Shortly after her appointment as the first woman conductor of the Vermont Symphony Orchestra, Kate Tamarkin responded to a question about her position being a novelty by stating, "A conductor must be competent—that's the main thing."[1] Competence is the main thing necessary for women in government, too, and is the basis for holding a succession of political offices. By competence, I mean having the necessary skills, expertise, experience, and confidence to fill a position or do a job. The rules are the same for either sex, but in our day women must also learn and practice perseverance.

Think of the path Madeleine Kunin took to the governor's office. It was fraught with frustration, punctuated with failures as well as successes, and stretched over many years. Although the same can be said for many men in politics—Governor Richard A. Snelling, is a good example—it is nonetheless true that many more women have to take the time, accept the risks involved in seizing leadership roles, and persevere in efforts to exercise political power if they are to achieve equal representation in the political process.

There is no affirmative action program for women in politics. As I look at the women with leadership potential that I have known in politics, frustration with failure at some step has derailed their movement up the ladder. To smooth this path for women, we need more women legislators to create the networks and support systems that men already have in place. Women know how to get elected at the local level and that success can be parlayed into leadership positions right to the top. Of course, there are barriers. There are colleagues who still think of us as "girls," mothers, grandmothers, and secretaries, but not speakers or governors. However, these people can and will be replaced.

As for the judiciary, the number of women lawyers has increased rapidly and we now have the precedent for women to enter judges' chambers, even at the state and federal supreme courts. Although the specific skills and experience are somewhat different, the same requirements—competence, patience, and perseverance—must be met for women to gain greater power in the judicial hierarchy. I have observed capable women lawyers advance in both the political and judicial arena even though a report by the Vermont Bar Association and the Vermont Supreme Court, entitled *Gender and Justice*, indicates that many barriers exist in Vermont's judiciary system, which prevent women's upward mobility. The study even suggests that gender affects the dispensation of justice. Unfortunately, the study shows that "gender bias can be imposed upon members of either sex by members of either sex."[2] Because men dominate the judiciary, however, the biases work overwhelmingly against women.

Now that we have acknowledged the problems, we may anticipate that reform will begin. Indeed, some changes occurred before the report was published. I served on the judicial nominating committee in 1990 and 1991 and some of the stinging criticism changed our procedures. I might also add that not all of the criticisms leveled against the judicial nominating committee were fair or accurate. Clearly, because of the Vermont system of nominating and appointing judges, having equal representation by women in all areas of government is the best way to alleviate the alleged and real problems.

It is my contention that women cannot depend on the goodwill of men in power to help us maintain the gains we have made or to grant us automatic equity. We can depend on men to support us when we demonstrate competence to do a job. Of course, party and power politics often prevent the most capable person from getting a position, but that is true for either sex. Again, we need perseverance to overcome such frustration and often injustice.

It is clear that even before women achieve an equal or dominant role in Vermont state government, we will have to take a leading role in resolving some very important and sensitive issues. Although they are issues that uniquely affect women, they are also issues involving religious, ethical and individual rights and, therefore, require the most thoughtful, selfless deliberations by all our best minds, male and female. But women must bring as much weight to bear as we possibly can, given our minority status at the table.

The most obvious of these issues for women is legal abortion. Because of some recent U.S. Supreme Court decisions and the possibility that *Roe v. Wade* will be overturned, states have become a battleground for abortion rights. Frank Olmstead has written a good study on Vermont abortion law and practice before and after *Roe v. Wade*. He states that a U.S. Supreme Court decision is not necessarily the last word on the issue.[3] Court decisions and laws are influenced by changes in society's beliefs and attitudes, technology, and scientific knowledge. Consider, for example, the technological changes that have already had an impact on abortion procedures, and the potential impact of the RU486 pill on attitudes and decisions about birth control by both men and women. But women must have a powerful voice as decisions are made about abortion and birth control methods that we use.

Equally as difficult to adjudicate, and closely related to issues of birth control, is the problem of defining and protecting rights in relation to a pregnant woman who uses drugs or alcohol and consequently threatens the health and welfare of a fetus.[4] Should a pregnant woman's behavior be monitored to protect the fetus? Should she be subjected to criminal penalties when she delivers an infant with fetal alcohol syndrome or some other obvious deficiency due to drug abuse? These are questions other state legislatures and Congress are already debating. Women cannot stand by and allow a male-dominated political and judicial system to make decisions without us.

Another area of political controversy where women have particular interest and expertise is the issue of surrogate motherhood. Should it be outlawed? Should we develop guidelines allowing it? Should we just let it happen without any legislation? I shudder when I read an article like the one Rita Arditti wrote in *Science for the People* in 1987.[5] She helps us understand the issues when she highlights potentially serious problems with allowing surrogate mothering. Resolving these sensitive issues will require a great deal of trust and cooperation between all parties involved. They deal very personally with women's bodies and demand guidance from us when our society makes legislative, administrative, and judicial decisions. However, these issues also involve beliefs and practices in the sphere of ethics, religion, social relations, and economics, and here all members of society have a legitimate voice.[6] Our challenge is to frame these issues broadly, rather than approach them possessively and narrowly as women's issues, but at the same time women must find ways to play an equal role in making the decisions that affect us.

To summarize, I put my faith in women's abilities to prepare for higher political office. Once increased numbers of women have the necessary competencies, we will climb into the seats of power, and once there, we can give other capable women the opportunities that lead to the highest state offices. It will take more time, but we are on the way. In the meantime, our challenge is to use what strength we have to push hard on the rudder of state government and influence not only decisions but the overall agenda.

NOTES

1. Amber Older, "Music, Ms. Maestro," *Vermont Times*, 4 July 1991, 1:2.

2. *Gender and Justice*, Report of the Vermont Task Force on Gender Bias in the Legal System. A joint project of the Vermont Supreme Court and the Vermont Bar Association, (January 1991), 50-60, xx.

3. Frank Olmstead, "Abortion Choice and the Law," *Vermont Law Review* 7:281-313.

4. See, for example, the article on fetal rights by Katha Pollitt, "Fetal Rights, A New Assault on Feminism," *The Nation*, March 26, 1990, 250, 409-411.

5. Rita Arditti, "'Surrogate Mothering' Exploits Women," *Science for the People* 19 (May/June 1987): 22-23. In my view, Arditti is less helpful when she charges that surrogacy is a plot to reinforce patriarchal views of women.

6. *Abortion, Religion, and the State Legislator after Webster: A Guide for the 1990s*, a report by the Park Ridge Center for the Study of Health, Faith, and Ethics (Chicago: 1990), 6-12.

Vermont's Citizen Legislature Can Be Preserved

William Doyle

en. Philip Hoff, Democrat and former governor, and Rep. Henry Carse, Republican and former Chair of the House Appropriations, Ways and Means, and Natural Resources committees, both agreed that longer and less disciplined sessions were a major factor in their decision to terminate their legislative careers.

According to Rutgers professor Alan Rosenthal, longer sessions are changing the character of state legislatures throughout the nation and a new breed of state legislator is replacing citizen legislators such as Hoff and Carse. Rosenthal describes the change this way:

> What distinguishes the full-time, professional politician from the part-time citizen-legislator is not only where they have come from but also where they are going to. Relatively few of the old-timers harbored career ambitions in politics. They intended to serve a while and return to private careers. Many of the new breed, by contrast, would like to spend their careers in government or politics. They find public office appealing and the game of politics exhilarating. They take pleasure in their status, delight in the exercise of power, and have policies they want to advance.[1]

If we use Rosenthal's definition, then Vermont still has a citizen legislature, since most legislators do have outside employment and rely upon it as their principal source of income. As sessions go long and longer, however, there will be less opportunity for those with occupations to serve.

To preserve our citizen legislature in Vermont and keep our sessions under control so we do not lose outstanding legislators, we should consider a number of changes in our state government procedures and practices.

(1) We should place some limitation on the length of legislative sessions, either by statute, through constitutional provisions, or by instituting a fixed annual

salary for legislators, which would provide an economic incentive to conduct their business more quickly and efficiently.

Only twelve states at present place no limit on the length of their legislative sessions. Thirty-two states have constitutional limitations, and six states have statutory or indirect limitations based upon cutoffs in legislative salaries. Vermont is one of the dozen states with no written session limitations and in the last four years the Vermont general assembly has met for 135, 136, 125, and 131 days respectively.

The State of Washington enacted session limitations in 1981. In 1984 Utah adopted a limit of forty-five days per session. Arizona and Iowa recently limited their sessions by legislative rule. In the 1970s Montana had annual sessions, but now the legislators only meet once every two years for ninety days. In 1988 the National Conference of State Legislatures (NCSL) reviewed the operations of the Alaska House of Representatives and recommended a session deadline. The legislature subsequently adopted a 120-day session, which now enjoys strong support.

(2) We should establish tighter deadlines for the introduction of bills, periods for committee consideration, and cutoff dates for floor consideration. These procedures, if implemented, tend to even out the work load and lessen the end-of-session logjam.

A 1983 NCSL study found that in seventy-nine legislative bodies the deadlines were too late in the session to be of benefit. The factors that distinguish the successful use of deadlines were as follows: The deadline schedule tends to be more detailed; deadlines for introducing legislation are usually earlier in the session than those in other states; the deadlines allow flexibility for major items such as tax and appropriations bills; legislative leaders rigorously enforce the deadlines.[2]

(3) We should establish rules that ensure that legislation is ready for committee study early in the session. In addition to deadlines, a number of states have adopted such rules. One rule requires members to file the majority of their bills prior to the tenth legislative day. Another rule requires that all executive branch bills be prefiled two weeks preceding the session. Executive branch bills usually represent about one-third of all bills introduced. The NCSL study indicated that in other state legislatures the deadline system helps manage time, establish priorities, allows for closer cooperation and coordination among committee chairs, assists scheduling for public hearings, floor discussion, and legislative work time.[3]

(4) We should make greater use of the "uni-bill," which is a bill introduced simultaneously in both houses carrying House and Senate bill numbers. Since a uni-bill lists the sponsors of both houses, it is not necessary to print two separate bills, thereby saving printing costs. The uni-bill works successfully in many states. Thirty percent of New York's bill introductions are uni-bills, and they are often major pieces of legislation.

(5) We should limit the number of bills that may be introduced in the second half of the biennium. The second half of the biennium should be limited to consideration of bills leftover from the first year, to committee bills, or to bills that could be introduced by rule exception. In the summer of 1984 a joint

committee of the Vermont House and Senate studied Vermont's political process. One of its recommendations was:

> The rules of each house should . . . provide that no bill may be considered at all in the second session of a biennium, unless it has either been introduced in the first session and held over, or has been drafted and approved for printing no later than December 15 preceding the second session of the biennium again unless a special exception were granted by the Rules Committee of that house.[4]

(6) We should use consent calendars to help speed the legislative process by reducing the number of votes that must be taken on noncontroversial items and reduce the time spent discussing these matters. Many bills and resolutions are noncontroversial, including technical bills and housekeeping bills. Fifty-seven of the ninety-nine legislative chambers in the nation use consent calendars for items that are noncontroversial. In New Hampshire each committee can vote to be placed on the consent calendar. Edward Pert, the clerk of the Maine House of Representatives, said that the consent calendar saves legislative and staff time and reduces legislative expenses.[5]

(7) We should adopt electronic voting. Most states now use this system. In Vermont, it could save a substantial amount of time over a roll call. More time could be spent on committee work and on the floor.

(8) We should consider filling leadership positions—especially committee chairs—within two or three weeks after an election, and we should make committee assignments in December. This could eliminate a considerable amount of dead time in the first week of the first session of the biennium. This idea, suggested by a 1971 Vermont legislative study,

> would give each new legislature an opportunity to hold party caucuses and to dispose of the selection of committees, the chairman and the leadership in advance of the session so that no time is lost in what is already regarded by some as a very short session. It would also give the leadership and the chairs a chance to consider the proper approaches for the work load to come.[6]

The constitutional provision for an early organizational session was introduced in the 1992 legislature, but died in the senate.

In recent years the Vermont legislature has begun to move towards some of these reforms. Two years ago the Vermont Senate established a consent calendar for the confirmation of gubernatorial appointees. In the spring of 1991 the Joint Rules Committee streamlined the process of electing legislative trustees to the state colleges and University of Vermont.

In July 1991 the Joint Rules Committee established a drafting request deadline of Friday, November 1, 1991, for all of the 1992 drafting requests from the Senate and the House. These requests received priority and were ready for introduction in January 1992. Requests after November 1, 1991, received no guarantee of when they would be printed. A similar procedure now applies to the executive branch.

The Joint Rules Committee of the House and Senate is reexamining deadlines for "crossover"—when bills must be out of Senate and House committees—and when those bills must leave the House of Representatives and the Senate in order to be eligible for consideration by the other chamber. The Joint Rules Committee is also exploring the possibility of wider use of consent calendars and having some of the major bills, such as the institutions bills and the pay act, originate in the Senate in order to even out the work load of both chambers and reduce the pressure on the Senate during the last few weeks of the session.

The Vermont legislature has made a good start in modernizing its legislative process. Further consideration of session limitations, bill limitations, consent calendars, electronic voting, and other procedures that have proven successful in other states will help to preserve our citizen legislature.

NOTES

1. Alan Rosenthal, *The Legislative Institution—Transformation and/or Decline* (New Brunswick, N.J.: Eagleton Institute of Politics, Rutgers University, 1987), 13-14.

2. Jan Carpenter, "Limiting Bill Introductions: A Re-examination," *State Legislative Report* 8 (December 1987): 1.

3. Carpenter, 2.

4. Report of the Committee on the Legislature, 1985, Vermont Legislative Council, 4.

5. Author's telephone conversation with Edward Pert, July 1991.

6. "Report of the Legislative Council Committee to Study Legislative Improvement," Legislative Council, 1971, 11.

Vermont Secretary of State James Douglas exhibits the multiple volumes of *Vermont Statutes Annotated* (left) and state *Administrative Rules* (right). 1982 photograph courtesy of the Office of Secretary of State, Montpelier, Vt.

Regulating Vermonters

James H. Douglas

Have you ever burned a little brush in the backyard without consulting your local fire warden? Have you ever fed garbage to a pig without boiling it for at least thirty minutes? Have you ever babysat for children from more than two different families without a license from the Office of Child Development? If you live along a highway, have you ever failed to trim the grass or weeds from the right-of-way by July 20? Have you ever gone hang gliding without a permit for the use of the launch site? Have you ever exploded fireworks without permission from the fire chief? Did you ever work at a charity auction without a license from the Secretary of State?

If you've ever done any of these things or engaged in any one of hundreds of other activities regulated by the state of Vermont or its municipalities, without proper authority, you have the right to remain silent, and anything you say will be used against you.

We are regulated literally from cradle to grave: a birth certificate proves that we arrived, and a death certificate is needed to verify our departure. We need a license to get married, to drive, or to fish. From abandoned property to zoo animals, we regulate every conceivable aspect of the lives of our citizens.

Isn't this supposed to be the land of the free? Isn't a basic tenet of our American system the sanctity of the individual and the right to strive and achieve according to our abilities, unfettered by the constraints of state plans and controls? Did our founding fathers intend that government would balloon into a massive bureaucracy, flexing its muscle to protect us from ourselves? How did all of this happen? Is Vermont unique? Is all of this regulation really necessary?

Andrew and Edith Nuquist, in their book *Vermont State Government and Administration*, note that regulation is as old as organized society itself. In medieval Europe, before the establishment of central governments, commercial and occupational guilds provided the oversight of their members. With the growth of the modern state, power was transferred from private organizations to the government.[1]

Regulatory laws were not diabolical schemes designed by public officials for their own purposes, but resulted from a public outcry against abuses by dishonest entrepreneurs. When private policing broke down, there was a resort to the power of society. That's the essence of legislation. Madison observed that if men were angels, we would need no laws. Until we reach that point, we'll have to rely on the legislative process, and the legislature will have to rely on the executive branch, which, in turn, will have to rely on what some have termed the fourth branch of government, the bureaucracy.

That society is organized to protect the people is an embodiment of Locke's theory of social contract. We agree to some limits on our freedom in order to promote public safety and protect the property of citizens. Government is formed by the consent of the governed, Locke and the American founding fathers tell us, for our mutual benefit and that of our descendants.

Let's look back at how governmental power flowed into this unelected fourth branch.

Following the lead of the thirteen colonies, the settlers of the New Hampshire Grants declared their independence on January 15, 1777, at a convention in Westminster. They proclaimed this land a "free and independent state" whose citizens had "the sole and exclusive and inherent right of ruling and governing themselves in such manner and form as by their own Wisdom they shall think proper."

Thomas Young, the Pennsylvania physician who gave Vermont its name and its early leaders their inspiration, wrote an open letter to the people of this state a few months after the Westminster convention. He said:

> . . . I esteem the people at large the true proprietors of governmental power. They are the supreme constituent power, and of course their immediate Representatives are the supreme Delegate power; and as soon as the delegate power gets too far out of the hands of the constituent power, a tyranny in some degree is established.[2]

This view of representative government was embodied in the state constitution, written later that year, which says in its current version in Article 6: "That all power being originally inherent in and consequently derived from the people, therefore, all officers of government, whether legislative or executive, are their trustees and servants; and at all times, in a legal way, accountable to them."

In the early days, state government consisted of little more than the state officers and members of the assembly, and it moved around from year to year. Despite the transient, temporary nature of Vermont's government in those days, the legislature in the first few years of statehood was not reluctant to impose regulatory controls. In fact, looking back, it is sometimes startling to see how far these early regulations reached. One particularly thorny issue was thistles. Thistles were both plentiful and a potential threat to livestock.

Consequently the assembly enacted a law in 1792 that required landowners to cut all thistles not only on their own property but on any public way abutting their property, before the thistles went to seed. Failure to comply resulted in a thirty-shilling fine for each offense.[3]

In 1797, the legislature moved to check what it viewed as the tricks and evasions of those engaged in commerce with an act that established standards for salting and shipping meat. It required

> that all barrels for packing beef or pork for exportation, shall be new and made of good white oak staves, and white-oak or good ash heading, and shall not be of less gauge than twenty eight, nor more than thirty gallons each, with, at least, twelve hoops on each barrel . . . to every barrel of beef, there shall be added four ounces of salt petre, and . . . all barrels . . . shall be branded on one of the heads, with the initial letter of the owner's christian name, and his sir name at full length.[4]

State government has always been interested in encouraging the development of manufacturing and industrial enterprises, but petitions to the 1792 legislature reveal that even at that early date there was concern about balancing industrial growth with environmental and health concerns. One set of petitions involved the raising and lowering of lake levels at Castleton Pond (now Lake Bomoseen). In this case the legislature decided the dam's "great utility" outweighed other concerns. At nearby Lake St. Catherine, however, the same legislature responded to a similar complaint by forcing the dam owners to lower their dam.[5]

Protecting the public health, or its safety or welfare, is the purpose of governmental regulation. No one would quarrel with that philosophical basis for the imposition of the state's police power on private endeavors. The problem comes when policymakers decide what situation requires intervention by the state. In spite of how much fun it is to point to its failures, government does not try to do wrong to us, yet it is often hard to explain to the general public the specific harm in doing what the law prohibits.

Consider, for example, what happened on August 1, 1909, at Berlin Pond, the water supply for Montpelier. K. W. Morse, who leased a cottage on the pond, went for a swim. An innocent act, except that the State Board of Health had ruled that no one could bathe or fish in the pond. No notice had been posted, and Mr. Morse had gone swimming there for years. But the Vermont Supreme Court said the judgment against him should stand. The regulation made sense; the public health was worth it.

The court quoted a treatise on nuisances, which explains that "every person yields a portion of his right of absolute dominion and use of his own property in recognition of an obedience to the rights of others, so that others may also enjoy their property without unreasonable hurt or hindrance." Therefore, the court concluded: "Whenever any of the rights of the individual come into conflict with those of the public which concern the interests named, the former must yield and the latter prevail."[6]

This is one of the first cases in Vermont's judicial history in which a regulation of a state agency is upheld as a legitimate exercise of the police power. From this swim in the pond, the state has come a long way toward regulating the use of land, water, and air for the sake of the environment, but in large measure the power the state exercises today began back in 1909, when Morse was arrested for swimming in Berlin Pond.

If we accept the proposition that regulation is appropriate in order to protect the public, what governmental entity has the authority and responsibility to regulate? It is one thing for the legislature to enact laws proscribing or constraining the behavior of the citizenry, but what about some agency or board or department or commission? That's okay, says the Vermont Supreme Court. The general assembly is the "supreme legislative power" under the constitution and although it may not delegate its purely legislative functions, it may authorize an administrative agency to adopt rules and apply the law to particular circumstances. Interestingly, one of the arguments in favor of this delegation, the court observed in 1912, was the brevity of the legislative session, which met once every other year in those days. The court found that it was even permissible to grant an executive branch entity functions that are judicial in nature, in order to effect the public policy articulated by the legislature. This does not offend the separation of powers doctrine, the court insisted, because decisions of administrative bodies and officials are always appealable to the courts.[7]

This judicial recognition of the authority of executive branch agencies to regulate has been recognized in other jurisdictions as well, but even if we accept the notion that the bureaucracy may regulate, how do people know what's going on? Legislative deliberations are usually conducted in the open, so the press and public are aware of the issues under debate. But an administrative edict could emanate from the desk of some functionary and receive no public notice until it slaps some unsuspecting citizen, like Mr. Morse, in the face.

This concern was particularly acute in the 1930s at the federal level, where many regulatory agencies were created under the aegis of the New Deal. The chairman of the Securities and Exchange Commission, William O. Douglas, proposed that each agency be abolished automatically at the end of ten years, to avoid co-option by the regulated industry. He was concerned that agencies would be caught in the revolving door, whereby today's regulator is tomorrow's regulated entrepreneur and vice versa. Although President Roosevelt was not persuaded by this suggestion, he asked the attorney general in 1939 to review the processes used by regulatory agencies to undertake their missions. It took a while, but in 1946 Congress enacted the Administrative Procedures Act, which spelled out requirements for public notice of proposed regulations and the methods undertaken by the agencies to administer them.[8] Eventually all the states adopted their own administrative procedure acts. Vermont's came into being in 1969.

Although it is fun to criticize the unelected fourth branch, rulemaking isn't an easy task. The Advisory Commission on Intergovernmental Relations, a group comprised of federal, state, and local officials, has noted that many laws enacted by the Congress are forged in the crucible of political compromise, and Congressional policy is not always clearly articulated. An act of Congress may be a profound expression of morality, but may give little if any legislative guidance to the administering agency.[9]

It became clear that, although an increasingly complex society requires the delegation of power to administrative agencies, the legislative branch needed a mechanism to ensure that the delegation was responsible and consistent with legislative intent. The courts were allowing great latitude, striking down rules only if they ranged beyond their intended purpose or neglected due process. To recapture their role in the regulatory system, legislatures acted to institute reviews of administrative rules.

The National Conference of State Legislatures reports that the first legislative rules review came in the 1930s, and now forty-one states have committees in place for that purpose.[10] The Vermont legislature took this step in 1976 by creating a joint legislative committee to review all new rules promulgated by executive branch agencies. Initially the general assembly sought to assign itself a veto power over administrative rules, but Governor Thomas Salmon vetoed that idea, citing the constitutional separation of powers. Accordingly, the joint committee would have to content itself with the duty to review and recommend changes if it found a rule repugnant to legislative intent, beyond the scope of the agency's authority, or arbitrary. It can also recommend repeal of a rule to the entire general assembly, which has the authority to act.

Assessments of the success of this system are mixed. It keeps agencies on their toes, to be sure, as they know someone is watching; but sometimes the signals from the committee are inconsistent, as its membership changes every biennium. In reviewing some rules, committee members bristle at what they perceive to be an agency overstepping its bounds. In other cases, they passively approve rules with little comment. The effect of disapproval by the committee is that the burden of proof in any challenge to the validity of the rule shifts from the aggrieved party to the agency.

Another form of legislative oversight of executive branch activity is the sunset process. As I noted, this was proposed by William O. Douglas in the 1930s, although he did not use the term, and then revived by Prof. Theodore Lowi of Cornell University in 1969. Conceptually, sunset is the periodic termination of a rule, a law, or even an agency itself. Colorado enacted the first sunset law in the mid-1970s; Florida was next, and Vermont followed in 1978. The theory of sunset is that legislators will be forced to reconsider the need for and value of a particular regulatory scheme at regular intervals, contradicting the thesis that, once created, a bureaucratic entity endures forever.

Regrettably, sunset laws have met with less than overwhelming success; indeed they have themselves been "sunsetted" in some states, including Vermont. The legislative will to actually bid a fond farewell to a government agency is often lacking, usually because each enjoys the support of some constituency. Florida reported in September 1990 that, although some agencies have been abolished, far more have been created.[11] The Vermont general assembly found the sunset process too onerous and replaced it with a sort of "dusk," whereby regulatory programs are reviewed by legislative staff (that is, if they remember or feel like it).

The concern for oversight of administrative rulemaking in recent years has heightened because there is much more regulatory activity than there used to be. The increasing complexity of government is one reason, of course, but so is the shift of regulatory responsibility from the federal to the state level. The Advisory Commission on Intergovernmental Relations suggests that our nation has had three major periods of federal regulatory activity: in the Progressive Era, during the early decades of this century; during the time of the New Deal, in the 1930s and 1940s; and again in the 1960s and 1970s.[12] Procedures were established in 1967 for consulting state and local officials in the course of federal rulemaking, with limited success. Then, in the 1980s, President Reagan initiated a course of deregulation which, while attempting to lighten the bureaucratic load on American business, in some respects made it worse.[13] Neil Peirce wrote in his syndicated column of April 10, 1988, that the Justice Department declined to pursue allegations of antitrust violations by more than thirty major insurance companies in 1986. As a result, a number of state attorneys general launched their own investigations and brought suit. So instead of an era of deregulation, American business faces, as the *National Journal*'s John Moore has put it, the "specter of 50 regulatory Rambos."[14]

Ironically, this return of regulatory foci to the states reverses an earlier trend. Our modern economy is based on the interstate transfer of goods, and modern technology and transportation offer many the opportunity to ply their trades all across the country and beyond. When the several states found it difficult to protect their citizens from the unscrupulous practices of mobile entrepreneurs, the federal government stepped in. In many cases, such as trademarks, consumer protection, environmental quality, and handicapped accessibility, state regulation is often relegated to a supplementary status.

Where the line between the federal government's legitimate preemption powers ends and the Tenth Amendment begins is not clear. Now that Congress has shifted responsibilities to the states and has no money to allocate to new programs, perhaps it will spend its time legislating and by extension, regulating.

Vast areas of governmental regulation belong principally to the states. Let's explore the development and effect of state regulation in one specific area: professional regulation, the licensing and discipline of some fifty thousand Vermonters and nonresidents who receive the permission of the state to offer their professional services to the public. It is the area with which I'm most familiar, since a majority of my staff and budget are dedicated to this program.

A license is the legal permission to do something that would otherwise be prohibited. The state has the responsibility to punish those who unlawfully attempt to use the forbidden license. We need a license to hunt, fish, own or operate a motor vehicle, or sell liquor, beer, or cigarettes. Licensure confers authority. No longer does a prospective consumer need to depend on the individual character or knowledge of the practitioner; an attractive certificate, displayed prominently on the office wall, stands out as a badge of legitimacy.

Usually the impetus for regulation comes not from consumers or public interest groups, but from the profession itself. Why, you may wonder, would a group of citizens trying to make a living embark upon a masochistic effort to subject themselves to government regulation? Several commentators have suggested that the reason is self-interest: protection from competition, since most new licensing laws exempt those already actively engaged in the field. These "grandfather clauses" provide that only newcomers are subjected to the rigors of proving themselves worthy of a professional license. Perhaps not coincidentally, licensing boards in most states, including Vermont, are comprised principally of licensees themselves.

The first licensing law was simple: God said to Adam, "You may pick fruit from any tree in the garden but one." Since then, however, the system has become much more complex. Earthly licensing schemes began with the guilds of medieval Europe, and the first requirement in this country was a New York City law in 1760 that required physicians to take an examination. Licensing for the medical profession is an excellent example to study in detail. At the time of the American Revolution, only about ten percent of doctors had any formal training, and about half of those had earned medical degrees. As a result, the New York statute was ignored, and unlicensed practice continued unabated.[15]

In the wake of this failed approach, legislatures granted licensing authority to medical societies. This was also ineffective, as the only penalty was denying the lack of access to the court system to recover debts. There was a simple remedy for this denial: unlicensed doctors would insist on payment in advance. In the unlikely event that a prosecutor preferred a charge of practicing without a license, juries refused to convict. Another shortcoming in this system was the fact that the societies relied on licensing fees to support their activities, so they rarely rejected an application. Why did this form of licensing persist, despite its ineffectiveness? Practicing physicians wanted to restrict entry into the field, and medical societies and schools wanted the revenue it ensured.[16]

In Vermont there were attempts in the 1820s and 1830s to restrict the practice of medicine to those who graduated from an accredited medical college. The legislature said that patients did not have to pay any medical provider without an acceptable degree. A group of Bennington County residents petitioned the assembly in 1834 urging repeal of that restriction. The law, they insisted, was "oppressive and unjust." They labeled "any law that gives to any class of men an advantage over their fellow-men repugnant to the spirit of the constitution of our country." The petitioners argued that if they were competent enough to vote for public officials, they were competent enough to choose their own doctors without any restrictions imposed by the state. They noted that practicing physicians were being denied the right to enforce payment, which was granted to everyone else in business in Vermont. "Each of our fellow-citizens should be permitted to stand or fall upon his own merits . . . there should be no exclusives by law."[17]

The Jacksonian era brought a strong distrust of monopolies, generally directed at business, but it affected the public's view of organized professionals as well. Like the Bennington residents who petitioned the 1834 legislature, people throughout the country felt that any intelligent American could practice a profession, and that government regulation was "an artificial imposition on their native intelligence." The number of states licensing attorneys dropped by two-thirds from 1800 to 1860. Legislatures repealed statutes licensing physicians as well, since it was clear that the public would no longer support the exclusivity of licensure. This attitude was similar and simultaneous to the antiMasonic fervor, wherein the public perceived an attempt to win advantages and business through a secret organization.[18]

After the Civil War, the public's resistance to licensing began to melt. Many states enacted laws regulating peddlers, so they would not compete with local tradesmen. The professions began enjoying success in promoting self-regulatory laws; they disarmed the opposition by the inclusion of grandfather clauses.[19] The first licensing agency in Vermont was the Board of Dental Examiners, created in 1882. Licensing grew incrementally: the first laws required only a diploma to practice a profession; next the boards were given the authority to judge the adequacy of the school granting it; later, applicants were required to pass licensing examinations. The relatively lax statutes were a boon to diploma mills, which offered no real education at all. To combat this trend, states began to require high school or college degrees as well, and then imposed a state exam for entrance into a professional school.

There was some resistance among professionals to a stronger level of regulation, but the proprietary medical schools wanted the business, and the locomotive of licensing was chugging along at full speed. In 1888, the U.S. Supreme Court, in *Dent v. West Virginia*, affirmed the right of the states to regulate the professions.[20] This judicial recognition of the state's power to license was a double-edged sword, however: the medical establishment achieved the control it sought, but it could not prevent other practitioners like chiropractors from gaining the same benefits of regulation.[21]

Licensing alone did not create the medical monopoly as we know it today. Paul Starr explains in *The Social Transformation of American Medicine* that governmental regulation of medicine has been bolstered by other institutional changes, such as the establishment of hospitals, the development of the health insurance industry, the restrictions on access to drugs, and the tax deductibility of some payments for health care. In fact, Starr argues, if licensure of physicians were eliminated today, the effect would be minimal. The cultural authority we have conferred on medical doctors, coupled with the health insurance system, would keep the system intact.[22]

Licensing of other professions has grown exponentially in this century. As an example, Oregon enacted the first licensing law for barbers in 1899, and every other state followed suit. The trend slowed somewhat during the 1960s and 1970s, when the Federal Trade Commission and Justice Department criticized licensure. In addition, there have been reports and studies by consumer groups and other private organizations that have caused legislatures to pause before creating more licensing boards, but the lag was brief. A study by the U.S. Department of Labor in 1980 listed approximately eight hundred different professions regulated somewhere among the fifty states.[23] Between 1986 and 1989, in Vermont, the legislature enacted a new professional regulatory program every year, and other groups are waiting in line. We have a law called "sunrise," which requires any profession seeking licensure to complete a lengthy questionnaire explaining the need for such a step, but most proponents are able to make a plausible case, sometimes with the aid of experienced lobbyists.

In 1958, the Commission to Study State Government, known as the Little Hoover Commission and chaired by Deane Davis, expressed its concern that dozens of licensing boards had sprouted up without any administrative connection to the rest of state government. Records were kept in the home or office of board members, with some hiring staff in various locations around the state. The commission noted the obvious inefficiency in this lack of administrative consolidation and recommended that the housekeeping tasks of the various boards be combined in the office of the secretary of state. The 1960 Special Session of the general assembly obliged, and all of the staff and records were moved to a single home.[24]

There is still a noticeable lack of uniformity in licensing standards, although a boiler plate bill drafted a decade ago by the legislature's staff helped, as did a 1990 act establishing some uniform grounds for unprofessional conduct and procedures to deal with disciplinary complaints. Nevertheless, each licensing law is enacted separately, by a different group of legislators, influenced by different lobbyists and public pressures, and, as a result, many inconsistencies remain.

When I took office in 1981, the licensing division of my office had nine employees; today it has twenty-eight, not to mention some part-time and contractual workers. It's a growth industry, and one ripe for some thoughtful reflection on whether we are regulating in the public interest.

Remember Mr. Morse, the man who swam unlawfully in Berlin Pond? He has something in common with all of us. The look on his face must have been excruciating. When government tells us we can't build on our own land, can't burn our trash in an old barrel in the backyard, can't drive a car that happens to have a rusted hole in the door, can't do what we want with our property, when there doesn't seem to be any palpable reason why not, we have to conclude that government has gone insane.

The problem is scope. At a legislative hearing, the committee hears the most horrifying stories of pollution, misuse of public waters, the burning of hundreds of old tires, the fraud of peddlers, frightful stories about doped-up surgeons, and beauticians with venereal disease, and the next thing you know there's a law against it. And too often, while there are legitimate reasons for the law in the first place, the big stick falls on the little guy who's just trying to save a few bucks by doing it his way.

The fact is that we overregulate all the time, every legislative session, every day the executive branch goes to work. Who's at fault? Is it the administrator who has to shrug and tell the poor applicant that's what the law says, even though it doesn't make sense? Is it the judge, who knows in his or her heart that the law is too broad, but who feels compelled to bow to legislative intent? Is it the legislature, or its constituents, or special interests? I don't know that it is worth assigning fault. I think we are all a little guilty of it, because we are human, and because we have a hard time being scientific about what long-term effects law and government will have in every case.

What shall we do, then, to extricate ourselves from this regulatory morass? Surely the state with the briefest constitution, the next-to-smallest population, and a government more accessible than most can find a solution that works. I suggest a four-pronged approach:

(1) We must eliminate unnecessary agencies. It's not easy, but we've done it before. Since I've been in Montpelier, the legislature has abolished the Interagency Child Coordinating Council, the Board of Elections, the Board of Radio and Television Technicians, the Committee on Administrative Coordination, the Vermont Metric Coordinating Council, and the Board of State Buildings. In addition, Governor Richard Snelling repealed a dozen or so advisory panels that had been created by executive order.

In some cases, boards and other entities could be combined. Many states have merged their boards of barbers and cosmetologists, or their boards of medicine and osteopathy. As the keeper of the state's archives, I fume at the fact that this small state has established the State Archives, the Vermont Historical Society, the Vital Records section of the Health Department, the Division of Public Records, the State Library, and the Special Collections unit at the University of Vermont, six different repositories of historical records and documents. Merger raises difficult issues of turf and jobs, but we need to economize and better serve those who use these resources.

(2) We must eliminate unnecessary rules and laws. It is not unprecedented in our state's history. In 1960, all administrative rules of all state agencies were sunsetted; in 1976, all professional licensing rules were terminated. In both cases, each promulgating agency was forced to reconsider the rationale and need for all its rules. The mechanisms in place to review administrative rules generally consider only newly proposed rules. They do not have time to look at those that have been in place for some time. A periodic wholesale review is essential: a few years ago, my office set about the herculean task of publishing all the administrative rules of state government.

A logical first step, it seemed to us, was to verify that the version of each rule on file in our office, which is the official text, was identical to the rule on file with the relevant agency. We discovered to our horror that literally half the rules were different! That means that, in some instances, agencies were enforcing rules that had no legal effect, and, in other cases, were not enforcing rules that were in effect. Is this just a meaningless exercise in bureaucracy? Hardly. The people of Bridport spent most of the 1980s trying to decide what to do with their junior high school students. They agonized over whether to build an addition to their school or send them on tuition to Middlebury. After five inconclusive special school district meetings, the State Education Department sheepishly admitted that because it had never formally adopted the rules, the department had no authority to enforce the standards that were the cause of Bridport's anguish.

Maybe we should sunset all rules again; maybe we should create a Deregulatory Commission (what, more bureaucracy?), but we need to keep a close eye on the regulatory fervor of state agencies and officials. New Jersey took this step a few years ago. Its Study Commission on Regulatory Efficiency reported in 1988 that the number of state regulations affecting business had more than quintupled between 1978 and 1985, and that the length of time required to secure all the necessary permits increased from ninety days in 1972 to eighteen months in 1984. It cost a business in that state an average of twenty-four thousand dollars to comply with state and federal regulations.[25] I have heard similar stories about occurrences in Vermont; we just have not documented them.

(3) We must consolidate the permit process. People trying to start or expand businesses do not confront a monolithic regulatory system, but rather a plethora of agencies and bureaucrats. Many regulators keep their heads down and do their work, but can't see what's on the other side of the wall from them, and they give the public a false sense of security that the ticket they're getting in this office is the last thing they need to have before they start.

In 1984 my office published a book called *The Regulation of Vermont*, in which we listed and described each regulatory program in state and local government in Vermont. As of 1987, there were 314 of them.[26] It had an impact. For the first time in history, somebody had actually identified all the permits and licenses and other kinds of permission people need from government. The State Planning Office, as a result of the publication, began to design a system of one-stop shopping for business permits. It was introduced a few years later with Gov. Madeleine Kunin sitting in front of a computer terminal in Barre pretending to open Madeleine's Restaurant and securing all the permits she needed. Regrettably, the experiment seemed to wither on the vine; in a short time, members of the committee appointed to implement this Permit Expediting Process (PEP) stopped showing up for meetings.

This solution also invades the sacred realm of bureaucratic turf, but government needs to begin thinking about the consumers of its services, rather than the convenience of the bureaucracy. We need to become user friendly. We should look to states like Washington and Minnesota, where the legislatures have established business permit centers, which offer true one-stop shopping. If this sounds like government-bashing, consider this: in Vermont, a developer who wants to build an apartment house needs twenty-four different permits from state and local agencies; to build a motel, one needs thirty-one permits; for a restaurant, it's thirty-five; for a manufacturing plant, thirty-six; and to build a grocery store, you need a grand total of forty-six different permits.[27] Surely we can design a system that works better than what we've got now.

(4) We need better communication. Business and consumer groups need to let government know what's wrong. Government needs to reach out and learn from the folks in the field. A state house conference on small business a few years ago provided one such opportunity. Citizens need to squawk to their elected representatives and the press, if all else fails. We've got to keep these issues on the front burner.

I believe these reforms will be beneficial to government as well as to the public. They will help us identify the legitimate role of government in the lives of individual Vermonters and promote the interests of common sense, fiscal stability, and public responsiveness.

There is an ironic twist to government regulation: it's like the yin and the yang. The people who rail against the excesses of the bureaucracy are often first in line to complain about the abuses of a competing enterprise and beg for intervention by some regulatory agency. We've got to decide where to draw the line between the freedom to do what we want and the protection offered by the rule of law. We've got to decide whether the imposition of the state's police power will serve the purpose for which it is intended. In what may have been an intentional response to James Madison, Senator Sam Ervin observed at the conclusion of the Watergate hearings in 1974 that law "does not make men good. This task can be performed only by ethics or religion or morality."

We now face the dilemma of trying on the one hand to use laws and regulations as impartial definitions and enforcers of morality and on the other of overloading our legislation and our government with regulations that appear to stifle citizens. Perhaps we should ask if there is a better way to hold citizens and public officials accountable to their responsibilities under the constitution and to society as a whole.

NOTES

1. Andrew E. Nuquist and Edith W. Nuquist, *Vermont State Government and Administration: An Historical and Descriptive Study of the Living Past* (Essex, Vt.: Essex Publishing Co., 1966), 438.

2. Dr. Thomas Young, "To the Inhabitants of Vermont, a Free, and Independent State." April 11, 1777, as quoted in *Governor and Council* 1: 394-395.

3. John Williams, ed., *State Papers of Vermont*, vol. 15, *Laws of Vermont, 1791-1795* (Montpelier: Office of the Secretary of State, 1967).

4. *Laws of Vermont, 1797* (Montpelier: Office of the Secretary of State).

5. Allen Soule, ed., *Vermont State Papers*, vol. 10, *General Petitions, 1793-1796* (Montpelier: Office of the Secretary of State, 1958), 126-7, 172-8.

6. John W. Redmond, ed., *Vermont Reports: Reports of Cases Argued and Determined in the Supreme Court of the State of Vermont* (Montpelier: Argus and Patriot Press, 1911) 84:387-400.

7. Redmond (Burlington: Free Press Printing Company, 1913) 86:347-391.

8. Benjamin Shimberg, *Occupational Licensing: A Public Perspective* (Princeton: Princeton University Press, 1982), 19-21.

9. Advisory Commission on Intergovernmental Relations, *Regulatory Federalism: Policy, Process, Impact, and Reform* (Washington, D.C., 1983), 12, 21.

10. Nancy Rhyme, *Legislative Review of Administrative Rules and Regulations* (National Conference of State Legislatures, 1990), 1-2.

11. Ibid., 3.

12. Advisory Commission on Intergovernmental Relations, 1-5.

13. Ibid., 28.

14. Neil Peirce, syndicated column (April 10, 1988).

15. Paul A. Starr, *The Social Transformation of American Medicine* (Hobart, Ind.: Basic Books, 1982), 40.

16. Ibid., 44-5.

17. Vermont State Archives, Manuscripts Vermont State Papers, vol. 63, 172.

18. Starr, 57-8.

19. Ibid., 103.

20. Ibid., 104-106.

21. Ibid., 126.

22. Ibid., 20, 27.

23. Shimberg, 7-8.

24. Nuquist, 471-2.

25. Roger A. Bodman, *State of New Jersey: Report of the Study Commission on Regulatory Efficiency* (1988).

26. Paul S. Gillies and David Healy, *The Regulation of Vermont* (Montpelier: Office of the Secretary of State, 1984 and Supplement, 1987).

27. Ibid.

The Disinfecting Light:

The Public Disclosure of Campaign Finances

Paul S. Gillies

Publicity is justly commended as a remedy for social and industrial diseases. Sunlight is said to be the best of disinfectants, electric light the most efficient policeman.

Louis Brandeis[1]

n the Vermont State Archives, there are twelve boxes, or twelve cubic feet, as the archivists like to describe it, of campaign finance filings from 1916 to 1990. These are the records of expenditures and contributions by candidates for public office during thirty-eight primaries, four special primaries (1923, 1931 and 1933, 1971), ten general elections for statewide and congressional candidates and statewide public questions, and two general elections for candidates for legislative and county office. This record series contains information on how campaigns for public office have been conducted, how money has been spent, and who contributes to public campaigns. To be candid, however, the archive is neither comprehensive or entirely reliable as a scientific data set, largely because of lax administration and lax reporting of campaign finances. Still, we must take it as it is for what it can tell us about campaigns. Understanding the law is a prerequisite to this study.

VERMONT CAMPAIGN FINANCE LAW

Money has been an issue in Vermont elections since the beginning of the twentieth century. In 1902 both candidates for governor, J. G. McCullough and Percival Clement, were accused of purchasing the votes of delegates to the Republican convention, in McCullough's case in amounts of five hundred to one thousand dollars per vote, in Clement's at five dollars for every ten votes at town caucuses that summer.[2] This was the first year since 1853 that the election was not determined at the state convention (or even at the general election, for that matter), since the legislature had to elect the governor when no one received a majority of the votes. The Republican machine had shown remarkable resilience, but from 1902 on nothing would be the same again. There would be in-fighting and arguments over which faction was the true Vermont party or the true Republican party; caucuses and state conventions would be contentious affairs and general elections would be lively and highly partisan.

After a difficult legislative battle, the general assembly of 1915 adopted the first Vermont law on primaries, which included a corrupt practices act, providing for a hundred dollar fine for soliciting, requesting or demanding money or anything of value to influence a vote or procure the vote of any other person. It also required the candidate to file, not less than ten days after the primary election, a sworn statement "setting forth each sum of money or thing of value, or any consideration whatever contributed, paid or promised by him, or by anyone for him, with his knowledge and acquiescence, for the purpose of securing, influencing or in any way affecting his nomination to such office," and "the sums paid as personal expense and state fully the nature, kind and character of the expenses for which the sums were expended separately, and the party to whom the sums were paid and the purpose for which such payments were made. . . ."[3] The 1915 act was approved in a statewide referendum of voters in March 1916 and remained in effect for fifty-six years, until the first comprehensive reform of campaign finance occurred in 1972.[4]

Disclosure of primary finances, without disclosure of finances for the general election, made sense in the first four decades of campaign finance reporting laws, because until the election of Democrat William Meyer for U.S. Representative in 1958 the primary always determined the outcome of the election. The Republican party was supreme in that time, and while there were sometimes colossal battles for the nomination for the major offices in the Republican primary, once that contest had been settled the nominee was guaranteed of victory.[5]

In 1961, limitations on campaign spending became the law of Vermont. No primary candidate for statewide office was authorized to spend or authorize anyone else to spend on his or her behalf more than $7,500, including costs for advertising paid for by the candidate or by others with the candidate's written consent. A $500 fine or imprisonment for ninety days for violating the law gave it some teeth.[6] The leading candidates for U.S. representative, governor, and lieutenant governor had each spent a good deal more than $7,500 in 1960.

The first reporting of general election expenses came in 1972, after the Federal Election Campaign (FEC) Laws were adopted, governing the disclosure of contributions and expenditures by candidates.[7] In 1972, Vermont adopted a new law requiring disclosures for the primary and general elections, limiting the contributions of individuals to candidates and political parties to one thousand dollars, and increasing spending limits to forty thousand dollars for candidates for governor and twenty thousand dollars for all other statewide candidates per election. Candidates for governor could then spend a total of not more than eighty thousand dollars for the primary and general elections.[8] The new law also defined "political committee" for the first time, as a formal or informal committee of two or more individuals accepting or spending over five hundred dollars in any one calendar year for the purpose of supporting or opposing one or more candidates. Political committees and political parties would have to file disclosures with the secretary of state.[9]

The FEC laws limited contributions to candidates for federal office to one thousand dollars from individuals to a candidate per election (primary and general considered as separate elections), twenty thousand dollars from an individual to a national party committee, and five thousand dollars from an individual to a political action committee. The federal law also limited the amount of money candidates could spend for election and re-election campaigns, but in 1975 the U.S. Supreme Court struck down all limits as a violation of the First Amendment to the U.S. Constitution in the case of *Buckley v. Valeo.*[10]

In 1976, responding to the *Buckley* case, the Vermont legislature repealed all limits, made reporting more specific, extended the first reporting date for disclosures to the fortieth—as opposed to the tenth—day before the day of election, and assigned the board of elections broad powers to investigate violations of the campaign finance law, among other duties. A year later, in 1977, the board was abolished. It had failed to regulate campaign finances[11] and made no serious investigation of campaign finance violations.

Other improvements in the campaign finance laws of Vermont were enacted in 1982, 1986, and 1988. The 1982 changes increased the threshold to fifty dollars for reporting the names of contributors, from the twenty-five dollar level set in 1976; established a threshold of five hundred dollars in expenditures or contributions for political party reporting; prohibited political committees from accepting more than five thousand dollars from any other political committee for any election; and extended coverage of the law to govern legislative, county, and local candidates spending or accepting five hundred dollars or more during any election.[12] In 1986, political committees reaching the five hundred dollar threshold in local elections were required to report.[13] The 1988 changes increased the name disclosure threshold to one hundred dollars in contributions and, responding to federal cases holding that the First Amendment prevented such regulations, eliminated contribution limits for political committees involved in supporting or opposing a public question.[14]

The evolution of campaign finance disclosure and limitation laws on Vermont elections shows the difficulty of regulating campaigns for public office. The First Amendment has limited the power of federal and state governments to prevent the infusion of ever-increasing amounts of money into the campaign arena. Even the limits that have been imposed constitutionally are easily circumvented. Moreover, the administration of campaign finance in Vermont is collegial and nonadversarial for the most part. No Vermont candidate's finances have been scrutinized any closer than by a review of the disclosures filed in the office of the secretary of state. Regulation is left principally to the sharp eyes of opposing candidates and reporters, and a nagging insistence by officials on the filing of reports. Even then, many minor party candidates simply fail to report, so the record is not in all cases complete.[15] This is in keeping with the record of administration of campaign finances since 1916. The files in the State Archives reflect timid requests to primary candidates for itemization or even for the required disclosure reports but often nothing more to justify the missing records or information.[16]

The problem is a lack of enforcement tools. With the exception of the short-lived Vermont board of elections, no Vermont law has given adequate investigatory authority to the secretary of state or other departments to audit the finances of candidates, parties, or political committees to ensure that the reports filed with the state are accurate and complete. The traditional empathy and trust shown toward Vermont politicians by the legislature (a body made up of politicians) has prevented vigorous enforcement of the laws on campaign finance.

The character of Vermont campaigns for public office is changing, however. Big money is now omnipresent and each new election promises to set records for contributions and expenditures. A weak law and tepid enforcement can predictably last only until the first discovery of underreporting or outright campaign fraud. There has been no evidence that any Vermont candidate has committed improprieties in campaign finances since the 1902 race for governor, but the temptation and the possibility are present, more so in a climate of lax enforcement of these laws.

WHAT THE REPORTS DISCLOSE[17]

The first campaign finance report among the records of the State Archives is the filing of Marshall Hapgood, candidate for governor in 1910, six years before mandatory reporting began in Vermont. Hapgood explained that he had made an unconditional agreement with the other candidates (except, as he points out, with the Rutland candidate—John Abner Mead, the man who won the primary) to report his expenses. The file, however, shows only Hapgood's report. He spent a total of $103.76 on his campaign for the primary, principally for advertising, postage, and printing. Hapgood explained that only seven of the state's papers charged him for this political advertising. In his report he said:

> I consider it a high honor that I am privileged to be the first one in the history of the state to file an account of election expenses. Especially considering the one-sided character of our state politics, I believe that the above amount is large enough for any candidate to be allowed to use. $500 should be the limit at the most. The general character and public record of a candidate is supposed to be well known at the state; and his principles and views upon public matters the press of the state are ever willing to publish without charge as a matter of general news and public interest. As a rule, the persons best

qualified for high office are those of comparatively, limited means who are not making the attainment of wealth as the chief object of their lives.[18]

Hapgood's philosophy failed to have an impact on subsequent candidates and a "ratchet" effect was already at work. Even if candidates were committed to limiting their expenditures or the amount of contributions they would accept, their ambitions would inevitably be challenged by an opponent intent on spending more money. If the conservative spender lost the election, his or her fate would become a lesson for those who followed. One such example was Frank E. Howe, a candidate who also filed prior to 1916, before the law required it. Howe was publisher of the *Bennington Evening Banner* and candidate for the Republican nomination for governor in 1914. He spent a total of $38.80 and lost the nomination to Charles Gates, who did not file.

When the primary reporting law took effect in 1916, the first reports revealed a battle of titans for the office of U.S. senator. Former governor Allen Fletcher spent $22,425, compared to incumbent Carroll S. Page's expenditures of $21,445. Fletcher hired the Hays Advertising Agency to run his campaign. The Hays Agency of Burlington quickly became a fixture of Vermont campaigning and served diverse candidates—always Republicans and almost always winning candidates—during elections for almost fifty years.[19]

Vermonters cherish the memory of George Aiken on the subject of campaign finance as the candidate who spent only the cost of one stamp on one of his reelection campaigns, but this level of expenditure is not unique to Aiken.[20] Many Vermont candidates for public office proudly noted that they spent that amount or less on their campaigns over the years. Perhaps this reflected the traditional fiscal conservatism of Vermonters. We see it in the 1916 files, for example, in the disclosure of Albert Ayers, Democratic candidate for attorney general, who spent thirty-three cents on his nomination. His report states that this involved a two-cent stamp for a letter to the secretary of state explaining that he would accept the nomination, and one thirty-one cent telephone call to the office relating to the form he wanted his name to take on the official ballot. Then there was Benjamin Gates, who in 1918 added this note to his disclosure of $3.30 for his primary campaign: "Used some old stationery I had and could not tell what it costs. Probably used 25 sheets of paper. Did nothing except send out my petitions, with requests for signatures." In other cases, spending nothing was an act of faith in the natural celebrity of a person's character and reputation and in an individual's conviction to "stand" as opposed to "run" for public office. "Not one dollar, not even one cent was expended by me or for me to obtain this nomination to the office of state treasurer," reported Democrat Otis Sawyer in 1920. In 1933, U.S. representative candidate Loren Pierce would write, "No contributions were received and no promises made."

Sorting out what should be disclosed from other expenditures has always been difficult. In 1918, Republican candidate for attorney general Frank Archibald reported $221.06 in expenditures, but added,

> I don't know whether the last six items ought to be included or not. Those represent sums paid for use of cars in carrying voters to and from the polls without much regard to how they were intending to vote. . . . I suppose the intention of the law is to require a candidate to disclose what he did pay out and for what purpose in order to prevent the corrupt use of money.

The 1920 files include a report from William Grant Webster, a candidate for president of the United States, who reported on his October 13 to 24 journey through Vermont, disclosing twenty-five cents for "sharpening razor"; his lodging expenses, including two nights for $1.50 at Mrs. Liberty's in Montpelier; and his meals. He even added an explanation for what might appear as underreporting of some of his meals—"I kept down the price of breakfast and lunch by buying rolls at bakeries at 15 cents a dozen. One dozen was enough for two breakfasts and two lunches, plus coffee [total for coffee: twenty cents]." Sensitivity to disclosure has made some candidates nervous, while others act carefully and disclose fully out of a concern for those who have contributed to their campaigns.[21]

The first contribution to a candidate for public office in Vermont was disclosed in the special primary of 1923 for the Second District U.S. Representative seat after Ernest Gibson accepted $775 from the Gibson for Congress Club.[22] This was not the beginning of a trend, however; the majority of statewide candidates prior to the end of World War II funded their own campaigns for the primary, and many prided themselves on accepting no contributions as a sign of independence from special interest or any individual or group. Robert Stafford, in his uncontested 1964 primary campaign for the U.S. Representative seat he had held since 1960, became the first candidate to contribute no money to his campaign. All of the $587 spent was contributed.

While the Gibson for Congress Club represented the first disclosed political committee, it was closely tied to the candidate and his campaign. The first separate organization to appear in the campaign finance files funding a candidate for public office was the Vermont Better Roads Association. It contributed $793 to the Hays Advertising Agency to support Roland Stevens's 1924 campaign for governor. Stevens, who also made use of the first reported moving picture film for his campaign (showing pictures of road construction, not Stevens), spent $3,387 that year on the primary, but still lost to Franklin Billings, who spent $387. The first disclosed contribution from a political party came in 1972, when the Republican State Committee gave $2,000 to John S. Burgess for his race against Leo J. Connor for the office of lieutenant governor. Now it is not uncommon for candidates to receive large amounts of money from national as well as political committees, such as the $50,000 contributed to John Easton by the National Republican Committee in 1984.

Sometimes candidates spend money on things we do not associate with traditional campaign expenses. Porter H. Dale, running for the nomination for U.S. Senate in the 1923 special primary, spent $31.59 of his $11,766 total on cabinets from the U.S. Clothespin Company. Harley Walter Kidder, Prohibition candidate for U.S. representative (Second District), spent $5.14 in 1928, most of it associated with keeping his car on the road—"wiring for timer, $1.10; cable for battery, $1.00." In the 1933 special primary for the U.S. representative seat (the reapportionment of the U.S. House left Vermont with a single member beginning in early 1933), one of the first women to run for statewide public office, Blanche Brown Bryant, spent $30 on gas for an airplane (the first reference to this as a campaign tool) and $3.50 for a translation for an Italian newspaper published in Vermont. Running for the Republican gubernatorial nomination in 1936, George Aiken spent $1.20 of his total war chest of $969.35 for light bulbs.

When reform of campaign finance is mentioned in federal circles today, one continuing issue is "soft money," that is, money spent by others, apart from the candidate, to influence the outcome. This is different from contributions to the candidate by political committees. John E. Weeks, candidate for the Republican nomination for governor in 1928, spoke of "soft money" when he wrote on his report, "There were certain advertisements that appeared in the newspapers in the state favorably affecting my nomination for governor. This was done at the instigation of my friends without my knowledge or acquiescence."

The purchase of campaign buttons is first disclosed in the files of Fred H. Babbitt and Curtis Emery, Republican candidates for governor in 1920. Babbitt and Emery both lost to James Hartness that year, and money may have been a factor in this race. Hartness, a candidate who had not served in public office before deciding to run for governor, spent $38,560.99—a new high for campaign spending and by far the most spent for a primary race—compared to Babbitt's $5,942, Emery's $1,798, and candidate Frank Agan's $5,294 totals. Hartness's record would not be broken until the special primary of 1971, when Richard Mallary spent $48,832 for the nomination for the office of U.S. representative. Adjusting for inflation, Hartness probably remained supreme in spending until the excesses of the 1980s.

The first reported use of radio in a Vermont campaign is found in the report of Frank C. Partridge, candidate for the 1931 special primary for U.S. senator. Partridge spent $544 of his $27,714 campaign on a payment to the General Electric Co. for radio addresses. From that moment on, radio became a permanent part of Vermont politics. While some candidates continued to devote most of their money to print, including newspaper advertising and handouts, radio was an immediate hit and eventually surpassed print. Partridge lost to Warren Austin in that election, however, in spite of his investment in new technology.

The first bumper stickers are reported as expenditures in the 1954 primary for governor in the files of Joseph Johnson.[23] Television arrives in the reports of Robert Stafford, running in 1956 for the Republican nomination for lieutenant governor. Stafford reported paying the Joseph Smith Advertising Agency $3,115 of his $6,192 total, a fee that included radio, newspaper, and television advertising on WCAX-TV in Burlington. In 1958, Lee Emerson used it in his race for U.S. senator against Winston Prouty, spending over two-thirds of his budget on radio and television advertising. Prouty outspent Emerson

$6,487 to $3,638, did not use television, and beat him two to one in the primary.

Beginning in 1944, nearly every candidate, Republican or Democratic, in any contested race, and often in uncontested races for statewide office, purchased an advertisement in the *Labor News*, published in Worcester, Massachusetts. Occasionally, as in Howard Armstrong's uncontested 1950 primary "race," when the Democrats did not nominate any opposition, the *Labor News* absorbed the entire treasury of the primary campaign. Why it held such power over candidates is unexplained from the record.

The treatment of minor parties is one of the greatest embarrassments of Vermont's election history. More than once candidates have been prevented from having their names printed on the ballot for apparently frivolous reasons.[24] The same policy appears to be in place in campaign finance reporting. Beginning in 1932, candidates for presidential elector for the Socialist and Communist parties were regularly required by the secretary of state's office to file campaign finance disclosures. Candidates for that office were nominated by caucus. In 1950, however, Attorney General A. G. Glifton ruled that those who seek nomination by certificate are exempt from filing campaign expense reports. No further reports appear in the files.

SPENDING THE MOST

The final question is whether more money means victory for a candidate. Here is good news for those who most fear that public offices are for sale in Vermont: Those who spend the most do not always win. There are other forces at work, ranging from the character and reputation of the candidate to the mood of the electorate, from the manner in which a candidate conducts the campaign (often an indicator of how the candidate will govern) to the ideas and principles with which the candidate wages the campaign itself. To test this statement, we need to compare the records of campaign finance and election results since 1916. Eliminating the non-contests, where there is only token opposition, we find in the files 132 primary and 51 general election contests that involve substantive expenditures. If we eliminate incumbency, because it confuses the issue of money and elections, we find eighty-four primaries and twenty general elections involving no incumbents. Of these, there are twenty-five primaries and three general elections where the winners spend substantially less than the losers.[25] These are candidates who won their primaries on something other than money or incumbency, and their victories—nineteen percent of the total—help justify the conclusion that money does not buy Vermont elections. In the 1923 primary Charles Plumley beat four opponents, even though he was outspent ten to one by his opponent Jeremiah Evarts ($1,096 to $11,942). In the Aiken/Flanders special primary for the U.S. Senate seat in 1940, Aiken spent $3,219 to Flanders's $18,698. In the 1980 primary for secretary of state, winner James Douglas spent $3,500 to Noble Smith's $54,000.[26]

This research is tentative, to be sure, but it does help answer the question of money and campaigns. While the mere expenditure of a great deal of money has not yet proven a reliable substitute for intelligence, character, or reputation, it is clear that money does have a place, and perhaps a more crucial place than it deserves in the conduct of elections. How much is too much? How much is enough?

Judging how much is spent requires a consideration of the competition, to be sure, but we cannot forget the restraint imposed by the law from 1961 to 1976, limiting expenditures in the primary to $7,500 for each candidate from 1961 to 1972, and to $40,000 for primary and general for candidates for governor (and $20,000 for each other statewide) from 1972 to 1976. Nevertheless, the cost of running for office in Vermont is growing faster than the rate of inflation or even the federal deficit. In the following table I have listed just a few of the high water marks for spending for some major state offices.

General Election Expenditures

Office/ Year	Winner/ Spending	Loser/ Spending
U.S. Senate 1986	Leahy $1.4 million	Snelling $1.2 million
U.S. Rep. 1990	Sanders $531,100	Smith $568,500
Governor 1988	Kunin $698,203	Bernhardt $457,808
Lt. Gov. 1990	Dean $121,551	Bernhardt $153,054
Treasurer 1990	Ruse $33,830	Crisman $28,255
Att. Gen'l. 1988	Amestoy $48,750	Flanagan $135,901

This listing of the expenditures of the candidates and political committees does not adequately reflect the astounding rise in campaign spending over the last ten years. Not until 1974 did the first candidates exceed $100,000 in spending on a general election campaign.[27] Today, no campaign for Congress or for the governor's seat would seem serious if a budget of at least two and a half times that amount were not planned. More alarming is the increase in the budgets of state legislative races, which have grown dramatically over the last three or four elections in counties and districts where competition is strong and divisive. Other more urban states have experienced ever more expensive campaigns for such offices. Nonetheless, for Vermont, numbers of this size seem troubling. Citizen government, that prized tradition of Vermonters, may not be able to withstand the assault of the professional campaign. Campaigning and governing, as Elizabeth Drew has suggested on the national level, have become identical.[28] The hunt continues for effective reform to limit the increases and control the excesses.

PARTING SHOT

Suppose we decided that we want to change the course of campaign finance. We know from the *Buckley* case that the First Amendment prohibits limits and from its progeny that some day even limits on individual contributions to candidates and political committees may be found unconstitutional. What then can be done to ensure that campaigns are run with a greater sense of modesty? Here are a few suggestions:

(1) Get voter commitment: taking a leaf from the temperance movement, we need to offer individual voters the opportunity to assert their lack of faith in any candidate who spends unreasonable amounts in campaigning. If a popular movement for self-control of candidates were successful (and were started early enough), it could change the habits of big-spending candidates.

(2) End the continuing campaign war chest: legislation at the state and federal levels could require closure of campaign accounts within a few months of an election and the elimination of any surplus through donation or other expenditure, to avoid carryover of campaign funds from one election year to the next.

(3) Give administrators enforcement tools: establish and fund an auditing unit, and give the administrators the tools to investigate whether disclosures are reliable.

(4) Limit the use of the franking privilege by prohibiting free mailings by incumbents to constituents in an election year.

(5) As the last resort, amend the U.S. Constitution to authorize laws limiting campaign expenditures: Some amendments relating to this issue have already been proposed in the Congress.

In any case, we see that the wonderful metaphor of Justice Brandeis quoted at the beginning of this paper has helped us define the problem of political campaign spending but has not, as he expected, solved it. Now that we have public disclosure of campaign finances, lobbyist expenditures, and the business of government through open meeting and access to public records laws, we must see if the public will take the next step and seek ways to act. Disclosure alone is no cure.

NOTES

1. Louis Brandeis, *Other People's Money & How the Bankers Use It* (1932).

2. Mason A. Green, *Nineteen-Two in Vermont: The Fight for Local Option, Ten Years After* (Rutland, Vt.: Marble City Press, 1912), 152, 172.

3. *Laws of 1915*, No. 4, § 22, 66-67.

4. *Laws of 1916 (Sp. Sess)*, No. 4, § 1, 467-68.

5. See Samuel B. Hand and D. Gregory Sanford, *The Star That Never Set: The Vermont Republican Party, 1854-1936* (Hanover, N.H.: University Press of New England, forthcoming).

6. *Laws of 1961*, No. 178, 203.

7. P.L. 92-225 (1971); P.L. 93-443 (1974); P.L. 94-283 (1976); P.L. 96-187 (1979).

8. *Laws of 1971* (Adj. Sess.), No. 259, 540-42.

9. The 1972 act was not perfect, however. The files for this year include a letter, sent by Secretary of State Richard Thomas to each candidate, explaining that "since the legislature omitted the requirement of filing the campaign contributions over $100 by source and amount and the disclosure of expenditures in primary elections, I have asked all the statewide candidates to voluntarily comply with the legislative intent of the Act for primary as well as general elections." They all did.

10. *Buckley v. Valeo*, 424 U.S. 1 (1975).

11. *Laws of 1977*, No. 34, § 3, 93.

12. *Laws of 1981* (Adj. Sess.), No. 197, 287-92. See also 1982 Op.A.G. 83-6 (September 14, 1982), relating to whether a statewide candidate violates Vermont's campaign finance law if he accepts a $1,000 contribution from a political committee that has its principal office outside Vermont, if that committee accepts funds in excess of $1,000 from individuals (answer: no).

13. *Laws of 1985* (Adj. Sess.), No. 198, 388.

14. *Laws of 1987* (Adj. Sess.), No. 263, 455-57. The cases include *First National Bank of Boston v. Bellotti*, 435 U.S. 765 (1978); *Citizens Against Rent Control v. City of Berkeley*, 454 U.S. 290 (1981).

15. The *Buckley* case suggested that mandatory reporting by minor party candidates may not be entirely appropriate, and subsequent rulings of the federal court have enlarged this idea to virtually eliminate prosecution of candidates of minor parties who fail to file disclosures.

16. In 1944, Secretary of State Rawson Myrick wrote Mortimer Proctor, Republican candidate for governor in the primary, that "This statement does not seem to be quite complete, especially as regards the names of the parties to whom the sums are paid, but we are placing it on file for the information it does contain." Myrick did not ask Proctor to file a corrected disclosure, and Proctor never did. Proctor's 1946 disclosure also lacks itemization.

17. It would be tiresome and redundant to review each of the filings in every campaign in this paper, since the reports themselves are often tiresome and redundant, but a summary of the files from 1916 to 1990 has been compiled and is available through the State Archives. This paper only reports trends and unusual findings.

18. All citations that follow are found in the *Election Records, Campaign Finance Series*, located in the State Archives, Office of the Secretary of State, Montpelier, Vermont. Hereafter cited as Campaign Finance Series, with a notation on the box number. Hapgood's report is found at the beginning of Subseries a, Box 1 (State Officers, 1916-1938). The other boxes in the series are as follows: Subseries a, Box 2 (State Officers, 1940-71); Subseries b, Box 1 (State Officers, 1972-1978), Box 2 (State Officers, 1980-1982), Box 3 (State Officers, 1984-1988); Subseries c, Box 1 (Congressional Officers, 1972-1974), Box 2 (Congressional Officers, 1976-1978), Box 3 (Congressional Officers, 1980), Box 4 (Congressional Officers, 1982-1984), Box 5 (Congressional Officers, 1986), Box 6 (Congressional Officers, 1986), Box 7 (Congressional Officers, 1986-1988), Box 8 (Congressional Officers, 1988), and Box 9 (Congressional Officers, 1988). Files on the 1990 election are located in the Elections Division temporarily but will be conveyed to the State Archives in 1992.

19. The last campaign of the Hays Agency appears to be the 1964 race for lieutenant governor, in the service of James Oakes, who lost the primary to Richard Snelling that year. The Hays Agency warrants further study. The file on the 1950 campaign of Winston Prouty for the U.S. representative seat includes all vouchers from the Hays Agency for that campaign.

20. Here is the entire campaign finance record of George Aiken: In 1934, running for lieutenant governor, Aiken spent $211.23 in the primary; in 1936, running for governor, his primary expenses totalled $969.35 (including $69.70 on radio); in 1938, for his second term, he spent thirty cents; in the special primary of 1940 for U.S. senator, following the death of Ernest Gibson, Sr., he spent $3,219.50 (to Ralph Flanders's $18,698.45); in 1944 and 1950, Aiken

spent nothing for reelection; in 1956, $1.08; in 1962, $4.48; in 1968, $17.09, for a total of $4,423.03.

21. One of the most interesting files is that of Fiore Bove, Democratic candidate for the U.S. senate nomination in 1970. Bove collected $1,424, spent only $1,291 before he lost the primary to Philip Hoff (who spent $15,184), and who then, in an act that can only be called refreshing by today's standards, returned the difference in a *pro rata* manner to his contributors.

22. Two other candidates that year also formed clubs to gather money and purchase political advertising and other things to assist in their campaign—John W. Gordon and James L. Stacy, both of whom were candidates for governor.

23. This reminds me of the old Vermont story about the man who sat on the porch all day watching the cars go by. A friend stopped by one evening and asked him, "Based on the number of bumper stickers, who would you say is most likely to win the governor's race this year?" The old man thought about it and then answered, "By my reckoning, Ausable Chasm is in the lead."

24. See *Schirmer v. Myrick*, 111 Vt. 255 (1940); *Abbott v. Thomas*, 130 Vt. 71 (1971).

25. By "less" in these equations, I have used a factor of one-third as the difference between the expenditures of one candidate and those of another. By "incumbent," I mean the person holding *that* office at the time of election. Frequently the governor runs for senate, the lieutenant governor for governor, and I have not considered these as incumbents, although they do naturally enjoy the advantage of an insider.

26. The others in this category are as follows, with the winner in bold (with their expenditures in parentheses): Republican primaries: 1916, lt. governor: Weeks ($330)-**Hurlburd** ($154); 1924, governor: **Billings** ($398)-Stevens ($3,387); 1926, governor: Farnsworth ($2,632)-**Weeks** ($5,612)-Powell ($9,038); 1930, U.S. rep.: Drennan ($2,434)-Vilas ($464)-**Weeks** ($89); 1934, governor: **Smith** ($3,557)-Williams ($5,754); 1936, governor: **Aiken** ($969)-Jackson ($5,247)-Moore ($2,022); 1948, lt. governor: **Arthur** ($811)-Prouty ($3,615); 1948, sec. of state: **Armstrong** ($584)-Bolles ($1,741); 1948, atty. general: Conley ($332)-**Parker** ($183); 1950, governor: Stacey ($5,007)-Bove ($6,740)-**Emerson** ($1,595); 1958, U.S. rep.: Cairns ($8,868)-Thurber ($5,733)-O'Neill ($1,528)-**Arthur** ($3,937)-Crispe ($12,881); 1960, U.S. rep.: **Stafford** ($9,070)-Dern ($423)-Gannett ($14,914)-Emerson ($723); 1968, sec. of state: **Thomas** ($3,730)-Riehle, Jr. ($5,349); 1978, U.S. sen.: Tufts ($2,466)-**Aiken** ($17); 1980, U.S. sen.: Buckley ($10,000)-Evslin ($164,000)-**Ledbetter** ($414,000)-Mullin ($670,000); 1984, governor: **Easton** ($173,000)-Wick ($233,000). Democratic primaries: 1962, U.S. sen.: **Johnson** ($314)-Meyer ($1,317); 1970, U.S. rep.: Morriseau ($6,098)-**O'Shea** ($25); 1970, sec. of state: Edmunds ($1,593)-**St.**

Peter ($448); 1984, U.S. rep.: **Pollina** ($3,000)-Forlenza ($11,000); 1988, U.S. rep.: **Poirier** ($52,000)-Welch ($86,000)-Guest ($81,400)-Sandoval ($10,000). General elections: 1972, governor: **Salmon** ($22,000)-Hackett ($45,000); 1976, lt. governor: Alden ($27,380)-**Buckley** ($16,441); and 1984, governor: Easton ($548,000)-**Kunin** ($408,000).

27. The Leahy/Mallary U.S. senate race in 1974 was the first.

28. Elizabeth Drew, *Money and Politics: The New Road to Corruption* (New York: MacMillan, 1983).

A Hardy Race: Forging the Vermont Identity*

D. Gregory Sanford

he search for identity inevitably leads to the past. Whether research-ing a family tree or the history of a state, the investigator will eventually examine historical records. Historical records are like mirrors, holding the reflections of past generations. Journals and dia-ries allow glimpses of how people perceived their society and themselves. Business and institutional records show how we evolved an economic and social identity. Government archives trace our efforts to translate our society's ideals into social action.

Too often, however, we approach the mirror like the queen in *Snow White*, demanding to know who is the fairest, while having in mind only one acceptable answer. Looking at the reflection, we see what we believe should be there, for believing is seeing. Thus we read George Washington's 1783 letter to Congress and take pride in his depiction of Vermonters as a hardy race, while ignoring his characterization, in the same sentence, of Vermonters as deserters from his army.[1]

If there is a recognizable Vermont identity, and the point after all is debatable, what better place to search for it than among the records of the government chosen by the people of Vermont? Manuscripts can only provide the perceptions, conditioned by personal experience and frozen in time, of individuals. The State Archives reveal how Vermonters, over the course of two hundred years, translated their social, economic, and ideological concerns into law and service.

It is within the framework of government that the Vermont of the Federalist and Jeffersonian, of Ernest Gibson and Lee Emerson, of the Northeast Kingdom and Chittenden County come together to find common

* This paper previously appeared in *Vermont History* 58 (Summer 1990): 201-206. Published by permission.

ground. That common ground should tell us something of the Vermont identity.

The advantage of government archives is that while the debate of the moment may change, the basic issues of governance remain constant. Thus our responses to these basic issues over time provide insights into our character as a people. For example, Vermont's 1777 constitution was the first state constitution to explicitly recognize the potential conflict between private property and the public interest. It did so not only by eschewing property qualifications for voters, but also in Article 2, Chapter 1, which states, in part, "that private property ought to be subservient to public uses when necessity requires it."

For over two hundred years we have debated not only what constitutes necessity but also what constitutes adequate compensation to property owners. We have debated these points as we developed our transportation network, built hydroelectric and flood control dams, established state parks and forests, sought to control billboards, sited solid waste dumps, and, of course, attempted to plan growth and development. Gubernatorial papers, legislative committee minutes, court decisions, and the reports of special commissions and boards give evidence of the persistence of this debate.

Yet we rarely use these records to provide a context for current debates or to measure the success or failure of past responses. Instead we argue over how Ethan Allen views Act 200. While Ethan thought reason is the only oracle of man, we seem to feel that Ethan is the only oracle of Vermonters. Like all good oracles Ethan never spoke directly on the subject, is open to multiple interpretations, and is unavailable for comment.

Why don't we use government archives? For one thing they *are* difficult to use. You must have the time and patience to wade through reams of memos, minutes, and directives. You must compare how the executive, judicial, and legislative branches interpreted an issue, as well as how the bureaucracy carried out programs. You must compile and manipulate data bases to see how political rhetoric and legislative intent translated into service.

In other words, government archives are not fun. How much more satisfying to seek refuge in the well-worn quotes that bolster our carefully cultivated self-image. After all, which is more satisfying: quoting Governor Weeks who after the 1927 flood announced that Vermont would take care of its own and not suppliantly ask for federal assistance, or tracing federal and state records detailing how we asked for and received over two million dollars in federal aid?

As this suggests, there are gaps between our impressionistic Vermont identity and the reality reflected in government archives. Let me cite two other examples. A key component of the Vermont identity is our citizen legislature. There are frequent expressions of concern about preserving this sacred Vermont institution. But what do we mean by citizen legislature? Is it the unicameral legislature that existed prior to 1836? Is it the one town/one representative legislature that existed prior to 1965? Is it the pre-1920 legislature that excluded women? Or is it the legislature that until relatively recently was governed by an informal rotation system that discouraged representatives from serving more than two consecutive terms? In other words, while our self-conscious identity suggests an immutable citizen legislature dating back to some pristine past, the reality has been a constantly evolving system of representation.

Another example. Local control is a cherished cornerstone of the Vermont identity. Many of our current debates are couched in terms of a centralized bureaucracy wresting control from local communities. Yet the pioneering work of University of Vermont historian Samuel B. Hand and others suggests a different reality. Since the 1880s Vermont's smallest communities used their legislative majorities to centralize services. They did so because their declining populations and tax bases denied them the financial and technical resources necessary to provide these services. By 1890 there was a clear trend to redistribute revenues through the state government to provide for education, public health, and transportation. Sam Hand has argued that Vermont's government was highly centralized by at least the 1920s. A careful search of the government archives bolsters this argument.[2]

So what does all this mean? At a minimum, promulgating a Vermont identity based on impressions rather than historical records diverts public debate from substantive discussion of issues. An unchanging, idealized identity masks changing realities. When we can no longer ignore the new realities, we are confused and angered by the discrepancy between our self-portrait, idealized and unchanging, and our actual life-style.

Too often we then retreat into xenophobia. If this is not the Vermont we always imagined, then the changes must have been sprung upon us by out-of-staters who have taken our government from us. Here is, by way of example, a January 1990 letter to the *Times-Argus*:

> Where have all the Vermonters gone? Who are these liberal outsiders running our government? How did they get there? Why were they allowed the opportunity? . . . Where have all of the old conservative, hardworking, honest natives gone? . . . I'll bet Ethan Allen, Gen. Stark, Cal Coolidge, and even my grandfathers are squirming in their graves . . . Come on, you conservative Vermonters, get off your butts, band together and throw these people out. They are not what our heritage is all about.

This xenophobic heritage is so strong that many cling to the belief that Vermont retains a right to secede from the Union. We even create mythical documents to substantiate this right. The State Archives regularly receives requests for the secession clause of the Vermont constitution. These requests come from the entire political spectrum, united by a desire to escape from, rather than work out solutions to, our problems. Let me assure you, no such escape exists.

There is another aspect of historical documents and identity that I will only briefly mention. One of the more daunting tasks confronting an archivist is determining which documents have continuing value. Which, and how, records are used play a role in determining what is preserved. If we continue to rely on an impressionistic Vermont identity, if we exclusively focus on the papers of the founders, then the archivist's efforts to preserve modern records become more difficult.

Lack of interest in public records leaves government to determine what has continuing value. In 1988, for example, gubernatorial commissions were exempted from the open meeting law, while in 1990 the Vermont Supreme Court ruled that governors could deny access to certain of their records through the exercise of executive privilege.[3] There is an obvious risk here. Since the days of Ira Allen, government officials have been more than happy to forge a Vermont identity.

Let me end on a more positive note by suggesting a way we can use public records to examine the Vermont identity. There is one area where government clearly has been involved in defining what makes us Vermonters. This is in government planning. At various times the government has promulgated plans to preserve the Vermont character through future generations.

The impulse for planning has come from two entirely opposite forces. Prior to 1960 most government plans were written in response to emigration and rural depopulation. After 1960 these plans grappled with preserving the Vermont identity in the face of large-scale immigration.

In the 1920s we turned to eugenics to preserve the Vermont character. Many Vermonters feared that emigration was making things a little murky in the gene pool. So we turned to progressive science to consciously engineer the perfect Vermonter. One report suggested that "the doctrine be spread that it is the patriotic duty of every normal couple to have children in sufficient number to keep up to par the 'good old Vermont stock.'"[4] Not willing to leave things to chance we passed sterilization laws and debated measures such as limiting the ballot to those who passed intelligence tests.

In the 1930s the eugenics survey gave birth to the Commission on Country Life. The commission mixed eugenics, tourism, education, and business components to develop a plan for the revitalization of Vermont. It wanted to preserve the Vermont identity and included a committee on tradition and ideals. This committee felt that the Vermont character "must be accepted by the unbiased student as indicating values in Green Mountain life . . . that merit consideration in any study of the state's future well-being."[5]

By the 1960s the problem was perceived quite differently. Gov. Philip Hoff's task force developed plans for preserving Vermont in the face of the state's largest population increase in well over a century. As its report noted, "Through state planning these changes can be directed and controlled . . . or the State can remain indifferent . . . until the change controls it."[6] Subsequent governors called for similar plans and we passed environmental and development guidelines. To promote these efforts the state produced films with titles such as "Planning Our Tomorrows" and "The Future Is Ours." Now in the 1990s we are debating whether the current plan, Act 200, preserves or dilutes the Vermont identity.

We are living in someone else's future, and there is much to learn from examining the various visions of Vermont put forth in these plans. What is it that each plan sought to protect? What changes did each attempt to control? Are there any consistent themes within these plans? Is our present the future envisioned by past planners?

When Europeans first came to Africa and encountered the zebra, they saw white animals with black stripes. Africans, however, saw the zebra as a black animal with white stripes. That is the problem when we only see things through our preconceptions. Until we take the time to use the historical record, we will never see the Vermonter beneath the stripes.

REPOSITORIES

Manuscript collections and archives important to understanding the Vermont identity are scattered throughout the state. Vermont's long tradition of local government and pride resulted in some of the state's most valuable collections being housed in municipal clerk offices and local historical societies. While there is no comprehensive guide to collections, over one hundred repositories are listed in *A Guide to Vermont Repositories* published by the Vermont State Archives (copies available upon request).

Four of the state's most important repositories are the **Vermont State Archives, Special Collections at the University of Vermont, Vermont Historical Society,** and the **Sheldon Museum** in Middlebury.

- The **Vermont State Archives** is responsible for acquiring, preserving, and making accessible permanently valuable state government records. Holdings cover the years from the formation of Vermont to the present and include gubernatorial and legislative records, as well as a wide range of eighteenth- and nineteenth-century petitions, legislative committee reports, town boundary surveys, and other government records. Additional government archival records are held by the Public Records Division.

- **Special Collections at the University of Vermont,** which includes the Wilbur Collection of Vermontiana, is the largest and best organized collection of Vermont manuscripts, maps, business records, and other historical documents. A large oral history and folklore collection provides additional sources for examining the Vermont identity.

- The **Vermont Historical Society** (VHS) was created in 1838 to collect material relating to Vermont. The VHS has acquired a wide range of material on the economic, social, and political evolution of Vermont.

- The **Sheldon Museum** (Middlebury), while focusing its collection policy on Addison County, contains the papers of numerous individuals who helped forge the Vermont identity (Nathaniel Chipman and Eben Judd are two examples). The Sheldon is in the process of creating a computerized retrieval system, which will make its collections easily accessible to researchers. In 1991 the Sheldon published an excellent guide to its collection, *Treasures Gathered Here*, which is an extract from a much larger computer database of its holdings.

SELECTED COLLECTIONS

The George D. Aiken Papers. Special Collections, Bailey/Howe Library, University of Vermont. To many, George Aiken was the quintessential Vermonter, at least in terms of the twentieth century. The papers are supplemented by an oral history collection, which includes a compilation of oral histories with Aiken providing a chronologically arranged autobiography.

The Henry Stevens, Sr., Collection. Vermont State Archives (Office of the Secretary of State). In the mid-nineteenth century, New York began publishing compilations of historical documents. These compilations ascribed less than pure motives to Vermont's founders. Stevens was consequently hired by the State of Vermont to collect documents to counter this sullying of the Vermont character by the Yorkers. His collection contains the papers of such founders as Ethan, Ira, and Levi Allen, Isaac Tichenor, and Thomas Chittenden, as well as early Vermont legislative, judicial, and executive records. Related collections gathered by Stevens can be found at the Vermont Historical Society and the University of Vermont's Special Collections.

NOTES

1. George Washington to Joseph Jones, in Congress, 11 Feb., 1783. The original letter is at the State Archives. A transcript of the letter is in E. P. Walton, *Records of the Governor and Council of the State of Vermont* (Montpelier: Steam Press of J. & J. M. Poland, 1875) 3:262-64. Washington was explaining why he did not think it appropriate to use the military to resolve the Vermont problem. The section of the letter most frequently quoted reads: "The inhabitants, for the most part, are a hardy race, composed of that kind of people who are best calculated for soldiers." What is not usually quoted is the next clause of the sentence: ". . . in truth, who *are* soldiers; for many, many hundreds of them are deserters from this army." One of the best examples of this selective quoting is found in the section on "The Conservation of Vermont Traditions and Ideals" in *Rural Vermont, A Program for the Future* (Burlington: Vermont Commission on Country Life, 1931), 371.

2. See Samuel B. Hand, Jeffrey Marshall, and Gregory Sanford, "'Little Republics': The Structure of State Politics in Vermont, 1854-1920," *Vermont History* 53 (Summer 1985): 141-66.

3. Act 256 of 1988. *Killington, Ltd. v. Lash* (February 16, 1990).

4. *Rural Vermont*, 32.

5. Ibid., 372.

6. *State Planning in Vermont* (Montpelier: Central Planning Office, 1964), 1.

Authors' Biographies

T. D. Seymour Bassett was curator of the Wilbur Collection of Vermontiana and University Archivist at the University of Vermont, until his 1977 retirement. His most recent work, *The Growing Edge: Vermont Villages, 1840-80*, is being published by the Vermont Historical Society in 1992.

Colin G. Calloway is associate professor of history at the University of Wyoming. He previously was editor and assistant director at the D'Arcy McNickle Center for the History of the American Indian at the Newberry Library in Chicago. Calloway has published widely on American Indians.

Deborah P. Clifford, a past president of both the Vermont Historical Society and the Sheldon Museum, specializes in the history of Vermont women. She is the author of biographies of Julia Ward Howe, *Mine Eyes Have Seen the Glory* (1979) and Lydia Maria Child, *Crusader for Freedom* (1992).

Eric L. Davis is professor of political science at Middlebury College, with special interests in American politics. Since 1982 he has broadcast weekly political commentaries and served as political analyst for radio station WDEV.

David Donath has been director of the Billings Farm & Museum in Woodstock, Vermont since 1985. Previously he directed Strawbery Banke, Inc., in Portsmouth, New Hampshire, managed historic sites and museums, and served in the Wisconsin State Historic Preservation Office.

James H. Douglas of Middlebury has been Vermont Secretary of State since 1981. Previously, he was elected to four terms in the Vermont House of Representatives where he was majority whip and majority leader. He served as Executive Assistant to the Governor in 1979-1980.

William Doyle has served in the Vermont State Senate since 1969 (R-Washington County). He is professor of government at Johnson State College, author of *The Vermont Political Tradition*, and co-editor of *Political Parties in New England* and *Vermont and the New Nation*.

Connell Gallagher is Library Assistant Director for Research Collections at the University of Vermont Bailey/Howe Library. He has served as president of the Vermont Library Association, New England Archivists, and the College and University Archives section of the Society of Archivists.

Paul S. Gillies, Vermont Deputy Secretary of State, writes extensively on governmental topics. He co-edited *Records of the Council of Censors of the State of Vermont* with D. Gregory Sanford and his bicentennial essays, "Confronting Statehood," were published by the Center for Research on Vermont.

Samuel B. Hand is professor of history at the University of Vermont. A national leader in oral history and widely recognized for his work on the Roosevelt and Truman administrations, he is past president of the Vermont Historical Society and helped found UVM's Center for Research on Vermont.

Richard Hathaway teaches at Vermont College of Norwich University, where he is professor of Liberal Studies. He has edited the *Correspondent* and *Current* magazines and is a trustee of the Vermont Historical Society and vice president of the Vermont Labor History Society.

Patrick Hutton is professor of history at the University of Vermont, where he teaches intellectual history and historiography and writes on the revolutionary tradition in France. A previous article on the print revolution and the drafting of written constitutions appeared in *Vermont History* in 1988.

Peter S. Jennison is chairman of the board of the Countryman Press, Woodstock, Vt. His books include *The History of Woodstock, 1890-1983*, *The Roadside History of Vermont*, and two novels. He is a trustee of the Norman Williams Public Library and the Vermont Historical Society.

Vi Luginbuhl served three terms as Vermont State Representative for District 6-2, South Burlington, and participated as a member of the House Education Committee. From 1979 to 1985, she served on the Vermont State Board of Education, which she chaired from 1983 to 1985.

William Mares served in the Vermont House of Representatives, was a member of the Vermont Bicentennial Commission, and is a trustee of the Fairbanks Museum. His books include *The Marine Machine*, *Working Together* (with J. Simmons), and *Real Vermonters Don't Milk Goats* (with F. Bryan).

Anne P. McConnell is associate professor of French and Spanish at Saint Michael's College. Her fields include French-Canadian and Franco-American culture. She is on the board of Chittenden County's La Société des Deux Mondes and is a member of the Vermont French Cultural Commission.

Wolfgang Mieder teaches German and folklore at the University of Vermont. He was named University Scholar in 1980, received the George Kidder Outstanding Faculty Award in 1987, has written numerous articles and books on proverbs, and edits *Proverbium: Yearbook of International Proverb Scholarship*.

Toby Morantz is assistant professor of anthropology at McGill University, teaching the ethnohistory of northeastern North America and the history of Indian-white relations. She has written on the fur trade in northern Quebec (*Partners in Furs*, with D. Francis) and on Algonquian society.

Nicholas Monsarrat teaches journalism at Saint Michael's College and is an editorial writer for the *Rutland Herald* and *Times Argus*. He has held numerous reporting and editing positions for the *Barre-Montpelier Times Argus*, the Vermont Press Bureau, and the *Rutland Herald*.

Willard S. Randall is the author of six books, including *Benedict Arnold: Patriot and Traitor* (1990) and *A Little Revenge: Benjamin Franklin and His Son* (1985), as well as numerous articles. He has taught history at the University of Vermont since 1985.

D. Gregory Sanford is Vermont State Archivist. He is former assistant director of the George D. Aiken Oral History Project and former coordinator of the M.I.T. Oral History Program. His most recent publication was *Records of the Council of Censors of the State of Vermont* (with co-editor Paul Gillies).

Richard H. Schein was formerly assistant professor of geography at Saint Michael's College and is now visiting assistant professor at Eastern Kentucky University. He has published on frontier settlement, urban geography, and the representation of human landscapes.

Gene Sessions has taught in the History Department of Norwich University and Vermont College since 1974, and edits *Vermont History*. He has published on nineteenth-century Vermont and serves on the Executive Committee of the Center for Research on Vermont at the University of Vermont.

Michael Sherman has been director of the Vermont Historical Society since 1985. He recently edited *A More Perfect Union: Vermont Becomes a State, 1777-1816* (1991) and is editor of *Vermont History News*.

Frank Smallwood is Nelson A. Rockefeller Professor Emeritus, Dartmouth College, and now teaches in the Public Administration program at the University of Vermont. A former Vermont State Senator, he has written numerous books on government and politics, including *Free and Independent*.

Robert E. Stanfield is professor of sociology at the University of Vermont, and from 1975 to 1990 was Executive Assistant to UVM's President. He is an actor and director who has appeared with Lyric Theatre, the Champlain Shakespeare Festival, the Saint Michael's Playhouse, and the Mozart Festival.

Esther Munroe Swift is librarian and archivist of the Billings Farm & Museum in Woodstock, Vermont, and is Vermont chairperson of the United States Place-Name Commission. Her history publications include: *Vermont Place-Names*, *The Brattleboro Retreat*, and *New Vermont Guide*.

Winn L. Taplin retired to Vermont in 1981 from a career as a Central Intelligence Agency operations officer. His research and writing interests have centered on early Vermont and intelligence topics. He currently serves as president of the Vermont Historical Society.

Marshall True has been teaching history at the University of Vermont since 1966. He is a former Director of the Center for Research on Vermont, a past editor of *Vermont History*, and is currently serving as director of UVM's Latin American Area Studies Program.

Jennie G. Versteeg is associate professor of economics at Saint Michael's College. She served as deputy-director of "We Vermonters" and was co-coordinator of "Lake Champlain: Reflections on Our Past." She is a member of the Executive Committe of the Center for Research on Vermont.

Ida H. Washington is professor emerita, University of Massachusetts at Dartmouth. She is the author of *Dorothy Canfield Fisher, A Biography*, co-author with Paul Washington of *Carleton's Raid*, co-translator with Carol Washington of *The Farm in the Green Mountains* by A. Herdan-Zuckmayer.

"We Vermonters: Perspectives on the Past"

Public Events Programming

With funding from the National Endowment for the Humanities, the Center for Research on Vermont of the University of Vermont, the Vermont Historical Society, and Burlington's Fletcher Free Library undertook two years of Vermont history programming. Between January of 1990 and December of 1991, eight programming periods of two months each brought more than sixty presentations before the general public. These were accompanied by exhibits and bibliographic handout materials.

The following pages list all of the events of this project in order of their original presentation. Papers in this volume are drawn from the presentation series, but sequencing of the pieces at times differs significantly from the original order. Local libraries wishing to duplicate some or all of these programs should contact the original presenters. Funding for program replication may be available through the Vermont Council on the Humanities' Speakers Program.

Exhibit materials have been retained by the Vermont Historical Society and are also documented in notebooks on file at the Fletcher Free Library and the University of Vermont's Special Collections at Bailey/Howe Library.

Part 1

"We Vermonters: A State of Mind"

January-February 1990

Sunday, January 7, 1990 at 4:00 P.M.
Opening Address: "Defining Ourselves: Peoples and Places"
John Engels, St. Michael's College
Bill Mares, State Representative and Author
Exhibit Opening: "A State of Mind"
Reception following

Wednesday, January 17, 1990 at 7:00 P.M.
"From Yankee Wit to Vermont Humor"
Richard Sweterlitsch, University of Vermont

Wednesday, January 24, 1990 at 7:00 P.M.
"'A Hardy Race': Forging the Vermont Identity"
Panelists: Elizabeth Dole Durfee, National Society
of the Colonial Dames of America
Connell Gallagher, University of Vermont
D. Gregory Sanford, Vermont State Archivist

Wednesday, January 31, 1990 at 7:00 P.M.
"Place Names as Footprints of History"
Esther Munroe Swift, Author and Librarian,
Billings Farm & Museum

Wednesday, February 7, 1990 at 7:00 P.M.
"Dorothy Canfield Fisher's Vermont Tradition"
Ida Washington, Biographer

Wednesday, February 14, 1990 at 7:00 P.M.
"Good Proverbs Make Good Vermonters"
Wolfgang Mieder, University of Vermont

Wednesday, February 21, 1990 at 7:00 P.M.
"Rudyard Kipling, Vermonter"
Performed by Robert Stanfield, University of Vermont

Wednesday, February 28, 1990 at 7:00 P.M.
"Gods of the Hills and the Valleys"
J. Kevin Graffagnino, University of Vermont

Part 2

"We Vermonters: Landscape, Townscape, Cityscape"

April-May 1990

Wednesday, April 4, 1990 at 7:00 P.M.
"Native American Perceptions of the Land"
Frederick Wiseman, Johnson State College
Exhibit Opening: "Landscape, Townscape, Cityscape"

Wednesday, April 11, 1990 at 7:00 P.M.
"Roadside History of Vermont"
Peter Jennison, Author

Wednesday, April 18, 1990 at 7:00 P.M.
"Clearing the Frontier"
Carl Reidel, University of Vermont

Wednesday, April 25, 1990 at 7:00 P.M.
"The Maritime Landscape of Vermont"
Art Cohn, Lake Champlain Maritime Museum

Wednesday, May 2, 1990 at 7:00 P.M.
"Agriculture and the Good Society"
David Donath, Billings Farm & Museum

Wednesday, May 9, 1990 at 7:00 P.M.
Keynote Address and Reception:
"Everyday Places: A Mirror of Vermont?"
Chester Liebs, University of Vermont

Wednesday, May 16, 1990 at 7:00 P.M.
"The Year 2050: Looking Back"
Panelists: Eric Gilbertson, Vermont Division
for Historic Preservation
Michael Monte, Burlington Community & Economic
Development Office
David White, Pomerleau Real Estate
Jennie Versteeg, St. Michael's College, Moderator

Wednesday, May 23, 1990 at 7:00 P.M.
"Burlington's Waterfront—Then and Now"
Lilian Baker Carlisle, Author

Part 3

"We Vermonters: Immigrants, Emigrants, Hearthminders"

July-August 1990

Sunday, July 1, 1990 at 4:00 P.M.
Keynote Address: "Stocking the State"
Samuel B. Hand, University of Vermont
Exhibit Opening: "Immigrants, Emigrants, Hearthminders"
Reception following

Wednesday, July 11, 1990 at 7:00 P.M.
"Legacies of Contact: Indians, Europeans,
and the Shaping of Vermont"
Colin Calloway, University of Wyoming

Wednesday, July 18, 1990 at 7:00 P.M.
"We Proprietors: The First Europeans"
Winn L. Taplin, Vermont Historical Society

Wednesday, July 25, 1990 at 7:00 P.M.
"The Franco-Americans of New England"
Anne P. McConnell, St. Michael's College

Wednesday, August 1, 1990 at 7:00 P.M.
"The Irish and the Jews"
Panelists: Vicent Feeney, University of Vermont
P. Jeffrey Potash, Trinity College
Vincent Bolduc, St. Michael's College, Moderator

Wednesday, August 8, 1990 at 7:00 P.M.
"*Like Lesser Gods*: The Italians of Barre"
Ruth Wallman, University of Vermont

Wednesday, August 15, 1990 at 7:00 P.M.
"Pirates, Gypsies, and Other White Trash"
Kevin Dann, Rutgers University

Wednesday, August 22, 1990 at 7:00 P.M.
"Hearthminders: Here and There"
Constance McGovern, University of Vermont

Part 4

"We Vermonters: Earning Our Keep"

October-November 1990

Wednesday, October 3, 1990 at 7:00 P.M.
Keynote Address: "The Evolution of Vermont's Economic Identity"
Jennie G. Versteeg, St. Michael's College
Exhibit Opening and Reception

Wednesday, October 10, 1990 at 7:00 P.M.
"Vermont Agriculture: Farming and Frustration"
Panelists: Austin Cleaves, Vermont Farmer of 1989
Harold Meeks, University of Vermont

Wednesday, October 17, 1990 at 7:00 P.M.
"Workers in the Mills, Quarries, and Railroads"
Panelists: Deborah Clifford, Author
Richard Hathaway, Vermont College of Norwich University
Gene Sessions, Norwich University
Michael Sherman, Vermont Historical Society, Moderator

Wednesday, October 24, 1990 at 7:00 P.M.
"Faces in the Parlor, Duties in the Yard"
Dawn Andrews, Independent Scholar

Wednesday, October 31, 1990 at 7:00 P.M.
"Trains, Planes, and Automobiles: Touring Vermont"
Michael Sherman, Vermont Historical Society

Wednesday, November 7, 1990 at 7:00 P.M.
"The Life of Vermont Teachers: Then and Now"
Panelists: Margaret Nelson, Middlebury College
Maida Townsend, Winooski High School

Wednesday, November 14, 1990 at 7:00 P.M.
"Shaping Our Economic Future: Twenty Years Hence"
Panelists: Hon. Paul Harrington, R-Washington-1
Arthur Woolf, State Economist
Malcolm Severance, Emeritus, University of Vermont, Moderator

Sunday, November 18, 1990 at 4:00 P.M.
"Child Labor in New England"
Karen Lane, Aldrich Public Library

Part 5

"We Vermonters: Hostilities and Hot Issues"

January-February 1991

Sunday, January 6, 1991, at 4:00 P.M.
Keynote Address: "Our Patriotic Identity"
Willard S. Randall, University of Vermont
Exhibit Opening: "Hostilities and Hot Issues"
Reception following

Wednesday, January 16, 1991, at 7:00 P.M.
"The Struggles That Shaped Vermont"
John Krueger, University of Vermont

Wednesday, January 23, 1991, at 7:00 P.M.
"The Citizen-Soldier at Peace and War"
Mark A. Stoler, University of Vermont
Commentary by Samuel B. Hand, University of Vermont

Wednesday, January 30, 1991, at 7:00 P.M.
"George Houghton: A Civil War Legacy"
Slide Presentation compiled by Harold and Pauline Barry,
Brattleboro Historical Society,
and Faith Pepe, Vermont College of Norwich University

Wednesday, February 6, 1991, at 7:00 P.M.
"Some Intolerant Vermonters"
T. D. Seymour Bassett, Emeritus, University of Vermont

Wednesday, February 13, 1991, at 7:00 P.M.
"The Global Crusade"
Panelists: Margaret Garland, Vermont Veterans Home
Eleanor Ott, Folklorist

Wednesday, February 20, 1991, at 7:00 P.M.
"A Haven in Vermont: Dorothy Thompson and Émigré Artists"
Ida Washington, Emerita, University of Massachusetts at Dartmouth

Wednesday, February 27, 1991, at 7:00 P.M.
"*Warriors' Women*: Vietnam Remembered"
Dorothy Tod, Filmmaker

Part 6

"We Vermonters: Frontier to Global Village"

April-May 1991

Wednesday, April 3, 1991, at 7:00 P.M.
Keynote Address: "Above the 'Optimum Climatic Area':
The Rise of the Global Village"
Frank Bryan, University of Vermont
Exhibit Opening, "Frontier to Global Village"
Reception following

Wednesday, April 10, 1991, at 7:00 P.M.
"Frontier Villages"
Richard Schein, St. Michael's College

Wednesday, April 17, 1991, at 7:00 P.M.
"Footlights and Spotlights in Vermont"
George B. Bryan, University of Vermont

Wednesday, April 24, 1991, at 7:00 P.M.
"Spreading the News"
Panelists: Nicholas Monsarrat, St. Michael's College
Dianne Lynch, St. Michael's College

Wednesday, May 1, 1991, at 7:00 P.M.
"Radio in Vermont: Crystal Sets to Satellites"
Ken Greene, WCAX-TV

Wednesday, May 8, 1991, at 7:00 P.M.
"From Nickelodeon to Multiplex"
Rick Winston, Savoy Theatre

Wednesday, May 15, 1991, at 7:00 P.M.
"Television Comes to the Green Mountains"
Stuart Martin, WCAX-TV

Wednesday, May 22, 1991, at 7:00 P.M.
"Kents Corners: From Global Village to Rural Retreat"
Cornelia Denker, Children's Art Exchange

Part 7

"We Vermonters: Freedom and Unity"

July-August 1991

Wednesday, July 10, 1991, at 7:00 P.M.
Keynote Address: "We Pledge Allegiance to . . .?"
Frank Smallwood, Dartmouth College
Exhibit Opening, "Freedom and Unity"
Reception following

Wednesday, July 17, 1991, at 7:00 P.M.
"Inventing Constitutions:
The Vermont Constitution in Historical Perspective"
Patrick Hutton, University of Vermont

Wednesday, July 24, 1991, at 7:00 P.M.
"The Citizen Legislature"
Panelists: William Doyle, Vermont Senate and Johnson State College
Micque Glitman, former member, Vermont House of Representatives
Ruth Stokes, Vermont House of Representatives

Wednesday, July 31, 1991, at 7:00 P.M.
"Biennial Government?"
Eric Davis, Middlebury College

Wednesday, August 7, 1991, at 7:00 P.M.
"Campaign Financing of Vermont Elections"
Paul Gillies, Deputy Secretary of State

Wednesday, August 14, 1991, at 7:00 P.M.
"Women in Government: Then and Now"
Panelists: Julie Bressor, Shelburne Farms
Vi Luginbuhl, Vermont House of Representatives

Wednesday, August 21, 1991, at 7:00 P.M.
"Red Scare in the Green Mountains"
David Holmes, Author

Wednesday, August 28, 1991, at 7:00 P.M.
"It Could Happen Here"
Robert Cochran, Emeritus, University of Vermont

Part 8

"We Vermonters: Echoes and Reflections"

October-November 1991

Wednesday, October 2, 1991, at 7:00 P.M.
"Finding the New World"
Toby Morantz, McGill University
Exhibit Opening, "Echoes and Reflections"
Reception following

Wednesday, October 9, 1991, at 7:00 P.M.
"Defining New England"
Marshall True, University of Vermont

Wednesday, October 16, 1991, at 7:00 P.M.
"Inventing Vermont"
Jere Daniell, Dartmouth College

Wednesday, October 23, 1991, at 7:00 P.M.
"Governing Vermonters"
Hon. John Dooley, Vermont Supreme Court

Wednesday, October 30, 1991, at 7:00 P.M.
"Celebrating Vermont"
Panelists: Nancy Graff, Historian and Author
Virginia Westbrook, Historian

Wednesday, November 6, 1991, at 7:00 P.M.
"Regulating Vermonters"
Hon. James Douglas, Vermont Secretary of State

Wednesday, November 13, 1991, at 7:00 P.M.
"Preserving Vermont"
Panelists: Tordis Isselhardt, Images from the Past
Tom Slayton, *Vermont Life*
Steve Wright, Sterling College

Wednesday, November 20, 1991, at 7:00 P.M.
"Portraying Vermont"
James Hayford, Poet